T0212722

Lecture Notes in Computer Science 9311

Commenced Publication in 1973
Founding and Former Series Editors:
Gerhard Goos, Juris Hartmanis, and Jan van Leeuwen

More information about this series at http://www.springer.com/series/7410

Raja Naeem Akram · Sushil Jajodia (Eds.)

Information Security Theory and Practice

9th IFIP WG 11.2 International Conference, WISTP 2015
Heraklion, Crete, Greece, August 24–25, 2015
Proceedings

 Springer

Editors
Raja Naeem Akram
ISG-SCC
University of London
Egham
UK

Sushil Jajodia
George Mason University
Fairfax, VI
USA

ISSN 0302-9743   ISSN 1611-3349 (electronic)
Lecture Notes in Computer Science
ISBN 978-3-319-24017-6   ISBN 978-3-319-24018-3 (eBook)
DOI 10.1007/978-3-319-24018-3

Library of Congress Control Number: 2015948704

LNCS Sublibrary: SL4 – Security and Cryptology

Springer Cham Heidelberg New York Dordrecht London

Printed on acid-free paper

Springer International Publishing AG Switzerland is part of Springer Science+Business Media
(www.springer.com)

Preface

Future ICT technologies, such as the concepts of Ambient Intelligence, Cyber-physical Systems, and Internet of Things provide a vision of the Information Society in which a) people and physical systems are surrounded with intelligent interactive interfaces and objects, and b) environments are capable of recognizing and reacting to the presence of different individuals or events in a seamless, unobtrusive, and invisible manner. The success of future ICT technologies will depend on how secure these systems are and to what extent they protect the privacy of individuals and individuals trust them.

In 2007, the Workshop on Information Security Theory and Practice (WISTP) was created as a forum for bringing together researchers and practitioners in related areas and to encourage interchange and cooperation between the research community and the industrial/consumer community. Due to the growing number of participants, the 2015 event became a conference – The 9th WISTP International Conference on Information Security Theory and Practice (WISTP 2015).

WISTP 2015 sought original submissions from academia and industry presenting novel research on all theoretical and practical aspects of security and privacy, as well as experimental studies of fielded systems, the application of security technology, the implementation of systems, and lessons learned. We encouraged submissions from other communities such as law, business, and policy that present these communities' perspectives on technological issues.

These proceedings contain the papers selected for presentation at the 9th WISTP International Conference on Information Security Theory and Practice (WISTP 2015), held August 24–25 in Heraklion, Crete, Greece.

In response to the call for papers 52 papers were submitted to the conference. These papers were evaluated on the basis of their significance, novelty, and technical quality. Each paper was reviewed by at least three members of the Program Committee. Of the papers submitted, 14 full papers and 4 short papers were selected for presentation at the conference.

There is a long list of people who volunteered their time and energy to put together the conference and who deserve acknowledgment. Thanks to all the members of the Program Committee and the external reviewers for all their hard work in evaluating and discussing papers. We are also very grateful to Damien Sauveron, Chair of the WISTP Steering Committee, for his guidance through all stages of the conference. Last, but certainly not least, our thanks go to all the authors who submitted papers and all the attendees.

We hope that you will find the proceedings stimulating and a source of inspiration for future research.

July 2015   Raja Naeem Akram
                                                                         Sushil Jajodia

Organization

WISTP 2015 was organized by FORTH-ICS, Greece

General Chair

Ioannis Askoxylakis   FORTH- ICS, Greece

Local Organizer

Nikolaos Petroulakis FORTH-ICS, Greece

Workshop/Panel/Tutorial Chair

Damien Sauveron   XLIM, University of Limoges, France

Publicity Chair

Ruggero Donida Labati Università degli Studi di Milano, Italy

Program Chairs

Raja Naeem Akram   Royal Holloway, University of London, UK
Sushil Jajodia   George Mason University, USA

Program Committee

Mohamed Ahmed Abdelraheem	The Technical University of Denmark/DTU Compute, Denmark
Claudio A. Ardagna	Università degli Studi di Milano, Italy
Ioannis Askoxylakis	FORTH-ICS, Greece
Selcuk Baktir	Bahcesehir University, Turkey
Lejla Batina	Radboud University Nijmegen, The Netherlands
Samia Bouzefrane	CEDRIC, Conservatoire National des Arts et Métiers, France
Lorenzo Cavallaro	Royal Holloway, University of London, UK
Hervé Chabanne	Morpho, France
Serge Chaumette	LaBRI, University of Bordeaux, France
Delphine Christin	University of Bonn, Fraunhofer FKIE, Germany
Mauro Conti	University of Padua, Italy
Kurt Dietrich	NXP, Austria
Sara Foresti	Università degli Studi di Milano, Italy
José María De Fuentes	Carlos III University of Madrid, Spain
Flavio Garcia	University of Birmingham, UK

Yong Guan	Iowa State University, USA
Gerhard Hancke	City University of Hong Kong, Hong Kong
Julio Hernandez-Castro	University of Kent, UK
Michael Hutter	IAIK, Graz University of Technology, Austria
Süleyman Kardas	TBITAK-BILGEM, Turkey
Mehmet Sabir Kiraz	TBITAK-BILGEM, Turkey
Andrea Lanzi	University of Milan, Italy
Maryline Laurent	SAMOVAR UMR CNRS 5157, Télécom SudParis, France
Albert Levi	Sabanci University, Turkey
Peng Liu	Pennsylvania State University, USA
Javier Lopez	University of Malaga, Spain
Federico Maggi	Politecnico di Milano, Italy
Vashek Matyas	Masaryk University, Czech Republic
Sjouke Mauw	University of Luxembourg, Luxembourg
Nele Mentens	KU Leuven, Belgium
Alessio Merlo	University of Genoa, Italy
Vladimir A. Oleshchuk	University of Agder, Norway
Jonathan P. Chapman	University of Bonn, Germany
Milan Petkovic	Eindhoven University of Technology, The Netherlands
Wolter Pieters	TU Delft and University of Twente, The Netherlands
Joachim Posegga	Institute of IT-Security and Security Law, Germany
Kai Rannenberg	Goethe University Frankfurt, Deutsche Telekom, Germany
Kui Ren	State University of New York at Buffalo, USA
Kouichi Sakurai	Kyushu University, Japan
Pierangela Samarati	Università degli Studi di Milano, Italy
Siraj Ahmed Shaikh	Coventry University, UK
Dave Singelée	KU Leuven, iMinds, COSIC, Belgium
Willy Susilo	University of Wollongong, Australia
Ulrich Tamm	TU Chemnitz, Germany
Li Tieyan	Huawei Technologies, Singapore
Denis Trcek	University of Ljubljana, Slovenia
Michael Tunstall	Cryptography Research Inc, USA
Umut Uludag	TBITAK-BILGEM UEKAE, Turkey
Omair Uthmani	West Lothian College, Livingston, UK
Stefano Zanero	Politecnico di Milano, Italy

Additional Reviewers

Ambrosin, Moreno	Anada, Hiroaki
Bilzhause, Arne	Carminati, Michele
Continella, Andrea	Dargahi, Tooska
Fukushima, Kazuhide	Garcia-Perez, Alexeis
González Manzano, Lorena	Jayasinghe, Danushka
Jonker, Hugo	Kalutarage, Harsha Kumara
Karaoğlan Altop, Duygu	Kasi, Mumraiz Khan

Le Vinh, Thinh
Ordean, Mihai
Quarta, Davide
Roman, Rodrigo
Tatli, Emin
Yang, Shuzhe
Yoshida, Hirotaka

Marktscheffel, Tobias
Polian, Ilia
Radu, Andreea-Ina
Spolaor, Riccardo
Tschersich, Markus
Yesuf, Ahmed Seid
Zeng, Qiang

Steering Committee

Angelos Bilas   FORTH-ICS & University of Crete, Greece
Konstantinos   ISG-SCC, Royal Holloway, University of London, UK
   Markantonakis
David Naccache   Ecole Normale Supérieure, France
Joachim Posegga   Institute of IT-Security and Security Law at the
                      University of Passau, Germany
Jean-Jacques Quisquater   DICE, Catholic University of Louvain, Belgium
Damien Sauveron   XLIM, University of Limoges, France

Scientific Support

IFIP WG 11.2 Pervasive Systems Security

Main Sponsors

The development of a strong program and Organizing Committee, and the WISTP relationship with high profile organizations, has further capitalized into direct financial support. This enabled the conference organizers to strengthen significantly their main objective for proposing a high standard academic event. The support helped significantly to keep the conference registration costs as low as possible and, at the same time, offer a number of best paper awards. Therefore, we would like to express our gratitude and thank Huawei for their support. We are also looking forward to working together for future WISTP events.

Contents

Challenges of Security and Reliability

Short Papers

Security and Privacy Services

On Secrecy Amplification Protocols

Radim Ošťádal, Petr Švenda, and Vashek Matyáš[(⊠)]

Masaryk University, Brno, Czech Republic
ostadal@mail.muni.cz, {svenda,matyas}@fi.muni.cz

Abstract. We review most important secrecy amplification protocols that are suitable for ad-hoc networks of devices with limited resources, providing additional resistance against various attacks on used cryptographic keys without necessity for asymmetric cryptography. We discuss and evaluate different designs as well as approaches to create new protocols. A special focus is given to suitability of these protocols with respect to different underlying key distribution schemes and also to open issues.

1 Introduction

Ad-hoc networks of nodes with limited capabilities often handle sensitive information and security of such networks is a typical baseline requirement. Such networks consist of a high number of interacting devices, price of which should be as low as possible – limiting computational and storage resources. On top of the limited capability of the devices, there usually comes also the requirement of avoiding expensive tamper resistance. As a detection of an attack with limited resources is quite difficult, systems secure by design with a strong focus on autonomous self-defense are desired. Lightweight security solutions are preferable, providing a low computational and communication overhead. When considering key management in nodes of limited capabilities, symmetric cryptography is the preferred approach, yet with a low number of predistributed keys. While all results we present can be applied to general ad-hoc networks, we present them directly on wireless sensor networks (WSNs) as typical representatives.

Our work targets scenarios with ad-hoc networks where a link between particular nodes can be compromised, yet the nodes themselves are not. A typical example comes with some schemes based on symmetric cryptography, requiring suitable key distribution schemes (KDSs). During the attack, an attacker learns a fraction of used keys, resulting in a partially compromised network.

Substantial improvements in resilience against node capture or key exchange eavesdropping can be achieved when a group of neighbouring nodes cooperates in an additional *secrecy amplification* (SA) protocol after the initial key establishment protocol. A strong majority of secure links (> 90%) can be obtained even when the initial network compromise is at 50% [15]. This technique can be utilized in a broad range of scenarios, even if the particular results depend on a particular key distribution scheme and attack strategy.

© IFIP International Federation for Information Processing 2015
R.N. Akram and S. Jajodia (Eds.): WISTP 2015, LNCS 9311, pp. 3–19, 2015.
DOI: 10.1007/978-3-319-24018-3_1

The *contributions* of our work are: 1) a comparative review of all SA protocols (we are aware of), together with unified notation and taxonomy; 2) extensive multicriterial evaluation of all these protocols; and 3) identification of open research challenges in this area.

The SA concept was originally introduced in [1] for the *key infection* plaintext key exchange, but can be also used for a partially compromised network resulting from node capture in probabilistic pre-distribution schemes of [6]. SA protocols were shown to be very effective, yet for the price of a significant communication overhead. The overall aim is to provide SA protocols that can secure a high number of links yet require only a small number of messages and are easy to execute and synchronize in parallel executions in the real network.

Let us briefly present the principles of SA protocols and their most important features. Due to an attacker action, the communication link between nodes A and B secured by a link key K can be compromised. When the group of neighbouring nodes of A and B cooperates in an additional protocol, communication link(s) protected by the previously compromised key K can be secured again, if a new key K' can be securely transported to both nodes. If this is the case, there has to exist at least one non-compromised path. The exact way the new key value K' is transported specifies a particular secrecy amplification (SA) protocol.

The network owner usually does not know which concrete link key was compromised by an attacker and which was not. SA can be executed as a response to a partial compromise already happened or as a preventive measure for potential future compromise. SA can be also executed as another layer of protection even if a particular link key might not be compromised at all. Different key distribution schemes and related attacks correspond to different compromise patterns as described in Section 1.1, influencing how successful a SA protocol will be. SA protocols can try all possible paths, yet for the price of a huge communication overhead. Proposed SA protocols therefore aim to find a good tradeoff between the number of paths tried and the probability of finding at least one secure path.

SA protocols consist of the following principal steps:

1. Selection of neighbouring nodes participating in a given SA protocol.
2. Generation of new key values (shares).
3. Transport of key values (shares) via transport path or multiple paths according to the given SA protocol.
4. Combination of transported key values (shares) and existing old key into a new link key with an appropriate one-way function. New key will be secure if either old key or at least one of shares was previously secure.

The paper roadmap is as follows: the next subsection provides a short introduction to networks where a partial compromise is inevitable and one has to deal with compromise patterns resulting from different key distribution schemes and corresponding attack strategies. Section 2 provides a unified taxonomy of SA protocols and surveys previous work. Section 3 evaluates properties of SA protocols based on performance, memory and transmission overhead as well as ease of synchronization during massively parallel executions. Section 4 highlights open research problems and conclusions are provided in Section 5.

1.1   Partial Network Compromise

A wide range of key distribution, establishment and management techniques was proposed for sensor networks, see [3] for an overview. Distinct key distribution schemes behave differently when a network is under an attack targeted to disturb link key security. Although various schemes differ significantly in the way how keys are distributed and managed, similar compromise patterns can be detected. A compromise pattern provides us with a conditional probability that link Y is compromised when another link X is compromised after a relevant attack. The characteristics of a particular compromise pattern may significantly influence the success rate of an SA executed later. We will perform analysis of SA protocols according to the following two most prominent compromise patterns, but our work can be as well extended to additional patterns.

1.2   Random Compromise Pattern

The random compromise pattern arises when a probabilistic key pre-distribution scheme of [6] and many later variants of [2,5,8,9] are used and an attacker extracts keys from several randomly captured nodes. In case of a node capture, all links to the captured node are compromised. If a probabilistic pre-distribution scheme is used, then some additional links between non-compromised nodes become compromised as well. Probabilistic key pre-distribution schemes exhibit an almost uncorrelated pattern resulting from node capture and extraction of randomly selected keys.

1.3   Key Infection Compromise Pattern

Compromised networks resulting from key distribution based on the idea of "key infection" [1] and later extended by [4,7,15] and others form the second inspected pattern. Here, link keys are exchanged in plaintext (no keys are pre-distributed) and an attacker can compromise them if the transmission can be eavesdropped by the attacker. The weakened attacker model assumes that an attacker is not able to eavesdrop on all transmissions, yet has a limited number of restricted eavesdropping nodes in the field. The closer the link transmission is to the listening attacker node and the longer the distance between link peers, the higher the probability of a compromise. An eavesdropping of the exchanged key in the key infection approach of [1] does not compromise nodes directly, but compromises links in the reach of eavesdropper's radio instead.

2   Protocol Survey

Different classes of SA protocols use different capabilities to improve security throughout the network. Although all SA protocols aim to setup new (possibly more secure) link key, three main distinct classes of SA protocols exist:

1. **A node-oriented protocol** sends key updates via every possible neighbour or neighbours by a simple protocol. Note that node-oriented protocol is executed for all possible k-tuples of neighbours in the network. A number of such k-tuples can be high, especially for dense networks.
2. **A group-oriented protocol** shares new key values inside a bigger group of cooperating nodes identified by their geographical areas in the form of relative distance to selected nodes.
3. **A hybrid-design protocol** uses sub-protocols (similarly to node-oriented), relative distances (similarly to group-oriented) and additionally utilize several repetitions of the whole process to achieve required success rate.

A summary of published protocols follows, with all details available in [13].

Table 1. Notation used for secrecy amplification (SA) protocols.

notation	description
A, B	identification of nodes for which the link key is strengthened during SA
C_i	identification of intermediate node(s) used during SA
N_C	identification of the central node during group-oriented SA protocols
N_P	identification of the node with a special role during group-oriented SA protocols
N_{d1_d2}	relative distance identification of a node with distance d_1 from N_C and d_2 from N_P
R_i	identification of a memory register
H	cryptographic one-way hash function

protocol instruction	description
NOP	no operation
$RNG\ N_a\ R_i$	generate a random value on node N_a into slot R_i
$CMB\ N_a\ R_i\ R_j\ R_k$	combine values from slots R_i and R_j on the node N_a and store the result to R_k; the combination function may vary on the application needs (e.g., a cryptographic hash function such as SHA-3)
$SND\ N_a\ N_b\ R_i\ R_j$	send a value from R_i on node N_a to slot R_j on N_b
$ENC\ N_a\ R_i\ R_j\ R_k$	encrypt a value from R_i on node N_a using the key from R_j and store the result to R_k
$DEC\ N_a\ R_i\ R_j\ R_k$	decrypt a value from R_i on node N_a using the key from R_j and store the result to R_k

2.1   Used Notation

SA protocols can be described in the common form of message exchanges and operations executed on communicating nodes. Alternatively, each node in the protocol can be modelled as a computing unit with a limited number of memory slots, where all local information is stored. Each memory slot can contain either a random value, encryption key or message. SA protocol is then a sequential series of primitive instructions, manipulating values in memory slots and exchanging values between nodes. Some protocols require only one memory slot, but protocols with more than five different memory slots were also published. Latter case is more suitable to describe non-deterministic protocols without a fixed set of communicating peers and with execution differing at actual network layout and nodes positions (e.g., group-oriented protocols). Table 1 summarizes the used notation.

Using this set of primitive instructions, a simple plaintext exchange of a new key for node-oriented protocols can be written as {RNG N_1 R_1; SND N_1 N_2 R_1 R_1;}, a Push protocol [1] as {RNG N_1 R_1; SND N_1 N_3 R_1 R_1; SND N_3 N_2 R_1 R_1;}, a Pull protocol [4] as {RNG N_3 R_1; SND N_3 N_1 R_1 R_1; SND N_3 N_2 R_1 R_1;}, a multi-hop version of Pull [4] as {RNG N_3 R_1; SND N_3 N_1 R_1 R_1; SND N_3 N_4 R_1 R_1; SND N_4 N_2 R_1 R_1;} and a multi-hop version of Push [1] as {RNG N_1 R_1; SND N_1 N_3 R_1 R_1; SND N_3 N_4 R_1 R_1; SND N_4 N_2 R_1 R_1;}. Group-oriented and hybrid-design protocols consist from of the same type of instructions, but are typically longer and more complex, see [13].

2.2 Node-Oriented Protocols

The multi-hop (two-hop) and multi-path (number of neighbours reachable from both A and B) SA protocol was described in [1]. Node A generates q different random key values and sends each one along a different path over an intermediate node(s) C_i to node B, encrypted with existing link key(s). Key infection compromise pattern was assumed and simulations for attacker/legal nodes ratio up to 5% are presented, showing that the plaintext key exchange followed by the Push protocol is suitable within this attacker model. More detailed and precise simulations were later performed in [4]. The Push protocol is used as a basis for an establishment of the intra-group link keys between multiple nodes belonging to different groups when more structured deployment is assumed [10]. Multi-hop version of the Push protocol is analyzed in [11]. For the comparison, we assume Push protocol with one (denoted[1] as NO_3PUSH04) and two (NO_4PUSH04) intermediate nodes.

A variant of the Push protocol called Pull protocol was presented in [4]. The initial key exchange is same as for the Push protocol, but node C_i generates fresh key values that are used to improve secrecy of the key shared between nodes A and B instead of node A as in the Push protocol. The basic idea here is that the area where eavesdropping nodes must be positioned to successfully compromise the link key is smaller than for the Push protocol. The resulting fraction of compromised keys is then lower as an attacker has a smaller chance to place eavesdropping nodes properly. For the comparison, we assume Pull protocol with one (denoted as NO_3PULL05) and two (NO_4PULL05) intermediate nodes.

A variant of initial key exchange mixed with the Push protocol (denoted as Commodity) without explicit SA is presented in [7] together with formal security proof. We omit the Commodity protocol from the comparison as it is only a variant of the Push protocol, does not provide SA as a separate operation and the fraction of secured links is lower than for the Push protocol alone.

A linear genetic programming in combination with network simulator was used to design a node-oriented protocol [15] for the key infection pattern.

---

[1] For the rest of the paper, we will name protocols consistently in the form *protocol-Class_protocolVariantYearOfPublication*, with additional compromise pattern designation when protocol was designed specifically for that pattern. E.g., NO_3PUSH04 means node-oriented protocol, Push variant with 3 participants, published in 2004.

Due to the nature of stochastic algorithms, a protocol was initially designed with up to 100 instructions storing intermediate values into up to 12 memory registers. Then was processed to omit all unused instructions and memory registers (based on performance provided by a network simulator), resulting in the 10 instruction protocol for four nodes (denoted as NO_EA09 for comparison).

As already mentioned, node-oriented protocols introduce a high communication overhead – all k-tuples of neighbours must be involved in a single execution of such a protocol. Another issue is an unknown number of direct neighbours and their exact placement. All neighbours can theoretically participate in the protocol and help to improve the fraction of secure links, but it is much harder to design an efficient protocol for ten nodes without unnecessary message transmissions instead of three or four nodes. Finally, due to the random placement of nodes in the sensor networks, the number of direct neighbours may vary significantly; a protocol constructed for a fixed number of parties can even fail due to an insufficient number of participants.

In short, the main advantage of node-oriented protocols is simple synchronization of multiple protocol executions running in parallel and generally low memory overhead. The main disadvantage is the high number of messages transmitted, especially for the dense networks (see section Section 3.3 for details).

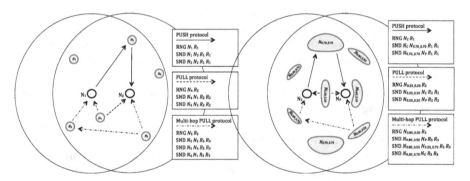

Fig. 1. Left: An example of instructions of a several node-oriented SA protocols. The Push, Pull and multi-hop version of Pull are included. A distance between nodes N_C and N_P is 0.5 of the maximal transmission range. **Right:** An example of instructions of a basic hybrid SA protocol. The Push, Pull and multi-hop version of Pull protocol are included. Selected node-relative identification (distance from N_C and N_P) of involved parties are displayed as the geographic most probable areas, where such nodes will be positioned. A probabilistic layout shown is for the case where the distance between nodes N_C and N_P is 0.5 of the maximal transmission range. Notation used is according to the Table 1.

2.3   Group-Oriented Protocols

In group-oriented protocols, an identification of the parties in the protocol is no longer "absolute" (e.g., node designation A, B, C), but it is given by the relative distance from other parties (we are using the distance from two distinct nodes).

It is assumed that each node knows the approximate distance to its direct neighbours. This distance can be approximated from the minimal transmission power needed to communicate with a given neighbour. If the protocol has to express the fact that two nodes N_i and N_j are exchanging a message over the intermediate node N_k, only relative distances of such a node N_k from N_i and N_j are indicated in the protocol (e.g., $N_{0.30\_0.70}$ is a node positioned 0.3 of the maximum transmission range from N_i and 0.7 from N_j). Based on the actual distribution of the neighbours, the node closest to the indicated distance(s) is chosen as the node N_k for a particular protocol run. There is no need to re-execute the protocol for all k-tuples (as was the case for node-oriented protocols) as all neighbours can be involved in a single execution, reducing the communication overhead significantly. Detailed description of group-oriented protocols is provided in [15].

Note that inferring the relative distance from the received signal strength indication (RSSI) is usually a burden with errors resulting from the generally unreliable propagation of wireless signal and also as the relation between distance and RSSI is not linear. Relative distances used in group-oriented protocols are robust against moderate inaccuracies as a precise node position is not required for a protocol to succeed.

The protocol described in [15] consists of twelve instructions (denoted as GO_EA09 for comparison), but protocols with a better success rate were also generated by [14] (GO_EA12_KI and GO_EA12_RP). Group-oriented protocols consist of multiple times more instructions when compared with node-oriented protocols.

Due to the stochastic nature of the linear genetic programming used to generate group-oriented protocols, many different group-oriented protocols can be constructed based on the defined evaluation metric (fitness function). Evaluation metric can guide genetic programming towards protocols not only maximizing the fraction of secured links, but also to lower the number of messages exchanged, see [14]. In principle, new protocols can be generated for a particular usage scenario on demand, which is an interesting option.

In summary, the main advantage of the group-oriented protocols is a significantly lower (compared to node-oriented protocols) number of messages transmitted. The main disadvantage is the complicated synchronization of the parallel executions and also complicated security analysis due to the high number of nodes involved (e.g., the best performing group-oriented protocol presented in [14] has 41 instructions and might include cooperation of up to 34 nodes. Compare this to the Push protocol with 3 instructions and only 3 nodes involved.).

2.4   Hybrid-Design Protocols

Hybrid protocols [12] combine properties of both node- and group-oriented protocols. A protocol consists of several primitive instructions as described in Table 1. They were constructed with an application of knowledge from node-oriented and group-oriented protocols (thus hybrid design) and statistical data about the most suitable placement of the participating intermediate nodes.

A hybrid protocol is executed for every pair of neighbouring nodes instead of every k-tuple – same approach as in case of group-oriented protocols. Other participating intermediate nodes are used for transmission of n different values in the same fashion as previously described basic node-oriented protocols. Participating intermediate nodes are not required to store any forwarded values and can erase them as soon as a message with the value is forwarded to the next node towards destination. This allows for a simpler synchronization even within large and dense networks.

Steps of a hybrid protocol are similar to those of group-oriented protocols and also exhibit only a linear increase in the number of messages sent with respect to the number of neighbours. The main difference is independence of separate SA protocols executions and the fact that the key is updated only between nodes N_C and N_P in the last step. Relative distance from special nodes N_C and N_P is also used in the same way as for group-oriented protocols. Hybrid protocols contain a lower number of instructions and their construction, analysis and implementation are simpler than for group-oriented protocols.

Hybrid-design protocols optimized separately for key infection (denoted as HD_PULLPUSH14_KI) and random compromise (HD_PULLPUSH14_RP) patterns as well as for better tradeoff between overall success rate and number of messages (HD_PULLPUSHOPT14_KI and HD_PULLPUSHOPT14_RP) were proposed in [12].

As was observed early in [4], multiple repetitions of an SA protocol can additionally improve the number of secured links, yet for the price of additional multiplication of the total number of required messages. Hybrid-design protocols designed in [12] use three repetitions with the total number of messages still lower then for node- and group-oriented design.

In summary, the main advantage of the hybrid-design protocols is simple synchronization of parallel executions and low number of messages. The main disadvantage is the longer execution time due to multiple amplifications repetitions (but with possibility for parallel executions).

2.5   Comparison of General Characteristics

Published SA protocols can be compared through several distinct characteristics:
Rules for selection of protocol participants – what neighbours and how they are included in SA protocol has a profound effect on the total number of protocol executions, overall number of messages transmitted and paths tested. Early protocols involved all neighbours indiscriminately (node-oriented) whereas later designs involved only nodes selected based on their relative positions w.r.t. to nodes controlling protocol execution (group-oriented and hybrid), resulting in probabilistic selection of nodes.
Design approach – early protocols were designed manually [1,4,7]; later came design with simulator-aided search for protocol settings, with stochastic optimization (genetic programming) [15] with semi-automatic postprocessing [12].
Number of involved intermediate nodes per single path – basic key exchange between A and B requires no intermediate node. If at least one intermediate node

is used then the protocol performs so-called *multi-hop amplification*. The path is compromised if an attacker is able to eavesdrop at least one link on the path. If more then one intermediate node is involved, a suitable end-to-end routing protocol must be available.

Communication overhead – significant metric influencing protocol practicality due to energy-intensive radio transmissions necessary to transmit new key values during an amplification protocol. Communication overhead can be proportional to the network density (number of neighbours). The lower the number of messages, the faster the amplification phase is and the lower are the energy requirements.

Number of required repetitions – an additional iteration of a SA protocol can provide better results as links newly secured in a previous iteration can be used in the current one. Some protocols are simpler, but expect multiple repetitions whereas others expect only a single iteration.

Synchronization requirements – a SA protocol is usually not executed only between two nodes in the whole network, but between many different nodes in parallel. Degree of required synchronization is therefore an important characteristic, influencing speed of the SA phase as well as memory requirements on every node.

Table 2. Basic characteristics of SA protocols. M/A means manual/automatic design approach respectively. Synchronization 1/3 means easy/difficult.

Protocol	# intermediates	design approach	#primitive instructions	#msg/execution	#msg/node(4 neigh)	#msg/node(7.5 neigh)	#msg/node(20 neigh)	#repetitions	synchronization (1-3)
NO_3PUSH04 [1]	1	M	3	2	24	98	784	1-2	2
NO_3PULL05 [4]	1	M	3	2	24	98	784	1-2	2
NO_4PUSH04 [1]	2	M	4	3	72	804	21509	1-2	2
NO_4PULL05 [4]	2	M	4	3	72	804	21509	1-2	2
NO_EA09 [15]	2	A	10	6	144	1609	43019	1	2
GO_EA09 [15]	1-8	A	12	9	36	68	183	1	3
GO_EA12_KI [14]	1-31	A	35	23	92	173	467	1	3
GO_EA12_RP [14]	1-33	A	41	24	96	180	487	1	3
HD_PULLPUSH14_KI [12]	1-4	A	14	9	108	203	548	3	1-2
HD_PULLPUSHOPT14_KI [12]	1-2	A/M	6	4	48	90	244	3	1
HD_PULLPUSH14_RP [12]	1-5	A	15	10	120	225	609	3	1-2
HD_PULLPUSHOPT14_RP [12]	1-2	A/M	6	4	48	90	244	3	1

Number of distinct paths used to send new key values – if more than one path is used then the protocol performs so-called *multi-path amplification*. An attacker must eavesdrop all paths to compromise the new link key. If two nodes A and B exchange a new key directly in one piece, then only one path is used. Basically all SA protocols can be classified as multi-path to some extent if different intermediates or multiple repetitions are assumed.

2.6   Practical Implementation

Practical implementation on the real nodes in existing work was provided only for hybrid-design protocols [12] on the TelosB hardware platform with the TinyOS 2.1.2 OS and tested with 30 nodes. The hybrid-design protocol implementation had a small memory footprint – additional $(N * 41)$ bytes of RAM are required (where N is the number of neighbours) and less then 3KB of additional code in EEPROM. Times required to finish different phases was highly dependent on the network density and the signal propagation characteristics of the surrounding environment. The radio discovery took most of the time to complete as multiple messages had to be sent from every node in the network to obtain a reliable averaged RSSI value. Reported time was roughly minutes or tens of minutes to finish. Rest of the protocol took only few seconds. The node-oriented protocols requires similar instructions to be executed on every node, therefore memory and computational requirements would be comparable. The radio discovery phase does not require lengthly averaging of RSSI values, but number of protocol runs is significantly higher, depending on the network density.

3   Comparison of Protocol Performance

SA protocols are able to provide a significant increase in secure links, e.g., from 50% of originally secured links to more than 90% [15]. To achieve such an improvement, there is a considerable overhead in communication and on-node processing. In the subsequent section, we compare and evaluate all SA protocols we are aware of – w.r.t. to various metrics, including fraction of secure links newly secured by a protocol, communication and memory overhead, synchronization requirements. All comparisons are done on different compromise patterns.

Different initial settings can be used as a basis for the comparison, resulting in high number of combinations where SA protocols can be evaluated. First axis is formed by the selected initial compromise pattern – either random compromise or key infection pattern. Second axis is formed by the network characteristics, most importantly by the network density. For the comparison, we provide only selected combinations with complete results available[2].

---

[2] http://crcs.cz/papers/wistp2015

3.1 Reference Network and Simulator

The following reference setting of simulator was used: network has 1000 deployed legal nodes and each node has 0.5 unit maximum transmission range. Target plane is a 13.8x13.8, 10.0x10.0 and 6.0x6.0 unit large that result in 4.0, 7.5 and 20.3 legal neighbours on average for networks with low, normal and high density respectively. Both random compromise and key infection patterns (see Section 1.1) were examined.

The evaluation of presented protocols is done using the same simulator that was developed specifically for security analysis of key distribution protocols and message routing by the authors of [15]. Commonly used simulators like ns2 or OMNeT++ work with an unnecessary level of details for our purposes (e.g., radio signal propagation or MAC layer collisions), significantly slowing evaluation of given network scenarios. The simulator is able to simulate a SA protocol on fifty networks with 1000 nodes each in about 5 seconds when executed on one core CPU @ 2.7 GHz. Compare this to several minutes necessary to process only one network on OMNeT++ simulator.

Protocols evaluated in the simulator are described in a metalanguage of proposed primitive instructions, see the second part of Table 1 for more details.

3.2 Upper Bound for Amplification Success

A modified Floyd-Warshall algorithm can be used to establish an upper bound for a given network, no matter what type of SA protocol is used. A single execution of the algorithm will find the shortest path between all pairs of vertices. When a graph is formed only from secure links, existence of the path between two nodes also implies possibility to transport and establish secure new key. As the precise compromise pattern for a given network is not known in advance (depends on an attacker, particular SA protocol, exact placement of nodes, etc.), we perform multiple evaluations for different networks to obtain an average result. As a side effect, we will also obtain lowest number of intermediate nodes necessary to transport new secure key.

There is a significant difference between two inspected compromise patterns. In the random compromise pattern, significantly more link keys can be secured than in the key infection compromise pattern. Also, that most benefit can be gained using only two intermediate nodes. With more nodes, the increase in secure links fraction is very small. Complete results of these experiments are provided in [13].

3.3 Number of Messages

The number of messages sent during the protocol execution mainly depends on the protocol type. Nonetheless, it also depends on the number of participating parties and the average number of neighbours. Node-oriented protocols exhibit a polynomial increase of messages with respect to the number of neighbours in the network and an exponential increase of messages with respect to the number of communicating parties in the protocol execution. Group-oriented protocols exhibit only a linear increase of messages and the same dynamics holds for hybrid protocols. The growth in the number of messages depends on the count of SEND instructions within a particular protocol.

Figure 2 shows the number of messages sent by every node in the protocol execution on networks with different average number of legitimate neighbours. It can be seen that node-oriented protocols have advantage for networks with low density about 4 neighbours in average. The group-oriented and hybrid protocols are more suitable for dense networks.

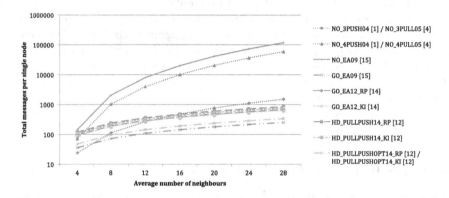

Fig. 2. Total number of messages per single node required by a particular SA protocol. Even when group-oriented protocols utilise more messages per single execution and hybrid protocols utilise several protocol repetitions, the total number of messages is smaller than in case of node-oriented protocols for networks with higher density. Number of messages grows polynomially with the number of neighbouring nodes for node-oriented protocols compared to linear increase in case of group-oriented and hybrid protocols. Note the logarithmic scale of the y-axis.

3.4 Success Rate

We compare and evaluate all published SA protocols we are aware of w.r.t. to the fraction of secure links secured by particular protocol and also we compare the protocol effectiveness, which means the number of newly secured links for one message sent.

All SA protocols perform better with a rising density of network. The improvement is bigger for the random compromise pattern than for key infection (where the compromised links are concentrated in particular areas around eavesdropping nodes).

The impact of tested protocols for the random compromise pattern is compared in Figure 3, with additional results including the key infection compromise pattern in [13]. The HD_PULLPUSH14 protocols give us the best results regarding the overall success rate for both random compromise and key infection patterns regardless of the network density. NO_EA09 and HD_PULLPUSHOPT14

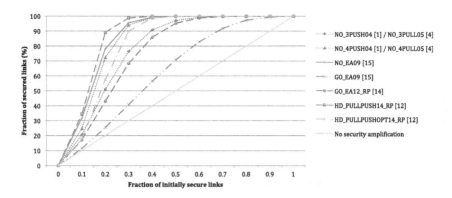

Fig. 3. Increase in the number of secured links after SA protocols in the random compromise pattern on network with 20.3 legal neighbours on average. With increasing number of neighbouring nodes the general effectiveness of protocol grows. As can be seen, a strong majority of secure links (> 90%) can be obtained even when the initial network had 80% of compromised links. The best performing protocol is HD_PULLPUSH14_RP and it sends only little bit more messages than GO_EA12_RP. As can be observed, the 4-party node-oriented protocols show very good results on networks with high density. The least successful protocol is GO_EA09 because it was optimized for key infection pattern.

perform similarly, but there is a big advantage for the HD_PULLPUSHOPT14 considering the communication overhead of both protocols. There is no difference between NO_3PUSH04 and NO_3PULL05 protocol in case of random compromise pattern. NO_3PULL05 performs slightly better than NO_3PUSH04 on key infection. Both protocols are constantly in the lower half of success rate rating for both random compromise and key infection compromise patterns, however we can take advantage of their effectiveness for networks with low density where they present the best improvement compared to number of messages sent.

An increase in the number of secured links for one message sent during the protocol execution is showed in Figure 4 for random compromise pattern. Efficiency of node-oriented protocols with respect to improvement per message rate decreases with rising network density and remain more constant for group-oriented and hybrid protocols. The NO_3PUSH04 and NO_3PULL05 protocols are the most efficient for network with low density regardless the compromise pattern. They perform worse for a higher network density, but they are still better than 4-party node-oriented protocols. For networks with normal and high density, the most efficient protocol is HD_PULLPUSHOPT14. HD_PULLPUSH14 and GO_EA12 present very similar results regardless the network density or compromise pattern. They are in the middle spectrum compared to the rest of protocols. 4-party node-oriented protocols NO_EA09, NO_4PUSH04 and NO_4PULL05 give the worst results regarding the efficiency per message. It drops very quickly with rising network density.

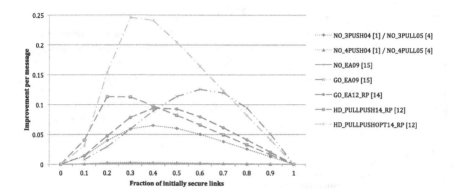

Fig. 4. Increase in the number of secured links divided by the number of exchanged messages during the protocol execution (random compromise pattern, 20.3 legal neighbours on average). Node-oriented protocols send significantly more messages with rising network density. This stands especially for 4-party node-oriented protocols, which are the least effective. The best tradeoff shows group-oriented and hybrid protocols, while HD_PULLPUSH14_RP also outperforms the rest of protocols with regards to success rate.

4   Open Research Questions

So far, we inspected two compromise patterns in detail – the highly correlated key infection pattern for which the term secrecy amplification was originally coined, and the random compromise pattern without a significant correlation. As we have demonstrated, differences in the patterns have a significant impact on the success rate of SA protocol, rendering some parts of protocol vital for one pattern ineffective in another one. Is there a better approach than testing all possible SA protocols to obtain well performing and message efficient protocol? Can we analyze the compromise pattern and directly select an appropriate SA protocol?

We examined compromise patterns relating directly to the link keys randomly extracted from a nodes or eavesdropped by an attacker. Other attacker models have to be considered, based on attacker's interaction with a node. We considered that all keying material could be exfiltrated and the the node may continue working in an unchanged manner. Yet what if the attacker installs some malware and the node is under her control? How can that malware affect the behaviour of the node and what will be resulting compromise pattern?

The SA protocols were evaluated mostly for a flat network topology, where no node has a special status (e.g., cluster head) and initial keys were established in the same way for all nodes (e.g., same number of predistributed keys). More optimal protocols might be designed when these differences are taken into account. For example, if some nodes are equipped with a tamper resistant hardware (smartcards), but others are not, routing more messages via more resistant nodes during the SA can secure more links per messages transmitted. The different communication paths can be selected once a SA protocol is used inside cluster-based networks.

The SA phase usually takes a predefined time interval, provides fresh session keys and then finishes. But what if SA is performed in a continuous manner, producing fresh keys during the whole network lifetime? As a network in the production phase is usually exchanging many messages, the continuous SA may "piggyback" on these transmissions using already transmitted values without an additional message overhead. Some directions were already proposed in [11], but new problems need to be solved – how to maintain consistency of the current key on communicating nodes without an additional overhead, especially when the wireless transmission medium with a high packet loss is used? Can an attacker adapt his strategies like a selective node capture during the longer time-frame?

In the principle, the more paths are used to distribute key shares, the better is the chance to find a non-compromised one. But as the new key is constructed from all key shares, a missing or corrupted key share will render the resulting key incorrect. Therefore, the tradeoff between the resulting confidentiality (probability of establishing the non-compromised key) and integrity (probability of establishing a same value of shared key) exists. Yet, this perspective was not yet inspected in detail, with existing publications focusing mainly on the confidentiality part of the schemes. Protocols for threshold cryptography could be used to limit the impact of the corrupted key share, but these have to be executable with significant performance limitations.

5   Conclusions

Secrecy amplification protocols can significantly improve the fraction of secure links in partially compromised networks. These protocols were originally introduced for the key infection plaintext key exchange, but can be used also for a partially compromised network resulting from a node capture for the probabilistic pre-distribution and other partially compromised networks.

Node-oriented protocols are simple to execute in synchronized parallel executions and able to secure a high number of previously compromised links, but require a significant transmission overhead. Group-oriented protocols significantly decrease the transmission overhead and still provide a high number of secured links, but synchronization of multiple runs of secrecy amplification protocols executed in parallel between multiple nodes is their critical issue. Hybrid-design protocols share similar internal design with group-oriented protocols, but exhibit a significantly simpler synchronization of parallel executions. Multiple repetitions are generally required to obtain the same success rate as for other designs, but a lower number of messages in a single iteration provides a lower transmission overhead in total.

Even though every SA protocol class has its advantages and disadvantages, we identified several patterns that hold for both key infection and random compromise patterns. The HD_PULLPUSH14 protocols showed us the best results regarding the overall success rate. Its optimised version HD_PULLPUSHOPT14 is the most efficient protocol for networks with normal and high density. For networks with low density, the NO_3PUSH04 and NO_3PULL05 protocols are the most efficient.

SA protocols can make a network almost completely secure (more than 95% of secure links) when 60% of links are initially secure (probabilistic pre-distribution) or less than 10% ratio of eavesdropping nodes are present (key infection). When appropriate, SA should be executed as an additional strengthening mechanism after a basic key establishment.

References

1. Anderson, R., Chan, H., Perrig, A.: Key infection: smart trust for smart dust. In: 12th IEEE International Conference on Network Protocols, pp. 206–215. IEEE (2004)
2. Chan, H., Perrig, A., Song, D.: Random key predistribution schemes for sensor networks. In: IEEE Symposium on Security and Privacy, pp. 197–213 (2003)
3. Chan, H., Perrig, A., Song, D.: Key Distribution Techniques for Sensor Networks, Wireless Sensor Networks, ISBN 1-4020-7883-8. Kluwer Academic Publishers (2004)
4. Cvrček, D., Švenda, P.: Smart dust security-key infection revisited. Electronic Notes in Theoretical Computer Science **157**, 11–25 (2006)
5. Di Pietro, R., Mancini, L.V., Mei, A.: Random key-assignment for secure wireless sensor networks. In: 1st ACM Workshop on Security of Ad Hoc and Sensor Networks, pp. 62–71 (2003)
6. Eschenauer, L., Gligor, V.D.: A key-management scheme for distributed sensor networks. In: 9th ACM Conference on Computer and Communications Security, pp. 41–47. ACM, Washington, DC (2002)
7. Kim, Y.-H., Kim, M.H., Lee, D.-H., Kim, C.: A key management scheme for commodity sensor networks. In: Syrotiuk, V.R., Chávez, E. (eds.) ADHOC-NOW 2005. LNCS, vol. 3738, pp. 113–126. Springer, Heidelberg (2005)
8. Liu, D., Ning, P.: Establishing pairwise keys in distributed sensor networks. In: 10th ACM Conference on Computer and Communications Security, pp. 52–61. ACM Press (2003)
9. Liu, D., Ning, P., Li, R.: Establishing pairwise keys in distributed sensor networks. ACM Trans. Inf. Syst. Secur. **8**(1), 41–77 (2005)
10. Liu, Z., Ma, J., Huang, Q., Moon, S.J.: Storage requirements for key distribution in sensor networks. In: Second International Conference on Sensor Technologies and Applications, pp. 631–638 (2008)
11. Liu, Z., Ma, J., Pei, Q., Pang, L., Park, Y.H.: Key infection, secrecy transfer, and key evolution for sensor networks. IEEE Transactions on Wireless Communications **9**(8), 2643–2653 (2010)
12. Ošť'ádal, R., Švenda, P., Matyáš, V.: A new approach to secrecy amplification in partially compromised networks (Invited Paper). In: Chakraborty, R.S., Matyas, V., Schaumont, P. (eds.) SPACE 2014. LNCS, vol. 8804, pp. 92–109. Springer, Heidelberg (2014)
13. Ošťádal, R., Švenda, P., Matyáš, V.: On Secrecy Amplification Protocols - Extended version, Technical report FIMU-RS-2015-01. Masaryk university, Brno (2015)

14. Smolka, T., Švenda, P., Sekanina, L., Matyáš, V.: Evolutionary design of message efficient secrecy amplification protocols. In: Moraglio, A., Silva, S., Krawiec, K., Machado, P., Cotta, C. (eds.) EuroGP 2012. LNCS, vol. 7244, pp. 194–205. Springer, Heidelberg (2012)
15. Švenda, P., Sekanina, L., Matyáš, V.: Evolutionary design of secrecy amplification protocols for wireless sensor networks. In: Second ACM Conference on Wireless Network Security, pp. 225–236 (2009)

Privacy-Respecting Auctions as Incentive Mechanisms in Mobile Crowd Sensing

Tassos Dimitriou[1,2](✉) and Ioannis Krontiris[3]

[1] Computer Engineering Department, Kuwait University, Kuwait City, Kuwait
tassos.dimitriou@ieee.org
[2] Research Academic Computer Technology Institute, Patras, Greece
[3] Huawei Technologies Duesseldorf GmbH, Munich, Germany
ioannis.krontiris@huawei.com

Abstract. In many mobile crowdsensing scenarios it is desirable to give micro-payments to contributors as an incentive for their participation. However, to further encourage participants to use the system, one important requirement is protection of user privacy. In this work we present a reverse auction mechanism as an efficient way to offer incentives to users by allowing them to determine their own price for the data they provide, but also as a way to motivate them to submit better quality data. At the same time our auction protocol guarantees bidders' anonymity and suggests a new rewarding mechanism that enables winners to claim their reward without being linked to the data they contributed. Our protocol is scalable, can be applied to a large class of auctions and remains both computation- and communication-efficient so that it can be run to the mobile devices of users.

Keywords: Mobile crowd sensing · Multi-attribute auctions · Incentive mechanisms · Security and privacy

1 Introduction

The availability of sensors in today's smartphones, carried by millions of people, has led to a new sensing paradigm, where people provide sensing capabilities to applications in order to map the environment and offer a better understanding of people's activities and their surroundings. This trend is often referred to as Mobile Crowdsensing (MCS) [1] or, using the more general term, as Mobile Crowdsourcing [2].

In this paradigm there is a platform provider who publicizes multiple sensing tasks from which people can choose and execute those that match their location and sensing capabilities. However, there are two factors that hinder the large-scale deployment of such applications. First, lack of proper incentives does not motivate users to participate, and second, in many cases data coming from users' smartphones can have a large impact on user privacy.

These two issues have been studied separately in existing research. For example, a number of MCS systems started incorporating different incentive features,

R.N. Akram and S. Jajodia (Eds.): WISTP 2015, LNCS 9311, pp. 20–35, 2015.
DOI: 10.1007/978-3-319-24018-3_2

including various forms of rewards based on monetary [3], social or gaming-related mechanisms [4]. The work from Zaman et al. present an overview of many available incentive mechanisms in MCS till today [5]. In particular, micro-payments have been shown to be effective in encouraging participation [6] and recently Rula et al. [7] presented additional experimental evidence that such a mechanism can increase the productivity of the participants.

One of the challenges in offering micro-payments to contributors is to determine the right amount they expect to receive as a payment for their effort in reporting sensing data. This amount may depend on personal preferences and the perceived cost of their participation, but also on the context and situation users are currently involved which can be different among individuals. One attractive solution to this problem is the use of *reverse* auctions, where the auction takes place among data providers (sellers) and data requester (buyers) of sensing data [3,8,9]. This mechanism is more attractive as it eliminates the need for the requester to set or guess the price which users consider reasonable for their data; instead it is the data provider who sets the price for the data it is willing to provide to the requester.

However, as mentioned above, privacy is an important factor that hinders user participation. Indeed, collecting data from users' devices has many privacy implications since user-sensitive information such as daily patterns, location and social relationships can easily be deduced from provided data [10,11]. It is thus imperative to address privacy in mobile crowdsensing systems. While several efforts already exist that suggest anonymizing users' contributions to protect user privacy (see for example [12]), it still remains an open problem on how to provide privacy protection when incentive mechanisms are also incorporated in the system.

Our Contribution: In this work, we suggest a privacy-respecting protocol that allows anonymous users to participate in reverse auctions employed by an MCS system. Our protocol consists of two main parts. The first part provides bidders' anonymity for the auction while it offers guarantees in terms of correctness and fairness of the auction process. The second part explores different options of rewarding users and suggests a new mechanism that enables winners of the auction to claim their rewards without being linked to their contributed data. Thus participants can have the highest privacy assurance, while the MCS platform operator can maintain the flexibility of offering incentives to users and encouraging participation. More specifically, our protocol (i) offers strong privacy protection by guaranteeing user anonymity and unlinkability of transactions, (ii) it is scalable and applicable to typical MCS applications, (iii) it offers resilience to compromised or colluding MCS entities, and (iv) it can support any type of reverse auction.

Organization: The rest of the paper is organised as follows. In Section 2, we overview work related to privacy and incentives for MCS systems, while in Section 3, we describe the system and adversarial models for our protocol. In this section we also present a *generic* auction mechanism that does not take privacy into account. Then, in Section 4, we add privacy by describing a scheme that provides for bidder anonymity in MCS auctions as well as different mechanisms that can be used to reward participating users. In this section we also specify the security properties expected by both the auction and rewarding schemes. The protocols' security guarantees and performance are analyzed in Section 5, while Section 6 concludes the paper.

2   Related Work

One of the earliest works that addresses the use of incentives for participatory sensing using auctions is [9]. Since then several other incentive models based on reverse auctions have been proposed [3,13,14]. At the same time, auction theory for electronic commerce continues to advance and multi-attributive auctions have gradually become a research hot spot, incorporating qualitative attributes to decide the winner [15]. This was shown to have many advantages for the MCS case, too [8].

Privacy is an important requirement in auctions which are used to facilitate the trade of goods. For example, Shi [16] proposes a sealed bid multi-attribute contract auction protocol that pays special attention on bid privacy and bidder anonymity. However, this and previous work [17–20] on conducting secure auctions has emphasized on attaining full privacy in which case bids remain secure even after the auction is over. This is typically achieved by distributing trust among bidders or by using multiple auctioneers. As a result, these works rely on heavier cryptographic operations and primitives (e.g. secret sharing techniques, multi-party computations, etc.) and as such they are not considered suitable for the MCS model described here. To this end, we have chosen to protect bids only during the bidding phase. Once this phase is over, all bids are revealed as they don't affect the correctness and fairness of the process or the privacy of users.

Some generic privacy-respective architectures for MCS exist that could be of interest in our discussion. For example, Gisdakis et al. [21] recently proposed the SPPEAR architecture, which supports anonymous users to contribute to sensing tasks and receive credits, as long as they submit at least n reports. In that sense it supports incentive mechanisms, but it concentrates mainly on the rewarding process.

Another recent work that places emphasis on rewards is given by Li and Cao [22], who propose two privacy-aware schemes for mobile sensing, where each data provider gets some credit for each contribution they make. The use of these credits/tokens may incentivize users to participate, however no auction mechanism is presented to help improve the quality of data provided.

Finally, Krontiris and Dimitriou [23] have proposed a solution to protect the privacy not only of data providers but also of data requesters. However, to the best of our knowledge, this is the first work that shows how to integrate more advanced incentive mechanisms, like auctions, in mobile sensing frameworks, while offering strong privacy protection guarantees.

3   Preliminaries

3.1   System Model

We consider a generic Mobile Crowdsensing (MCS) system that consists of the following three actors.

Service Providers: These are the requesters of sensing data. We assume that a requester has a specific budget and wants to collect real-time sensing data from a specific area of interest. To ensure data is real-time, the requester defines short time periods T_i, within which data are to be collected from a given area.

Users: They participate in the sensing process using various types of mobile devices such as smartphones or wearable devices. These devices come equipped with different types of sensors such as cameras, microphones, GPS, etc.

Auction Infrastructure: For the sake of modularity we separate this into three different servers, even though they can belong to the same entity: The Task Server, which is responsible of publishing the sensing tasks, the Auction Server, which is responsible for running the auction process, and the Report Server, which collects the reports from the auction winners and forwards them to the Service Provider.

Participating users first contact the task server to see if there are any tasks that match their preferences and context. Then, they decide which ones to download and execute. The advantage of this approach is that users do not reveal private information, like context or location, to the task server in order to execute the sensing task. At the network level, we assume the existence of an *anonymizing* network which can be used to protect the network identities of the communicating devices as in [12].

3.2   Threat Model

We assume that both internal and external adversaries could try to compromise the system. External adversaries can monitor communications, in order to extract information about user activities. They can also manipulate the collection of information by submitting unauthorized data or replaying data of benign users. Typically, these attacks can be mitigated using traditional cryptographic mechanisms to provide confidentiality and integrity guarantees. External attackers can also target system availability by launching jamming and DoS attacks, but here we assume that these are handled by the network operators and so they fall outside the scope of this work.

Internal adversaries, on the other hand, can be malicious users or MCS system entities that target the auction and/or rewarding processes. For example, adversarial users could try to obtain rewards without offering contributions or could try to double-spend already redeemed quotas. Internal adversaries can also target the privacy of participating users, by trying to profile them and reveal their identities by colluding with other entities in the system. Thus, with respect to user privacy, our goal would be to ensure that bids, reports and rewards cannot be linked to a particular user even if that user has submitted multiple bids and has accepted multiple rewards for the data it has provided.

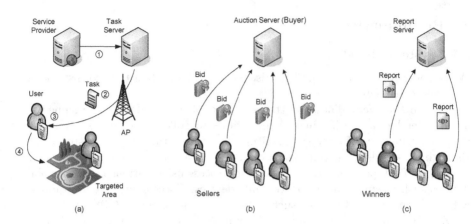

Fig. 1. Acquisition of sensing data.

Attacks where malicious users submit false sensing data are outside the scope of this work, as these can be addressed by different methods, such as anonymous reputation schemes [24].

3.3 A Generic Auction Mechanism

The goal of this section is to give a description of a generic MCS system, integrating an auction mechanism, without, however, taking privacy concerns into consideration. Then, in the next section, we will pose our security and privacy requirements and add all the mechanisms required.

As we mentioned in Section 2, many auction mechanisms proposed for MCS systems are mainly based on reverse auctions [3,9,13,14]. However, reverse auctions constitute a sub-optimal solution because they incorporate only the expected price into the user's auction bid and they do not allow participants to negotiate on *data quality* as well. In MCS applications, sensing data may be of different qualities and this has to be considered in the auction mechanism in order for better data to reach the service providers.

A more general form of auction is the *multi-attributive* auction, which enables service providers also pose quality criteria on the sensed data they are looking to buy, in addition to the price. This, however, does not affect our privacy solution, which is generic and can work with any reverse auction variant. In Figure 1, we highlight the three main phases of the auction process. The specific steps involved are described below, however for a more detailed discussion the reader is referred to [8].

Step 1: The Task Server (TS) publishes the tasks received by the Service Providers. Once a task is published, the bidding phase for this task begins and lasts for a fixed amount of time T_i. This deadline is announced in the description of the task, which also contains other details like the *acceptance conditions* C_i which define the required sensors, termination conditions, etc., and a *utility function* $S(x)$ for this task, setting the ground for which mobile devices qualify for executing it. The role of the utility function is to allow the service provider to announce its budget and quality requirements in order to be addressed by the mobile user (seller) when bidding for this task.

In summary, each task contains the following information: (i) Geographic area of interest, (ii) Acceptance Conditions C_i, (iii) Utility Function $S(x)$, and (iv) Bid duration T_i.

Step 2: The mobile devices periodically check with the Task Server to see if there are any tasks available for them, filtered based on their acceptance criteria which may also include other local, user-defined conditions like remaining battery level of the mobile device, and so on.

Step 3: If the user/mobile device decides to execute a task, then it bids for it by calculating and sending the value of the utility function $S(x)$ to the Auction Server (AS), during the bidding phase of this task. The value of $S(x)$ is calculated *locally* at the mobile device, as all necessary information is already available to the device.

One important attribute that affects the calculation of $S(x)$ is the price that the user expects for this task. However, besides the price, additional attributes can be integrated into the bid using multi-attribute auctions. More precisely, a bid can be expressed as a n-dimensional tuple of attributes x_i, represented as $x = (x_1, \ldots, x_n)$, which can be weighted together to compute the overall utility of a bid in terms of a *utility score*.

Typical examples of attributes x_i that can be incorporated in the utility function include the distance from the desired location, the location accuracy, the sampling frequency, etc.

Step 4: Before submitting their bids, the users can see their utility score, and if not satisfied, they can choose to improve it by adjusting the various attributes. For example, a user could set a lower price, move closer to the sensing area in order to provide more accurate data (see Figure 1(a)), and so on. When the utility score can no longer be improved, the bidder submits her bid to the AS (Figure 1(b)). We stress again that the user's bid is *not* comprised of the actual sensed data but is equal to the computed utility score.

Step 5: Once the bidding phase for a task is over, the *opening phase* begins where the winning bidders will be determined. More specifically, the Auction Server determines the winners to be those with the n highest utility scores (n does not have to be equal to 1). These winners are publicly announced by the Auction Server.

Step 6: The actual sensing data of the winning bidders are submitted to the Report Server (Figure 1(c)). Once the RS verifies the provided data match the utility scores promised in the bid, the winners collect their rewards for this task, typically the price that they have asked for in their bids.

4   Privacy-Respecting Auction and Rewarding Protocols

So far we have not considered security and privacy in the auction protocol. Here we pose such requirements and we demonstrate how they can be satisfied in an efficient way.

The participants of the protocol include the m bidders (potential sellers of sensing data) and the Auction Server (buyer) who will get the data from the bidder(s) with the maximum utility scores. The auction consists of two main phases: the *bidding* and the *opening* phase. During the bidding phase, each bidder commits to a bid that is kept secret from the other participants. When the bidding phase is over, the Auction Server (AS) opens the bids and determines the winners with the highest utility scores. These bidders are the winners of the auction and they will be rewarded for their participation once they upload their sensing data.

4.1   Security and Privacy Requirements

The following properties are expected from our protocol.

- *Correctness and Fairness*: The result of the auction is determined according to the rules described in the previous section. In our case the first $n < m$ bidders (e.g. $n = 2$) that made the highest utility bid win the auction and get rewarded. Additionally, no bidder can obtain an unfair advantage over the rest of the bidders by determining or changing its own bid based on information revealed about other bids.
- *Bidders' privacy*: Bidders remain anonymous throughout the whole process of the auction. This means that the identity of the bidder cannot be linked in any way to the bids they submit. Moreover two different bids from the same user cannot be linked with each other, thus nobody can build a profile and reduce users' anonymity. Finally, the claim of a reward by a winning bidder cannot be linked with either a bid or a user ID.
- *Confidentiality of bids*: All bids remain secret until the opening phase. If the Auction Server (AS) or any other party can recover some of the bids before the opening, he can inform a colluding bidder in order to cheat and win the auction. Contrary to prior work [16]-[20] that requires distribution of shares among participants or the use of heavy zero-knowledge schemes which are not easy to apply in the participatory sensing paradigm, we will develop a lightweight, yet secure protocol, that guarantees bid secrecy up until the opening phase.
- *Public verifiability*: The correctness of the auction process should be easy to verify by any interested party. This includes assurance about the validity of the bids, as well as winner selection.
- *Non-repudiation*: No bidder should be able to change its mind (e.g. deny or modify its bid) once the bid is submitted. Our protocol will ensure this property by requiring the bidders to commit to their bids prior to the opening phase.

4.2 Auction Protocol

In what follows we assume that bidders are aware of the public key K_{AS} of the auction server. They can use this to send confidential information to AS and authenticate messages signed by the AS. We denote by $H()$ a secure cryptographic hash function with at least 256 bits of output. In this context 'secure' means that $H()$ is one-way and collision resistant. Thus inverting the hash function or finding x and y satisfying $H(x) = H(y)$ is computationally infeasible.

We also assume the existence of a "bulletin board" that is used to communicate messages between the bidders and the Auction Server (AS). Once a message is posted to the bulletin board, anybody (even third-parties) can read it. However, erasing from the bulletin board is not possible. Thus, the bulletin board is nothing more than a public channel where broadcasted messages are received by anybody and can be verified by any third party [25].

The two main phases of the auction are bidding and opening, however, there is also an implicit, *registration* phase in which the AS sets up the bulletin board, publishes its public key and announces various parameters of the auction like the auction ID, starting/ending time, duration of each phase, and so on. Upon registration, each bidder i sends to the AS a pseudonymous ID (*BidderID*) to represent its identity during the auction along with a *one-time* public key K_i. AS publishes this information to the bulletin board and every bidder can verify it has been properly registered for the auction.

Bidding: During the bidding phase, each bidder i computes its utility score S_i, masks it with a random number r_i and sends a commitment C_i of the form

$$C_i = Sig_i(AuctionID\|BidderID\|h_i), \tag{1}$$

where $h_i = H(S_i\|r_i)$. Thus the auction server receives a bid, however it cannot read this bid before the opening phase. Additionally, these values are published in the bulletin board so that anybody can verify that its bid has been correctly accounted for.

Opening: When the auction server marks the end of the bidding phase, each bidder reveals both S_i and r_i that have been used in the computation of the commitment C_i. The server goes through the values C_i and recovers the n highest utility scores as the winners of the auction. Then it sends a signed message

$$Sig_{AS}(AuctionID, \langle BidderID_{i_1}, K_{i_1}, S_{i_1}, r_{i_1}\rangle,$$
$$\langle BidderID_{i_2}, K_{i_2}, S_{i_2}, r_{i_2}\rangle, \ldots) \tag{2}$$

which contains the pseudonymous IDs of the winners along with their public keys and the committed values that have been opened in the beginning of the phase. Thus, any participant can verify correctness by computing $H(S_i\|r_i)$ and comparing with the signature C_i received during the bidding phase. In the next section we discuss how the winning bidders can be rewarded for the data they provide.

4.3   Rewarding Mechanisms

Once the winning bidders are selected, they contact the Report Server (RS) in order to transmit their sensed data (recall Figure 1(c)). Each winning bidder i provides RS with the winning notification shown in (2) (alternatively the auction server can forward this directly to the RS) and submits its sensed data as follows:

$$Bidder_i \rightarrow RS : \langle BidderID, AuctionID, D, \sigma \rangle, \tag{3}$$

where $\sigma = Sig_i(BidderID, AuctionID, H(D))$ and D is the sensed data for the relevant task. The Report Server goes on to verify if the signature comes from a winning bidder whose public key is listed in the winning notification shown in (2) and evaluates the utility function on the received data D. If the utility score matches the one shown in the winning notification, it proceeds to reward the bidder for the data provided[1]. In the following, we demonstrate how this can be achieved using (i) an existing payment service (e.g. a Bank) along with an e-cash scheme, and (ii) a decentralized token-based scheme.

While the e-cash scheme may be easier conceptually, it suffers from a potential loss of privacy if the report server and the Bank collude together to reveal the bidder's identity. To mitigate this possible loss of trust, we have developed a decentralized variant where the RS is the sole issuer of rewards that can be redeemed by the bidder.

Using e-cash: An e-cash scheme in its general form is a set of cryptographic operations that allows a party S (in our case the report server) to withdraw electronic money from a bank in order to purchase something from a second party B (the bidder), and B to deposit the money in its bank account. E-cash schemes are distinguished between "on-line" and "off-line" ones depending on whether the bank has to be actively involved in the purchase protocol. The auction protocol that we present here works with both schemes, however an off-line scheme is more preferable as the bidder does not have to query the bank for the validity of the payment it will receive from the report server. We therefore abstract away the actual implementation details of the digital cash protocol used and describe a coin as tuple $\langle c, \sigma_{Bank}(c) \rangle$, where c basically denotes the value of the coin and $\sigma_{Bank}(c)$ is the signature of the bank. Other information such as expiration day, or details that might help in extracting the ID of the owner in case of double-spending are omitted here [27].

Once the Report Server receives the data sent by the winning bidder in message (3), it sends back to the bidder a coin $\langle c, \sigma_{Bank}(c) \rangle$ *encrypted* with

---

[1] An issue may arise if the provider refuses to reward the bidder after obtaining the sensed data. Although there are cryptographic protocols to mitigate this type of behavior [26], we chose to keep the protocol as simple as possible since (i) the damage to the reputation of the provider will be much higher than any gains for data received but not paid, and (ii) the provider runs the risk of losing potential bidders which goes against the idea of introducing payments in the first place as a means to enhance user participation in crowdsensing applications.

the bidder's public key. The value of the coin matches the price agreed in the specification of the utility function. The RS does not need to know who the bidder is, only that it is one of the winners of the auction. The encryption of the coin is required so that only the bidder can recover (and use) the coin. Thus, anyone else who eavesdrops on the communication line cannot steal and spend the coin. The bidder now can either deposit the coin to the Bank or spend it if the coin is transferable. This depends on the underlying digital cash protocol used.

Another alternative, that avoids the use of digital cash but still uses a centralized payment service, is for the Report Server to authorize a payment *directly* with the bank. In this scheme, the winning bidder computes

$$\mu = F(H(D), N),$$

where F is a secure one-way function, D is the data submitted and N is a new unpredictable number. Then it includes μ in the message and the signature σ shown in (3). Once the Report Server receives and validates the signature, it produces a payment $p_{RS} = Sig_{RS}(\langle H(D), \mu, Amount \rangle)$, where *Amount* corresponds the price for the data received, and forwards p_{RS} to both the bidder and the payment service. To claim the money from the bank, the bidder has to reveal N used in the computation of μ. Once the bank verifies the signature of RS on p_{RS} and validates μ, it credits the bidder with the specified amount.

Both schemes presented here protect the bidder's anonymity as long as the Report Server and the payment service/Bank do not collude to reveal the bidder's identity. If the payment service is not trusted, we can use a decentralized variant where the bidder itself constructs the coins to be redeemed by the RS. This is explained below.

Using a Decentralized Scheme: To eliminate the need for a centralized payment service, we can use the Report Server as an *issuer* of reward tokens that can be redeemed by the bidder. However, since it is the RS who issues these tokens we must be sure that tokens cannot be used to track bidders. A similar token service was developed in [28], however for use in a different setting. There, a querier Q wishing to access an MCS network for sensor data could use tokens issued by the application owner to pay for data received by some producer P.

In our setting there is no querier for data, however we can leverage this technology to allow a winning bidder to obtain rewards for the data provided once the auction is over. This approach can still be thought as a lightweight e-cash scheme, yet without the requirement of a trusted payment service. However, in this case, double-spending detection becomes an important property as bidders may be tempted to redeem these tokens more than once. In what follows, we explain how to adapt these ideas to build a rewarding mechanism for auctions. In particular, we will explain (i) how tokens can be constructed during submission of sensing data without compromising bidder privacy, and (ii) how tokens can be redeemed.

Token construction: To create such a token, the collaboration of both the bidder and the Report Server is needed. The bidder has to introduce some *private* piece of information (a unique ID) to the token T so that upon redemption, the RS can tell if T is already spent. The token will also contain a *public* part, introduced by the RS, minimally containing the value of the coin but perhaps an expiration date, etc. To make these tokens untraceable, blind signatures will be used to blind the private information introduced to the token by the bidder before it is signed by the RS. When the blinding factor is later removed, the token will bear the signature of the RS but the only identifiable information on the coin will be its public part.

To introduce this unique ID to the token and make double-spending possible, we leverage the identification scheme of Schnorr [29]. The bidder first selects two primes p and q, where $q|p-1$. Then it chooses at random two numbers $s, r \in Z_p$ and computes $u = g^{-s} \bmod p$ and $v = g^r \bmod p$, where g is a generator of order q in Z_p^*. The token ID now is comprised of the two values u and v, which has to be further blinded by the bidder and signed by the RS as mentioned above (details omitted due to space restrictions, however the interested reader is referred to [30]). After the signature by the RS, the bidder will have in its possession a token T of the form

$$T = Sig_{RS}(\langle u, v, Value, Expiration \rangle). \tag{4}$$

Token spending: When, at some future time t, the bidder wants to spend T, it has to prove it knows s, r. This is possible using a non-interactive zero-knowledge proof. In particular, the bidder sends along with the token T, the pair $\langle y, t \rangle$, where t is the date/time of the transaction, $e = H(T, t)$ and $y = r + es \bmod q$. The RS verifies the authenticity of the token by first checking its signature on T and then wether $v = g^y u^e \bmod p$. If both tests succeed, the token is considered *valid*. However, RS still needs to check that T has not been used before.

So, RS looks in its database of spent tokens for a token with the same ID $\langle u, v \rangle$. If no such token exists, T is accepted and RS records the tuple $\langle T, y, t \rangle$. If, however, a token T with the same ID already exists, there will be two tuples $\langle y, t \rangle$ and $\langle y', t' \rangle$ of token T such that $v = g^y u^e \bmod p$, $v = g^{y'} u^{e'} \bmod p$, $y = r + es$ and $y' = r + e's$. From these two last values, RS can obtain the secret value $s = (y - y')/(e - e')$ and subsequently r. Thus, two submissions of the same token will result in evidence that the coin has already been spent. However, as these values are not tied to the bidder's identity, its privacy is maintained even in the case of double-spending.

In summary, the protocol ensures that i) tokens are not tied to bidder identities, and ii) the RS is protected by malicious bidders who try to double-spend tokens. A snapshot of both data submission and token construction phases is shown in Figure 2 (although Steps 1a and 1b are shown separate for presentation clarity, they can be merged into one.)

Winning Bidder B_i **Report Server** RS

Data submission and token generation

D is the sensed data
Set $\sigma = Sig_i(BidderID, AuctionID, H(D))$

1a: $\langle BidderID, AuctionID, D, \sigma \rangle$ →

Verify signature σ.
Is B_i a valid winner?

Pick random numbers $s, r \in Z_p$
Set $u = g^{-s} \bmod p$, $v = g^r \bmod p$
Create blinded token ID $\langle u^*, v^* \rangle$
Obtain blind signature

1b: $\langle u^*, v^* \rangle$ →

←   2: $Sig_{RS}(\langle u^*, v^*, Val, Exp \rangle)$

Send signed, blinded token

Remove blinding factor
$TokenT = Sig_{RS}(\langle u, v, Val, Exp \rangle)$

Fig. 2. Data Reporting and Token Generation.

5 Evaluation

In this section we first emphasize on how our solution satisfies the security and privacy requirements posed in Section 4.1. Then, we also discuss performance issues.

- *Confidentiality of bids.* Since bids are opened only after the bidding phase, nobody can compute the bids before they are opened. This is because the bids at this time consist of only a commitment of the form $h_i = H(S_i \| r_i)$. The one-wayness of the hash function H ensures that bid values remain hidden, eliminating the possibility of collusion since no bidder or the Auction server can leak any information about anybody else's bidding. It is only after the opening phase that bids are revealed to all.
- *Correctness & Verifiability.* Since all values are published in the bulletin board anybody can verify the correctness of the auction. This is possible as all bidders reveal their utility scores S_i and the random numbers r_i used in the computation of the signed bid commitment h_i. Hence no new values can be introduced at this point (all values must already exist in the bulletin board) or changed (due to the collision resistance of the hash function H). A value that is not available in the bulletin board at the end of the opening phase automatically excludes the bidder for the remaining of the auction. Additionally, anybody can compare and verify if the winning bidders published in message (2) by the AS are indeed the ones with the highest utility scores. Thus, correctness of the auction is assured.
- *Non-repudiation.* Since each bid carries the bidder's signature, nobody can deny its bid. The collision resistance of the hash function also ensures that it is not possible to find a different set of (S_i', r_i') such that $H(S_i' \| r_i') = H(S_i \| r_i)$. Hence nobody can deny its bidding price once the bids are opened. Furthermore, if a dispute arises over the winning bids, the bid commitment

can be used to resolve the dispute: the values (S_i, r_i) and the bidder's signature can be used to prove authenticity of a bid.

- *Unlinkability between bids.* This property is related to the privacy of the bidder. In particular, we would like to be sure that it is not possible to relate two bids submitted at *different* auctions by the same bidder. It should be clear that this property holds as bidders participate in auctions using different pseudonyms and public keys. Hence it is not possible to relate the bids.[2]

- *Unforgeability/Unreusability of tokens.* The zero knowledge proofs used during token spending ensure that only a bidder who knows the representation of u and v in the token ID can supply these proofs. Furthermore if the bidder supplies two different proofs for the same token, the secret values r, s used in the construction u and v can be extracted, thus providing a proof of double-spending. Thus, a token can be used only once, satisfying the unreusability property.

- *Bidder privacy/Unlinkability of tokens.* When a user tries to redeem a token and provides the server (directly or indirectly through a proxy) the zero knowledge proof, the server cannot tell which bidder created the token as the only visible part during the token construction is the public part $\langle Val, Exp \rangle$ of the token.

    There are, however, other *side channels* that can be used to infer bidder information. Consider, for example, the case where the IP address of a bidder is visible when the user submits sensed data/retrieves a token to/from the server and then tries to spend this token. Obviously, in such a case additional mechanisms are required to ensure that a connection cannot be made with the reporting bidder. However this can be avoided by using an anonymizing network at the network layer, as we mentioned in our system model.

    Another side channel is the structure of the token's public part $\langle Val, Exp \rangle$. If the value of the token or its expiration date is an unusual quantity, both can be used to associate the data with the bidder upon redeeming the token. Hence these values must be drawn from a universe that does not allow for this kind of discrimination. For example, expiration dates can be set to the end of the current year and token values can be *coarsely* defined. This would exclude tokens with unusually precise values, e.g. \$1.236743. A simpler alternative, however, is to use a trusted proxy or representative that can redeem these rewards on behalf of a user.

Performance

The bid submission protocol is very simple, requiring the submission of just a single message (recall the bidding message shown in (1)). The bidder has to compute a hash value $H(S_i \| r_i)$ on the utility score S_i and random r_i, along

---

[2] This, however, necessitates the use of an anonymity service so that bid submissions cannot be linked to an internet identifier such as the IP address of the bidder. Hence the use of services like TOR mentioned in the system model.

with a signature C_i on this data. A typical signature using a 1024-bit signing key on a 450MHz processor takes approximately 30ms as shown in [31], which is well within the capabilities of modern-day phones incorporating much faster CPUs. Similarly, the opening phase requires one more message in which each bidder reveals the committed values S_i and r_i.

Perhaps it is more instructive to consider the token rewarding protocol we developed in Section 4.3, as this actively involves the bidder in the token generation process. Here we argue that the most expensive operation is the actual transmission of the sensed data submitted by the user (Step 1a in Figure 2). The creation of the token requires two modular exponentiations for u and v, and two modular multiplications for the blinding and unblinding of the u^* and v^*. However, these operations are well within the capabilities of modern phones as mentioned above. Token redemption requires the user to prove knowledge of the values u and v, however this requires only one extra addition and multiplication to compute $\langle T, y, t \rangle$. The burden is on the side of the server who has to verify the corresponding signature, but this overhead is negligible given the capabilities of the RS.

Finally, from a storage point of view, the server has to maintain only the collection of tokens that have not expired yet. As the sensor data collected along with these tokens are perhaps orders of magnitude larger, the overhead for the Report Server is again minimal.

6   Conclusions

In this paper we have presented a protocol for privacy-protecting auctions in mobile crowdsensing systems. Users of mobile devices can participate anonymously in the auctions and define the price they expect for contributing sensing data. On the other side, the buyer of the data can select the winners based not only on the price, but also on the quality of the offered data. The winners of the auction can then collect their price without linking their real identity to the data they contributed. Our solution uses a lightweight and decentralized rewarding scheme eliminating the need for a single trusted payment system.

As future work, we plan to extend our protocol to address some research questions that remain open. In particular, we plan to incorporate a mechanism for encouraging users who lose the auction, to return, so that the system maintains its base of participants. We also think it is important to include user credibility as one of the attributes that determine the winners of the auction. In order to do that, we plan to show how to integrate an anonymous reputation mechanism in our auction protocol so that winners can collect reputation points based on the quality of their submitted data.

Acknowledgments. The first author would like to acknowledge support of this work by Kuwait University, Research Grant No. QE 01/13.

References

1. Guo, B., Yu, Z., Zhou, X., Zhang, D.: From participatory sensing to mobile crowd sensing. In: Proceedings of the IEEE PERCOM Workshops, pp. 593–598, March 2014
2. Chatzimilioudis, G., Konstantinidis, A., Laoudias, C., Zeinalipour-Yazti, D.: Crowdsourcing with smartphones. IEEE Internet Computing **16**(5), 36–44 (2012)
3. Yang, D., Xue, G., Fang, X., Tang, J.: Crowdsourcing to smartphones: incentive mechanism design for mobile phone sensing. In: Mobicom 2012, Istanbul, Turkey, pp. 173–184 (2012)
4. Di, B., Wang, T., Song, L., Han, Z.: Incentive mechanism for collaborative smartphone sensing using overlapping coalition formation games. In: IEEE Globe Communication Conference (Globecom), Atlanta, USA, pp. 1705–1710 (2013)
5. Zaman, S., Abrar, N., Iqbal, A.: Incentive model design for participatory sensing: technologies and challenges. In: International Conference on Networking Systems and Security (NSysS), pp. 1–6 (2015)
6. Reddy, S., Estrin, D., Hansen, M., Srivastava, M.: Examining micro-payments for participatory sensing data collections. In: Proceedings of the 12th ACM International Conference on Ubiquitous Computing (UbiComp), pp. 33–36 (2010)
7. Rula, J.P., Navda, V., Bustamante, F.E., Bhagwan, R., Guha, S.: No "one-size fits all": towards a principled approach for incentives in mobile crowdsourcing. In: Proceedings of the 15th Workshop on Mobile Computing Systems and Applications (HotMobile), pp. 3:1–3:5 (2014)
8. Krontiris, I., Albers, A.: Monetary incentives in participatory sensing using multi-attributive auctions. International Journal of Parallel, Emergent and Distributed Systems **27**(4) (2012)
9. Lee, J.S., Hoh, B.: Sell your experiences: a market mechanism based incentive for participatory sensing. In: Proceedings of the IEEE International Conference on Pervasive Computing and Communications (PerCom), pp. 60–68 (2010)
10. Christin, D., Reinhardt, A., Kanhere, S.S., Hollick, M.: A survey on privacy in mobile participatory sensing applications. Journal of Systems and Software **84**(11) (2011)
11. Wang, Y., Huang, Y., Louis, C.: Respecting user privacy in mobile crowdsourcing. ASE Science Journal **2**(2) (2013)
12. Shin, M., Cornelius, C., Peebles, D., Kapadia, A., Kotz, D., Triandopoulos, N.: AnonySense: A system for anonymous opportunistic sensing. Journal of Pervasive and Mobile Computing **7**(1), 16–30 (2010)
13. Zhang, X., Yang, Z., Zhou, Z., Cai, H., Chen, L., Li, X.: Free market of crowdsourcing: Incentive mechanism design for mobile sensing. IEEE Transactions on Parallel and Distributed Systems **25**(12), 3190–3200 (2014)
14. Koutsopoulos, I.: Optimal incentive-driven design of participatory sensing systems. In: Proceedings of IEEE INFOCOM, pp. 14–19 (2013)
15. Pham, L., Teich, J., Wallenius, H., Wallenius, J.: Multi-attribute online reverse auctions: Recent research trends. European J. of Oper. Research **242**(1), 1–9 (2015)
16. Shi, W.: A sealed-bid multi-attribute auction protocol with strong bid privacy and bidder privacy. Security and Communication Networks **6**(10), 1281–1289 (2013)
17. Peng, K., Boyd, C., Dawson, E.: Optimization of electronic first-bid sealed-bid auction based on homomorphic secret sharing. In: Dawson, E., Vaudenay, S. (eds.) Mycrypt 2005. LNCS, vol. 3715, pp. 84–98. Springer, Heidelberg (2005)

18. Brandt, F.: How to obtain full privacy in auctions. Intern. Journal of Information Security **5**(4), 201–216 (2006)
19. Zheng, S., McAven, L., Mu, Y.: First price sealed bid auction without auctioneers. In: Proceedings of the International Conference on Wireless Communications and Mobile Computing (IWCMC), pp. 127–131 (2007)
20. Nojoumian, M., Stinson, D.R.: Efficient sealed-bid auction protocols using verifiable secret sharing. In: Huang, X., Zhou, J. (eds.) ISPEC 2014. LNCS, vol. 8434, pp. 302–317. Springer, Heidelberg (2014)
21. Gisdakis, S., Giannetsos, T., Papadimitratos, P.: SPPEAR: security & privacy-preserving architecture for participatory-sensing applications. In: Proc. of the 7th ACM Conf. on Security and Privacy in Wireless and Mobile Networks (WiSec), pp. 39–50 (2014)
22. Li, Q., Cao, G.: Providing efficient privacy-aware incentives for mobile sensing. In: Proceedings of the 34th IEEE International Conference on Distributed Computing Systems (ICDCS), pp. 208–217 (2014)
23. Krontiris, I., Dimitriou, T.: A platform for privacy protection of data requesters and data providers in mobile sensing. Computer Communications **11**, 43–54 (2015)
24. Christin, D., Rosskopf, C., Hollick, M., Martucci, L.A., Kanhere, S.S.: Incognisense: an anonymity-preserving reputation framework for participatory sensing applications. In: Proceedings of the IEEE PerCom, pp. 135–143 (2012)
25. Cohen, J.D., Fischer, M.J.: A robust and verifiable cryptographically secure election scheme. In: Proceedings of the 26th Annual Symposium on Foundations of Computer Science (SFCS), pp. 372–382 (1985)
26. Rial, A., Preneel, B.: Optimistic fair priced oblivious transfer. In: Bernstein, D.J., Lange, T. (eds.) AFRICACRYPT 2010. LNCS, vol. 6055, pp. 131–147. Springer, Heidelberg (2010)
27. Chaum, D., Fiat, A., Naor, M.: Untraceable electronic cash. In: Goldwasser, S. (ed.) CRYPTO 1988. LNCS, vol. 403, pp. 319–327. Springer, Heidelberg (1990)
28. Dimitriou, T., Krontiris, I., Sabouri, A.: PEPPeR: A querier's privacy enhancing protocol for PaRticipatory sensing. In: Schmidt, A.U., Russello, G., Krontiris, I., Lian, S. (eds.) MobiSec 2012. LNICST, vol. 107, pp. 93–106. Springer, Heidelberg (2012)
29. Schnorr, C.P.: Efficient signature generation by smart cards. Journal of Cryptology **4**(3), 161–174 (1991)
30. Chaum, D.: Blind signatures for untraceable payments. In: Advances in Cryptology Proceedings of Crypto. no. 3, pp. 199–203 (1982)
31. Lauter, K.: The advantages of elliptic curve cryptography for wireless security. IEEE Wireless Communications **11**(1), 62–67 (2004)

Electrical Heart Signals can be Monitored from the Moon: Security Implications for IPI-Based Protocols

Alejandro Calleja, Pedro Peris-Lopez$^{(\boxtimes)}$, and Juan E. Tapiador

Universidad Carlos III de Madrid, Avenida de la Universidad 30,
28911 Leganes, Madrid, Spain
pperis@inf.uc3m.es

Abstract. Inter-Pulse Intervals (IPIs) have been proposed as a source of entropy for key generation and establishment algorithms in Implantable Medical Devices (IMDs) and Body Area Networks (BANs). Most of the proposed protocols built on top of this biometric feature assume that reliable measures of the IPIs are only available to devices maintaining physical contact with the user. However, computer vision techniques have proved to be able to obtain estimates of heart timings from a video recording of the user's face. In this paper, we study the impact of these techniques on IPI-based authentication protocols, comparing a heart signal captured using a traditional contact-based approach against a signal retrieved using such a contactless technique. One key finding is that quantization is a crucial step in the process and we report our empirical assessment of the main approaches proposed so far. Our results show that up to 70% of the information obtained by means of the contact-based method can be also obtained through contactless techniques.

Keywords: Implantable medical devices · Inter-pulse intervals · IMD Security · Security protocols

1 Introduction

Implantable Medical Devices (IMDs) allow physicians to treat medical conditions such as heart or neurodegenerative diseases. Similar kind of devices are increasingly being used in Wireless Body Area Networks (WBANs), in which wireless sensors deployed over the patient are able to monitor her physical status. The current trend in the design of this sort of devices is making totally unnecessary the intervention of patients, thus facilitating the remote operation by the physician with the aim of programming them or performing diagnostic tasks. As this family of devices evolves and becomes more sophisticated, new challenges arise concerning their security and more efficient protection mechanisms are demanded [1]. For instance, the inclusion of wireless radio communication capabilities in IMDs has given rise to several concerns regarding the privacy and integrity of information exchanged between the physician and the device.

© IFIP International Federation for Information Processing 2015
R.N. Akram and S. Jajodia (Eds.): WISTP 2015, LNCS 9311, pp. 36–51, 2015.
DOI: 10.1007/978-3-319-24018-3_3

As the patient's privacy and physical safety are the main assets involved, security plays a vital role for these new technologies. Several authors have shown the potential risks derived from deploying security-lacking protocols in these scenarios, including the modification of the implant's operational parameters or the leakage of the patient's private information [2–4]. It is also worth mentioning that IMDs suffer from important limitations regarding their computational capabilities and energy consumption, which so far has hindered the use of strong and well-known security protocols, for example those based on public-key cryptography algorithms [1]. This has motivated experts to seek more lightweight alternatives in the field of biometry. Specifically, one of the most promising approaches so far relies on the use of the Inter-Pulse Intervals (IPIs) obtained from the patient's heart signals via electrocardiography (ECG) or photoplethysmography (PPG). The use of this information comes supported mainly by the high degree of entropy contained in IPIs [5–8] and by the simplicity and consistency in the measuring process, which allows the retrieval of nearly the same values in different body parts. Overall, this fact makes such signals very resilient against noise.

All the proposed protocols built on top of this feature assume that IPIs cannot be retrieved if there is no physical contact between the patient and a measuring device (i.e., a set of electrodes). This peculiarity has been proposed as an additional security warranty, since if a potential attacker is not touching the patient, she will be unable of authenticating herself against the implanted device or the WBAN and, therefore, unable to inject fraudulent information or modifying the applied therapies. Nevertheless, driven by the rise of telemedicine, new techniques with the ability to retrieve heart signals such as ECG or PPG without establishing physical contact with patients have emerged [9,10]. These techniques are roughly based on the amount of light reflected by the human skin when the blood flows through capillaries located near the skin surface. The variations in the reflected light are totally imperceptible to the human eye, but could be enhanced and magnified using video processing and computer vision techniques [10]. Despite the fact that these techniques could threaten the need of physical contact assumed in IPI-based protocols, to the best of our knowledge their potential impact has not been yet explored.

In this paper, we study how contactless techniques developed to retrieve heart signals that can be used as the basis for security protection mechanisms on-board of IMDs. To do so, we present a comparison of heart signals obtained by means of a contact-based and a contactless method. Our approach uses commodity hardware to show that, following a process akin to those presented in related works, it is possible to extract nearly equal IPIs using both methods. Particularly, our final results show that up to 70% of the information contained in the signal obtained through the contact method can be extracted from the signal retrieved using the contactless technique.

The rest of this paper is structured as follows. In Section 2 an overview of cardiac signals and feature extraction is introduced. Section 3 presents our proposal, attending to important aspects such as signal retrieval, preprocessing, and feature extraction. The experimental setting and our results are presented in Section 4. In Section 5, we discuss the applicability of our approach and the potential impact to the IPI-based protocols proposed so far. Finally, in Section 5 we present our conclusions and future research lines.

2   Background

During the past few years, several biometric features have been proposed to be used in human identification and other security-related scenarios. For instance, biometric traits like fingerprints, the voice pitch, or iris pigmentation have been successfully used as verification or identification mechanism [11–13]. The rise of mobile health services and telemedice have forced the experts to seek new biometric features that could be measured in a more continuous and ubiquitous way, i.e., without requiring the interruption of the patient's activity. Furthermore, as many kinds of WBANs and IMDs exist, it is desirable for a candidate biometric trait to be accessible in almost every part of the body. Nowadays, the most promising features are those related to the heart activity, particularly those related to the Heart Variability (HV), i.e., the variation in the time intervals between heartbeats, which can be measured by the analysis of different cardiac biosignals such as the ECG or the PPG.

The ECG signal describes the variations in the electrical activity of the heart within a time interval. An ECG graph can be used to obtain a clear representation of the HV through the analysis of the QRS complex, a set of waves representing the fluctuations of electrical potential due to depolarization of heart muscles during a heartbeat. As depicted in Figure 1(a), the QRS complex is composed by the superposition of several waves (Q, R, and S) with different amplitudes and duration. The ECG signal can be retrieved by using a set of sensors or electrodes attached to different body parts and connected to a measuring device that interprets and stores the collected data. Nowadays it is possible to find small and wearable versions of these devices, resulting in a measuring process that does not interfere with the normal activity of the patient [14].

On the other hand, the photoplethysmogram (PPG) signal, also known as pulse signal, describes the variation in the amount of blood flowing in a certain body area during a time interval. Like the ECG signal, a PPG signal can be retrieved using a sensor attached to some body parts such as a finger, an earlobe, or the forehead. The PPG is obtained by illuminating the skin with a light pulse and measuring the amount of reflected or absorbed light, which varies depending on the volume of blood that flows in a given instant. These variations can be represented in a graph such as the one depicted in Figure 1(b). As it can be seen, the PPG also contains local maxima similar to those that can be observed in the ECG graph. This means that the same heartbeat (i.e., the R peak) can be detected in both signals.

2.1   The Inter-Pulse Interval Feature

Depending on the purpose of the biometric system, one-to-one or one-to-many comparisons are performed for verification and identification, respectively. In these comparisons, it is unusual to compare all the raw-biometric material, but rather a set of features extracted from it. For instance, when using fingerprints, it is possible to extract many features such as the fingerprint size, its shape, or the distance between ridges. Instead of using the whole set of features, only a subset is commonly employed. This is done because using all extracted features could affect the protocol performance, for instance by increasing the probability of false positives or negatives. Therefore, the common approach is to choose a representative set of features and build a robust protocol on top of them.

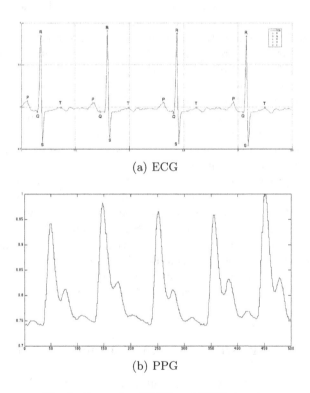

(a) ECG

(b) PPG

Fig. 1. Example of ECG and PPG signals.

In the case of the cardiac signals, several authors have shown the existence of certain features that can be used for security purposes due to their randomness [5–7]. This is the case of the Inter-Pulse Intervals (IPIs). An IPI is the temporal distance between two heartbeats (i.e., the inverse of the heart rate). Thus, given a cardiac signal, an IPI can be extracted by just measuring the temporal distance between two R peaks, which are correlated with the heartbeats. As said before, a heartbeat is detectable in both the ECG and the PPG signal, so the IPI feature can be extracted from these two signals.

Since the R wave is the most prominent in the QRS complex, its detection is easier than in the case of other signal features. This greatly simplifies the measuring process, given the fact that it relaxes the need of having a large set of sensors attached in order to obtain a reliable dataset. In practical terms, just one or three electrodes would suffice for the acquisition of the PPG and ECG signals, respectively.

2.2 Digitalization

In order to use the retrieved IPI, it must be digitally represented using an encoding process. Digitalization is approached in previous works by means of a quantization algorithm. The use of one quantizer or another will affect the overall system performance. Quantization consists in mapping the image set of an analog and continuous signal (representing, for example, a voltage signal) into a small set of discrete values. Combining this process with a subsequent binary codification, it is possible to obtain a digital representation of an analog signal. It is important to note that the quantization process introduces a noise component due to the rounding errors between the real values and the approximated discrete values. The amount of noise varies depending on several parameters such as the quantization step (i.e., the distance between the discrete values the real values are mapped to) or the quantization algorithm employed.

Choosing a particular quantization algorithm and its parameters is a crucial step in the development of IPI-based protocols, as this will affect the amount and the quality of the obtained digital representation. Surprisingly, despite this fact, only a few of the publications in this field explain in detail the particular quantization process used. Furthermore, even those works that facilitate details about the process usually only provide details about the precision used in the encoding process, i.e., the number of bits used to encode the quantized values. In Section 3.3, the quantification alternatives included in our study are described in detail.

3   Biosignal Retrieval: Physical Contact vs Contactless

The high levels of entropy that can be found in the IPIs of cardiac signals make it a very attractive feature to be used in the generation of shared keys between an IMD and a programmer device. Besides, as the extraction of IPIs requires physical contact, it prevents that this information could be retrieved by a third party without the implant owner noticing it. However, this last assumption has been overridden by contactless biosignal retrieval techniques such as the one mentioned above. Thus, if it is possible to achieve a similar signal resolution using contactless techniques as that achieved with contact-based ones, this would mean that an attacker might try to defeat the security of IPI- based protocols without needing physical contact with the user.

With the aim of exploring the impact of this threat, we carried out an effective comparison between two heart signals retrieved by both methods. The first will be retrieved by a traditional contact-based technique. Specifically, we use a pulse sensor similar to the ones used in medical environments to obtain a PPG signal. The second signal will be recorded using a contactless method. In our case, we will use a heart rate monitor software based on real time video analysis to estimate heart variability. This signal will be compared against the first one, which will be considered as a control signal, extracting the same features and measuring their similarity.

To extract the features from the signals, we followed a procedure similar to the one proposed by previous works on IPI-based protocols. First, we identify the R peaks in both signals with the aim of detecting when a heartbeat happens. The number of heartbeats identified on each signal will be used as a preliminary metric of similarity. After this, we calculate the IPIs on both signals and apply a quantization algorithm in order to get their binary representations. After that, we use traditional techniques such as Hamming distance and entropy analysis to measure the similarity between both signals at low level.

Our final goal is to measure the impact of contactless biosignal retrieval techniques on security solutions for IMDs. To do so, we have followed a similar approaches to the one described for the paring stages of protocols such as IMD-Guard [15] or H2H [8]. The following sections present a more detailed description of the experimental process and the obtained results.

3.1 Signal Acquisition

The signal retrieval process has been carried out by using commodity hardware and software. In order to capture the control signal, we have used a DIY pulse sensor[1] attached to an `Arduino` microcontroller[2], which acts as interface between the sensor and the computer used for storing the signal. The sensor is supposed to be placed in an area where the blood flow could be easily measured, such as a fingertip or an earlobe. The microcontroller was loaded with a program that reads every 50 ms the analog input to which the sensor is connected and sends it to the computer through its serial interface. The sensor circuitry roughly consists of a LED that emits a light pulse and a light-dependent resistor that changes its value depending on the amount of light that it receives from the environment. As explained above, the amount of light reflected by the skin changes when a heartbeat happens. In this way, it is possible to get an approximation of the blood flow and the HV. The computer to which the microcontroller is connected runs a simple process that periodically reads the serial port and saves the read data.

On the other hand, the contactless signal has been taken using the built-in webcam of an Apple MacbookPro laptop. The camera is used as a real-time video source for an open-source pulse monitor software that is able to approximate

---

[1] http://pulsesensor.myshopify.com/

[2] http://www.arduino.cc/

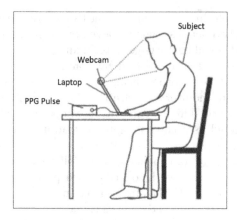

Fig. 2. Experimental Setup

the patient's PPG signal. This software locates the forehead of the subject using the OpenCV[3] computer vision library and performs spectral power analysis to approximate the heart rate and its corresponding PPG signal. In our setup, the subject is located in front of the camera, at a distance of around 50 cm from the laptop. The recorded video resolution is 640x480 pixels at a frame rate of 30 fps and the color scheme used is RGB with 8 bits per channel. This software has been slightly modified for the purpose of our experimentation.

3.2 Preprocessing

The experimental setup described before, sketched in Figure 2, has been used for retrieving 13 pairs of samples from subjects of ages between 20 and 40 years old with no known heart condition and Caucasian skin tone. All signals have a length of 60 seconds. The frequency of the sensor signal is 100 Hz while the frequency of the webcam signal is 14.7 Hz.

Once the two raw signals were gathered, a preprocessing stage is needed prior to the detection of the R-peaks. As a first step, both signals were resampled to the same frequency. In this case, we decided to resample the signal sampled at the highest frequency (the sensor signal) to the lowest one in order to reach the same temporal resolution in both of them. Following this approach, the sensor signal has been resampled to 14.7 Hz. The next step was to apply a filtering strategy to reduce in both signals the noise components introduced during the measuring process. A low-pass filter with a 3 Hz threshold frequency was applied in order to remove higher frequencies. This parameter has been tuned according to the highest heart rate considered, which is 180 heartbeats per minute. After filtering, the next step is to identify the R-peaks in both signals for further digitalization and comparison. Figure 3 depicts the result of applying the filtering process,

---

[3] http://opencv.org/

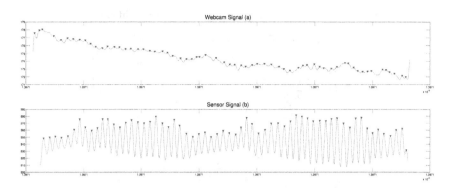

Fig. 3. Processed signals with marked peaks

Table 1. R-peaks (beats) detected on each sample.

Sample	Beats Webcam Signal	Beats Sensor Signal	Error
sample 1	62	64	2
sample 2	68	71	3
sample 3	59	59	0
sample 4	63	60	3
sample 5	60	62	2
sample 6	60	59	1
sample 7	66	65	1
sample 8	69	69	0
sample 9	62	60	2
sample 10	85	81	4
sample 11	61	65	4
sample 12	69	70	1
sample 13	68	69	1
Mean Error	-	-	1.69

where the red dots represent the heartbeats detected on each graph—webcam on top and PPG sensor at the bottom.

As it can be seen in Fig. 3, in the case of the PPG sensor all the R-peaks corresponding a heartbeat have been detected. However, in the webcam case it is easy to observe the presence of false peaks (red dots located very close each other) or real peaks not marked with a red dot (the distance between two marked peaks is anomalously wide). This translates into a different number of heartbeats detected on the retrieved signal pairs. In fact, in only 2 of the 13 subjects we obtained a perfect match in the number of detected beats. In Table 1 we show a comparative analysis between the number of heartbeats detected in both signals. In most cases, although the number of beats is different, the mean error is lower than 2 heartbeats, which is lower than previously reported results [9]. Even though this is by no means a concluding evidence of its similarity, it shows a certain degree of closeness between both signals.

More preprocessing can be applied to the webcam signal to match as much as possible the peaks detected by the PPG signal. We implemented a simple algorithm to find hidden peaks (i.e., those that were not initially detected) and

Table 2. Average IPI values and and average IPI differences.

Sample	Mean IPI value PPG Sensor	Mean IPI value Webcam	Difference(s)
sample 1	1.0296	1.198	0.2188
sample 2	0.928	0.9394	0.1364
sample 3	1.0092	1.0681	0.2348
sample 4	0.9884	0.9685	0.3506
sample 5	0.9525	1.025	0.2512
sample 6	1.0071	1.038	0.1694
sample 7	0.9855	1.0167	0.1570
sample 8	0.8576	0.8924	0.2649
sample 9	0.9148	0.958	0.1684
sample 10	0.6756	0.7032	0.0676
sample 11	0.9137	0.9973	0.1951
sample 12	0.8472	0.9048	0.1570
sample 13	0.8586	0.8816	0.1182

to discard false peaks (i.e., those located very close to each other). The procedure is described next. First, the IPI vector is extracted from the webcam signal and the mean value ($meanIPI$) is computed. We next compare $meanIPI$ to each IPI and, if the rate between the $meanIPI$ value and the detected IPI is bigger than a predefined experimental value N, we conclude that there is a hidden beat that has not been detected, so a new IPI is added to the extracted IPI vector. This new IPI has the value $meanIPI$. Otherwise, if the rate is lower than another experimental factor M, then we conclude that one of the heartbeats from which the IPI has been extracted is not real. In this case, the first heartbeat of the pair is deleted and the IPI vector is recalculated.

By applying this algorithm and tuning the $\{N, M\}$ parameters, the same number of heartbeats can be found in both signals. In order to measure the error of approximating the IPI locations, we have performed a preliminary comparison between the mean of the IPI values for each sample and then computed the mean error between both signals. Table 2 shows the result of this comparison. The mean and standard deviation of the difference between the mean IPI obtained using the camera signal and using the PPG sensor are 0.191 and 0.073, respectively. As these are very small values, we consider them as another preliminary evidence of the similarity between both sources of features.

3.3 Quantization

Having the same number of heartbeats (and thus the same number of IPIs) in both signals, the next step was to encode the signals into their binary representation. To proceed with the quantization process, we first studied different available alternatives: scalar, uniform, and dynamic quantization.

A scalar quantizer is the simplest type of quantization algorithm. It consists of a direct mapping from the input values (in this case, the time intervals between heartbeats) into a set of integers. The parameters of this algorithm are the codebook and the set of boundary points. The set of boundary points contains the values to which the input values will be rounded. That is, it contains values between the minimum and the maximum input values incremented by a quantization step obtained as a result of dividing the distance between limit values by the number of codes considered. The smaller this step is, the less quantization error will appear in the final result. The codebook contains the different values associated to each boundary point. The cardinality of these two sets depends on the desired characteristics of the output value. In order to emulate the approaches followed by previous works on IPI-based protocols [15], we encoded each quantized value as an 8-bit unsigned integer, so $2^8 = 256$ codes have been used.

On the other hand, an uniform quantizer unifies the process of quantizing and encoding the output value. It follows a similar approach to the scalar quantizer algorithm and, as a final step, it maps the output value into an integer of the desired precision. The parameters of this algorithm are the maximum and minimum input value and the precision of the desired encoded output value. In our case, we established this parameter to 8 bits as explained above.

Finally, we also implemented the quantization algorithm employed by Rostami et al. in the H2H protocol [8], known as dynamic quantization. This algorithm assumes that the perturbation of the signal (i.e., the remainder of subtracting the signal baseline) can be modeled with a normal distribution with mean $\mu = 0$ and a standard deviation of σ. Knowing this, the Normal Cumulative Distribution Function (NCDF) is calculated for each value in the raw signal. This yields a set of values between 0 and 1 that allows us to multiply them by a roof factor to obtain values between this threshold and 0. We set this roof factor to 256 (2^8) in order to have the same resolution than in the other quantizers. Finally, the quantized values were encoded as 8-bit unsigned integers.

Once the IPI values are quantized using one of the three mentioned algorithms, its Gray code representation is calculated. This is done with the aim of eliminating (or, at least, reducing) the differences between the contact and contactless signals.

4   Results and Discussion

To analyze and measure the similarity between the PPG sensor and the webcam signals, we performed two experiments. In the first experiment, we evaluate the similarity of both signals by comparing the decimal digits of each IPI. To do so, we have grouped the decimal digits of the IPIs in four groups: two first decimal digits, three first decimal digits, second and third decimal digits, and third and fourth decimal digits. For each group, we have converted the digits into an unsigned integer, then transformed it into its 8-bit binary representation (10 bits in the case of the second group, as it includes values from 0 to 999), and finally computed the Hamming Distance (HD) between the value obtained from the PPG sensor and the value captured from the webcam. We have computed an overall similarity value (i.e., % of bits that are equal for all IPI decimals in each sample) for each sample. The results are shown in Table 3 and clearly show a similarity higher to the one that would be obtained by pure chance between both signals.

Table 3. Signal similarity of InterPulse Intervals (IPIs) at digit level

sample	2 first decimals	3 first decimals	2nd and 3rd	3rd and 4th
Sample 1	56.96%	51.80%	57.50%	65.36%
Sample 2	62.31%	55.67%	56.71%	63.61%
Sample 3	58.40%	56.37%	61.20%	61.20%
Sample 4	63.98%	51.52%	56.77%	57.41%
Sample 5	56.14%	44.90%	51.63%	61.68%
Sample 6	59.91%	54.48%	63.14%	65.51%
Sample 7	61.71%	52.18%	54.29%	65.82%
Sample 8	59.74%	48.67%	57.16%	61.94%
Sample 9	59.11%	48.81%	54.66%	62.92%
Sample 10	69.68%	59.10%	63.59%	65.93%
Sample 11	56.05%	56.40%	54.88%	61.71%
Sample 12	64.67%	58.84%	59.96%	58.51%
Sample 13	65.99%	58.08%	58.63%	60.29%
Overall	61.13%	53.60%	57.70%	62.45%

Table 4. Percentages of similar bits and entropy values obtained with the dynamic quantizer for all samples.

Bit	Hit Probability (%)	Entropy	
		Sensor	Webcam
1 (MSB)	62.157	0.979	0.946
2	65.071	0.947	0.959
3	49.88	0.991	0.951
4	55.741	0.781	0.959
5	47.010	0.905	0.977
6	49.880	0.997	0.961
7	51.555	0.657	0.983
8 (LSB)	52.990	0.9290	0.999
Last 4 bits	50.358	0.959	0.999
Overall	54.41	0.990	0.999

In the second experiment, we applied the quantization algorithms explained in previous subsections to obtain the binary representations of the IPI values. We have conducted the same experiment for the three different quantization algorithms. We quantized all the IPI values of each sample (the IPI values were previously normalized) and then converted them to their binary representation. This process was applied to all samples of all signals captured by both devices. Finally we computed an overall similarity measure between the binary representations of both IPI strings (PPG sensor and webcam) belonging to all the samples in our dataset. For a better understanding of what exactly is happening here, we have also computed the similarity at the bit level (Hit Probability). Table 4 and Table 5 summarize the similarity and entropy results obtained for all the signals using the dynamic and the scalar quantizers. Due to space reasons, we do not include the results obtained with the uniform quantizer, as they are very similar to those obtained with the dynamic quantizer.

As it can be observed, the best results are obtained with the scalar quantizer. Even when the entropy is high, the Hit Probability is over 60% for the majority of the bits, including the four Least Significant Bits (LSB), which is particularly remarkable as these bits have been pointed out by previous works as the most suitable for cryptographic purposes due to their high degree of randomness [5]. In the case of the dynamic quantizer, it is evident that the results do not improve

Table 5. Percentages of similar bits and entropy values obtained with the scalar quantizer for all samples.

Bit	Hit Probability (%)	Entropy	
		Sensor	Webcam
1 (MSB)	70.095	0.714	0.868
2	61.483	0.941	0.689
3	61.004	0.898	0.762
4	62.918	0.929	0.709
5	58.688	0.959	0.816
6	94.976	0.143	0.228
7	82.775	0.0.266	0.593
8 (LSB)	70.095	0.719	0.764
Last 4 bits	76.883	0.718	0.657
Overall	70.37	0.782	0.708

a blind guessing approach for the last four bits, although it is possible to observe a higher hit ratio in certain high entropic bits, for instance in the most significant bit. Though we are not completely guessing the bits, these results show that the webcam provides insights about the heart beat of the subjects. In the case of the scalar quantizer, the percentage of equal bits is 70% (overall value), which again supports the hypothesis of signal similarity between the PPG sensor and the heartbeats derived from the webcam.

5   Applicability and Impact

We next analyze the potential impact of our results in a recently proposed ECG-based protocol in which IPI values are extracted from ECG chunks. In particular, we focus our efforts in the H2H (*Heart-2-Heart*) scheme proposed in 2013 by Rostami et al. [8]. In H2H, the authors developed cryptographic authentication and pairing protocols for IMDs such as pacemakers or Holter monitors. The proposed protocol is based on a comparison between a set of IPIs obtained from the implanted device (α) and another set of IPIs simultaneously taken by an external programmer (β). If both sets are nearly equal, the programmer is authenticated to the IMD and, hence, both are able to interchange commands.

As ECG signals contain a certain amount of noise, a perfect match between both set of features is rarely achieved. Thus, a similarity threshold must be established in order to have a trustworthy evidence of sameness between the compared features. However, if this threshold is naively established, it would be possible for an attacker to circumvent the protocol security by replacing a legit ECG signal with another one randomly generated. In the H2H scheme, the authors propose an statistical characterization for ECG authentication that allows to discern if the signal provided by a programmer device has been retrieved by means of physical contact or else if an attacker is trying to replace it with a fraudulent one. To do so, the authors base their approach on the statistical distribution of the error rates found in a legit comparison (both signals are retrieved synchronously by means of physical contact) and the error rate found in a fraudulent signal, which is assumed to be 0.5 (as the attacker is assumed to be unable to doing better than random guessing). In detail, the authors assume that

Table 6. Results of False Positive rates values achieved for different N and FN_{req}.

N-IPI values	$FN_{req} = 1 \times 10^{-3}$	$FN_{req} = 1 \times 10^{-4}$
5	3.591×10^{-1}	5.440×10^{-1}
10	7.37×10^{-2}	1.555×10^{-1}
15	1.11×10^{-2}	3.28×10^{-2}
20	1.4×10^{-3}	5.6×10^{-3}
25	1.687×10^{-4}	8.1912×10^{-4}

an IPI feature set β can be accepted as a legit sample if and only if the likelihood ratio between the probability distributions of the error rates for a fraudulent read $(P(u))$ and a legit read $(Q(u))$ is bigger than a computed threshold τ. This threshold comes associated with a false positive ratio (FP) that indicates the probability of accepting a fraudulent β set of IPI features as a legit one. Mathematically:

$$\log\left(\frac{P(u)}{Q(u)}\right) > \tau \tag{1}$$

Rostami et al. modeled $Q(u)$ as a binomial distribution $B(N, p)$, where N represents the number of IPIs in the feature set and p represents the mean error rate for the four LSBs of the IPI, obtained from a comparison between two legitimate signals. On the other hand, the $P(u)$ distribution is also modeled as a binomial distribution with the same N parameter and $p = 0.5$.

It is important to note that, as shown in Table 4, the dynamic quantization algorithm employed in H2H returns results that are not much better than 50% for the LSBs—only better results are obtained for the MSBs. Nevertheless, as depicted in Table 5, we are able to obtain substantially better results that blind guessing (having a hit ratio of 76.9% for the four LSBs) when using the scalar quantizer. Having results better than blind guessing makes necessary to calculate new false positive rates. To do so, we used the algorithm provided by the authors in the original paper (see Algorithm 1 in [8]). The inputs to this algorithm are P, the vector of the error rates in the four LSBs, N the number of IPIs to be compared, and FN_{req} the false negative ratio yielded by a legit programmer (i.e., meaning that a legit programmer will fail once in 10000 attempts).

In Table 6 we show our results after calculating the false positive rate for different FN_{req} and N values. As it can be seen, the false positive rates are much bigger when the adversary error rates decrease from 50% to 23%. A consequence of this difference is that, in order to achieve the same false positive rate, it is needed to retrieve more IPIs, extending the duration of the IPI retrieval process. This result can be more clearly observed in the following graphs. In Figure 4, it is possible to observe how the false positive rate decreases as the number of retrieved IPIs grows. This represents the variation for the H2H case, in which the error rate of the attacker is estimated to be 0.5. However, if a lower error rate is considered (i.e., the attacker is more accurate than random guessing), it is needed to retrieve a larger number of IPIs to achieve the same false positive rates. This can be observed in Figure 5, where the attacker error rate is set to 0.23, i.e., one minus the hit probability 0.77 shown in Table 5 for the scalar quantizer.

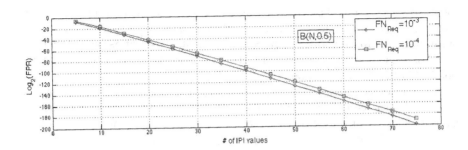

Fig. 4. Error rate equal to 0.50 (dynamic or uniform quantizer)

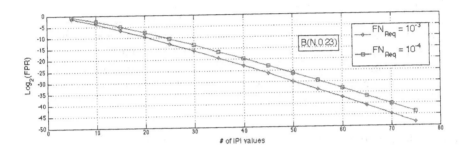

Fig. 5. Error rate equal to 0.23 (scalar quantizer)

Fig. 6. Variation of the FP rate with the number of retrieved IPIs for attacker's error rates equal to 0.50 and 0.23.

6   Concluding Remarks and Future Work

We have presented a study on the security of IPI-based security protocols when the attacker can obtain heart signals by means of a contactless method, in particular through video recording via webcam. We have analyzed the information extracted from both signals and presented a comparative study of the achieved similarity. The study has been done with different quantization algorithms, and the use of one to another will greatly affect the similarity of both signals and, therefore, the success probability of an attack. Finally, we have used the approach followed by Rostami et. al in H2H scheme to validate our hypothesis [8].

   We have shown how using freely available commodity hardware it is possible to remotely gather useful information of cardiac signals. Through an analysis of the retrieved data, we have shown that even when the data obtained using contact-based techniques is highly entropic, the data obtained through a contactless technique represent up to the 70% of that information, which is clearly better than randomly guessing. Particularly, two main conclusion should be extracted from our study. First, quantization is a critical step for IPI-based schemes, so protocol designers should put more emphasis on selecting an appropriate scheme. Second, entropy should not be the only criterion used for determining the most appropriate bits for generating cryptographic material such as keys; other criteria should include, for instance, bits that are more resistant to leakages via a webcam, as shown in this paper.

Our dataset is composed of 13 pair of signals retrieved from different volunteers, which is certainly a reduced sample for extracting strong conclusions. One immediate future work is to further validate our results with an extended dataset. It is also interesting to study how physiological parameters of the volunteers could affect the final results. For example, since all the volunteers share roughly the same skin tone, the performance of our proposal when considering volunteers with other skin tones remain unknown. We also found out that the quality of the data retrieved with the webcam strongly depends on environmental conditions such illumination or the distance between the camera and the subject. Because of our limited experimental setup, it is unclear if the use of better equipment (e.g., a camcorder with much higher resolution) will translate into a performance increase. Experimentation in open environments with a natural source of light and arbitrary distance between the subject and the camera will be also necessary.

Acknowledgements. This work was supported by the MINECO grant TIN2013-46469-R (SPINY: Security and Privacy in the Internet of You) and the CAM grant S2013/ICE-3095 (CIBERDINE: Cybersecurity, Data, and Risks).

References

1. Halperin, D., Kohno, T., Heydt-Benjamin, T.S., Fu, K., Maisel, W.H.: Security and privacy for implantable medical devices. IEEE Pervasive Computing **7**, 30–39 (2008)
2. Li, C., Raghunathan, A., Jha, N.K.: Hijacking an insulin pump: Security attacks and defenses for a diabetes therapy system. In: 13th IEEE International Conference on e-Health Networking Applications and Services (Healthcom), pp. 150–156. IEEE (2011)
3. Radcliffe, J.: Hacking medical devices for fun and insulin: Breaking the human scada system. In: Black Hat Conference Presentation Slides, vol. 2011 (2011)
4. Halperin, D., Heydt-Benjamin, T.S., Ransford, B., Clark, S.S., Defend, B., Morgan, W., Fu, K., Kohno, T., Maisel, W.H.: Pacemakers and implantable cardiac defibrillators: Software radio attacks and zero-power defenses. In: IEEE Symposium on Security and Privacy, SP 2008, pp. 129–142. IEEE (2008)
5. Poon, C.C., Zhang, Y.T., Bao, S.D.: A novel biometrics method to secure wireless body area sensor networks for telemedicine and m-health. IEEE Communications Magazine **44**, 73–81 (2006)
6. Bao, S.D., Poon, C.C., Zhang, Y.T., Shen, L.F.: Using the timing information of heartbeats as an entity identifier to secure body sensor network. IEEE Transactions on Information Technology in Biomedicine **12**, 772–779 (2008)

7. Bao, S.D., Zhang, Y.T., Shen, L.F.: Physiological signal based entity authentication for body area sensor networks and mobile healthcare systems. In: 27th Annual International Conference of the Engineering in Medicine and Biology Society, IEEE-EMBS 2005, pp. 2455–2458. IEEE (2005)
8. Rostami, M., Juels, A., Koushanfar, F.: Heart-to-heart (h2h): authentication for implanted medical devices. In: Proceedings of the 2013 ACM SIGSAC Conference on Computer & Communications Security, pp. 1099–1112. ACM (2013)
9. Poh, M.Z., McDuff, D.J., Picard, R.W.: Non-contact, automated cardiac pulse measurements using video imaging and blind source separation. Optics Express **18**, 10762–10774 (2010)
10. Wu, H.Y., Rubinstein, M., Shih, E., Guttag, J.V., Durand, F., Freeman, W.T.: Eulerian video magnification for revealing subtle changes in the world. ACM Trans. Graph. **31**, 65 (2012)
11. Jain, A.K., Dass, S.C., Nandakumar, K.: Soft biometric traits for personal recognition systems. In: Zhang, D., Jain, A.K. (eds.) ICBA 2004. LNCS, vol. 3072, pp. 731–738. Springer, Heidelberg (2004)
12. Zhu, Y., Tan, T., Wang, Y.: Biometric personal identification based on iris patterns. In: International Conference on Pattern Recognition, vol. 2, pp. 2801–2801. IEEE Computer Society (2000)
13. Kumar, A., Wong, D., Shen, H., Jain, A.: Personal verification using palmprint and hand geometry biometric. In: Kittler, J., Nixon, M. (eds.) AVBPA 2003. LNCS, vol. 2688, pp. 668–678. Springer, Berlin Heidelberg (2003)
14. Guennoun, M., Abbad, N., Talom, J., Rahman, M., El-Khatib, K.: Continuous authentication by electrocardiogram data. In: 2009 IEEE Toronto International Conference on Science and Technology for Humanity (TIC-STH), pp. 40–42. IEEE (2009)
15. Xu, F., Qin, Z., Tan, C.C., Wang, B., Li, Q.: Imdguard: Securing implantable medical devices with the external wearable guardian. In: Proceedings IEEE INFOCOM, pp. 1862–1870. IEEE (2011)

Private Minutia-Based Fingerprint Matching

Neyire Deniz Sarier[✉]

Department of Computer Engineering, MEF University, Istanbul, Turkey
sarierd@mef.edu.tr

Abstract. In this paper, we propose an efficient biometric authentication protocol for fingerprints particularly suited for the minutia-based representation. The novelty of the protocol is that we integrate the most efficient (linear complexity) private set intersection cardinality protocol of Cristofaro et al. and a suitable helper data system for biometrics in order to improve the accuracy of the system. We analyze the security of our scheme in the standard model based on well-exploited assumptions, considering malicious parties, which is essential to eliminate specific attacks on biometric authentication schemes designed for semi-honest adversaries only. Finally, the complexity is compared to the existing provably secure schemes for fingerprint matching, which shows that the new proposal outperforms them both in semi-honest and malicious security models.

Keywords: Secure remote authentication · Biometrics · Set difference · Private set intersection · Standard model

1 Introduction

Over the last decade, it has been shown that biometrics have some advantages in authentication systems compared to password-based systems, as passwords can be easily lost, forgotten or compromised using various attacks.

However, biometrics is sensitive data, thus, biometric data, either stored on a central database or on a tamper-proof smartcard, should be protected using cryptographic techniques. For instance, biometric cryptosystems such as fuzzy extractors, fuzzy vault and bipartite biotokens are used for biometric key generation, key binding and key release, respectively. Juels and Wattenberg [20] introduce the fuzzy commitment scheme as a cryptographic primitive, which is is applicable for biometrics that can be represented as an ordered set of features. However, biometrics can be affected from two types of noise, i.e. white noise that represents the slight perturbation of each feature and the replacement noise caused by the replacement of some features. Thus, Juels and Sudan have developed the *fuzzy vault* [19], which assumes that biometrics consists of an unordered set of features and is designed for the set difference metric. Specifically, fuzzy vault [19] is a key binding system that hides an encoded secret among some chaff points, where the secret key is encoded as the coefficients of

© IFIP International Federation for Information Processing 2015
R.N. Akram and S. Jajodia (Eds.): WISTP 2015, LNCS 9311, pp. 52–67, 2015.
DOI: 10.1007/978-3-319-24018-3_4

a polynomial that is evaluated at the biometric feature locations such as fingerprint minutia coordinates. Implementation of fuzzy vault for fingerprints are given in [8] and [32,33], where the latter two include helper data constructed from the high curvature points of the fingerprint minutia, which does not leak any information about the minutia locations and used for easing the alignment of the query fingerprint to the original template.

However, the implementation of biometric cryptosystems come along with various attacks that question the security of them [27,28]. In fact, the first paper that considers provable security in biometric remote authentication is the work of Bringer et al. [6] that proposed a hybrid protocol distributing the server side functionality in order to detach the biometric data storage from the authentication server. The common point of this work and the following papers designed for security against semi-honest adversaries -where security is guaranteed if each party follows the protocol- is that they are all implemented for biometric data represented as a binary string such as Iris. Hence, they depend on the hamming distance metric for the matching operation of the verification protocol. For this particular metric, an efficient face-identification protocol between a client C and server S are described in [22] that is based on Secure Function Evaluation (SFE) -a special case of Secure Multiparty Computation-. Within the same framework, biometric identification [2,3] and authentication [29] protocols are described for iris and fingerprint (in particular fingercode), all of which are based on euclidean distance metric.

Finally, one should note that the most popular and widely used techniques in fingerprint identification extract information about minutiae from a fingerprint and store that information as a set of points in the two-dimensional plane as in fuzzy vault. Fingerprint matching can also be performed using a different type of information extracted from fingerprint image, i.e. FingerCode, that uses texture information from a fingerprint scan to form fingerprint representation. Although FingerCodes are not as distinctive as minutiae-based representations, [2,3] describe privacy-preserving protocols for FingerCodes due to the efficient implementation within the euclidean distance.

2   Related Work

It is quite surprising that despite the various papers on minutia-based biometric cryptosystems [8,19,30–33] designed for the set difference metric, the only paper that describes a private minutia-based fingerprint authentication protocol based on SFE and set difference metric is [12]. In particular, the authors of [12] design an efficient minutia-based biometric authentication scheme for a client server architecture based on the Private Set Intersection (PSI) protocol of [13] that is secure against semi-honest parties in the standard model and malicious adversaries in the random oracle model (ROM). This PSI protocol is based on homomorphic encryption and polynomial interpolation and its computation complexity is quadratic, although the number of modular exponantiations can be reduced to $O(n \log \log m)$. Here, m denotes the size of the client set and

n denotes the size of the server set with $m \approx n$ in the authentication mode. Besides, [3, 29] describe private minutia-based fingerprint matching using homomorphic encryption for euclidean distance, the former considering semi-honest adversaries only in a system based on garbled circuit evaluation. The latter is also based on polynomial interpolation idea of [13] but it is much more complex compared to the original scheme as it can be deduced from the computation complexity that is $O(nmwh)$ for the semi-honest case, where w and h denote the pixel sizes of the fingerprint image.

As one can notice, current minutia-based biometric authentication schemes, whose security is proven against semi-honest attackers are based on PSI, in particular the combination of homomorphic encryption and polynomial interpolation. A natural question is whether there exists more efficient constructions of PSI that is applicable to input sets that can be represented as an unorderded set of elements such as fingerprint minutia. To answer this, we need to inverstigate several techniques that realize PSI protocols such as Public-Key-Based PSI, Circuit-Based PSI, OT-Based PSI and Third Party-Based PSI as summerized in [23]. Specifically, the first PSI protocol based on the Diffie-Hellman (DH) key agreement scheme was presented in [16] without any security analysis. This protocol is based on the commutative properties of the DH function and was used for private preference matching, which allows two parties to verify if their preferences match to some degree. The Diffie-Hellman-based protocol of [16], which was the first PSI protocol, is actually the most efficient w.r.t. communication (when implemented using elliptic-curve crypto) [23]. Therefore it is suitable for settings with distant parties which have limited connectivity. Lastly, it is possible to incorporate a relatively efficient zero-knowledge proof and authenticated inputs that each party is following the protocol honestly, so that active cheating by either party will be detected. In this context, [10] extends the protocol of [16] for malicious server and semi-honest client by incorporating zero-knowlege proofs and two additional communication rounds and provides a simulation based proof in ROM in order to build a Private Set Intersection Cardinality (PSI-CA) protocol. Similarly, [18] also extends the protocol of [16] so that security is guaranteed for malicious parties (both C and S) in ROM. The protocols in [10,18] provide linear complexity in the sizes of the two input sets, however the PSI protocol in [18] cannot be converted to a PSI-CA scheme due to its ROM based security proof that reveals the common elements of the intersection set to one of the parties (C or S).

2.1 Motivation and Contributions

When confronted with the PSI problem, most novices come up with a solution where both parties apply a cryptographic hash function to their inputs and then compare the resulting hashes. Although this protocol is very efficient, it is insecure if the input domain is not large or does not have high entropy, since one party could easily run a brute force attack that applies the hash function to all items that are likely to be in the input set and compare the results to the received hashes. This is exactly the case for minutia based fingerprint data.

To avoid this attack, our solution is to incorporate a malicious-secure PSI to biometric authentication.

First of all, when designing a secure biometric authentication protocol, one should consider three major points: The matching should be performed privately for both sides, namely, for the two parties, a client C and a server S who jointly compute a function of their private inputs, the parties should only learn the output of the matching and nothing else. Secondly, the protocol should consider both honest-but curious adversaries and malicious adversaries. This is required for a secure biometric system in order to protect against the attack of [1], which regenarates the enrolled biometric image from a random template with a hill climbing attack, that depends on the matching score. However, a recent publication [15] shows that with malicious behaviour against the cryptographic identification protocol SciFI [22] designed for the semi-honest adversaries, one can reconstruct a full face image with the help of computer vision techniques although SciFI does not output any matching score. The attack relies on the fact that a dishonest adversary is able to input vectors of any form, not just vectors that are properly formatted [15]. The attack learns the client's face code bit-by bit through the output of $'match'$ or $'nomatch'$ decision. Thus, the new protocol should be designed in the malicious security model so that neither learning the matching score nor the accept/reject decision could help a malicious party to learn additional information about the private data of the other party including the common elements of the intersection set as in PSI schemes. Finally, the protocol should be practical and efficiently implementable with linear complexity (in terms of computation and communication cost) and it should depend on widely adopted representations of biometric data.

With these goals in mind, we present a new minutia-based fingerprint authentication protocol for set difference metric between a client and a server based on PSI techniques. In particular, the only work within this framework is the work of [12], that depends on the PSI scheme of [13].

Specifically, our protocol is inspired by the PSI-CA scheme of [10] although our scheme is defined on an elliptic curve group that simplifies the PSI-CA protocol of [10] slightly by removing the last step of the protocol (i.e. hashing), but more importantly, the need for a random oracle which questions the security of the systems when the ROM is replaced by a real hash function. In fact, certain artificial signature and encryption schemes are known which are proven secure in the ROM, but which are trivially insecure when any real function is substituted for the random oracle [7]. This way, we also reduce the communication complexity since the communication overhead of [10] amounts to $2(m + 1)$ $|p|$-bit values with $|p| = 1024$ or $|p| = 2048$, whereas our protocol requires $2(m + 1)$ $|q|$-bit values with $|q| = 160$ or $|q| = 224$. Thus, our scheme is a scalable and efficient protocol with linear complexity and its security relies on well exploited cryptographic assumptions (DDH and l-DDHI) in the standard model. Besides, our protocol reveals neither the server nor the client the elements of the intersection set S, but only the size of the intersection set $d = |S|$ is learned by a single party (C or S). Similar to the scheme of [12], the computation complexity of [29] is also quadratic, i.e. $O(nmwh)$ for the semi-honest case, where w and h denote the pixel sizes of the fingerprint image. Thus, our proposal is more efficient compared to the current private fingerprint matching schemes [12,29] that are based on Oblivious Polynomial Evaluation (OPE) of [13].

Furthermore, we discuss the security of our scheme in malicious model in order to prevent the attacks presented in [1,15]. Unfortunately, the PSI-CA scheme of [10] can only achieve one-sided simulatability in ROM, i.e. the scheme only provides privacy of the server against a semi-honest client. Thus, we extend the security of our protocol so that both parties can be corrupted by a malicious adversary in standard model.

To the best of our knowledge, the proposed scheme is the first private minutia-based fingerprint authentication protocol for set difference metric that achieves complexities linear in the size of input sets, i.e. set of user's minutia that is secure in the standard model both for semi-honest and malicious adversaries.

3   Building Blocks

3.1   Fingerprint Data

The approach that forms the basis for the biometric data representation of our scheme is the Minutiae Fuzzy Vault Implementation of Uludag et al. [32,33]. Our system operates on the fingerprint minutiae that are generally represented as (x_i, y_i, θ_i) triplets, denoting their row indices (x_i), column indices (y_i) and angle of the associated ridge, respectively. Next, we concatenate x_i and y_i coordinates of a minutia as $[x_i|y_i]$ to arrive at the data unit b_i for $i \in [1, m]$. To account for slight variations in minutiae data (due to fingerprint distortions), raw minutiae data are first quantized. We require an alignment step where the query minutiae templates are aligned to the registered template based on using auxiliary alignment data aux, i.e. helper data derived from the orientation field of fingerprints. Naturally, it is required that the helper data does not leak any information about the minutiae-based fingerprint template. Another approach could be the use of alignment-free features, i.e. features that do not depend on the finger's rotation or displacement. The reader is referred to [32,33] for the details of this representation.

3.2   Cryptographic Tools

Since our system works in set difference metric, we need to compare/match aligned query template to the registered template in a private manner. In particular, our protocol is inspired by the (reversed) PSI-CA scheme of [10] that enables two parties, i.e. a client C which has a set $B' = (b'_1, ..., b'_m)$ of size m and a server S which has a set $B = (b_1, ..., b_n)$ of size n to compute the size of the intersection of their respective sets without disclosing anything about their inputs including the common elements of the intersection set. After the computation the server has obtained the size of the intersection $d = |B \cap B'|$ and the client has learnt nothing other than the accept/reject notification based on the system threshold t.

In short, PSI and PSI-CA can be achieved using OPE [13], Oblivious Pseudo-Random Functions (OPRF) [17], Bloom filters [11] and blind signatures [10], where the latter is the primitive we require in our protocol to achieve linear complexity. As different from the scheme of PSI-CA of [10] we eliminate the last step of the protocol, namely hashing the result of the verification and computing the size of the intersection on these hashes. Besides, we swap the roles of the server and the client in [10], thus, the biometric server obtains a signature on its input without disclosing it. This simplification is caused by describing our protocol on a suitably chosen elliptic curve group where DDH (and l-DDHI) assumption holds, whereas PSI-CA of [10] works on groups where DDH (and One-More-Gap-DH) assumption holds. Thus, the client performs $2(m+1)$ exponentiations and server computes $(m+n)$ modular exponentiations modulo p-bit prime with $p = 1024$ or $p = 2048$, whereas in our scheme the same operations are performed modulo q-bit prime with $q = 160$ or $q = 224$. In [10], communication overhead amounts to $2(m+1)$ p-bit values and n κ-bit values, where κ is a security parameter of $H':\{0.1\}^* \rightarrow \{0.1\}^\kappa$. Since, we eliminate H' and work on an elliptic curve group, the communication complexity is reduced from p-bit values to q-bit values. To provide client and server privacy against malicious adversaries, we employ standard techniques of cryptography such as zero knowledge proof of knowledge (PoK).

3.3   Security Model

We provide efficient biometric authentication protocols with security in the presence of both semi-honest and malicious adversaries. Here, the term adversary refers to insiders, i.e., protocol participants. Outside adversaries are not considered, since their actions can be mitigated via standard network security techniques. Informally, we have the following goals for our protocols.

Client Privacy: No information is leaked about client C biometrics, except an upper bound on its size m and the matching score, i.e. the number of common elements between the biometric template registered at the server and the client's fresh template.

Server Privacy: C learns no information beyond an upper bound on the size of his registered feature set n at the server and the accept/reject notification.

Unlinkability: Neither party can determine if any two instances of the protocol are related, i.e., executed on the same input by client or server, unless this can be inferred from the actual protocol output [10].

Our first protocols for authentication are presented in the semi-honest model, i.e. adversaries that are honest-but-curious, who follow the protocols and try to gain more information than they should on the other parties' inputs. An honest-but-curious party is a party that follows the instructions of the protocol, but may record the communications it receives and try to infer extra information using such recordings. In this case, the traditional real-versus-ideal definition is applied in the security proof. Basically, the protocol privately computes a function for an honest-but-curious Client C (resp. Server S) if there exists a PPT algorithm SIM that is able to simulate the view of C (resp. S), given only Client's (resp. Server's) (private and public) input and output. The random variable representing the view of Client (resp. Server) during an execution of the protocol with Client's private input $B' = \{b'_i\}$, Server's private input $B = \{b_i\}$ is denoted here by $View_S(B, B', P)$ (resp. $View_C(B, B', P)$).

Definition 1. *(Privacy against Honest-but-curious Adversaries).*
Let $View_S(B, B')$ be a random variable representing server's view during execution of PSI-CA with inputs B, B', P. There exists a PPT algorithm SIM that is able to simulate the view of Server (resp. Client), given only Server's (resp. Client's) respective (private and public) input and output; i.e., $\forall (B, B', P)$:

$$View_S(B, B', P) \overset{c}{\equiv} SIM_S(B, P, |B \cap B'|))$$
$$(resp.\ View_C(B, B', P) \overset{c}{\equiv} SIM_C(B', P))$$

The security of our protocols relies on the following assumptions.

Definition 2. *Decisional Diffie-Hellman (DDH). Let $x, y, z \overset{R}{\leftarrow} \mathbb{Z}_q^*$ and $g \in \mathbb{G}$ be a random generator of the prime order group $\mathbb{G}$. Given (g, g^x, g^y) distinguishing between the distributions (g, g^x, g^y, g^{xy}) and (g, g^x, g^y, g^z) is hard.*

Definition 3. *l-Diffie-Hellman inversion problem (l-DHI). Let $l \in \mathbb{Z}$, $z \overset{R}{\leftarrow} \mathbb{Z}_q^*$ and $g \in \mathbb{G}$ as above. Given $(g, g^z, g^{z^2}, ..., g^{z^l})$ computing $g^{\frac{1}{z}}$ is hard.*

Definition 4. *l-Decisional Diffie-Hellman inversion problem (l-DDHI). Let $l \in \mathbb{Z}$, $z \overset{R}{\leftarrow} \mathbb{Z}_q^*$, $g \in \mathbb{G}$. Given $(g, g^z, g^{z^2}, ..., g^{z^l}, v)$ deciding whether $v = g^{\frac{1}{z}}$ is hard.*

In section 7, we present our last protocol for authentication in malicious model, where a malicious adversary uses any kind of strategy to learn information. A malicious party is a part that does not necessarily follow the instructions of the protocol. Finally, the number of minutiae used in the protocol, namely n and m, are considered to be public. If privacy of the number of minutiae is required, C and S can simply agree on a size (or two sizes) beforehand and then adjust the number of minutiae they use as input by either omitting a number of minutiae or adding a number of chaff minutiae to their set.

4   The New Protocol

As a warm up, this section presents our first construction in authentication mode, secure in the presence of semi-honest adversaries in the ROM. An overview of the scheme is given in Fig. 1. Although our scheme integrates the PSI-CA of [10], its security is based on a different assumption. Besides, we work on a group $\mathbb{G}$ implemented using a group of points on a certain elliptic curve with generator g of prime order q and require a MaptoPoint hash function (modeled as a random oracle) H: $\{0.1\}^* \rightarrow \mathbb{G}$ together with two random permutations $\mathbf{P}$ and $\mathbf{P'}$.

The client C registers his biometric features b_i for $i \in [1, n]$ at the server S as described in section 3.1 and stores the helper data aux publicly. For verification, C presents his fresh biometrics, aligns it with the help of aux, and obtains $\{b'_i\}$ for $i \in [1, m]$. Next, C makes an authentication request and the server S replies by masking the hashed biometric feature set items corresponding to the client C with a random exponent $k \in \mathbb{Z}_q$ and sends resulting w_i's to C, which blindly exponentiates them with its own random value $\alpha \in \mathbb{Z}_q$. Next, C shuffles these v_i's and sends to S the resulting u_i's together with the exponentiations of client's items $\mathrm{H}(\underline{b}'_j)'$s to randomness $\alpha \in \mathbb{Z}_q$ as x_j's. Finally, S tries to match these x'_j values received from C with the shuffled u_i values, stripped of the initial randomness $k \in \mathbb{Z}_q$. S learns the set intersection cardinality (and nothing else) by counting the number of such matches and notifies C based on the system threshold t with an accept/reject decision.

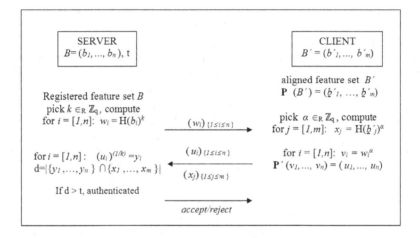

Fig. 1. Protocol in ROM: $m \approx n$

Lemma 1. *The proposed scheme achieves client privacy against a semi-honest server based on the l-DDHI assumption in the random oracle model.*

Lemma 2. *The proposed scheme achieves server privacy against a semi-honest client based on the DDH assumption in the random oracle model.*

Due to page limitations, the proofs will appear in the full version of the paper.

By designing the protocol for an elliptic curve group $\mathbb{G}$, we do not require a second hash function H', hence our scheme is less complex compared to [10], since the elements of $\mathbb{G}$ are already 160 or 224-bits instead of 1024 or 2048-bit as in [10]. Hence, the comparison performed over the H' values as in [10], can be performed on x'_js and y'_is directly. Since the protocol is designed for semi-honest adversaries, the attack of [1] does not work since the parties are passive attackers and do follow the protocol specifications. However, the distance/matching score or accept/reject notification could be useful for a malicious server for a brute force attack against the privacy of the client or the opposite, namely, a malicious client trying to impersonate a user. In other words, this information is only helpful as in the case of malicious behaviour by one of the parties. However, to prevent malicious behaviour as presented in [1,15], where the latter attack is able to break the secure face identification scheme SciFI even if no matching score or distance information is output by the protocol, one should extend the security of the new scheme for malicious adversaries.

5   Security in Standard Model

As described above, our protocol requires one hash function that is assumed as a random oracle. However, by slightly modifying the protocol, we are able to prove the security of our scheme in the standard model. In particular, instead of extracting the input set of each party via the random oracle queries as in [10], we use the Proof of Knowledge (PoK) to extract the randomness k used by each party and determine the input set as in [17,18]. Hence, we use the input set of the semi-honest (resp. malicious) party directly in the simulation due to the extraction of sender's inputs given this randomness that is obtained by running the extractor algorithm for PoK with the semi-honest party to extract k, such that it satisfies the commitment g^k sent by that semi-honest party. As an example application, we can replace the hash function with the MapToPoint hash function of [4,14], we are able to prove the security in the standard model.

For instance, [14] relies on a variant of Dodis-Yampolskiy's Pseudo-Random Function (PRF) based on the Boneh-Boyen unpredictable function [17]. The Boneh-Boyen function is $f_y(x) = g^{1/(y+x)}$ where $g \in \mathbb{G}$ generates a group $\mathbb{G}$ of prime order q, and y is a random element in $\mathbb{Z}_q^*$. This function is unpredictable under the computational l-DHI assumption on $\mathbb{G}$ [17]. Thus, the decisional l-DHI assumption on group $\mathbb{G}$ implies that the Boneh-Boyen function is a PRF. Besides, the OPRF construction of [17] is also based on the Boneh-Boyen PRF with the sole modification being a substitution of a prime-order group $\mathbb{G}$ with a group whose order is a safe RSA modulus.

Lemma 3. *The proposed scheme achieves client privacy against a semi-honest server in the standard model.*

Proof. We show that server's view can be efficiently simulated by a probabilistic polynomial time algorithm SIM_S. The server's view includes his inputs B, randomnesses he uses, and messages he receives. The server has inputs of the registered feature set $B = \{b_i\}$ and randomness $k \in \mathbb{Z}_q$. We follow a similar proof technique that is presented in [17]. The simulator is constructed as follows:

1. Upon receiving g^k, π_1 and $w_1, ..., w_n$ from the server, if the server succeeds in the proof π_1, then SIM_S runs the extractor algorithm for π_1 with the server to extract k. Then when getting the randomness k from S, SIM_S tries every possible input in the range of the hash function -which is identical to

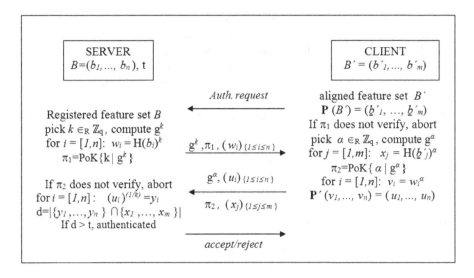

Fig. 2. Protocol in standard model: $m \approx n$

the Boneh-Boyen PRF- to reconstruct the set B as in OPRF proof of [17]. This can be performed due to the fact that the domain of this hash/PRF is polynomially-sized [17].

2. SIM_S picks at random $\alpha \leftarrow \mathbb{Z}_q$, computes g^α, computes π_2 and adds distinct pairs $(H(b_i), x_i) = (h_i, x_i)$, where $x_i = H(b_i)^\alpha$ and b_is (i.e. the set B) are computed as in the previous step. SIM_S computes $v_i = w_i^\alpha$ and sends $\mathbf{P}'(v_1, ..., v_n) = (u_1, ..., u_n)$ and $(x_1, ..., x_m)$ to the server. Here, $(x_1, ..., x_d)$ denotes the intersection of the client and server's input set constructed by selecting a random subset of $x_i = H(b_i)^\alpha$ values with size $|d|$. For the remaining $m - d$ elements, the simulator padds the set with random values, i.e. c_i^α for $i \in [d+1, m]$.

Server learns nothing either interacting with the real world client or interacting with SIM_S, therefore, the environment (distinguisher) D's views in the real world and ideal world are indistinguishable. Now we show that this SIM_S does a successful simulation. Consider the following series of games:

1. In the first game, the public parameters are generated as in the definition of the protocol, and then the adversary A interacts with the real world party as defined above.

2. In the second game, the parameters are generated the same way, but now A interacts with a $\overline{SIM}$ which behaves as the real protocol for step 1, but then behaves as SIM_S for step 2. The only difference then is that this simulator padds the set with random values, i.e. c_i^α for $i \in [d+1, m]$ for the remaining $m - d$ elements. This differs from the first game only in that the elements not common with the set B and the simulated set B' are randomly chosen in order to simulate the fresh biometric reading of the client biometrics which

cannot be equal to the registered biometric set B totally due to the nature of biometrics. Thus, this is indistinguishable from the first game by the randomness of these padded elements chosen from the underlying group.

3. In the last game, the public parameters are generated the same way, and then adversary A interacts with SIM_S. This differs from the second game only in that SIM_S extracts k from the proof, and uses this k to form the registered biometric set of the authenticating client at the server. Note that if the proof is sound, then this set will be identical to that used in the previous game. Thus this is indistinguishable from the previous game by the extraction property of the ZK proof system.

Since the first game is indistinguishable from the third, the probability that the adversary A can detect the simulation in each game can differ only negligibly. Thus, the simulation is successful.

Lemma 4. *The proposed scheme achieves server privacy against a semi-honest client in the standard model.*

Due to page limitations, the proof will appear in the full version of the paper.

6   Use of Multi-modal Biometrics for High-Entropy Inputs

One factor limiting the security of biometric cryptosystems is the entropy of the biometric feature data. To increase the entropy of biometric data and to achieve higher privacy levels in biometric cryptosystems, one combines the information of several biometric traits (e.g. fingerprints with finger vein, or face with iris) or several instances of the same biometric trait, denoted as multi-biometrics systems. Compared to traditional (uni)biometric authentication, multibiometric systems offer several advantages such as better recognition accuracy, increased population coverage, greater security, flexibility and user convenience. For these systems, different fusion approaches exist, and in [21], fusion at the feature level is performed for both multi-modal and multi-instances that the key entropy in the biometric cryptosystem is increased to sufficient levels required in security applications. In [24–26], another fusion at the feature level is described in the context of biometric IBE in order to avoid the collusion attacks inherent in fuzzy IBE systems. Considering our biometric matching system, one can follow a similar strategy as described in [28]. Specifically, 2048 bits Iriscode b has inherent entropy of 249 bits. If we implement the Iris fuzzy commitment scheme of [5], we can see this Iris code as $z = b \oplus c$, where c is a codeword that is stored in form of $H(c)$ as a helper data together with z. If we concataneted to each biometric feature (for instance fingerprint minutia value) this c, each of the biometric data has enough input entropy for the hash function. To further increase the input-entropy, a client password can be concatanated to the biometric inputs, where a randomly generated 8-character password can have 52-bit entropy [21].

7   Security in Malicious Model

Consider a malicious client (or an adversary trying to impersonate a user) that implements one of the attacks presented in [1,15] against the biometric authentication system. To prevent this, the security should be guaranteed considering malicious behaviour of both parties. We note that the PSI-CA protocol of [10] provides security against semi-honest server and malicious client, when the roles of server and client are swapped, namely the protocol provides one-sided simulatability in ROM.

To upgrade our scheme presented in Fig. 2 to malicious parties in the standard model, we add one additional zero-knowledge proof π_3 as in [10], where $\pi_3 =$ PoK $\{\alpha | (\prod_{i=1}^{m} w_i)^{\alpha} = \prod_{i=1}^{m} u_i\}$ since a proof of logical *and* of n separate statements $w_i^{\alpha} = u_i$ would reveal the relationship between each index i of w_i and corresponding index j of u_j with $w_i^{\alpha} = u_j$ after permutation $\mathbf{P}'$ allowing the server to determine which elements belong to the intersection, rather than just how many [10]. We note that considering our protocol in a group equipped with a bilinear map does not solve the problem since the server can check $\hat{e}(w_i, g^{\alpha}) = \hat{e}(u_j, g)$ for each u_j until he determines all the common elements instead of just their cardinality.

The commitments g^k, g^{α} together with the proofs of knowledge allows the simulator to extract the malicious party's input and may help to ensure that the inputs are consistent and that the same values are used along the protocol. However, since any logical *and* of n separate PoK as in the above sense would reveal the common elements themselves instead of just their total number, a challenge/response mechanism similar to the one in [10] is needed to guarantee that the same α is used on each w_i. An overview of the protocol is presented in Fig. 3.

Lemma 5. *The proposed scheme achieves client privacy against a malicious server in the standard model.*

Sketch of the Proof. A malicious server against a honest client can behave arbitrarly as in the following ways.

Case 1: A malicious server can pick a random set of inputs instead of the registered user information B or does not apply the same random exponent k that is committed in $w_i = \mathrm{H}(b_i)^k$ and g^k. To avoid this, one can include a zero knowledge proof in order to prove the honest client that the malicious server knows the underlying registered biometric feature hashes and another zero knowledge proof to prove that the committed value in g^k is consistently used in all w_is. However, as it is proven in [18], the server (i.e. the receiver of the PSI scheme of [18]) cannot change its input set B after sending the w_is since the server's input set is committed in the first and only message he sends regarding the biometric data. With this behaviour, the server does not gain any advantage since the honest client can detect the malicious behaviour from the authentication result (i.e. a reject decision for a honest client that should be accepted) as the malicious server cannot compute the matching score and

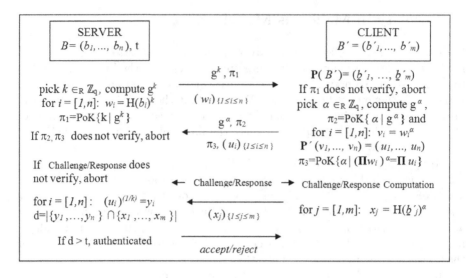

Fig. 3. Protocol in malicious model: $m \approx n$

returns a random accept/reject notification or aborts the protocol without any notification. We note that an accept decision of that server for a honest client that should be authenticated remains undetected. Hence, to prove that the committed input set of the server belongs to the particular client that tries to authenticate to the system, authorization of server input must be enforced. This can be achieved via the signature of the sensor on the inputs of the server during the registration phase of each client to the server, since the sensor, which captures the biometric data of each client is fully trusted in any biometric authentication system [6]. An example application in a different context is presented in the Authorized PSI-CA scheme of [10], which we can integrate into our construction with the sole modification of substitution the prime-order group $\mathbb{G}$ with a group whose order is a safe RSA modulus N. It is shown that prime-order groups also imply that the Boneh-Boyen function in a composite-order group N remains a PRF under the l-DDHI assumption on such groups (and hardness of factoring) and the same generic-group argument which motivated trust in the l-DDHI assumption on the prime-order groups carries to composite-order groups as well [17]. Hence, if we use the MapToPoint hash function of [14] that is identical to the Boneh-Boyen PRF, we can integrate authorization of server inputs via the signatures of the trusted sensor at the registration.

Case 2: Hence, the only misbehaviour left for the malicious server is to abort without sending the final decision although it computed the (correct) matching score. This can be eliminated by providing fairness via integrating an optimistic fairness protocol, i.e. a semi-trusted offline third party arbiter. Fairness is out of the scope of this paper.

Lemma 6. *The proposed scheme achieves server privacy against a malicious client in the standard model.*

Due to page limitations, the proofs will appear in the full version of the paper.

8   Comparison

As it is noted in [23], the Diffie-Hellman-based private matching protocol of [16], which was the first PSI protocol, is actually the most efficient w.r.t. communication (when implemented using elliptic-curve crypto). Besides, the PSI scheme of [18], PSI-CA scheme of [10] and our scheme are based on small variations of the protocol in [16], this protocol is suitable for settings with distant parties which have limited connectivity. To the best of our knowledge, the only schemes that provide private fingerprint matching protocols with a concrete security analysis based on fingerprint minutia representation are described in [3], [29],[12], where the latter considers set difference metric, whereas the others implement the protocols for euclidean distance. All three of the protocols provide security against semi-honest adversaries, although the scheme of [29] includes an extention of his semi-honest protocol for malicious adversaries without any security analysis. Thus, the comparison is based on the protocols for semi-honest adversaries for consistency and we assume $m \approx n$ for the authentication mode since the total number of minutia m registered at the server and captured at the client side n will be close to each other as opposed to the identification mode as in [3].

Table 1. Comparison of time complexity

	Complexity Estimate, i.e. Number of exponentiations	Underlying Method
Blanton et al.* [3]	quadratic in m + m OT protocols	Homomorphic encryption and Garbled Circuits
Shahandashti et al. [29]	quadratic in m	OPE
Feng et al.† [12]	quadratic in m	OPE
Our Construction‡	linear in m	PSI-CA

*:in authentication mode;
†: [13] reduces the number of exponentiations to $O(n \log \log m)$ using Horner's rule and hashing for bucket allocation; ‡ $m \approx n$ with $20 < m < 40$.

Therefore, our construction is the most efficient authentication protocol for minutia-based fingerprint authentication based on PSI techniques, in particular the OPE of [13]. In addition, our protocol is more efficient compared to the garbled circuit-based construction of [3], as it is shown in [9], the PSI and PSI-CA constructions of [10] are more efficient compared to garbled-circuit based constructions. Finally, the only scheme that considers malicious parties is [29] (without any security analysis). Similar to the comparison in the semi honest model, our scheme outperforms [29] also in malicious model due to the additional PoKs at each step of the protocol which is already complex enough for semi-honest model.

9   Conclusion

In this paper, we design an efficient biometric authentication protocol for a client-server architecture based on one of the most efficient PSI-CA technique. Our scheme is suitable for any type of biometrics that can be represented as an unordered set of features similar to the constructions of fuzzy vault. We provide the security in standard model based on the well-exploited assumptions and consider malicious parties, which is essential to eliminate specific attacks on biometric schemes. A future work could be integration of fairness protocol to prevent a malicious abort of the server.

References

1. Adler, A.: Vulnerabilities in biometric encryption systems. In: Kanade, T., Jain, A., Ratha, N.K. (eds.) AVBPA 2005. LNCS, vol. 3546, pp. 1100–1109. Springer, Heidelberg (2005)
2. Barni, M., Bianchi, T., Catalano, D., Di Raimondo, M., Donida Labati, R., Failla, P., Fiore, D., Lazzeretti, R., Piuri, V., Scotti, F., Piva, A.: Privacy-preserving fingercode authentication. In: MMSec 2010, pp. 231–240. ACM (2010)
3. Blanton, M., Gasti, P.: Secure and efficient protocols for Iris and fingerprint identification. In: Atluri, V., Diaz, C. (eds.) ESORICS 2011. LNCS, vol. 6879, pp. 190–209. Springer, Heidelberg (2011)
4. Boneh, D., Franklin, M.: Identity-based encryption from the Weil pairing. In: Kilian, J. (ed.) CRYPTO 2001. LNCS, vol. 2139, p. 213. Springer, Heidelberg (2001)
5. Bringer, J., Chabanne, H., Cohen, G., Kindarji, B., Zemor, G.: Optimal iris fuzzy sketches. In: BTAS 2007, pp. 1–6. IEEE (2007)
6. Bringer, J., Chabanne, H., Izabachène, M., Pointcheval, D., Tang, Q., Zimmer, S.: An application of the Goldwasser-Micali cryptosystem to biometric authentication. In: Pieprzyk, J., Ghodosi, H., Dawson, E. (eds.) ACISP 2007. LNCS, vol. 4586, pp. 96–106. Springer, Heidelberg (2007)
7. Canetti, R., Goldreich, O., Halevi, S.: The random oracle methodology, revisited. J. ACM **51**(4), 557–594 (2004)
8. Clancy, T.C., Kiyavash, N., Lin, D.J.: Secure smartcard based fingerprint authentication. In: WBMA 2003, pp. 45–52. ACM (2003)
9. De Cristofaro, E., Tsudik, G.: Experimenting with fast private set intersection. In: Katzenbeisser, S., Weippl, E., Camp, L.J., Volkamer, M., Reiter, M., Zhang, X. (eds.) TRUST 2012. LNCS, vol. 7344, pp. 55–73. Springer, Heidelberg (2012)
10. De Cristofaro, E., Gasti, P., Tsudik, G.: Fast and private computation of cardinality of set intersection and union. In: Pieprzyk, J., Sadeghi, A.-R., Manulis, M. (eds.) CANS 2012. LNCS, vol. 7712, pp. 218–231. Springer, Heidelberg (2012)
11. Dong, C., Chen, L., Wen, Z.: When private set intersection meets big data: an efficient and scalable protocol. In: ACMCCS 2013, pp. 789–800. ACM (2013)
12. Feng, Q., Su, F., Cai, A.: Privacy-preserving authentication using fingerprint. IJICIC **8**(11), 8001–8018 (2012)
13. Freedman, M.J., Nissim, K., Pinkas, B.: Efficient private matching and set intersection. In: Cachin, C., Camenisch, J.L. (eds.) EUROCRYPT 2004. LNCS, vol. 3027, pp. 1–19. Springer, Heidelberg (2004)
14. Goyal, V., O'Neill, A., Rao, V.: Correlated-input secure hash functions. In: Ishai, Y. (ed.) TCC 2011. LNCS, vol. 6597, pp. 182–200. Springer, Heidelberg (2011)

15. Grauman, K., Gerbush, M., Luong, A., Waters, B.: Reconstructing a fragmented face from a cryptographic identification protocol. In: WACV 2013, pp. 238–245. IEEE (2013)
16. Huberman, B.A., Franklin, M., Hogg, T.: Enhancing privacy and trust in electronic communities. In: Proceedings of the 1st ACM Conference on Electronic Commerce, EC 1999, pp. 78–86. ACM (1999)
17. Jarecki, S., Liu, X.: Efficient oblivious pseudorandom function with applications to adaptive OT and secure computation of set intersection. In: Reingold, O. (ed.) TCC 2009. LNCS, vol. 5444, pp. 577–594. Springer, Heidelberg (2009)
18. Jarecki, S., Liu, X.: Fast secure computation of set intersection. In: Garay, J.A., De Prisco, R. (eds.) SCN 2010. LNCS, vol. 6280, pp. 418–435. Springer, Heidelberg (2010)
19. Juels, A., Sudan, M.: A fuzzy vault scheme. Des. Codes Cryptography 38(2), 237–257 (2006)
20. Juels, A., Wattenberg, M.: A fuzzy commitment scheme. In: ACM CCS 1999, pp. 28–36 (1999)
21. Kanade, S., Petrovska-Delacre'taz, D., Dorizzi, B.: Multi-biometrics based cryptographic key regeneration scheme. In: IEEE 3rd International Conference on Biometrics: Theory, Applications, and Systems, BTAS 2009, pp. 1–7. IEEE (2009)
22. Osadchy, M., Pinkas, B., Jarrous, A., Moskovich, B.: Scifi - a system for secure face identification. In: IEEE Symposium on Security and Privacy, pp. 239–254 (2010)
23. Pinkas, B., Schneider, T., Zohner, M.: Faster private set intersection based on OT extension. In: Usenix 2004, pp. 797–812. USENIX Association (2014)
24. Sarier, N.D.: A new biometric identity based encryption scheme. In: International Symposium on Trusted Computing - TrustCom 2008, pp. 2061–2066. IEEE (2008)
25. Sarier, N.D.: A new Biometric Identity Based Encryption Scheme secure against DoS attacks. Security and Communication Networks 3(1), 268–274 (2010)
26. Sarier, N.D.: Generic constructions of biometric identity based encryption systems. In: Samarati, P., Tunstall, M., Posegga, J., Markantonakis, K., Sauveron, D. (eds.) WISTP 2010. LNCS, vol. 6033, pp. 90–105. Springer, Heidelberg (2010)
27. Sarier, N.D.: Security notions of biometric remote authentication revisited. In: Meadows, C., Fernandez-Gago, C. (eds.) STM 2011. LNCS, vol. 7170, pp. 72–89. Springer, Heidelberg (2012)
28. Sarier, N.D.: Biometric Cryptosystems: Authentication, Encryption and Signature for Biometric Identities. PhD thesis, Bonn University, Germany (2013)
29. Shahandashti, S.F., Safavi-Naini, R., Ogunbona, P.: Private fingerprint matching. In: Susilo, W., Mu, Y., Seberry, J. (eds.) ACISP 2012. LNCS, vol. 7372, pp. 426–433. Springer, Heidelberg (2012)
30. Tams, B.: Absolute fingerprint pre-alignment in minutiae-based cryptosystems. In: BIOSIG 2013, pp. 1–12. IEEE (2013)
31. Tams, B.: Attacks and countermeasures in fingerprint based biometric cryptosystems (2013). CoRR, abs/1304.7386
32. Uludag, U., Jain, A.: Securing fingerprint template: fuzzy vault with helper data. In: CVPRW 2006. IEEE (2006)
33. Uludag, U., Pankanti, S., Jain, A.K.: Fuzzy vault for fingerprints. In: Kanade, T., Jain, A., Ratha, N.K. (eds.) AVBPA 2005. LNCS, vol. 3546, pp. 310–319. Springer, Heidelberg (2005)

Secure Resource Sharing
and Access Control

Secure Resource Sharing for Embedded Protected Module Architectures

Jo Van Bulck, Job Noorman, Jan Tobias Mühlberg$^{(\boxtimes)}$, and Frank Piessens

iMinds-DistriNet, KU Leuven, Celestijnenlaan 200A, 3001 Leuven, Belgium
jo.vanbulck@student.kuleuven.be,
{job.noorman,jantobias.muehlberg,frank.piessens}@cs.kuleuven.be

Abstract. Low-end embedded devices and the Internet of Things (IoT) are becoming increasingly important for our lives. They are being used in domains such as infrastructure management, and medical and health-care systems, where business interests and our security and privacy are at stake. Yet, security mechanisms have been appallingly neglected on many IoT platforms. In this paper we present a secure access control mechanism for extremely lightweight embedded microcontrollers. Being based on Sancus, a hardware-only Trusted Computing Base and Protected Module Architecture for the embedded domain, our mechanism allows for multiple software modules on an IoT-node to securely share resources. We implement and evaluate our approach for two application scenarios, a shared memory system and a shared flash drive. Our implementation is based on a Sancus-enabled TI MSP430 microcontroller. We show that our mechanism can give high security guarantees at small runtime overheads and a moderately increased size of the Trusted Computing Base.

Keywords: Protected module architecture · Internet of things · Embedded file system · Access control · Resource sharing · Trusted computing

1 Introduction

Ongoing developments in our ever-changing computing environment have led to a situation where every physical object can have a virtual counterpart on the Internet. These virtual representations of things provide and consume services and can be assigned to collaborate towards achieving a common goal. This Internet of Things (IoT) brings us unpreceded convenience through novel possibilities to acquire and process data from our environment. With numerous applications in domains such as infrastructure management, transportation, and medical and healthcare systems, the increasing growth of the IoT raises questions regarding the safe and secure deployment and use of extremely interconnected devices. Computing nodes in the IoT are often equipped with inexpensive low-performance microcontrollers that provide just enough computing power to periodically perform their intended tasks, e.g., obtain sensor readings and pass them on to other nodes. As a result, well established concepts and mechanisms

© IFIP International Federation for Information Processing 2015
R.N. Akram and S. Jajodia (Eds.): WISTP 2015, LNCS 9311, pp. 71–87, 2015.
DOI: 10.1007/978-3-319-24018-3_5

from desktop and server environments – hierarchical protection domains, virtualisation, virus scanners, firewalls, etc. – are either not available or cannot easily be employed on IoT-nodes [17].

The problem of trustworthiness and trust management of low-power low-performance computing nodes has previously been discussed in the context of sensor networks [8,14]. Most techniques proposed for this domain focus on observing the communication behaviour and on validating the plausibility of sensor readings to assess the trustworthiness of nodes, which is shown to reliably detect the systematic failure nodes. Yet mechanisms to protect software and data on a node are rare as most work in this domain focuses on efficiency and handles security and privacy requirements as second-class citizens at best.

Contributions. In this paper we describe and evaluate an approach to implement and securely enforce application-grained access control policies for IoT-nodes. Our access control mechanism can manage access to various system resources such as a file systems, Memory-Mapped I/O (MMIO) devices or specific devices attached to an external communication bus. While incurring low overheads, our mechanism guarantees at runtime that only authenticated software modules gain access to resources as specified in the policy; the internal state of the access control implementation is protected and cannot be tampered with.

Our approach is based on Sancus [16], a lightweight hardware-only Trusted Computing Base (TCB) and Protected Module Architecture (PMA) [18]. Sancus targets low-cost embedded systems which have no virtual memory. Recent research on Program Counter Based Access Control (PCBAC) [19] shows that, in this context, the value of the program counter can be used unambiguously to identify a specific software module. Whenever the program counter is within the address range associated with the module's code, the module is said to be executing. Memory isolation can then be implemented by configuring access rights to memory locations based on the current value of the program counter. Sancus also provides attestation by means of built-in cryptographic primitives to provide assurance of the integrity and isolation of a given software module to a third party, which we use to authenticate software modules.

We evaluate a prototypic implementation of our access control mechanism in two application scenarios that facilitate secure data sharing between software modules, (1) through a shared memory implementation and (2) through peripheral flash memory and the Coffee [20] file system. Our evaluation shows that module isolation and access control impose relatively low overheads that should be acceptable in deployment scenarios with stringent safety and security requirements. The application scenarios run on a Sancus-enabled TI MSP430 microcontroller, a single-address-space architecture with no memory management unit. The source code of the evaluation scenario is available at https://distrinet.cs.kuleuven.be/software/sancus/wistp2015/.

2 Protected Module Architectures and Sancus

As mentioned in the introduction, our work is built upon Sancus [16], a lightweight PMA [18] specifically designed for embedded systems. Sancus guarantees strong isolation of software modules, called Sancus Modules (SMs), through low-cost hardware extensions. Moreover, Sancus provides the means for local and remote parties to attest the state of, or communicate with, the isolated software modules. This section gives a detailed introduction of the features of Sancus we use in the rest of this paper.

Isolation. Like many PMAs, Sancus uses PCBAC [19] to isolate SMs. Software modules are represented by a *public text section* containing the module's executable code and a *private data section* containing data that should be kept private to the module. The core of the PCBAC model is that the private data section of a module can only be accessed from code in its public text section. In other words, if and only if the program counter points to within a module's code section, memory access to this module's data section is allowed. Note that on systems that use MMIO, an SM can get exclusive access to a device by mapping its private data section around the MMIO region of the device.

To prevent instruction sequences in the code section from being misused by external code to extract private data, entry into a module's code section should be controlled. For this purpose, PMAs allow modules to designate certain addresses within their code section as *entry points*. Code that does not belong to a module's code section is only allowed to jump to one of its entry points. In Sancus, every module has a single entry point at the start of its code section. Table 1 gives an overview of the access control rules enforced by Sancus.

Table 1. Memory access control rules enforced by Sancus using the traditional Unix notation. Each entry indicates how code executing in the "from" section may access the "to" section. The "unprotected" section refers to code that does not belong to a SM.

From/to	Entry	Text	Data	Unprotected
Entry	r-x	r-x	rw-	rwx
Text	r-x	r-x	rw-	rwx
Unprotected/				
Other SM	r-x	r--	---	rwx

SM Identification. Sancus allows SMs to reliably identify each other. To this end, Sancus assigns a unique ID to each SM when its isolation is enabled. The instruction `sancus_get_id` can be used to retrieve the ID of an SM at a specific address. This can be used to, for example, verify the expected SM is isolated at a specific location before calling its entry point.

To enable the implementation of access control policies, Sancus keeps track of the ID of the previously executing SM. This ID can be queried using the `sancus_get_caller_id` instruction. SMs typically use this feature to restrict access to their entry point to some specific SMs.

Besides enabling SMs to identify each other, Sancus also provides cryptographic primitives for modules to *attest* each other's state. That is, to verify that a module's code section has not been tampered with before the isolation was enabled and that its code and data sections are loaded at the correct addresses. For this, Sancus employs an elaborate key management scheme that is beyond the scope of this paper. Suffices to say that SMs can be deployed with a Message Authentication Code (MAC) of the code section and load addresses of a module it needs to attest and Sancus provides instructions to verify that the actual isolated module corresponds to this MAC.

Sancus Module Compilation. To securely create SMs for Sancus, a number of specifics have to be considered. For example, every SM needs a separate stack in its private data section to ensure the integrity of control data and local variables. Also, whenever exiting an SM, registers need to be cleared to avoid data leakage. The Sancus distribution includes a C compiler to automate the process of creating SMs. The compiler generates the necessary entry and exit stubs to deal with intricacies mentioned above. Moreover, the compiler allows for the definition of multiple entry points that are dispatched from the single physical entry point supported by Sancus. A generic approach to securely compiling high-level code to low-level language with fine-grained memory access control is presented in [1].

3   Motivation and Related Work

In this section, we introduce the need for a secure embedded file system and discuss this in the light of recent related research. In a wider context, our prototype demonstrates the feasibility of encapsulating and controlling access to a shared system resource through a lightweight trusted software layer on top of hardware-enforced mechanisms.

3.1   Embedded File System Security

Existing embedded file systems [5,6] focus mainly on performance aspects: flash specific optimisations, RAM usage and energy consumption, whereas file protection is non-existing or remains very limited. This is in line with the original concept of a single static unprotected embedded application. Indeed, the design notes for Matchbox, a file system for TinyOS, state literally: "We do not need: Security in any form, [...]" [7]. As another example, Contiki features the Coffee file system [20], a dedicated lightweight flash file system without any form of access control. LiteOS [4] provides its own LiteFS UNIX-like file system in which files may represent data, binaries or devices. It also offers a coarse-grained user-oriented protection mechanism that classifies all users in one of three levels, each with its own rwx mode bits.

We argue that in an embedded context, featuring a dynamic multi-stakeholder deployment model, it is software modules rather than users that represent the unit of file protection. Indeed, recall from Sec. 2 that an SM represents the unit of memory protection and authentication. Extending these guarantees with SM-grained protection for shared system resources would thus be valuable.

File protection on a per-SM-basis would furthermore be interesting as it differs from conventional UNIX-like user-oriented file protection [2]. UNIX decides file access based on the identity of the owner of the currently executing program. This coarse grained scheme does however not shield a user from malicious programs that run with her permissions [3]. Moreover, fine-grained file protection is hindered by the default owner/group/others file attributes. Capability-based process-specific file protection for UNIX has been proposed [3] as a countermeasure and fine-grained access control can be accomplished with access control lists [9].

3.2   Secure Resource Sharing

PMAs reorganise an unprotected single-address-space into a set of hardware-delimited protected SM enclaves. Secluding SMs in their respective protection domains allows strong security guarantees on the one hand, but also limits the overall flexibility of the system. Indeed, Sancus [16] does not natively support complex policies, such as dynamically allocating and sharing of protected memory, or fine-grained peripheral access control. In this respect, our protected file system serves as a case study on how to encapsulate a typical shared system resource (i.e. secondary storage) in its own protection domain with flexible SM-grained access control policies.

Self Protecting OS Modules. An SM should either fulfil its own needs or rely on the services of an untrusted OS to interact with the outside world. This implies poor trade-offs between flexibility and protection. Consider for example an SM that wants to save confidential data in a file system or read secret values from a sensor. Without additional support this SM would have to either claim the file system / sensor for itself, effectively denying others access to the resource, or accept to use it in an unprotected way.

The key idea we explore in our secure file system prototype is to mitigate this flexibility vs. protection trade-off by adding a level of indirection. In our setup, we build upon the existing Sancus primitives to provide a dedicated module SM_{server} with exclusive access to a system resource and we implement a thin software layer on top to enforce flexible access control policies. Sancus' hardware logic ensures SM_{server} is solely responsible for the resource it encapsulates. This shows that even though this intermediate SM performs a typical OS task – shared resource management – it differs significantly from a conventional omnipotent trusted kernel software layer.

Secure resource sharing for PMAs thus requires a disjoint set of *self protecting OS modules*. Every such module encapsulates and controls access to a platform resource (e.g. a protected memory buffer, a file system, a keyboard, a network

interface, etc.). This way, client SMs that use its services are offered availability
and access control guarantees.

Zero-Software Microkernel. The idea of implementing the OS as a set of non-
privileged modules echoes the widely known microkernel approach [12,13]. In a
microkernel architecture all non-essential OS services – such as device drives, file
systems, process management, etc. – are implemented as regular user programs,
known as *servers*. The main task of the privileged microkernel is to separate the
applications from each others and provide inter-process communication between
them. User programs and servers always communicate indirectly through the
microkernel. From a security perspective, a true microkernel limits the TCB by
reducing the kernel's size. The actual OS services are implemented in user space
on top of these abstractions.

There is no consensus on which mechanisms should be implemented in the
microkernel. In a way, the Sancus platform is a truly minimal zero-software
microkernel that provides two basic mechanisms to SMs: memory isolation and
authentication. The question then becomes whether such a zero-software microkernel is sufficient to securely implement OS-like services on top. In this respect,
Liedtke [12,13] identifies only three basic abstractions for his minimalist second
generation L4 software microkernel: address spaces, inter-process communication and threads. He argues a microkernel has to "hide the hardware concept
of address spaces, since otherwise, implementing protection would be impossible." [12]. The Sancus platform provides fine-grained hardware-enforced protection domains in a single-address-space. Furthermore, Liedtke identifies the need
for a microkernel to "establish a communication channel which can neither be corrupted nor eavesdropped" and states "uids are required for reliable and efficient
local communication" [12]. This clearly resembles Sancus' hardware-supplied
unique SM IDs and attestation features.

Our protected file system prototype, SM_{sfs}, demonstrates Sancus' hardware-
enforced mechanisms are sufficient to realise SM-grained logical file access restrictions. SM_{sfs} offers security guarantees similar to those of user-space file system
server which is effectively shielded from other protection domains. Moreover, a
client is ensured confidentiality and integrity when communicating with SM_{sfs}.
Importantly, Sancus realises these security guarantees without any trusted software layer. Its hardware-enforced protection scheme indeed makes an omnipotent
kernel layer inherently impossible.

3.3 Application Scenarios

The problem domain of low-end embedded devices is characterised by conflicting
interests between economic considerations on the one hand and security requirements on the other. Sancus presents the SM as the unit of lightweight memory
isolation and authentication. Our protected file system SM_{sfs} module supple-
ments these hardware-enforced security properties with logical file access control
guarantees by means of an explicit software TCB. It thus shows the feasibility
of securely sharing system resources on a per-SM-basis.

Protected Shared Memory. Being able to pass a moderate sized buffer securely between protection domains is useful in many contexts. A first scenario concerns parameter passing of large values. Indeed, one can only pass parameters securely through a limited number of CPU registers when calling an SM [16].

Protected shared memory is also useful in the context of secure I/O. Recall from Sec. 2 that an SM can be provided with exclusive access to a MMIO peripheral. As an example, a keyboard driver module $SM_{keyboard}$ could offer an entry function to get an input line confidentially from the user. The module may then use protected shared memory to pass the result to a client SM.

Secondary Storage. Several authors identify an emerging application area for embedded platforms using secondary storage file systems [5,6,20]. In a multi-stakeholder model with software extensibility by multiple untrustworthy vendors, fine-grained access control for secondary storage resources is essential. Consider for example a low-end extensible wearable device. One application could save sensitive medical logs in the file system; another one could simultaneously use the file system to save privacy-sensitive data such as environment sensor data, recordings, GPS locations, etc. Needless to say reliable and fine-grained memory protection and file access control is imperative in such a system.

4   Design and Implementation of a Protected File System

In this section, we present a protected file system for the Sancus platform [16]. The file system is encapsulated in its own SM_{sfs} protection domain with exclusive access to the storage device, ensuring file system integrity. Furthermore, our file system realises SM-specific access control, allowing fine-grained access control policies for logical file sharing between SMs.

4.1   Layered Design

The protected file system depicted in Fig. 1 features a layered design with a *front-end* access control layer deciding access to a private *back-end* software layer, encapsulating the actual resource. From the point of view of the front-end, the back-end is an abstract Contiki File System (CFS) interface implementation that can be plugged in when compiling the SM_{sfs} module. We provide two different back-end implementations. Section 4.3 discusses an implementation that operates on a Sancus-protected memory buffer, allowing a form of protected shared memory between SMs. Section 4.4 plugs in a real-world embedded flash file system, realising SM-grained protection on a shared system resource.

From a security perspective, the front- and back-end are merely a logical structure, as the entire file system runs in a single protection domain SM_{sfs}. The front-end offers the public interface (i.e. SM_{sfs}'s entry points) towards clients, whereas the back-end is called through private non-entry functions. As the PMA hardware guarantees a protection domain can only be entered from

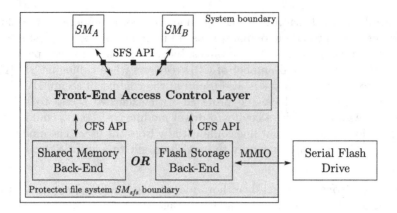

Fig. 1. Our protected file system SM_{sfs} module consists of a generic public front-end access control layer controlling access to a pluggable private back-end software layer, encapsulating the actual resource.

its predefined entry points, a client is effectively prohibited from bypassing the access-control front-end and calling the back-end directly.

The division of responsibilities between the front- and back-end is as follows. The front-end presents a transparent UNIX like file system interface towards client SMs to provide them with the concept of a contiguous logical file with offset-addressable content. Internally however, the front-end is only concerned with SM-oriented access control policies and maintains the data structures to do so. It relies on the back-end CFS implementation for the concept of a logical file. The back-end in its turn encapsulates the actual file system implementation and is completely unaware of any access control going on. It is important to note here that the front-end has no notion of persistence and stores all its access control data structures in volatile protected memory. Our SM_{sfs} prototype does not support persistent SM-grained file protection (c.f. Sec. 6) since it uses Sancus' unique hardware IDs that do not last over multiple boot cycles [16].

4.2   Generic Front-End Access Control Layer

The front-end is conceived as a wrapper implementation that associates an access control list (ACL) of (ID, permissions_flag) pairs per logical file to validate the caller's permissions before passing the call to the back-end.

Software-Module-Grained Access Control. Recall from Sec. 2 that the IDs, uniquely identifying a Sancus module within one boot cycle, are inherently unforgeable as they are exclusively managed by hardware. They can therefore safely be used for subsequent client authentications in a software layer. Essentially, the front-end accomplishes its access control guarantees through the sancus_get_caller_id hardware instruction, which it uses to reliably retrieve the ID of the client – i.e. the SM that entered the currently executing module.

To realise our protected file system prototype SM_{sfs}, we build upon Sancus' hardware-enforced security guarantees in two ways. On the one hand, Sancus' memory isolation techniques grant SM_{sfs} exclusive access to its back-end resource. On the other hand, Sancus' SM identification scheme provides SM_{sfs} with a reliable client authentication mechanism that allows implementing a thin software layer to realise flexible access control policies for its private back-end resource.

Interface. We based our Sancus File System (SFS) interface on the UNIX-like Contiki File System (CFS) interface [20], modifying it where needed and extending it with SM-specific access control functions. Specifically, we had to replace the `cfs_read` and `cfs_write` functions, requiring a pointer to an unprotected memory buffer and a length argument, with `sfs_getc` and `sfs_putc` functions, which pass the arguments and return values securely through CPU registers. For the same reason we had to replace file name strings with single chars.

In addition, our interface supports SM-specific access control. Using the `sfs_chmod` function, the software module that first created a file can assign or revoke fine-grained permissions for a specific SM via a bit flag. Currently our prototype supports read-only, write-only and read-write permissions, but due to the generic access control scheme, more advanced policies such as append-only could be added relatively easy. Client SMs open files through a modified `sfs_open` function, requiring a permissions flag argument and an initial size hint which is passed to the back-end.

Data Structures. Our prototype stores all access control data structures in its protected private data section. It employs a linked list for logical files, each with a corresponding SM-grained permission ACL. This allows a two phase permission lookup procedure when specifying a file by name. The file list is first traversed to locate the file, using the name as a key. Thereafter, the corresponding ACL is searched using the calling SM's ID as a key. To speed up future accesses, using a file descriptor, we employ a fixed-sized file-descriptor-indexed array with pointers to the corresponding ACL entry.

On each function call, before translating the call to the CFS back-end, the front-end validates the caller's permissions. If the caller passes a file descriptor, the implementation first checks whether it is in the expected range and points to an ACL entry that belongs to the caller. Furthermore, to allow safe revocation of earlier assigned permissions, SM_{sfs} closes any remaining open file descriptors when revoking a permission – as opposed to the POSIX standard [10] which leaves such behaviour implementation-defined.

As Sancus [16] requires the protected memory section of an SM to be fixed-sized during the SM's lifetime, SM_{sfs} should fulfil its own dynamic protected memory requirements. To do so, our implementation enforces a maximum number of open file descriptors, pre-allocates a fixed number of file and permission structs at compile time and maintains them in a free list at run time. When running out of protected memory, the front-end rejects requests to create additional files.

4.3   Protected Shared Memory Back-End

In the protected shared memory implementation, the back-end operates on a fixed-sized Sancus-protected memory buffer. Internally, we use a dynamic memory allocation `malloc` implementation on this buffer, allowing clients to transparently claim a portion of the buffer through a UNIX-like API.

Logical files in the protected shared memory back-end have a fixed size during their lifetime. When creating a new file, the implementation uses the initial size argument to allocate a buffer of the corresponding size. From then on, it does proper bounds checking, refusing to seek beyond the buffer's end.

Files are arranged in a linked list, each element containing a pointer to a location inside the private `malloc` buffer and the corresponding size. As in the front-end, we maintain a file-descriptor-indexed array to speed up common file operations and to store the current client-specific logical file offset. This bookkeeping information must also reside in protected memory. To support a dynamic number of logical files, the prototype implementation allocates the required structs using its own protected `malloc` buffer.

4.4   Protected Shared Flash Storage

The research presented here adopts Contiki's open source Coffee FS [20] as our case study flash file system back-end. Coffee FS is highly optimised for small flash memories, requires a small and constant RAM footprint per open file and does not provide any existing file protection mechanism.

The shared flash storage back-end introduces the important issue of *secure peripherals* [11]. Indeed, SM_{sfs} should be provided with exclusive access to the flash drive to ensure file system integrity and confidentiality. For peripherals that are being accessed through the memory address space, Sancus' program counter based memory access control scheme grants a dedicated driver SM exclusive access to a resource by including the relevant MMIO addresses in its private data section [16]. The driver module then mutually authenticates with SM_{sfs}, using attestation as discussed in Sec. 2, to realise end-to-end file system protection.

5   Experimental Evaluation

In this section we evaluate the protected file system SM_{sfs} prototype; our implementation and evaluation suite are available online. We discuss runtime overhead as well as the induced memory footprint and code size. We define total runtime overhead from a client SM's perspective as the additional number of CPU cycles needed to call an SM_{sfs} entry function, compared to calling the respective function of an unprotected file system. Furthermore, we split the overall overhead into a Sancus-dictated component, induced by switching Sancus protection domains, and an implementation-dependent component caused by the access control layer. Finally, we provide the relative overhead for the protected shared memory and Coffee flash file system back-ends.

All experiments were conducted on a Sancus-enabled MSP430 FPGA running at 20 MHz. The FPGA is connected to a Micron M25P16 serial flash drive, using the Coffee file system from Contiki release 2.7. For technical details on the MSP430 and Sancus extensions we refer the reader to [16].

Sancus Protection Domain Switching. As explained in Sec. 2, SMs need entry and exit code stubs that take care of private call-stack switching and clearing of CPU registers to avoid leaking of confidential data. These code stubs thus incur overhead for function calls that switch protection domains. The exact number of cycles needed for such a function call varies with the number and size of the arguments and return value. Calling an unprotected function from within a module SM_A takes between 120 and 170 cycles, whereas calling an SM_B entry function from within SM_A requires between 210 and 280 cycles.

These results indicate an additional Sancus-dictated overhead of roughly 100 cycles for client SMs calling our protected SM_{sfs} module, as opposed to calling an unprotected file system. Note that this overhead is solely caused by encapsulating the file system in its own protection domain SM_{sfs}, independent from any additional access control logic.

Access Control Overhead. We first provide micro benchmarks of the access control front-end layer. The last column of Table 2 shows the total number of CPU cycles needed for a protected client SM_A to call our protected file system SM_{sfs} configured with a dummy back-end. The "Sancus Induced" column lists the number of cycles thereof caused by calling the respective Sancus entry function, depending on the number of arguments. These numbers are responsible for the vast majority of cycles, illustrating how SM_{sfs} realises SM-grained access control policies through a thin software layer on top of Sancus.

Table 2. The number of cycles needed for SM_{sfs} configured with a dummy back-end, assuming a single open file with one ACL entry. The "Sancus Induced" column lists the number of cycles needed to call the respective SM_{sfs} entry function. The next two columns show the overhead of the front-end and the last column lists the summation.

| SFS API | | Sancus | Front-End Induced | | Total |
function	case	Induced	ACL checks	back-end call	
format		211	181	17	409
open	creat	279	120	69	468
open	exist	259	95	69	423
seek		259	18	58	335
getc		229	46	59	334
putc		234	55	63	352
close		229	56	24	309
remove		226	138	27	391
chmod	add	247	120	0	367
chmod	revoke	247	158	0	405

We further detail the overhead induced by the front-end. The "back-end call" column of Table 2 lists the number of cycles needed by the front-end to call the back-end – the downside of a layered design. The "ACL checks" column shows the number of cycles needed to traverse the access control data structures, in the case of a single file and ACL entry. The impact of using the file-descriptor-indexed array is clearly visible, resulting in a constant and low access control overhead for the functions `seek`, `getc`, `putc` and `close`. As explained in Sec. 4.2, our prototype uses linked lists, resulting in a linear growing access control overhead for functions without a file descriptor. We experimentally verified the worst-case overhead indeed grows linearly with a reasonable factor of about 12 extra cycles per additional logical file or ACL linked list entry.

The memory overhead of our SM_{sfs} prototype is bounded at compile time by pre-allocating the file descriptor array and a maximum number of structs for logical files and ACL entries, which is common practice in embedded file systems (as in the Coffee back-end). Both structs occupy 6 bytes. In our test setup, we configured the SM_{sfs} module with a maximum number of 10 ACL entries, 5 files and 8 file descriptor entries, resulting in a total memory usage of 106 bytes. In terms of code size, the access control layer of SM_{sfs} occupies 1.9 KB, whereas the Coffee back-end requires 5.3 KB. Our front-end access control layer thus increases the code size with a factor of 0.36.

Protected Shared Memory Back-End. To investigate the runtime overhead of the protected file system module SM_{sfs} configured with a shared memory back-end, we compare it to the case where two SMs communicate via an unprotected dynamically allocated shared memory buffer in the single-address-space. The "shm" column of Table 3 thus shows our baseline, i.e. the number of cycles needed to create a shared buffer of size 100 via an unprotected `malloc` call, read/write a character and `free` it.[1] The next two columns list the number of cycles needed for our protected shared memory SM_{sfs} module and the absolute overhead.

The key thing to note here is that, once the unprotected dynamic memory is allocated, read and write accesses are equivalent to normal memory accesses and thus require very few cycles. Our SM_{sfs} protected shared memory setup however adds a level of indirection, implying a huge relative overhead for memory accesses. Moreover, setting up the memory buffer takes longer as the meta data structures should be initialised and clients have to open the logical file before accessing it. Emulating flexible access control policies on top of Sancus' native protection model is however for the moment the only way of realising complex protected interactions between SMs.

Protected Shared Flash Storage Overhead. We investigate the runtime overhead of our protected SM_{sfs} file system prototype on top of Contiki's Coffee FS [20], a typical real-world embedded flash file system. The "coffee" column

---

[1] Recall from Sec. 4.2 that we cannot support a multi-byte read/write API. Reading/writing a buffer will thus need multiple calls to `getc`/`putc`.

Table 3. The overhead for a client SM_A that uses SM_{sfs}'s services for each back-end, assuming a single open file with one ACL entry. The "Shared Memory" columns list from left to right: the number of cycles needed by SM_A to use unprotected dynamic memory, SM_{sfs} with a shared memory back-end and the absolute overhead. The "Flash Storage Back-End" columns list from left to right, the number of cycles needed for SM_A to call: an unprotected Coffee file system, SM_{sfs} with a Coffee back-end; the absolute and relative overhead and the overhead percentage induced by the ACL lookup.

API		Shared Memory			Flash Storage Back-End				
		baseline		*overhead*	*baseline*		*overhead*		
function	case	shm	sfs-shm	shm-abs	coffee	sfs-coffee	abs	rel	acl
format		-	584	584	360 E6	360 E6	286	0	63
open	creat	192	1,326	1,134	76,133	76,436	303	0	40
open	exist	-	706	706	2,604	2,862	258	10	37
seek		-	322	322	430	594	181	44	10
getc		2	342	340	902	1,081	179	20	26
putc		4	351	347	1,288	1,485	197	15	28
close		-	539	539	317	498	181	57	31
remove		192	670	478	8,033	8,293	260	3	53
chmod	add	-	367	367	-	367	367	-	33
chmod	revoke	-	405	405	-	405	405	-	39

of Table 3 lists our baseline, i.e. the total number of CPU cycles needed for a protected client SM_A to call an unprotected Coffee flash file system. The "sfs-coffee" column shows the number of cycles needed by SM_A to call our SM_{sfs} protected file system module, configured with a Coffee back-end. Note that these numbers reflect the ideal case where the front-end as well as the back-end implementation and flash driver share the same protection domain SM_{sfs}. In our test setup the Coffee file system and the flash driver operate in unprotected mode, see also Sec. 6. We thus arrived at the presented data by carefully subtracting the fine-grained overhead of switching Sancus protection domains.

The "abs" column of Table 3 lists the absolute number of overhead cycles caused by the protected file system implementation, as compared to the unprotected Coffee setup. To interpret these numbers, the next columns provide the relative overhead and the percentage of the total overhead that is caused by the access control front-end implementation. These results indicate the overhead of protected resource sharing on top of a real-world flash file system is reasonable. Due to the delay of the flash I/O and the file-descriptor-indexed array, the relative number of additional cycles remains limited for commonly used file operations: under 20 % for getc and putc; it even drops to zero for I/O-heavy operations such as format, creat and remove. Moreover, the additional SM-specific chmod access control function consumes a number of cycles of the same magnitude as the unprotected in-memory file operations, such as seek. Finally, the front-end access control software layer shows to be lightweight in the sense that over half of SM_{sfs}'s overhead – in the case of a single file and

ACL entry – can be attributed to calling the respective Sancus entry function and the back-end function call.

Comparing the two back-ends reveals another characteristic of SM interactions: the relative overhead of switching protection domains decreases as the execution time of the callee module increases. Specifically, the relative overhead of SM_{sfs} with a flash back-end is reduced by the flash I/O delay, whereas fast unprotected memory access aggravates overheads in the protected shared memory case.

6   Discussion

In this section, we discuss the security guarantees and limitations of our protected file system SM_{sfs} prototype.

Trusted Computing Base. Our SM_{sfs} module builds upon Sancus' existing hardware primitives [16] to supplement the hardware-enforced security guarantees of its clients with logical file access restrictions. Clients using SM_{sfs} naturally incorporate it in their TCB. Our approach differs significantly from a traditional trusted OS computing base however for two major reasons.

Firstly, *only* client SMs using SM_{sfs} have to trust SM_{sfs} and Sancus offers strong authentication to verify SM_{sfs}. A client can attest an SM, guaranteeing that, i.e., SM_{sfs} has not been tampered with and was loaded correctly, with exclusive access to the MMIO flash drive addresses. This results in a small explicit TCB, as opposed to the implicit TCB induced by an omnipotent trusted kernel.

Second, the SM_{sfs} module is solely entrusted its dedicated file system task, echoing the well known principle of least privilege. Thus, a faulty SM_{sfs} module can only tamper with or leak the file system data it is entrusted. A client SM still preserves exclusive access to its private section. In this, SM_{sfs}'s security guarantees are similar to those of a microkernel file system running in user space as it is shielded from other protection domains. Notably, Sancus does not rely on any trusted kernel software layer to enforce this separation.

Limitations. We acknowledge several limitations in our SM_{sfs} prototype. Firstly, in our test setup, the Coffee file system back-end runs in unprotected mode. We believe that protecting the Coffee implementation by an SM is relatively easy, albeit out of scope for the work presented in this paper.

A second limitation concerns the protected flash driver. Currently Sancus' program counter based memory access control hardware logic only allows a single contiguous private data section per Sancus module [16]. This implies that a module including a MMIO address range in its private data section, cannot at the same time have protected data. Moreover, as it cannot safely provide the stack needed by higher level programming languages, its corresponding code section should be entirely implemented in assembly. We therefore need a separate dedicated flash driver SM, exclusively communicating with SM_{sfs}. From a security perspective, there is no real issue here, but switching protection domains decreases the performance, as explained in Sec. 5. In a real-world setup however, Sancus' program counter based access control logic [16] could relatively easy be extended to allow a MMIO address range as well as another contiguous protected address range in a single protection domain SM_{sfs}.

Finally, SM_{sfs} ensures confidentiality and integrity of logical files as long as it is up and running (which can be verified by the client), but does not persist these guarantees across reboots. Indeed, since the IDs assigned to SMs by Sancus, do not persist after reboots (see Sec. 2), they may change when redeploying an SM. We argue that extending SM_{sfs}'s file protection guarantees across reboots is non-trivial, as anything could happen between crashing of the node and successful redeployment of SM_{sfs}. In this respect, our protected file system does also not protect against physically removing and reading out the flash drive. This matches Sancus' attacker model [16] which does not consider attackers with physical access to the hardware. The only way to protect against such attacks and to support persistent file protection would be to encrypt all data on the flash disk with SM_{sfs}'s Sancus-provided private key. Such an approach would however dramatically reduce performance, especially since all data is transferred safely through CPU registers on a byte-per-byte basis. Moreover, there would be little advantage over the situation where clients encrypt the data themselves before passing it to SM_{sfs} or even an unprotected file system.

We therefore consider our protected file system SM_{sfs} module as a way for SMs to extend their fixed sized private data section considerably, while at the same time offering flexible access control guarantees. In this respect, it could be an interesting future work direction to ensure the hardware automatically clears the flash drive on system boot – even before SM_{sfs} is deployed – to enforce the non-persistence of file system data.

7 Conclusion

Low-end embedded devices are becoming increasingly present and interconnected in our everyday lives. Adequate software isolation for these platforms is crucial in a multi-stakeholder context. In this perspective, PMAs offer strong hardware-enforced memory isolation and authentication guarantees, but cannot realise flexible access control policies for shared system resources. SMs should either claim the resource for themselves or rely on the services of an untrusted OS when interacting with the outside world.

In this paper we presented a protected file system SM_{sfs} module that builds upon existing PMA hardware primitives to construct a software layer that realises access control, i.e. logical file protection guarantees for client SMs. In a broader perspective, this demonstrates the feasibility of supplementing the hardware-enforced security properties offered by PMAs with SM-grained access control guarantees enforced by a protected software TCB.

While our implementation is based on Sancus [16], a hardware-only TCB for lightweight embedded microcontrollers, our approach is fairly general and can be implemented with other PMAs that provide (1) memory isolation, (2) attestation guarantees and (3) exclusive use of MMIO ranges. Yet, to the best of our knowledge, Sancus is the only PMA satisfying all these requirements in the embedded world. In server and desktop computing, our approach can be implemented using a trusted hypervisor and a PMA such as Intel's SGX [15]. Since SGX enclaves cannot claim MMIO ranges directly, a rather large software TCB would be necessary.

In the future we will further investigate the effectiveness and efficiency of our access control mechanism based on extended evaluation scenarios that allow for meaningful macro-benchmarks. A particularly interesting scenario would be to provide access control for I/O devices connected to a peripheral bus.

Acknowledgements. This research is partially funded by the Research Fund KU Leuven, and by the FWO-Vlaanderen. Job Noorman holds a PhD grant from the Agency for Innovation by Science and Technology in Flanders (IWT).

References

1. Agten, P., Strackx, R., Jacobs, B., Piessens, F.: Secure compilation to modern processors. In: IEEE CSF 2012, pp. 171–185. IEEE (2012)
2. Bach, M.J.: The design of the UNIX operating system, vol. 5. Prentice-Hall (1986)
3. Berman, A., Bourassa, V., Selberg, E.: TRON: Process-specific file protection for the UNIX operating system. In: USENIX TCON 1995, pp. 165–175. USENIX Association (1995)
4. Cao, Q., Abdelzaher, T., Stankovic, J., He, T.: The liteos operating system: Towards unix-like abstractions for wireless sensor networks. In: IPSN 2008, pp. 233–244. IEEE (2008)
5. Escolar, S., Carretero, J., Isaila, F., Lama, S.: A lightweight storage system for sensor nodes. In: PDPTA, pp. 638–644 (2008)
6. Farooq, M.O., Kunz, T.: Operating systems for wireless sensor networks: A survey. Sensors 11(6), 5900–5930 (2011)
7. Gay, D.: Matchbox: A simple filing system for motes, August 21, 2003. http://www.docs.tinyos.net/tinyos-1.x/doc/matchbox.pdf
8. Granjal, J., Monteiro, E., Silva, J.S.: Security in the integration of low-power wireless sensor networks with the internet: A survey. Ad Hoc Networks 24(Part A), 264–287 (2015)
9. Grünbacher, A.: Posix access control lists on linux. In: USENIX TCON 2003, pp. 259–272. USENIX Association (2003)
10. IEEE. Std 1003.1 (2004). http://pubs.opengroup.org/onlinepubs/009695399/
11. Koeberl, P., Schulz, S., Sadeghi, A.-R., Varadharajan, V.: Trustlite: a security architecture for tiny embedded devices. In: EuroSys 2014, pp. 10:1–10:14. ACM (2014)
12. Liedtke, J.: On μ-kernel construction. In: SOSP 1995, pp. 237–250. ACM (1995)
13. Liedtke, J.: Toward real microkernels. Comm. ACM 39(9), 70–77 (1996)
14. Lopez, J., Roman, R., Agudo, I., Fernandez-Gago, C.: Trust management systems for wireless sensor networks: Best practices. Comput. Commun. 33(9), 1086–1093 (2010)

15. McKeen, F., Alexandrovich, I., Berenzon, A., Rozas, C.V., Shafi, H., Shanbhogue, V., Savagaonkar, U.R.: Innovative instructions and software model for isolated execution. In: Proceedings of the 2nd International Workshop on Hardware and Architectural Support for Security and Privacy, pp. 10:1–10:1. ACM (2013)

16. Noorman, J., Agten, P., Daniels, W., Strackx, R., Van Herrewege, A., Huygens, C., Preneel, B., Verbauwhede, I., Piessens, F.: Sancus: Low-cost trustworthy extensible networked devices with a zero-software trusted computing base. In: USENIX SEC 2013, pp. 479–494. USENIX Association (2013)

17. Roman, R., Najera, P., Lopez, J.: Securing the internet of things. Computer **44**(9), 51–58 (2011)

18. Strackx, R., Noorman, J., Verbauwhede, I., Preneel, B., Piessens, F.: Protected software module architectures. In: ISSE 2013, pp. 241–251. Springer (2013)

19. Strackx, R., Piessens, F., Preneel, B.: Efficient isolation of trusted subsystems in embedded systems. In: Jajodia, S., Zhou, J. (eds.) SecureComm 2010. LNICST, vol. 50, pp. 344–361. Springer, Heidelberg (2010)

20. Tsiftes, N., Dunkels, A., He, Z., Voigt, T.: Enabling large-scale storage in sensor networks with the coffee file system. In: IPSN 2009, pp. 349–360. ACM/IEEE (2009)

Secure Obfuscation of Authoring Style

Hoi Le[✉], Reihaneh Safavi-Naini, and Asadullah Galib

Department of Computer Science, University of Calgary, Calgary, Canada
{leh,rei}@ucalgary.ca, asadullah.al.galib@hotmail.com

Abstract. Anonymous authoring includes writing reviews, comments and blogs, using pseudonyms with the general assumption that using these pseudonyms will protect the real identity of authors and allows them to freely express their views. It has been shown, however, that writing style may be used to trace authors across multiple Websites. This is a serious threat to privacy and may even result in revealing the authors's identities. In obfuscating authors' writing style, an authored document is modified to hide the writing characteristics of the author. In this paper we first show that existing obfuscation systems are insecure and propose a general approach for constructing obfuscation algorithms, and then instantiate the framework to give an algorithm that semi-automatically modifies an author's document. We provide a secure obfuscation scheme that is able to hide an author's document *securely* among other authors' documents in a corpus. As part of our obfuscation algorithm we present a new algorithm for identifying an author's unique words that would be of independent interest.

We present a security model and use it to analyze our scheme and also the previous schemes. We implement our scheme and give its performances through experiments. We show that our algorithm can be used to obfuscate documents securely and effectively.

Keywords: Obfuscation · Stylometry · Privacy · Anonymity

1 Introduction

Creating accounts on Websites under pseudonyms and using them to write reviews or post comments is a common practice, with the general belief that authors remain anonymous and can freely express their opinions and views. Although major review Websites do not allow mass collection of data by outsiders, it is possible to collect substantial number of reviews and posts from Websites such as IMDB and Netflix and so a natural question is whether authors can be traced across websites that they have posted their blogs, reviews and comments.

Authorship attribution techniques are based on the observation that people write in their own individual styles. Authorship attribution techniques have made

---

A. Galib—This work is supported in part by Alberta Innovates Technology Futures, in the Province of Alberta, Canada.

© IFIP International Federation for Information Processing 2015
R.N. Akram and S. Jajodia (Eds.): WISTP 2015, LNCS 9311, pp. 88–103, 2015.
DOI: 10.1007/978-3-319-24018-3_6

significant progress. Today, with sufficient amount of data it is possible to identify an author among a large number (e.g. 100,000) of authors [1]. An author's writing style is referred to as the *writeprint* and can be extracted as a feature set from the documents written by them, and used to identify their anonymously written documents with accuracy above 90% [2]. Examples of writeprint features are syntactic features (such as part-of-speech tags, function words) and lexical features (e.g., word frequencies, word n-grams). Using writing style to link an author on multiple web sites was proposed in [3,4]. It was shown that this can pose a real threat to the user's anonymity and allow adversaries to learn more about a user than they intended to reveal, including access to their private information such as photos, places that they live and work. In some cases, if the information can be linked to websites such as forums of universities that include the users' real names, the user identity will be revealed. In [3], Narayannan et al. showed that attackers who know a small amount of information about a Netflix subscriber can identify the subscriber in the dataset. Similarly through a linkability study of Yelp reviews [4] authors showed that using letter distribution of alphabet, up to 83% of anonymous reviews can be linked to their authors. To summarize, analysis of writing style allows one to breach users' privacy by tracing their activities across the Internet. This is particularly concerning because users are unaware of the fact and could inadvertently reveal sensitive information.

This problem can be alleviated if authors' writing style is obfuscated. A direct approach is to imitate another author's style by analysing their style using a set of documents on the same topic, learning the style characteristics and modifying one's own style to match those characteristics. This however would be a tedious process that needs sufficient automation and computer support to become acceptable. To support users in hiding their writing styles, a number of approaches have been proposed. Unfortunately, these approaches [5,6] are vulnerable to attacks that allow the adversary to narrow down the number of users and in some cases recover the original author. We review previous works and present our attacks on these works in Section 2.

We also propose a new approach to obfuscation of writing style and give details of an instance of the approach, its security analysis and experimental results supporting feasibility and practicality of the approach.

Our Contributions: Our contributions can be summarized as follows:

– We present attacks on the schemes [5,6] and show the attacks substantially reduce the claimed security and in some cases completely reverse the obfuscation. The attacks exploit the deterministic nature of the algorithms and are successful in revealing the original author of an obfuscated document. In the case of Anonymouth (an instantiation of [6]) which is not completely deterministic, using the data set and experiments that are reported in the paper, we can identify a set of size 2 that includes the author, with probability $\frac{14}{32} = 0.438$. In this experiment, in total 10 authors were considered and so random guessing of a set of size 2 that includes the author would have the success chance of $\frac{9}{\binom{10}{2}} = 0.2$. Hence, our attack doubles the success chance of the attacker compared to this random guess.

– We propose a general approach for designing stylometry obfuscation schemes and give an instantiation that provides a secure obfuscation system. In this approach, a document is represented by a set of *features*. One can obfuscate a document with respect to a subset of features as described below. Consider a corpus of documents of N authors and assume the corpus is used to determine a set of features for both a user that is represented by a set of documents, and a single document. A feature f_i^D in a document D has value w_i^D, and is also referred to as a *feature point* (e.g. frequency of occurrences, a measure of the uniqueness of the feature, etc.). To obfuscate a document D of the user U with respect to a subset of features $\mathcal{F}^D$, the following steps are applied to elements of $\mathcal{F}^D$ in sequence. For a feature $f_i^D \in \mathcal{F}^D$, a feature point $w_i^{u'}$ of another author U' is selected and w_i^D is modified so that it becomes "close" to $w_i^{u'}$. Here "close" means the distance between w_i^D and $w_i^{u'}$ is made small under a distance measure. The resulting document will be used as the input of the same process for the next feature in the sequence.

In our instantiation of this approach we will use Basic-9 as the feature set. A feature point is a non-negative real number representing one of 9 characteristics of a user's writings. Moving "close" to a feature point means a user modifies their document such that the corresponding feature in that document becomes close to that target feature point.

We also present a new unique word identification algorithm using information theoretic measures and use it as an identifying feature for users during obfuscation. This algorithm may have other applications and would be of independent interest.

– We present a security model for stylometry obfuscation algorithms and will use it to analyse other schemes as well as our scheme. The model provides a framework for the evaluation of style obfuscation systems. In this model, we describe attackers' capabilities, discuss possible attack strategies and define the success of their attacks.

The rest of the paper is organized as follows. Section 2 summarizes the related works and we present attacks to the security flaws of those previous works. In Section 3 and 4 we introduce our approach and implementation. We provide a security analysis in Section 5. Section 6 presents our experimental results. We conclude the paper in Section 7.

2   Related Work

Rao and Rohatgi suggested round trip machine translation (for example, English - German - English) as a possible method for document anonymization [7]. However, with the improvement in machine translation, it has been shown empirically that round trip machine translation is not effective in obfuscating writing style. There are also proposals to allow users to obfuscate their writing styles in an automated or semi-automated way. Kacmarcik et. al [5] used word frequencies in one's writings as the writing style. WinMine is a tool that uses Decision Tree algorithm and is used as the core of their work. Each author's writing is represented by a set of features (a feature is a word with a frequency attached to it). Inputs of the algorithm are feature sets of K authors, and the output is the root of the Decision Tree which is the most discriminating feature between these authors. This root is removed and included in the *most important feature set*. The procedure is repeated with the rest of the features from the authors to get the next most discriminating one until the set of the most important features is completed. The algorithm also provides a threshold for each feature that helps distinguish the authors. For example, if the feature f_i weight is less than 0.034, it belongs to author U_1, if its weight is greater than 0.074, it belongs to author U_2 (suppose $K{=}2$). The system will suggest to an author how to adjust their features so that the weights of the features are close to the corresponding weights of the farthest authors of those features. In their implementation of the approach they considered $K = 2$, and in experiments changes were only made to features in order to evaluate the obfuscation results (no actual changes were made in the document).

McDonald et al. [6] used Basic 9 feature set in their work (a brief description of this feature set is presented in Section 4). Their system helps the user to semi-automatically anonymize their document using the following approach. Consider an author U who wants to obfuscate their writing style in a document D. Suppose there exists a set of sample documents from other authors as well as a sample set from U. Features extracted from all authors are clustered (for each feature type separately) such that each cluster has at least K features. For each cluster, the following weight is then measured: $W = num\_elements \times (centroid - f_i^u)$, where $num\_elements$ is the number of elements in the cluster, $centroid$ is the centroid of that cluster, and f_i^u is the feature weight of the corresponding feature extracted from sample documents of U. The cluster that has the greatest weight will be selected, and author U should adjust their corresponding feature in D to be close to that cluster's centroid.

As we will describe in Section 2.1, the main drawback of the above two algorithms is that the obfuscated documents could be linked to the original authors.

There are other works [8,9] on automatic replacement and style transformation. However, these works either provide a general approach or are not acceptable in practice. In [8], it is suggested to transform the writing style of a document incrementally using a loop, where in each run of the loop, the style is slightly changed and this is repeated until some target condition is satisfied. An example of this latter category is [9] where all the words in a document are automatically replaced with their synonyms. This may decrease the readability, and could significantly affect the semantic of the document.

2.1   Attacks on the Existing Text Obfuscation Approaches

The algorithm in [5] is deterministic, and the steps of the algorithm can be perfectly reversed, as we present below.

Attack on the system in [5]: Consider a document D written by U which is anonymized following the algorithm described in [5], together with the initial training set. From the initial training set, we can obtain the most important feature set $\mathcal{F}$ from the obfuscated document D_O and for each feature in $\mathcal{F}$, compare its feature point with the same feature of authors from the training set. If an author U' in the training set results in the highest distance for every feature in $\mathcal{F}$, then U' is the original author of the anonymized document D_O.

Attack on the system in [6]: Suppose the obfuscated document is D_O, and the initial training documents of other authors and U are given. We can de-obfuscate the document D_O as follows: (i) Cluster each feature point of all authors into clusters, (ii) Compare centroids of these clusters with the corresponding feature point in D_O. The cluster that has centroid match with feature point of D_O is the cluster that was used in the obfuscation process. Call these clusters which are collected from all feature types is CLS. (iii) For each candidate author c, calculate its weight W with each cluster in CLS; (iv) If a candidate author U' which has the highest W values with every cluster in CLS, U' is the original author of D_O.

Anonymouth is an implementation of the algorithm [6] in which some randomness has been used for the initial stage of the K-mean algorithm. However, the resulting clusters from the K-mean algorithm stay mostly the same. Hence, we will show that this would not be enough to protect the obfuscated document. We exploit the fact that the targets in the obfuscation process can be calculated and they are related to the features which also can be extracted from the obfuscated document. We represent this relation by the distances between the possible targets and the extracted features of the obfuscated document. To normalize these distances over different types of features, the distances are converted into percentages. An average distance over all features is then calculated for each candidate author and all candidates are sorted in increasing order of this distance. This distance for obfuscated document and its real author must be small, and so the smaller distance means that it is more likely to be the real author. Hence we consider the top 2 of this list. The result is the original author appears at these positions with probability $\frac{14}{32}$ while the random chance is 0.2. This shows that this attack can be used to narrow down the set of possible authors quite effectively.

Due to limited space, our detailed attack will be introduced in a longer version of this paper.

3   Secure Stylometry Obfuscation

3.1   Problem Description

An author U wishes to obfuscate their writing style in a document D.

We assume there is a corpus $\mathcal{C}$ that contains public documents of U and also of other authors. The total number of authors is N. Writing styles of U and other authors are represented by a set of features that can be extracted from their authored documents.

3.2   A General Approach to Secure Obfuscation

Assume that the feature set of an author U_k in $\mathcal{C}$ consists of ℓ features, denoted by $\mathcal{F}_k = \{f_1^k, f_2^k, \cdots, f_\ell^k\}$. For sufficiently long documents, a document can be seen as a collection of sub-documents and so the algorithm used for extracting a user's feature set can be used to extract a feature set for a document. This means that we can extract the same feature set $\mathcal{F}_D$ from a document D that needs to be obfuscated, $\mathcal{F}_D = \{f_1^D, f_2^D, \cdots, f_\ell^D\}$.

In order to hide a feature f_i^D among the same feature of other authors in the corpus $\mathcal{C}$, we cluster authors' features $f_i^1, f_i^2, f_i^3, \cdots, f_i^N$ into a number of clusters and randomly select one as the target cluster for hiding f_i^D. The target cluster should not contain extreme values that are abnormal such as too small or too large.

1. Input:
– $\mathcal{C}$: corpus of N authors.
– K: number of clusters
– D: the document that needs to be obfuscated.
2. Algorithm:
(a) Consider feature i of N authors in the corpus $\mathcal{C}$. Denote this set as $PublicFeatures = \{f_i^1, f_i^2, f_i^3, \cdots, f_i^N\}$
(b) Run K-means algorithm to cluster $PublicFeatures$ into K clusters.
(c) User selects a target cluster (which could be randomly).
(d) The algorithm selects a random point p in the selected cluster.
(e) Modify D to corresponding feature in p, and output a temporary document D_{tmp}. Set $D = D_{tmp}$.
3. Perform step 2 for all features in the feature set of document D. Use classifier δ (described later) to classify D_{tmp}. If D_{tmp} is classified to user U with a probability less than or equal to a random chance, output $D_O = D_{tmp}$. Otherwise, replace $D = D_{tmp}$, and repeat from step 2.

The elements in the approach are described in detail as follows.

Parameter K. K is the number of clusters for each feature and ranges from 1 to $N-1$. Choosing K depends on the number of features that a user wants in a target cluster, specially level of privacy, and the distance that the user is willing to move their document. Users may prefer many features in a cluster, or resulting in small distances to adjust. In the worst case, K and the target cluster may be chosen randomly by the user or the program (if there are too many features in the feature set), which still guarantees that the obfuscation system is secure as we will analyse in Section 5.

Feature set. This approach in general can work for any feature set. In our implementation, we use Basic-9 feature set which is widely used in experiments on text classification and text obfuscation [6,10] as well as more feasible for users to modify them compared to other complex features.

Text classifier δ. There is a wide range of text classifiers to perform text classification. Many of these text classifiers are implemented in Weka [11] which is a common tool set used in text classification related research. The tool set includes implementations for SVM, NaiveBayes, Neural Network, Decision Tree, etc. To select an appropriate classifier with respect to the corpus $\mathcal{C}$, the classifiers should be evaluated using cross-validation method: **N**-fold cross-validation splits a data set into **N** folds and runs classification experiment **N** times, each time one fold of data is used as test set and the classifier is trained on the other $\mathbf{N}-1$ folds of data. The classification accuracy is averaged over the results of **N** runs, and the classifier that gives higher accuracy is the one should be selected as δ for the obfuscation process.

K-mean clustering algorithm. K-mean clustering algorithm starts by dividing members in a dataset into K clusters, with at least one item in each cluster. The data points are randomly assigned to the clusters resulting in clusters that have roughly the same number of data points. The distance between each data point to each cluster's mean is then measured, and the mean is defined for each problem normally as the average value of all elements in a cluster. If the data point is not closest to its own cluster, it is moved to the closest cluster. This step is repeated until there is no data point moving from one cluster to another.

The above approach is flexible and the set of features can be chosen so that the document change is acceptable by the user.

4   Our Implementation

In this section, we present an implementation of the above approach using Basic-9 feature set. This set can be divided into subsets, (i) *Sentence related features* including: Average Sentence Length, Sentence Count, (ii) *Lexical features* including: Unique Word Counts, Average Syllables per Word, Character Count, Character Count without Space, and (iii) *Readability related features* including: Gunning Fox Readability Index, Complexity, Flesch Reading Ease Score. These features are described in Table 1. In stylometry Basic-9 feature set is less powerful than Writerprints which consists of low-level features such as frequencies of 1-, 2-, 3-grams. Basic-9 feature set, however, is convenient to provide suggestions to change the document for the users following these suggestions.

4.1   Preprocessing

We implemented all Basic-9 features except Unique Word Count, using the standard definitions of these features [12]. For Unique Word Count we defined a new algorithm using the information theoretic measure of mutual information, defined as follows.

For two random variables X and Y with joint probability distribution $P(X, Y)$, the mutual information measure is defined as the reduced uncertainty of variable X when variable Y is known, or vice versa. Our Unique Word Count extractor works as follows.

Table 1. Descriptions of Basic-9 feature set.

Feature	Description
Unique Word Counts	Number of unique words
Average Sentence Length	Average number of words in a sentence
Sentence Count	Number of sentences in a document
Average Syllables per Word	Average number of syllables per a word used
Gunning Fox Readability Index	A weighted average of the number of words per sentence, and the number of long words per word: $(= 0.4[\frac{words}{sentences} + 100(\frac{complex\ words}{words})])$
Complexity	equivalent to lexical density of a document $(= \frac{N_{lex}}{N_{tok}})$ N_{lex} is the number of lexical words token, N_{tok} is the total number of tokens.
Character Count	Number of characters used in a document
Character Count without Space	Number of characters used in a document (without spaces)
Flesch Reading Ease Score	The readability of a document: the higher values are, the easier to read. $(= 206.83 - 1.015\frac{total\ words}{total\ sentence} - 84.6\frac{total\ syllables}{total\ words})$

Unique Word Extractor. To extract a list of unique word for an author U from a corpus $\mathcal{C}$ we will do the following. Let W_U denote the list of all the words that U used in the documents in the corpus $\mathcal{C}$.

The importance of a word $w_i \in W_U$ to U is modelled by the mutual information between two random variables X_U that represents the presence of U in the corpus, and X_{w_i} that represents the presence of the word w_i in the corpus. The mutual information is calculated as,

$$I(w_i, U) = I(X_U, X_{w_i}) = H(X_{w_i}) - H(X_{w_i}|X_U)$$

Here $p(X_{w_i} = 1)$ is the probability that w_i appears in a document in $\mathcal{C}$, $p(X_U = 1)$ is the probability that U is the author of a document in $\mathcal{C}$, and $p(X_{w_i} = 1, X_U = 1)$ is the probability that w_i appear in a document written by U in $\mathcal{C}$. These probabilities are calculated as relative frequencies,

$$p(X_{w_i} = 1, X_U = 1) = \frac{n_{w_i \wedge U}}{n}$$
$$p(X_{w_i} = 1) = \frac{n_{w_i}}{n}$$
$$p(X_U = 1) = \frac{n_U}{n}$$

where n is the number of documents in the corpus, $n_{w_i \wedge U}$ is number of documents in $\mathcal{C}$ that are written by U which contain w_i, and n_{w_i} is number of documents in $\mathcal{C}$ contain w_i, and n_U is number of documents written by U.

Mutual information of words in W_U with U are ranked, and the top ℓ words are selected to the most important or "unique" word set.

The advantage of extracting "unique words" as above instead of the standard approaches, as in [13], is that the resulting extracted words are more representing for one's writing. Using the standard definition, words which appear once in a particular context would be selected as unique words, thus, do not necessarily represent one's writings.

4.2 Obfuscation Algorithm

Algorithm 1 is our instantiation of the approach described in Section 3.2.

The user must select the number of clusters $K_i (i = 1, 2, ..., 9)$, and then after applying the clustering algorithm, select one of the resulting clusters (which could be done randomly). Each K_i in the K set ranges from 1 to $N - 1$, where N is the total number of authors in the corpus C.

Among a number of choices for the classifiers in the Weka set, by running 10-fold cross-validation analysis over the training corpus, in Section 6, SVM is selected as the best classifier for our scheme.

5   Security Analysis

We present an attacker model $\mathcal{A}$ for a text obfuscation system and use it to evaluate our system. Let D be a document that is to be obfuscated using an algorithm Π, with respect to a corpus $\mathcal{C}$, a classification algorithm δ and a feature set $\mathcal{F} = \{f_1, f_2, \cdots, f_\ell\}$. The attacker can be modelled as follows.

Attacker capabilities:
– Attacker knows the obfuscation algorithm Π;
– Attacker knows the corpus of training documents from all authors $\mathcal{C}$;
– Attacker can extract the same feature set $\mathcal{F}$ for an author or a document as in the obfuscation algorithm Π;
– Attacker use the same text classifier δ as used in the obfuscation algorithm Π.

The attackers will use the following attack strategies:

1. Backtracking.

In backtracking, the adversary takes the steps of the obfuscation algorithm in the reverse order, starting from the obfuscated document, and taking reverse steps. This adversary will have success chance of 1 in some deterministic obfuscation algorithms.

2. Exhaustive search on authors in the corpus.

In exhaustive attack, the attacker considers each author in the corpus as the candidate author. The distance for the features of each candidate and the obfuscated document can be derived (such as the distance in Section 2.1) and used to select the most likely author. For example, the author who has the closest distance is the original author.

We also consider the effect of using a different classification algorithm and show that the attacker will not have a higher chance if they use a different classification algorithm.

Suppose U is the original author of an obfuscated document D_O. Consider an attacker with capabilities as above, the attacker will try to make the candidate set $\mathcal{S}$ as small as possible. We define the success of the attack by the size of a set $\mathcal{S}$ that includes the original author. An attack is $(\Delta, \mathcal{S}, t)$ - successful if the probability that the author is in $\mathcal{S}$ is at least $1 - \Delta$ and $|\mathcal{S}| \leq t$ (with $\Delta \geq 0$ and $1 \leq t \leq N$):

$$P_t[\text{Author in } \mathcal{S}] \geq 1 - \Delta$$

Input : document D, corpus $\mathcal{C}$, and
$K = \{K_1, K_2, K_3, K_4, K_5, K_6, K_7, K_8, K_9\}$.

Output: obfuscated document D_O

1 $FeatureExtractor(\mathcal{C}) \longleftarrow (\mathcal{F}_1, \mathcal{F}_2, \cdots, \mathcal{F}_N)$

2 /* Each $\mathcal{F}_k$ includes 9 elements of Basic-9 features:
   $\mathcal{F}_k = \{f_1^k, f_2^k, f_3^k, f_4^k, f_5^k, f_6^k, f_7^k, f_8^k, f_9^k\}$ */

3 $FeatureExtractor(D) \longleftarrow \mathcal{F}_D$

4 /* $\mathcal{F}_D = \{f_1^D, f_2^D, f_3^D, f_4^D, f_5^D, f_6^D, f_7^D, f_8^D, f_9^D\}$ */

5 Select a classifier δ.

6 **for** *each feature i in the Basic-9 feature set* **do**

7 $\quad$ /* Clustering $f_i^1, f_i^2, \cdots, f_i^N$ into K_i clusters   */

8 $\quad$ $SimpleKmeans(f_i^1, f_i^2, \cdots, f_i^N, K_i)$

9 $\quad$ U selects a cluster

10 $\quad$ /* A target t_i is chosen randomly in that cluster.   */

11 $\quad$ $t_i = RandomSelection()$

12 $\quad$ U modifies D to adjust feature f_i^D to the target t_i.

13 $\quad$ Output a temporary document D_{tmp}. Set $D = D_{tmp}$.

14 **end**

15 $\delta(D_{tmp})$ /* Reclassify D_{tmp}.   */

16 **if** $\delta(D_{tmp}) \longleftarrow U_i$ **and** $U_i \neq U$ **and** $P[\delta(D_{tmp} \leftarrow U] \leq \frac{1}{N}$ **then**

17 $\quad|$ output $D_O = D_{tmp}$.

18 **end**

19 **if** $D_O \equiv \emptyset$ **then**

20 $\quad|$ Re-run the algorithm. /* Now $D = D_{tmp}$ */

21 **end**

Algorithm 1. Secure Obfuscation

The most identifying attack is when $t = 1$.

We showed that the backtracking attack was successful against deterministic algorithms to determine the author in Section 2.1.

Evaluation of Secure Obfuscation. Given the obfuscated document D_O and the public corpus $\mathcal{C}$, the attacker can extract its feature set using the same feature extractor algorithm as the obfuscator. Suppose all feature weights in the feature set match the target values generated by the obfuscation process, so $\mathcal{F}_{D_O} = \{t_1, t_2, t_3, t_4, t_5, t_6, t_7, t_8, t_9\}$ (t_i is the target generated in the obfuscation process for feature f_i^D of the document D). According to our algorithm, these target values are selected in chosen clusters by a random algorithm $RandomSelection()$. As these clusters are chosen by the user, if this information is not leaked, the attacker cannot determine which clusters that the values in $\mathcal{F}_{D_O}$ belong to, and only can guess these clusters with a random chance. The attackers are also unable to find the link between the user and their chosen clusters.

The exhaustive search was successful against Anonymouth in reducing the size of potential authors from the full author set to a limited set $\mathcal{S}$ with $|\mathcal{S}| = 2$ and $P_2[\text{Author in } \mathcal{S}] = \frac{14}{32}$.

In *Secure Obfuscation*, the targets in the obfuscation process are chosen randomly, hence the attacker cannot perform the same attack to our algorithm as on Anonymouth in Section 2.1. Instead, we perform a *similar* attack on the documents which are obfuscated by our scheme (Section 6). The attack generates a sorted list of the candidate authors for each obfuscated document based on the average distance measured between the obfuscated document's features and a candidate author's (instead of targets from clusters as in the attack on Anonymouth). Note that we allow the user to appear at the top two elements of the list, the success probability of the attack is $P_2[\text{Author in } \mathcal{S}] = \frac{3}{20}$ that is smaller than a random chance as $P_2[\text{Author in } \mathcal{S}] = \frac{2}{10} = 0.2$.

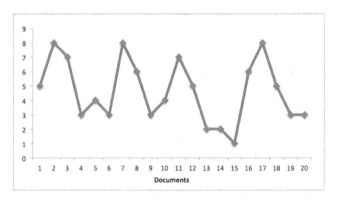

Fig. 1. The tested obfuscated documents as the x-axis, the positions of the original authors in the sorted candidate lists as the y-axis.

We note that as the backtracking strategy cannot continue after the *RandomSelection*() step. Hence combinations of backtracking with other strategies also cannot proceed after this point. In other words, backtracking strategy cannot improve the strength of other attacks.

Cross-classifier attack. Consider our obfuscation scheme which is based on a classification algorithm δ and assume we obfuscate a document D of author U to D_O such that δ classifies D_O to U'. There is a chance that δ misclassifies D_O, which means that D_O may still link to U. Therefore, if the attacker uses another classifier δ' which can link D_O to the real author, he may gain success. We analyzed the success chance of the attacker which is:

$$Succ = \tfrac{1}{N-1}\left((1 - p_\delta)\,p_{\delta'} + p_\delta\,(1 - p_{\delta'})\right) \le \tfrac{1}{N-1}$$

where p_δ and $p_{\delta'}$ are the precision rates of δ and δ' respectively. This shows that, with this attack, the attacker cannot gain a success with a chance better than a random chance which is $\frac{1}{N}$.

6   Experiments

In our experiments, we demonstrate that our algorithm obfuscates documents successfully with Basic-9 feature set, and examine the effect of changing the background corpus on the obfuscation results. In our experiments, the background corpus is Brennan-Greenstadt Adversarial Stylometry Corpus [6] and is comprised of documents from 10 authors. In this corpus, there are at least 5 documents for each author, each document consisting of 500 words. These documents are written about different topics. We asked 10 participants to contribute their documents and join our experiments.

Each participant submitted at least 6 documents of at least 500 words. One document was used to obfuscate and the rest was used as training data. All the documents were in English and extracted to plaintext forms. We asked each participant to obfuscate at least 2 documents.

To select an appropriate classifier for our data set we followed the approach in Section 3.2. We ran ten-fold validation analysis on various classifiers (J48, Neural Network, Naive Bayes, etc.) in the Weka classifier set. The analysis was performed on the public corpus of authors' documents. SVM was selected as it yielded in high classification accuracy of 86%.

For each document, we output for users a list of suggested target values of features respecting to that corpus and a list of unique word. Guidelines on how to change these features in their documents to achieve these target values were suggested to users, e.g. removing or rephrasing unique words (note that we did not ask users to increase or decrease their number of unique words), reduce the sentence count by combining sentences together. We transformed number of characters to an approximate number of words, so that changing character counts related features would become changing number of words.

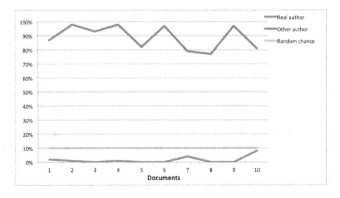

Fig. 2. Authorship attribution results of the obfuscated documents.

The temporary document which was output after changing the features was then re-classified using the SVM classification algorithm. Using above approach 19 out of 20 document were obfuscated after users change their features. On average, it took users one round of modifying features to anonymize the documents. In Figure 2 we demonstrate the authorship attribution results of the first 10 obfuscated documents. These documents were attributed to the original authors with less than or equal to a random chance which was $\frac{1}{10}$ and also were attributed to other authors with more significant chances.

6.1 Effect of Background Corpus on the Obfuscation Results

The background corpus, or set of reference authors and documents, is important for document anonymization as the algorithm calculates the target value for each feature based on the background corpus and suggests changes to users based on these target values.

We tested if documents anonymized using one background corpus are also anonymized against a different background corpus. To test this, we added 3 more authors to the existing corpus. The documents from these authors were about different topics (similar to the documents in the initial background corpus). The results (Figure 3a) showed that the effectiveness of the anonymization could change if the background corpus is changed. Although all the obfuscated documents were still anonymized however the chances that those documents were classified to the original authors might slightly increase or stay the same. This was also true for the case when we added 6 authors to the existing corpus.

We also tested the results using the whole new 10-author corpus. When we switched to the new background corpus, the chances that those obfuscated documents were attributed to the original authors all increased (Figure 3b). This was predictable as the documents were anonymized respecting to a different background corpus.

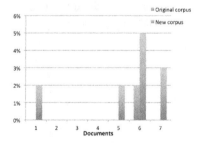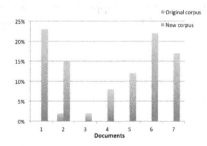

Fig. 3. Authorship attribution accuracy of the obfuscated documents in a new background corpus: (a) 3 authors were added to the original corpus, (b) new 10 authors were used.

6.2   An Example of an Obfuscated Document

A Short Paragraph Before Being Obfuscated: "This work does not make big improvement comparing to the previous works, the reasons are follows. In Obana's work, the adversarial cheating probability is defined as the overall failure probability for all the players that adversary control. We can not compare the cheating probability under the different definition of cheating success probability. In the proof of theorem 1, the authors show the cheating probability is... But I don't know how they get the probability less than... In Obana's proof of cheating probability, he got the probability from the forging probability of strong universal hash functions of strength t + 1. But in this proof, the g(X) is not proved to be the strong universal hash function, so they can not directly get the probability less than 1 q. There are some mistakes of writing: in page 8, kil+1,it+1 should be kit+1,it+1 . There are similar mistake in this page. To sum up, the authors do not define the cheating probability in the same way as Obana's work and do not explain the relation between two definitions. The improvement of sharing size is small comparing with Choudhury's work. The proof of theorem 1 is not well explained. I suggest the paper should consider the above issues."

The Obfuscated Paragraph: "This work does not make a big improvement comparing to the previous works, the reasons are follows. In the previous work, the adversarial cheating probability is defined as the overall failure probability for all the players that adversary control. We can not compare the cheating probability with the different definition of cheating success probability. In the proof of theorem 1, the authors show the cheating probability is..., and they get the probability less than... In proof the previous work about the cheating chance, he got the probability from the forging probability of strong universal hash functions of strength t + 1. But in this proof, the g(X) is not proved to be the strong universal hash function, so they can not directly get the probability less than 1 q. There are some mistakes of writing: in page 8, kil+1,it+1 should be kit+1,it+1 . There are similar mistake in this page. To sum up, the authors do not define the cheating probability in the same way as the previous work and do not explain the relation between two definitions. The improvement of sharing size is small comparing with previous work. The proof of theorem 1 is not well written. I suggest the paper should address the above issues."

Remark: In the above example, we highlighted some of the modifying applied by the author to the document. Author increased the sentence length by adding sentences together. Unique words were replaced or removed in the document. Author also adopted new words that they did not normally use in their document to change the complexity score of the document. The classification result of the obfuscated document with SVM classifier and Basic-9 feature set is presented in author 6 in Figure 2. The result shows that the probability that the obfuscated document is classified to the original author is nearly zero.

6.3   Performance Evaluation

Over 10 participants, we estimated that on average, obfuscation process requires 17 to 20 minutes depends on each user for a 500 word document. The time started from the time that the program output the suggested targets and the user knew about the task clearly, and also had a basic guide on how to change feature weights in their documents as noted above. This is reasonably efficient for document obfuscation. During our experiments, after modification process and if the document was already anonymized, we did not ask participants to change the *readability-related features* that had been affected because of the change in other features.

7   Concluding Remarks

We considered privacy of authors on anonymous websites by considering obfuscating their writing styles. We showed that the current research does not guarantee security and proposed secure obfuscation as an approach to hiding an author's identity among other authors in a corpus. We implemented our scheme using Basic-9 feature set and SVM classifier.

Our work provides a clear analysis of security for stylometry obfuscation schemes, and our algorithm can help users to obfuscate documents in practice. Refining our work to include other feature types will be an interesting direction for future research.

References

1. Narayanan, A., Paskov, H., Gong, N.Z., Bethencourt, J., Chul, E., Shin, R., Song, D.: On the feasibility of internet-scale author identification. In: Proceedings of the 33rd Conference on IEEE Sympsoium on Security and Privacy. IEEE (2012)
2. Stamatatos, E.: A survey of modern authorship attribution methods. J. Am. Soc. Inf. Sci. Technol. **60**, 538–556 (2009)
3. Narayanan, A., Shmatikov, V.: Robust de-anonymization of large sparse datasets. In: Proceedings of the 2008 IEEE Symposium on Security and Privacy, SP 2008, pp. 111–125. IEEE Computer Society, Washington, D.C. (2008)
4. Mishari, M.A., Tsudik, G.: Exploring linkablility of community reviewing. CoRR, vol. abs/1111.0338 (2011)
5. Kacmarcik, G., Gamon, M.: Obfuscating document stylometry to preserve author anonymity. In: Proceedings of the COLING/ACL on Main Conference Poster Sessions, COLING-ACL 2006, pp. 444–451. Association for Computational Linguistics, Stroudsburg (2006)
6. McDonald, A.W.E., Afroz, S., Caliskan, A., Stolerman, A., Greenstadt, R.: Use fewer instances of the letter "i": toward writing style anonymization. In: Fischer-Hübner, S., Wright, M. (eds.) PETS 2012. LNCS, vol. 7384, pp. 299–318. Springer, Heidelberg (2012)
7. Rao, J.R., Rohatgi, P.: Can pseudonymity really guarantee privacy? In: Proceedings of the 9th Conference on USENIX Security Symposium, SSYM 2000, vol 9, pp. 7–7. USENIX Association, Berkeley (2000)

8. Khosmood, F., Levinson, R.A.: Automatic natural language style classification and transformation. In: Proceedings of the 2008 BCS-IRSG Conference on Corpus Profiling, IRSG 2008, pp. 3–3. British Computer Society, Swinton (2008)
9. Khosmood, F., Levinson, R.: Automatic synonym and phrase replacement show promise for style transformation. In: Proceedings of the 2010 Ninth International Conference on Machine Learning and Applications, ICMLA 2010, pp. 958–961. IEEE Computer Society, Washington, D.C. (2010)
10. Brennan, M., Greenstadt, R., Brennan, M., Greenstadt, R.: Practical attacks against authorship recognition techniques emerging applications track
11. Hall, M., Frank, E., Holmes, G., Pfahringer, B., Reutemann, P., Witten, I.H.: The weka data mining software: An update. SIGKDD Explor. Newsl. **11**, 10–18 (2009)
12. Mitchell, T.M.: Machine learning. McGraw Hill, New York (1997)
13. Le Thi, H., Safavi-Naini, R.: An information theoretic framework for web inference detection. In: Proceedings of the 5th ACM Workshop on Security and Artificial Intelligence, AISec 2012, pp. 25–36. ACM, New York (2012)

DET-ABE: A Java API for Data Confidentiality and Fine-Grained Access Control from Attribute Based Encryption

Miguel Morales-Sandoval[✉] and Arturo Diaz-Perez

Laboratorio de Tecnologias de Informacion, CINVESTAV-LTI, Parque Cientifico Y
Tecnologico de Tamaulipas, 87130 Ciudad Victoria, TAMPS, Mexico
{mmorales,adiaz}@tamps.cinvestav.mx

Abstract. Many works in the literature have proposed information
security mechanisms relying on Paring Based Cryptography (PBC),
for example, Ciphertext Policy Attribute Based Encryption (CP-ABE).
However, a public set of software modules that allow integrating that
kind of encryption for data security of information systems in an easy
and transparent way is still missing. Available APIs like PBC (C-based)
or jPBC (Java-based) are focused on low level arithmetic operations and
several non trivial issues must still be addressed to integrate a functional
PBC/ABE scheme into end-user applications for implementing end-to-
end encryption. We present a novel and portable Java library (API) to
ensure confidentiality and access control of sensitive data accessed only
by authorized entities having as credentials a set of attributes. Novel
encryption and decryption processes are defined, using the digital envelope technique (DET) under a client-server computing model. The new
DET-ABE scheme supports standard security levels (AES encryption)
and provides the user with an easy interface for transparent use of next
generation cryptography, hiding the complexity associated to PBC (field
and group arithmetic, curve selection) and ABE (setup, key management, encryption/decryption details). Running times of main API's modules at server (ABE setup and key generation) and client (DET-ABE
encryption/decryption) side are presented and discussed. From these
results, it is concluded that the proposed API is easy to use and viable
for providing confidentiality and access control mechanisms over data in
end-user applications.

Keywords: Pairings · Cryptographic API · Attribute based encryption

1 Introduction

Since ancient times, human beings have had the necessity to protect information
in a way that only authorized entities have access to it. Nowadays, cryptographic
schemes are vital to provide information security services to IT applications, such
as confidentiality, integrity, authentication and non-repudiation [19].

© IFIP International Federation for Information Processing 2015
R.N. Akram and S. Jajodia (Eds.): WISTP 2015, LNCS 9311, pp. 104–119, 2015.
DOI: 10.1007/978-3-319-24018-3_7

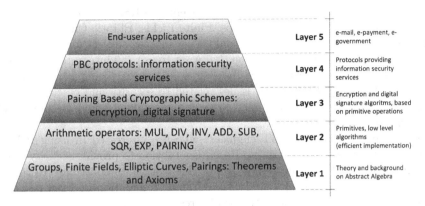

Fig. 1. Layered view of secure end-user applications based on Pairing Based Cryptography (PBC).

A relative novel field in cryptography is Pairing Based Cryptography (PBC) [5]. It is based on mathematical mappings defined on algebraic structures of abstract algebra. PBC provides elegant solutions to open problems of the past, such as Identity Based Encryption [6], where cryptographic operations are performed in function of the public identity of participants. Thus, under this approach digital certificates and their costly PKI (Public Key Infrastructure) are not required [7].

Research on PBC has increased recently. Currently, there are academic forums completely dedicated to it as the Pairings[1] and ECC[2] Conference series. A useful web resource for PBC is *The Pairing-Based Crypto Lounge* Barreto's website[3]. Attribute Based Encryption (ABE) [14,25] is a kind of public key encryption constructed over the foundation of PBC. ABE is a relatively new research topic, ideal to provide a fine-grained and non-interactive access control mechanism of encrypted data. Although several contributions on ABE exist at theoretical level, there are very few on the practical side [21].

Secure end-user applications as e-mail, e-payment, e-government, etc., can be seen as several layers, where the upper ones rely on the security and efficiency of the lower ones. Using PBC, the layered view of a secure application can be seen as shown in Figure 1.

In the past, some software modules have been published and made available for the community to serve as building blocks in the construction of applications at upper layers. Two of the most known are PBC [18] and jPBC [9]. Others for example, have been proposed to target specifically computing constrained devices [1,17,22,26]. However, these APIs are mainly focused for layer 2 of Figure 1 and provide some specific implementations for layer 3, leading to a gap for an easy incorporation of PBC and ABE in IT information systems

---

[1] http://www.ieccr.net/2013/pairing2013/

[2] http://www.eccworkshop.org

[3] http://www.larc.usp.br/~pbarreto/pblounge.html

at layer 5. Unlike other public key cryptosystems, as RSA [23], the mathematical background of PBC (Cyclic Groups, Finite Fields, Elliptic Curves, modular arithmetic, pairing computation,...) could be a complex subject for IT engineers without a cryptography specialization that want to use and integrate PBC-based protocols to enable security services in their applications. Going from layer 3 to layer 5 implies several important issues related to security and efficiency when using pairings in cryptography [13]. That decision taking could discourage IT engineers to use PBC.

This paper is mainly for IT engineers who are interested in using Pairing Based Cryptography and Attribute Based Encryption to provide security information services in IT systems. The aim of this work is to contribute to reduce the gap between the pairing based cryptographic foundation and the practical use of it. As main contribution, this work presents the design and implementation results of a set of classes written in Java that encapsulate the implementation details from layer 1 to layer 4 in Figure 1 (underlying algorithms, security parameters, type and size of the elliptic curve) and provide an easy interface to IT security implementers for using this type of next generation encryption at layer 5 in Figure 1.

The novel security modules proposed in this work are based on the Digital Envelope Technique (DET) [24]. In this work, an AES-key k used for bulk encryption [20] is protected by means of CP-ABE encryption [4], which is a specific type of ABE. Once encrypted, the encrypted data (with AES) together with the encrypted AES-key (with CP-ABE) can be securely distributed over insecure networks or stored in a honest but curious untrusted third party (i.e Cloud storage provider). Thus, DET allows to achieve confidentiality and CP-ABE enable fine-grained control access mechanisms. Only those authorized entities with a valid set of attributes could decrypt and recover the AES-key k to launch the AES decryption process over the encrypted data. Under this solution approach, typical applications as securing digital medical records or storing and sharing of digital documents in the Cloud could be easily implemented. As an application example, in this paper we provide a performance evaluation of the proposed security modules for encryption and decryption of digital documents (.doc and .pdf files). Due to the layered and highly modular design of the publicly available set of software modules, they can be further optimized to meet specific timing requirements.

The rest of this paper is organized as follows. Section 2 presents main aspects related to the use of pairings in cryptography as well as the general concept of Attribute Based Encryption. Section 3 describes the proposed approach for new DET-ABE encryption and decryption using pairings. Section 4 describes with details the design of the proposed set of Java classes that implement DET-ABE with PBC. Also, this section shows a practical use of the proposed API for confidentiality and access control of digital documents. Section 5 presents and discusses the running time of the main software modules for setup, encryption, decryption and key generation. Finally, section 6 gives the concluding remarks of this work and points out future work.

2   Foundations of PBC and ABE

A cyclic group $\mathbf{G}$ is a set of elements S together with a binary operation $\diamond$ where exists an element $g \in S$ such that for all $h \in S$, h can be obtained by applying the operation $\diamond$ over g $d-1$ times [11,15] (d is a positive integer number). This is denoted as $h = g^d$ using a multiplicative notation or $h = d \times g$ using an additive notation. The element g is named generator of $\mathbf{G}$ and written as $\mathbf{G} =< g >$. The most common cyclic group is $Z_r = \{0, 1, ..., r-1\}$, where r is a prime and $\diamond$ is the addition modulo r operation, being r the order of Z_r.

Let $\mathbf{G}_0 =< g_0 >$, $\mathbf{G}_1 =< g_1 >$, and $\mathbf{G}_T$ be cyclic groups of prime order r. A bilinear pairing or bilinear mapping is an efficient computable function $e : \mathbf{G}_0 \times \mathbf{G}_1 \rightarrow \mathbf{G}_T$, such that:

1. $\forall a, b \in Z_r, e(g_1^a, g_2^b) = e(g_1, g_2)^{ab}$
2. $e(g_0, g_1) \neq 1$

The tuple $(r, g_0, g_1, \mathbf{G}_0, \mathbf{G}_1, \mathbf{G}_T)$ defines an *asymmetric* bilinear pairing. If $\mathbf{G}_0 = \mathbf{G}_1 = \mathbf{G}$, and $\mathbf{G} =< g >$, the tuple $(r, g, \mathbf{G}, \mathbf{G}_T)$ defines a *symmetric* bilinear pairing [12].

In practice, many cryptographic protocols based on pairings have used a subset of points in an elliptic curve [13] as the cyclic group $\mathbf{G}$. An elliptic curve $E(F_q)$ is a set of pairs (x, y), with x, y elements of a finite field F_q satisfying an elliptic curve equation $E(x, y)$. The properties of such equation categorize the elliptic curve and determines its secure properties for practical use in cryptographic applications. So, in practice, pairings $\mathbf{G}_0$ and $\mathbf{G}_1$ are subgroups of the elliptic curve $E(F_q)$ and G_T is a subgroup of $F_{q^k}^*$ (an extension field of F_q). The number k is named the *embedded degree*. The security parameters to take into account when defining a paring over elliptic curves are: the size q of the finite field F_q, the embedding degree k, and the order l of $\mathbf{G}_0$, $\mathbf{G}_1$, and $\mathbf{G}_T$. These security parameters must be chosen carefully to ensure that the discrete logarithm problem is hard to compute in the three groups.

In our proposed set of security modules, the selection of this security parameters and the corresponding pairing is transparent to the programmers. The parameters selection is in function of the security level chosen by the programmer, which is one of those recommended by international standards, as the National Institute for Standards and Technology (NIST): 80-bit (low-term security, not recommended anymore), 128-bit (minimum security level), 192-bit (mid-term security), and 256-bit (long-term security) [2]. In our proposed DET-ABE scheme, programmers only need to specify the security level to use, the pairing security parameters will be selected internally.

2.1   Attribute Based Encryption

Firstly introduced by Sahai and Waters [25], Attribute-based Encryption (ABE) is a mean for complex access control on encrypted data. In this kind of cryptography, ciphertexts are not necessarily encrypted to one particular user as it occurs in traditional public key cryptography. Contrarily, ciphertexts and their corresponding private keys that decrypt them are associated with a set of *attributes* or a policy over attributes. This way, if there is a match ciphertext-private key, the ciphertext will be decrypted by that private key. In [4], Betancourt et al., present Ciphertext-Policy Attribute-Based Encryption (CP-ABE), a method conceptually closer to traditional access control techniques such as Role-Based Access Control (RBAC). In CP-ABE attributes are used to describe users credentials, and an entity encrypting data determines a policy for who can decrypt. When an entity encrypts data, it specifies an associated *access structure* over attributes. This case, any other entity will only be able to decrypt a ciphertext if that entity's attributes pass through the ciphertexts access structure. What Betancourt et al proposed as access structure is a tree structure where its nodes represent threshold gates (AND, OR) and the leaves describe attributes. An AND gates is constructed as n-of-n threshold gate and an OR gate is a 1-of-n threshold gate. Generalizing, threshold gates are of the form m-of-n. Complex access controls including numeric ranges are also addressed by converting them to small access trees.

Basic modules in CP-ABE are constituted by four fundamental algorithms [4]:

1. **ABE-Setup:** Select an elliptic curve and the associated security parameters to define a pairing. As it was stated previously, it is the tuple (r,g_0,g_1,$\mathbf{G}_0$,$\mathbf{G}_1$, $\mathbf{G}_T$). With the pairing and associated cyclic groups, this module produces a public key PK and a secret master key MK.
2. **ABE-Encrypt:** The encryption algorithm uses PK to encrypt a message M under an access structure A over the universe of attributes U. As a result, the ciphertext is CT, which will be only decrypted by an entity possessing a set of attributes S that satisfies the access structure A. It is assumed that CT implicitly contains A.
3. **ABE-KeyGen:** The key generation algorithm uses MK to produce a private key SK, related to a specific set of attributes S.
4. **ABE-Decrypt:** The decryption algorithm uses PK and SK associated to a set of attributes S to decrypt a ciphertext CT, which contains an access structure A. If S satisfies A, this module will decrypt CT and return the original message M.

The main components of CP-ABE are described in Table 1, considering both symmetric [4] and asymmetric pairings [16].

The construction of the CP-ABE modules involve many computations over groups and finite field (some of them are shown in Table 1). In the proposed set of security modules, all these computations are encapsulated and hidden from user. As part of CP-ABE encryption and decryption, main operations include tree traversal, boolean function (policy) evaluation, hashing and creation of private keys by computing several pairings, polynomials generation and evaluation, and computation of Lagrange's coefficients. All those operations as well as the internal representation and the storing and recovery processes of main components in CP-ABE (PK, SK, CT, MK) are not required to be understood by CP-ABE users. In our proposal, these modules are treated as blackboxes.

Table 1. Main components in Ciphertext Policy Attribute Based Encryption (CP-ABE)

Component	Definition on a symmetric pairing	Definition on an asymmetric pairing
Public key PK	$\{g, h = g^{\beta}, e(g,g)^{\alpha}\}$	$\{g_0, g_1, h = g_0^{\beta}, e(g_0,g_1)^{\alpha}\}$
Master key MK	$\{\beta, g^{\alpha}\}$	$\{\beta, g_1^{\alpha}\}$
Private key SK	$\{D, d_j, d_j'\}$, where $D = g^{(\alpha+r)/\beta}, \forall j \in S$: $d_j = g^r \times H(j)^{r_j}$ $d_j' = g^{r_j}$ $r, r_j \in Z_r$ (random) $H : \{0,1\}^* \to G$	$\{D, d_j, d_j'\}$, where $D = g_1^{(\alpha+r)/\beta}, \forall j \in S$: $d_j = g_1^{\tau} \times H(j)^{r_j}$ $d_j' = g_0^{r_j}$ $r, r_j \in Z_r$ (random) $H : \{0,1\}^* \to G_1$
CipherText CT	$\{A, C', C\}$, where $C' = M \times e(g,g)^{\alpha s}$, $C = h^s$ $\forall$ leaf node $y \in A$, having $j \in S$, compute: $[C_y, C_y']$, where $C_y = g^{q_y(0)}$ $C_y' = H(j)^{q_y(0)}$ $H : \{0,1\}^* \to G$	$\{A, C', C\}$, where $C' = M \times e(g_0,g_1)^{\alpha s}$ $C = h^s$ $\forall$ leaf node $y \in A$, having $j \in S$, compute: $[C_y, C_y']$, where $C_y = g_0^{q_y(0)}$ $C_y' = H(j)^{q_y(0)}$ $H : \{0,1\}^* \to G_1$
Access Structure A	Tree structure where each internal node represents a k-of-n gate, and leaves represent attributes.	

3 Security Services from the Digital Envelope Concept with PBC and ABE

The digital envelope technique (DET) [24] is a method for key exchange, not used by all key exchange protocols [10]. DET is used generally for secure transporting of a session key, that is, a secret key to be used by a symmetric encryption algorithm for protecting all traffic exchanged by a sender and receiver in a communication session. In DET, the secret key is usually encrypted with public-key cryptography (PKC).

One advantage of DET is that end-users may switch secret keys as frequently as they would like. Switching keys often is beneficial because it is more difficult for an adversary to find a key that is only used for a short period of time. Another advantage of DET is the increase in performance which is obtained by using symmetric ciphers to encrypt the large and variably sized amount of message data, reserving PKC for encryption of short-length keys. In general, symmetric ciphers are much faster than public key cryptosystems [19].

So, in this work, data (text, image, sound, video,...) is encrypted using as symmetric cipher the Advanced Encryption Standard (AES) [20] in a way that the AES session key is protected and securely embedded in the ciphertext by using CP-ABE encryption. In this work, we re-define each main module in the original CP-ABE scheme by Betancourt et al. in [4], leading to new building blocks for data encryption using the digital envelope technique with CP-ABE, we name it DET-ABE.

3.1   DET-ABE Setup

Setup involves the selections and settings for PBC and ABE. This includes the selection of the elliptic curve and the associated security parameters to define a pairing. The setup is performed in a *trusted third party*, that is responsible of generating and managing the public key *PK* and a secret master key *MK*.

In DET-ABE setup, the single parameter specified by the user is the security level to use in the encryption process. That security level is one recommended by the current standard for symmetric encryption, AES. According to NIST, security can be either minimum (128 bits), medium (192) or high (256). The elliptic curve and associated security parameters are internally selected to be consistent with the security level required. Table 2 shows the association of a given AES security level with a set of elliptic curves recommended for use in PBC and ABE. As it has been demonstrated and well documented in the literature [18], the best attacks over the groups with prime order r defining the pairing require $\sqrt{r}$ operations, so at least the order of $\mathbf{G}_1, \mathbf{G}_2, \mathbf{G}_T$ is twice the security level to achieve.

Table 2. Security settings

AES Security(bits)	Curve type	$\log_2 r$	Embedding degree
128 (minimum)	A (symmetric pairing)	256	2
192 (medium)	F (asymmetric pairing)	384	12
256 (high)	F (asymmetric pairing)	512	12

Pairing-based cryptographic settings given in Table 2 ensure that the discrete logarithm problem will be intractable in each group $\mathbf{G}_0, \mathbf{G}_1, \mathbf{G}_T$. In our construction, we have selected type A curves with embedding degree $k = 2$ for the security level of 128. This curve defines a symmetric pairings ($\mathbf{G}_0 = \mathbf{G}_1 = \mathbf{G}$). Also, the type F curves also known as Barreto-Naering (BN) curves [3] having embedding degree of 12 are used for the security levels 192 and 256 bits.

In this work, the generation of *PK* and *MK* are based on the definition given in [4] when using type A elliptic curves. For the case of type F curves defining an asymmetric pairing, *PK* and *MK* are derived as previously defined in [16].

As in CP-ABE, the DET-ABE setup module is executed in the trusted third party (server). As part of the DET-ABE setup process, a set of attributes U containing N distinct strings must be defined and administrated in the trusted entity.

3.2   DET-ABE Encryption

DET-ABE encryption is a client module of the trusted entity that encrypts a sequence of bytes (*data*) specified in a binary file. Main tasks in this module include:

1. Internally, an AES-key (k) is generated from a security level s given by the user.
2. With k, AES is used to encrypt *data* producing the ciphertext CT_{AES}.
3. Then, CP-ABE is used to encrypt k, given a policy P over a set of valid attributes S. Being P a boolean expression over S, it is evaluated to be logically well formed and the corresponding access structure A is generated. With A, k is encrypted using CP-ABE and the resulting ciphertext CT is stored together with CT_{AES} and the policy A in a binary file.
4. For CP-ABE encryption, the client connects to the trusted third party (server) to retrieve the public key PK created during the DET-ABE setup module and associated to the security level s.
5. The policy P is specified by the client, and the attributes are retrieved and validated from the server.
6. The result is the tuple $T_E = \{CT_{AES}, CT, A, s\}$.

The client executing the DET-ABE encryption module requires three elements: the *data* to encrypt, the security level s (see Table 2), and the policy P as a boolean expression of valid attributes S. The tuple T_E resulting from the DET-ABE encryption process can be either stored locally in the client side or uploaded to a public repository.

3.3   DET-ABE Decryption

The DET-ABE decryption module is used to decrypt previously encrypted data represented by the tuple $T_E = \{CT_{AES}, CT, A, s\}$. The following tasks are performed during the execution of DET-ABE decryption:

1. The decryption client process requires T_E and the list L of user's attributes.
2. The decryption client starts a connection with the trusted third party (server), asking a private key from L. The client sends L to the server and the security level $s \in T_E$.
3. The server (trust party) validates the user's attributes L. The pairing parameters (curve type) associated to s are selected in the server side and the corresponding *private key SK* is computed by the server using those settings. SK is send back to the client together with the public key PK associated to s.
4. With SK, the client executes CP-ABE to decrypt $CT \in T_E$, and recovers the session AES-key k, which is used to decrypt $CT_{AES} \in T_E$.

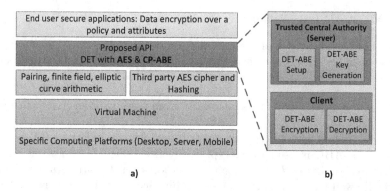

Fig. 2. a) Layered view of components for building secure applications using the digital envelope technique (DET) with AES and CP-ABE. b) Main components in the proposed API, executing the main tasks for DET-ABE data encryption/decryption under a client-server architecture.

4   Proposed API for DET-ABE

Our proposal is to integrate the concept of DET and CP-ABE in a set of software modules as a kind of middleware that allows programmers to build secure applications by mean of data encryption over a policy and a set of attributes. Figure 2 shows the layered view of modules needed to construct and execute secure applications based on the DET-ABE scheme proposed in this paper. The proposed set of security modules are written in Java and built on top of the jPBC library [9] that performs low level finite field, group and pairing computations. The use of Java allows a broader range of applications as the security scheme is able to be used over different platforms (server, desktop, mobile).

4.1   Attributes Management

Attributes management and how policies are constructed are dependent on the end-user application. Although attributes can be administrated in the trusted authority responsible for DET-ABE setup and key management, another trusted entity could be used specifically for attributes management. This entity (AA authority) should be responsible for registering and authenticating users in DET-ABE, either those that encrypt data (producers) or those that access encrypted data (consumers). When a user registers itself with the AA entity, a set of attributes are assigned to it, depending on the application specifications. For an authenticated producer U_p, it is the AA entity that authorizes the encryption operation by providing it the attributes required to construct the policy needed by DET-ABE encryption. In the case of an authenticated consumer U_c, the AA entity authorizes the decryption process by giving U_c its corresponding attributes, assigned according to the user application restrictions. Communication between the AA entity and the user must be secured for example using TLS/SSL.

4.2   The Server Side

The server modules run in a trusted central authority as specified in the CP-ABE scheme. Communication between the server and clients is secured by means of the SSL/TLS protocol. The server is able to manage the three security levels in Table 2, having a specific set of curve parameters for each of those. That selection is based on recommended elliptic curves in [9] and [18]. The server executes the DET-ABE setup module and generates CP-ABE private keys for clients executing DET-ABE decryption. The server keeps a pair $\{PK, MK\}$ for each security level supported. When clients connect to the server, they inform the security level to use and the server uses the correct curve parameters and keys. If keys are not already created for the demanded security level, the DET-ABE setup for that specific security level is launched.

4.3   The Client Side

A client properly authenticated in the AA entity can execute the DET-ABE encryption or decryption modules. In any case, a secure connection is established with the server at a specific port. During an encryption operation over a tuple T_E, the client asks the server for the public key PK associated to the security level $s \in T_E$. Also, the client constructs and validates the policy P. As PK is public, it is cached in the client side for future encryption operations using the same security level s. All the encryption operations (AES and CP-ABE) are executed in the client side. During a decryption operation, the client sends to the server the security level and its set of attributes, previously retrieved in a secure manner from the AA entity. The server constructs the private key from the client's attributes and returns that key to the client. All the main decryption operations are performed in the client side. Exceptions could be thrown during a DET-ABE encryption or decryption process due to connectivity problems. On success, during an encryption operation a file with extension .detabe is created containing the serialized version of tuple T_E. In a decryption operation, the .detabe extension is removed from the input file, which contains the decrypted data of $CT_{\mathrm{AES}} \in T_E$.

4.4   Keys Management

The PK and MK keys are generated in the server side according to the arithmetic operations shown in Table 1. All the resulting values that characterize these keys are stored in server (trusted authority) only. The random numbers α and β used for their creation are local variables that are destroyed after the keys are created. While PK can be read by the server and sent to clients performing an encryption operation, MK is used exclusively in the server side. The private keys for clients used in CP-ABE are created only in the server side and securely sent to clients.

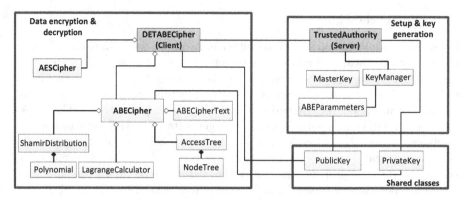

Fig. 3. Proposed set of Java classes for DET-ABE.

4.5   The Proposed Java Library for DET-ABE

The new set of classes comprising the new DET-ABE library are shown in
Figure 3. The set of software modules in the client comprises classes for AES,
CP-ABE encryption/decryption, and DET-ABE encryption/decryption. The set
of software modules in the server side are classes for DET-ABE setup, CP-
ABE setup, CP-ABE private key generation and DET-ABE key management.
As explained in section 5, the AES class in Figure 3 is actually a wrapper for
the AES implementation provided by Java SE. This wrapper adds the required
methods to interface the symmetric cipher with CP-ABE for implementing the
DET technique.

4.6   Using the Proposed API

In this section we show how the proposed API for DET-ABE can be used. We
target the application of encryption and decryption of digital documents (.doc,
.pdf). After encrypting these files they can be either locally saved in the client
or stored at a cloud storage provider. The DET-ABE encryption of a digital
document is shown in Listing 1.1.

```
import com.detabe.client.encryption.*;

public static void main(String args[]) {
    String policy = "(directive AND level = 7) OR (
    accountant AND level >= 3)";

    DETABECipher cipher = new DETABECipher();
    cipher.encrypt("contract.pdf", 128, policy);
}
```

Listing 1.1. Encrypting a digital document using DET-ABE

The encrypt() method of objetc cipher at line five in listing 1.1 implements all the logic specified in section 3.2. What is only specified by the programmer is the file to be encrypted (contract.pdf), the security level (128 bits) and the policy ((directive AND level = 7) OR (accountant AND level >= 3), with four attributes). An exception can be thrown at line five in the following cases: *i*) the given security level is not supported, *ii*) the policy is a bad boolean equation, and *iii*) the attributes are not previously registered in the server. The result of encrypt() method is the encrypted file contract.pdf.detabe.

The DET-ABE decryption of the file privateLetter.doc.detabe is shown in Listing 1.2.

```
import com.detabe.client.cipher.*;

public static void main(String args[]){
        List<String> attributes = new LinkedList<String>();
        attributes.add("directive");
        attributes.add("level = 5");
        attributes.add("accountant");
        attributes.add("level = 4");

        DETABECipher cipher = new DETABECipher();
        cipher.decrypt("privateLetter.doc.detabe", attributes)
    ;
}
```

Listing 1.2. Decrypting a ciphertext with DET-ABE

For decryption, the client only provides to the server its set of attributes. The server validates them and generates the corresponding private key for the client. The input encrypted file privateLetter.doc.detabe contains the ABE ciphertext, the the access structure, and pairing parameters. With all these elements together with the received private key from the server, the client recovers the original file privateLetter.doc performing all the steps described for DET-ABE decryption in section 3.3.

Before running the client programs the server must be launched, for example, by executing java com.detabe.server.ABETrustedAuthority. Also, in the client side the configuration file configuration.cfgt must have the correct IP or host name where the server (trusted authority) is running.

5   Implementation and Performance Results

In this section we present the running times of the main modules in the proposed API. The experimentation was carried out on a desktop machine 32-bit Intel Core2 Quad 2.40GHz, 4GB RAM with Windows7 as operative system. The main objective to present the execution time of DET-ABE scheme is to show the feasibility of using the proposed API in IT end-user applications. Further optimizations could be done over specific modules in order to get the API running faster. The implementation of classes described in Figure 3 were built on top of jPBC, a Java API [9] that provides specialized modules for pairing computations and is defined over PBC[18].

All classes shown in Figure 3 except AES were implemented and validated. For AES, we use the implementation provided by Java in the packages `javax.crypto` and `javax.crypto.spec`. To support security levels above 128-bit, we use the Java Cryptography Extension (JCE) Unlimited Strength Jurisdiction Policy Files. All modules were integrated and the execution paths of DET-ABE main modules were validated performing unit and functional tests, ensuring that the result of each cryptographic function was correct.

In all tests, the client and server run on the same machine. Table 3 shows timing result of the DET-ABE setup module, that comprises the generation of pairing parameters, the master and the public keys. That module is executed once, and the previously generated keys are chosen and used by each client connection for DET-ABE encryption or decryption.

Table 3. Running times for DET-ABE setup.

Module	Timing (secs)		
	128-bit	192-bit	256-bit
Curve param. generation	30.78	8.47	24.03
PK and MK generation	2.26	2.32	4.45

Figure 4 shows the running time for DET-ABE encryption, DET-ABE decryption and CP-ABE key generation. For all experimentations, we used a PDF document of size 182Kbytes and considered the three standard security levels of 128-bit (symmetric pairing with type A elliptic curve), 192-bit, and 256-bit (asymmetric pairing with type F elliptic curve). The size of data being encrypted does not impact significantly the overall timing of DET-ABE as the number of attributes and security level do. Data size only affects the running time of the block cipher AES, which is proved to have a complexity $O(1)$ [8].

Figure 4 a) shows the running time for DET-ABE encryption. Note that more considerable time is spent in case of using a symmetric pairing (128-bit security). While a linear time with respect to the number of attributes is demanded for 128-bit encryption, that is not true for 192-bit and 256-bit. The same behaviour is exhibited in Figure 4 b), that shows the time required for CP-ABE private key generation. Figure 4 c) shows the decryption time. For 128-bit and 256-bit security levels the time is very similar whereas a security level of 192-bit achieves the better timing. Finally, Figure 4 d) contrasts the timing for each DET-ABE operation considering the three security levels. For this last experiment, a PDF file of 182Kbytes size and 6 attributes were used.

As it is observed, 128-bit encryption and private key generation using type A elliptic curves are by far the most time consuming operations. In case of 192-bit

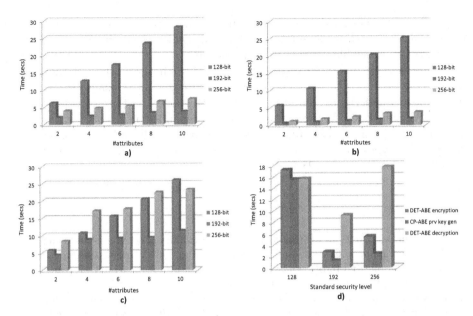

Fig. 4. Running times of DET-ABE main modules considering different number of attributes, a 182Kbyte digital document, and the three standard security levels. a) DET-ABE encryption. b) CP-ABE private key generation to open the digital envelope. c) DET-ABE decryption. d) Contrasting the three main DET-ABE modules using 6 attributes and the three standard security levels.

and 256-bit security levels, significant reduced time is obtained except for DET-ABE decryption, which remains with high timing costs. As it was previously stated, the proposed modules can be optimized to reduce the timing, for example, the optimized versions of jPBC can be used to speed up the low level operation (abstract algebra arithmetic).

6   Conclusion

We presented a set of Java classes aiming to reduce the existing gap for using Pairing Based Cryptography (PBC) and Attribute Based Encryption (ABE) in end-user IT applications. We presented the DET-ABE scheme for data encryption over a set of attributes, thus providing confidentiality and fine grained access control under an end-to-end encryption approach. DET-ABE is the result of using the Digital Envelope Technique (DET) together with CP-ABE and AES. The proposed DET-ABE software modules are built on top of libraries for low level computations in finite fields and groups. The complexity associated to the operations and settings for a secure implementation of cryptographic algorithms (adequate pairing parameters as the elliptic curve type and properties) are encapsulated in the proposed API, facilitating the use of those modules in end-user applications. The efficacy of proposed software modules was verified in a simple application for securing digital documents. Further optimizations specially at low level modules can be done to outperform the achieved running times, which have shown to be viable in practical applications.

Future work is planned to explore implementation alternatives of the proposed API, for example with multi-threading programming using GPUs and multi-cores as underlying computing platforms to speed up the execution time of DET-ABE modules. As the running time also depended on the pairing parameters and elliptic curves used, further research will be conducted to explore other elliptic curve types to achieve faster computations, for example, to use alternative elliptic curves for the 128-bit security level.

References

1. Ambrosin, M., Conti, M., Dargahi, T.: On the feasibility of attribute-based encryption on smartphone devices. In: Proceedings of the 2015 Workshop on IoT Challenges in Mobile and Industrial Systems, IoT-Sys 2015, pp. 49–54. ACM, New York (2015). http://doi.acm.org/10.1145/2753476.2753482
2. Barker, E., Barker, W., Burr, W., Polk, W., Smid, M.: Recommendation for key management part 1: general(Revision 3). In: NIST Special Publication 800-57, pp. 1–147 (2012)
3. Barreto, P.S.L.M., Naehrig, M.: Pairing-friendly elliptic curves of prime order. In: Preneel, B., Tavares, S. (eds.) SAC 2005. LNCS, vol. 3897, pp. 319–331. Springer, Heidelberg (2006). http://dx.doi.org/10.1007/11693383_22
4. Bethencourt, J., Sahai, A., Waters, B.: Ciphertext-policy attribute-based encryption. In: Proceedings of the 2007 IEEE Symposium on Security and Privacy, SP 2007, pp. 321–334. IEEE Computer Society, Washington, DC (2007). http://dx.doi.org/10.1109/SP.2007.11
5. Boneh, D.: Pairing-based cryptography: past, present, and future. In: Wang, X., Sako, K. (eds.) ASIACRYPT 2012. LNCS, vol. 7658, p. 1. Springer, Heidelberg (2012)
6. Boneh, D., Franklin, M.: Identity-based encryption from the weil pairing. In: Kilian, J. (ed.) CRYPTO 2001. LNCS, vol. 2139, pp. 213–229. Springer, Heidelberg (2001)
7. Braun, J., Volk, F., Buchmann, J., Mühlhäuser, M.: Trust views for the web PKI. In: Katsikas, S., Agudo, I. (eds.) EuroMPI 2013. LNCS, vol. 8341, pp. 134–151. Springer, Heidelberg (2014)
8. Daemen, J., Rijmen, V.: The Design of Rijndael. Springer-Verlag New York Inc., Secaucus (2002)
9. De Caro, A., Iovino, V.: jPBC: Java pairing based cryptography. In: 2011 IEEE Symposium on Computers and Communications (ISCC), pp. 850–855, June 2011
10. Diffie, W., Van Oorschot, P.C., Wiener, M.J.: Authentication and authenticated key exchanges. Des. Codes Cryptography 2(2), 107–125 (1992). http://dx.doi.org/10.1007/BF00124891
11. Escofier, J.P.: Galois Theory, Graduate Texts in Mathematics, vol. 204. Springer, New York (2001)
12. Galbraith, S.D., McKee, J.F.: Pairings on elliptic curves over finite commutative rings. In: Smart, N.P. (ed.) Cryptography and Coding 2005. LNCS, vol. 3796, pp. 392–409. Springer, Heidelberg (2005)

13. Galbraith, S.D., Paterson, K.G., Smart, N.P.: Pairings for cryptographers. Discrete Appl. Math. **156**(16), 3113–3121 (2008). http://dx.doi.org/10.1016/j.dam.2007.12.010
14. Goyal, V., Pandey, O., Sahai, A., Waters, B.: Attribute-based encryption for fine-grained access control of encrypted data. In: Proceedings of the 13th ACM Conference on Computer and Communications Security, CCS 2006, pp. 89–98. ACM, New York (2006). http://doi.acm.org/10.1145/1180405.1180418
15. Herstain, I.N.: Abstract Algebra, 3rd edn. Wiley (1996)
16. Jahid, S., Mittal, P., Borisov, N.: Easier: Encryption-based access control in social networks with efficient revocation. In: Proceedings of the 6th ACM Symposium on Information, Computer and Communications Security, ASIACCS 2011, pp. 411–415. ACM, New York (2011). http://doi.acm.org/10.1145/1966913.1966970
17. Liu, W., Liu, J., Wu, Q., Quin, B.: Android PBC: A pairing based cryptography toolkit for android platform. In: Communications Security Conference, CSC 2014, pp. 1–6. IEEE, May 2014
18. Lynn, B.: On the implementation of pairing-based cryptosystems. Ph.D. thesis, Stanford University, Department of Computere Science (2007)
19. Menezes, A.J., Vanstone, S.A., Oorschot, P.C.V.: Handbook of Applied Cryptography, 1st edn. CRC Press Inc., Boca Raton (1996)
20. Miller, F.P., Vandome, A.F., McBrewster, J.: Advanced Encryption Standard. Alpha Press (2009)
21. Pang, L., Yang, J., Jiang, Z.: A Survey of Research Progress and Development Tendency of Attribute-Based Encryption. The Scientific World Journal **2014**, 1–13 (2014)
22. Picazo-Sanchez, P., Tapiador, J.E., Peris-Lopez, P., Suarez-Tangil, G.: Secure publish-subscribe protocols for heterogeneous medical wireless body area networks. Sensors **14**(12), 22619 (2014). http://www.mdpi.com/1424-8220/14/12/22619
23. Rivest, R.L., Shamir, A., Adleman, L.: A method for obtaining digital signatures and public-key cryptosystems. Commun. ACM **21**(2), 120–126 (1978). http://doi.acm.org/10.1145/359340.359342
24. Rosenberg, B.: Handbook of Financial Cryptography and Security, 1st edn. Chapman & Hall/CRC (2010)
25. Sahai, A., Waters, B.: Fuzzy identity-based encryption. In: Cramer, R. (ed.) EUROCRYPT 2005. LNCS, vol. 3494, pp. 457–473. Springer, Heidelberg (2005). http://dx.doi.org/10.1007/11426639_27
26. Xiong, X., Wong, D.S., Deng, X.: TinyPairing: A fast and lightweight pairing-based cryptographic library for wireless sensor networks. In: 2010 IEEE Wireless Communication and Networking Conference, pp. 1–6. IEEE, April 2010

WSACd - A Usable Access Control Framework for Smart Home Devices

Konstantinos Fysarakis[1]([⊠]), Charalampos Konstantourakis[2], Konstantinos Rantos[3], Charalampos Manifavas[4], and Ioannis Papaefstathiou[1]

[1] Department of Electronic and Computer Engineering,
Technical University of Crete, Chania, Greece
kfysarakis@isc.tuc.gr, ypg@mhl.tuc.gr
[2] Department of Computer Science, University of Crete, Heraklion, Greece
harconst@csd.uoc.gr
[3] Department of Computer and Informatics Engineering,
Eastern Macedonia and Thrace Institute of Technology, Kavala, Greece
krantos@teiemt.gr
[4] Department of Informatics Engineering, Technological Educational Institute of Crete,
Heraklion, Greece
harryman@ie.teicrete.gr

Abstract. Computing devices already permeate working and living environments; a trend which is expected to intensify in the coming years. However, the direct interaction smart devices often have with the physical world, along with the processing, storage and communication of private sensitive data pertaining to users' lives, bring security concerns into the limelight. This paper presents Web Service Access Control for devices (WSACd), a framework that combines access control provided by the eXtensible Access Control Markup Language (XACML) with the benefits of Service Oriented Architectures through the use of the Devices Profile for Web Services (DPWS). Based on standardized technologies, it enables fine-grained policy-based management of the heterogeneous embedded devices that may be found in a smart residential setting. The proposed framework is implemented in full and its performance is evaluated on a test-bed featuring devices expected to be found in a typical residential environment.

Keywords: Policy-based access control · XACML · Service architectures · DPWS · Smart home · Ubiquitous computing

1 Introduction

In recent years, massive advancements in computing and communication technologies have led to significant changes in terms of how people perform the various tasks comprising their everyday lives; a development enabled by the ubiquitous presence of computing devices in all aspects of modern life. These major changes could not leave the residential environment unaffected, with smart homes gradually becoming a reality, i.e. homes featuring sophisticated lighting (e.g. smart light bulbs), ambient environment controls (e.g. heating, ventilation and air conditioning via smart thermostats),

© IFIP International Federation for Information Processing 2015
R.N. Akram and S. Jajodia (Eds.): WISTP 2015, LNCS 9311, pp. 120–133, 2015.
DOI: 10.1007/978-3-319-24018-3_8

appliances (smart -fridge, -oven, -washing machine, -coffee makers etc.), communication systems (including smart phones), entertainment (e.g. smart TVs), and home security (smart cameras, door and window controls etc.) devices. Moreover, the residential environment integrates with other ubiquitous computing applications, like smart metering and e-health, found in the smart home ecosystem. Nevertheless, as said devices typically handle personal sensitive data and often feature direct interaction with the physical world, a key factor in the wider adoption and success of these new technologies will be the effectiveness with which the various security [1][2] and privacy [3] concerns are tackled. A necessary instrument in successfully addressing these issues is the presence of robust access control mechanisms.

This paper presents Web Service Access Control for devices (WSACd), a scheme which aims to address the above requirements by defining a policy-based Access Control (AC) mechanism based on the eXtensible Access Control Markup Language (XACML [4], an OASIS standard), thus providing the means to control access to the resources of smart home nodes based on policy constraints centrally managed by the system owner. Typical XACML deployments require the setup of complex infrastructures to enable entities' interaction and policy retrieval (e.g. via LDAP); such an approach may be acceptable for corporate environments but is not suitable in the context of consumer applications and the average home user. To this end, the proposed framework leverages the benefits of Service Oriented Architectures (SOAs) by implementing key entities using the Devices Profile for Web Services (DPWS [5]), also an OASIS standard, which allows the deployment of devices aligned with the Web Services technologies, thus facilitating interoperability among services provided by resource-constrained devices. The adoption of DPWS facilitates seamless Machine-to-Machine (M2M) discovery and interactions, allowing the deployment of the framework's entities to any platform, anywhere on the home network, with minimal involvement on behalf of the user. By combining the above technologies, new devices can easily join existing networks and offer services protected by a predefined or dynamic policy set. Based on the policy rules set by the system owner, the proposed architecture provides fine-grained AC over the plethora of devices and services that may be found in smart home environments. Thus, WSACd assists in the use of the various smart devices aiming to enhance consumers' lives, while addressing their security concerns.

This work is organized as follows: Section 2 provides the rationale behind this work, and relevant research efforts identified in the literature. Section 3 presents the proposed framework and its key entities, along with our approach to implementing the framework. Section 4 includes the performance evaluation of the developed solution on typical devices that may be found in a smart home environment. Finally, Section 5 concludes the article, containing pointers to areas that future work could explore to further enhance the presented scheme.

2   Rationale and Related Work

In a typical ubiquitous-computing-enhanced residential setting, various smart devices are expected to be present on appliances (e.g. smart fridge) and automation-enabled structures (e.g. smart doors), also including environmental sensors and actuators. Moreover, these are typically complemented by purpose-built devices intended to organize, manage and enhance the functionality of the rest of the smart infrastructure, like energy monitors and control nodes (e.g. a computing system with touch-based input to allow seamless monitoring and interaction with the devices).

This heterogeneous assortment of devices will feature a variety of services, each with its own intrinsic characteristics (some being critical in terms of the residents' safety, others dealing with private sensitive data etc.), thus requiring a different protection profile. For example, all residents should be able to control the smart doors and windows of a house, but, perhaps, children should not be able to tamper with a subset of those (e.g. front door) at certain timeframes (e.g. during the night). In another scenario, visitors may have the rights to monitor the environmental sensors of the residence, but not to set the climate control at their will. Moreover, the residence owners may decide they feel alright with visitors checking the contents of their smart fridge, but they, expectedly, should not be able to add goods to the shopping lists. Assuming the presence of e-health devices in the smart home ecosystem, it is anticipated that the patient, her spouse and medical staff should be able to monitor the various readings and control the actuators that deliver the prescribed medicine, but only the latter group should have access to the service that controls the drug dosage. In cases where the residence is equipped with smart-metering devices, authorized power company staff should be the only ones able to adjust and/or reset the meters (for billing purposes), but, nevertheless, the owners should be able to access the consumption readings. A more thorough analysis on the security risks associated with smart homes can be found in [6]; a report which identified threats, with high exposure, to all of the smart home assets, including the human inhabitants.

Furthermore, a survey [7] on smart home users revealed that inflexibility (often forcing users to adopt solutions offered by a single manufacturer) and difficulties in achieving security constitute significant barriers to the broader adoption of pertinent technologies and devices.

From the above, and considering that, typically, the only pervasive protection mechanism present in home environments is the access to the wireless network, it is evident that strong and interoperable access control mechanisms are required to safeguard a variety of aspects pertaining to the operation of a smart home environment. Additionally, this should be achieved in a flexible, platform-agnostic manner, acting as an enabler instead of introducing new (or further exacerbate existing) obstacles to the adoption of "smart" devices and services.

To this end, the presented framework is based on standardized mechanisms, which also allows leveraging work already carried out both in terms of Web Services as well as XACML policy definitions. DPWS can enable user-to-machine and M2M interactions in a unified manner, moving on from the current state of the field, where consumer electronics manufacturers offer a variety of proprietary protocols which are not interoperable and essentially lock-in consumers, forcing them to use a specific vendor/ecosystem. With regard to XACML, the scheme can trivially be expanded to cater for additional specific concerns, such as privacy issues and/or the handling of sensitive data (e.g. healthcare, as covered by the relevant XACML profile [8]).

2.1   Service-Oriented Architectures

SOAs evolved from the need to have interoperable, cross-platform, cross-domain and network-agnostic access to devices and their services. This approach has already been successful in business environments, as web services allow stakeholders to focus on the services themselves, rather than the underlying hardware and network technologies.

The Devices Profile for Web Services (DPWS) specification defines a minimal set of implementation constraints to enable secure Web Service messaging, including discovery, description, interactions and event-driven changes on resource-constrained devices. DPWS was introduced in 2004 and is now an OASIS open standard (at version 1.1 since July 2009). It employs similar messaging mechanisms as the Web Services Architecture (WSA), with restrictions on complexity and message size, allowing the provision of totally platform- and language-neutral services, similar to those offered by traditional web services, allowing system owners to leverage the SOA benefits across heterogeneous systems that may be found in the various smart environments (residential, enterprise etc.).

In this context, the work of Leong et al [9] presents a rule-based framework for heterogeneous smart-home systems management. Their work focuses on the use of SOAP for interoperability and uses an Event-Condition-Action (ECA) mechanism for machine-2-machine interactions and orchestration of the devices. The SOAP-based interoperability framework has been further extended by Perumal et al [10] with the addition of a service stub to facilitate the addition of new devices and a database module to handle the queries of the SOAP messages (including home service functions, operation logic and access to other local or remote databases).

SOA-DOS [11] is a SOA-based distributed operating system proposed in the relevant literature, aiming to manage all embedded devices in a home network and facilitating interoperability between the various systems. The work manages to provide a SOA-based solution that is also applicable to very resource-constrained platforms (like sensor nodes), but deviates from standardized mechanisms, e.g. resorting to the use of the JSON [12] format instead of XML for data exchange.

The use of SOA concepts to tackle the dynamic and heterogeneous nature of home-control applications has also been proposed by Bourcier et al [13]. The authors introduce an implementation of their approach based on open source, standardized platforms, providing bridges to seamlessly integrate disparate devices (including DPWS devices) and their services into their home control infrastructure.

The DPWS stack also forms the basis of iVision [14], a purpose-built hardware platform used to add context-awareness to a service architecture for controlling home appliances, and its accompanying architecture. In the above work, the context information extracted by the iVision camera and all the necessary smart home appliance communications are exposed as web services using DPWS.

The use and benefits of DPWS have also been studied extensively in the context of various other applications areas, including automotive and railway systems [15], industrial automation [16], smart grid [17], eHealth [18] and wireless sensor networks [19]. All of the above are positive indicators for the future of the technology chosen as the underlying implementation and communication mechanism for the presented framework, and its potential for ubiquitous adoption.

2.2   Access Control

Among the studied access control schemes proposed for systems with different requirements and properties, a cross-platform solution that meets the requirements of all types of embedded systems and provides interoperability (which is crucial for next-generation pervasive computing devices), is based on eXtensible Access control Markup Language (XACML) policies. XACML defines the structure and content of access requests and responses exchanged among access control entities. In this work, the typical policy based access control architecture, combined with XACML, is mapped to a SOA network of nodes to provide protected access to their distributed resources.

A survey of the literature reveals a wealth of related work, including various diverse approaches and attesting to the applicability of XACML in the context of smart homes.

Kim et al [20] have proposed the use of an OSGi (Open Services Gateway initiative) -based framework to integrate heterogeneous smart-home devices and services, including an access control model, combining XACML mechanisms with OSGi services to appropriately create the queries that will be forwarded to the entity responsible for access control decisions (i.e. the Policy Decision Point, PDP). While the proposed approach theoretically supports a variety of protocols (including DPWS devices), the presented analysis and proof of concept implementation are mainly based on Universal Plug and Play (UPnP), a protocol lacking in many respects (e.g. security & scalability). Furthermore, the performance of the proposed mechanisms – an important aspect considering the resource-constraints of many smart devices – is not evaluated.

Busnel et al [21] present a case study for remote healthcare assistance in smart homes. Most of the smart home security & dependability requirements are discussed extensively, identifying the use of SOAs along with XACML as the most applicable technologies to fulfill these requirements. An XACML-based authorization solution is applied using the security pattern approach to satisfy security requirements typically existing in such environments. This work presents the outline of such a framework, but not an actual implementation of the SOA and XACML mechanisms, nor a performance evaluation. The resource-constrained nature of the target devices and the use of appropriate security mechanisms do not appear to have been considered during the design phase.

Researchers have also studied the use of access control mechanisms to safeguard the users' privacy, a key concern in the context of smart environments. Faravelon et al [22] outline such an architecture in the context of SOA-enabled pervasive environments, using a medical scenario as a test case. The interoperability with DPWS is considered, among other SOA technologies, but a non-standardized approach is adopted for the access control functionality.

Privacy issues have also been considered by Jung et al [23], who have presented a generic concept of access control for home automation gateways, aiming to safeguard the privacy and security of users and their data. The scheme is based on a customized SOAP message structure that integrates XACML attributes within SAML-based access token. However, the initial, theoretical evaluation of the proposed scheme indicates that this approach is quite costly (especially in terms of packet size), which questions its applicability in the context of embedded smart home devices. The authors acknowledge this drawback and indicate it will be investigated, as future work, on actual platforms.

Müller et al [24] have also proposed the combined use of DPWS with XACML, but focusing on end-user content (e.g. the distribution of multimedia files) and the use of proxies to establish trust relationships across smart home domains (an approach which could be exploited in WSACd as well). Moreover, the authors did not exploit DPWS in the implementation and deployment of the XACML architecture.

3   Proposed Model and Implementation Approach

This section aims to detail the basic components of the proposed solution, as well as the toolkits chosen to develop the proof of concept implementation.

3.1   XACML Implementation

In the proposed framework, the following key entities are present and can be deployed on different smart home nodes, depending on their role and resources:

— *Policy Enforcement Point (PEP):* Makes decision requests and enforces authorization decisions. This is expected to be present in every smart device (appliances, sensors, e-health devices, energy monitoring or smart metering devices etc.) which provides its resources to the end users, and which need to be protected by the active policy set.
— *Policy Decision Point (PDP):* Evaluates requests against applicable policies and renders an authorization decision. It is expected to be deployed on more feature-rich nodes, typically a personal computer or an embedded system that acts as a controlling node for the whole smart home infrastructure
— *Policy Administration Point (PAP) & Policy Information Point (PIP):* The former creates and manages policies or policy sets, while the latter acts as a source of attribute values. These two entities will typically be deployed on the same feature-rich node, facilitating direct interaction with end-users (e.g. home owners). A desktop computer or a laptop are good candidates for this role.

As is evident from the above, and considering that nodes embedded in a smart home may not have the computing resources to accommodate expensive mechanisms, the core decision process is undertaken by more powerful nodes expected to operate within the node's trusted environment. Such an approach allows requests to be directly addressed to the node in question, while maintaining the capability to centrally manage and control access to these nodes. An overview of the architecture can be seen in Fig. 1.

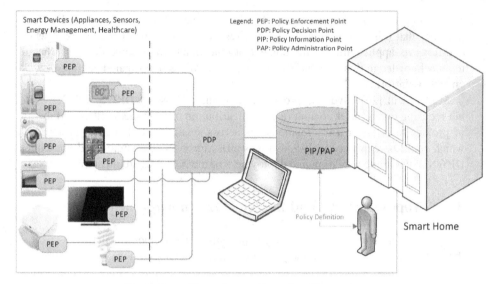

Fig. 1. Smart Home Access Control architecture

There are various open-source and commercial implementations of XACML that could be used as a basis for the AC entities needed to implement the proposed framework. We chose to use Sun's Java-based XACML implementation for all the infrastructure components, as it remains popular among developers and is actually the basis of various current open-source and commercial offerings.

3.2 DPWS Implementation of the XACML Entities

All of the framework's entities are exposed to the network using DPWS, thus leveraging the benefits provided by SOAs. There are a variety of APIs available for DPWS development, including the tools provided by the Web Services for Devices (WS4D) initiative and the SOAs for Devices (SOA4D) toolkits, based on various programming languages (C, C++, Java etc.) and each featuring its own intrinsic characteristics. Nevertheless, when focusing on key features such as code portability, deployment on heterogeneous platforms, support for IPv6 (necessary for ubiquitous computing applications) and, most importantly, active development and support of the tools, WS4D-JMEDS currently stands out as the most attractive choice. It is the most advanced and active work of the WS4D initiative, supporting most of the existing DPWS features and providing portability to a wide range of platforms; it is also our toolkit of choice to develop the DPWS entities presented in this work.

The XACML features are exposed as follows:

— *PEP to PDP implementation:* The Policy Enforcement Point must reside on every device with resources that must be protected from unauthorized access. Other than the functional elements of the devices which the framework intends to protect (e.g. access to its sensors), two extra operations must be present on each DPWS device.

These operations, in essence, constitute the PEP functionality and its communication with the PDP. The latter acts as a DPWS client which accesses these PBAC-specific operations. More specifically, the first operation is the "SAREvent" (Service Access Request Event), referring to an operation following the WS-Eventing specification to which devices can subscribe. When fired, the operation outputs "SAROut", a message which includes all the information the PDP needs to have in order to evaluate a request (i.e. Subject, Action and Resource). The second operation is "PDPResponse" (Policy Decision Point Response), which is invoked by the PDP to relay an answer to a pending access request.

— *PDP to PIP/PAP implementation:* In terms of the discovery and information exchange that must take place between infrastructure entities (PDP, PIP, PAP), an extra operation must reside with the entity that stores the active policy set (namely the PIP/PAP). This extra operation is named "PIPOperation" (Policy Information Point Operation). It features an input for the request issued by the PDP (requesting all applicable policy rules), and an output containing all the pertinent information (i.e. policies and rules) that the PIP has identified.

The above DPWS operations and the sequence of events that take place when an access request is received for a protected resource are depicted in Fig. 2.

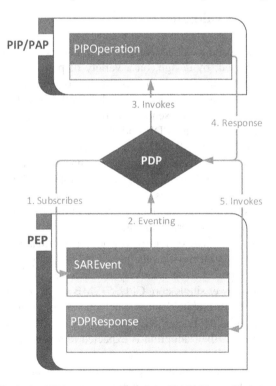

Fig. 2. DPWS implementation of the XACML mechanisms.

3.3   Security Considerations

The effectiveness of any access control mechanism can easily be compromised unless appropriate security mechanisms are deployed to protect policy messaging. A malicious entity would otherwise be able to eavesdrop, replay or tamper with the access control messaging, overriding the offered protection to provide access to unauthorized entities or denying access to authorized ones. When feasible, deployments over trusted and/or secure networks (e.g. over a Virtual Private Network, VPN) can address most of these concerns, but an alternative mechanism has to be considered for deployments where these provisions are not realistic.

The Web Services Security Specification (WS-Security or WSS, [25]) is part of the WS-* family of specifications published by OASIS. The protocol specifies integrating security features in the header of SOAP messages. Working in the application layer, it ensures the end-to-end integrity and confidentiality of SOAP messages.

Therefore, a variation of the proof-of-concept implementation was developed as well, adopting the security mechanisms specified in WSS. These mechanisms authenticate entities and safeguard the integrity and confidentiality of the policy messaging exchanged by the framework's entities.

4   Performance Evaluation

The use of platform-agnostic technologies (i.e. DPWS and Java) enables the proposed framework to be deployed, by design, on a variety of platforms and operating systems. However, in order to realistically assess the performance of the proposed framework and its impact on the target devices, the developed entities have to be deployed on devices expected to be present in smart home environments. Therefore, the infrastructure entities, namely the PDP and PIP/PAP, were deployed on a laptop (quad core CPU at 2.6GHz, 4GB RAM), as a personal computer is typically available in home environments and is expected to act as a management hub through which the residents monitor and control their smart residence. A total of 50 policies were stored in the policy repository, which we consider a realistic approximation of the number of policies needed, considering the relatively limited number of devices expected to reside in a smart home. Tests were also carried out with 500 policies, to assess the impact more policies would have on the framework's performance.

Regarding the target platforms – i.e. the platforms featuring the services that need to be protected – we chose to use relatively resource-constrained smart embedded devices (600MHz low power single core CPU, 512MB RAM) running a popular open source operating system for mobile devices. Such operating systems are already found in many smart commercial appliances (e.g. smart fridges) offered by the various consumer vendors. Moreover, their adoption is expected to spread as more sophisticated home devices become available to end users; thus, the above platform can be considered a realistic choice for evaluating the performance of the proposed mechanisms.

The DPWS device deployed on the smart platform not only featured the access control related operations (as depicted in Fig. 2) but also featured three simple operations, emulating part of the functionality of a smart appliance. Via the above operations, the user can get the current temperature, subscribe to a service that periodically informs of said temperature and also set the desired temperature when needed. A basic touch GUI was developed for this device, which can be seen in Fig. 3.

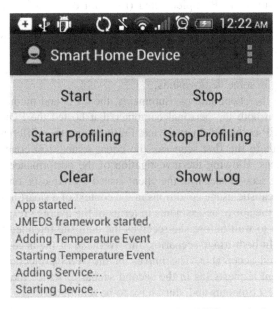

Fig. 3. Screen capture of the (access control-protected) DPWS test device deployed on the touch-enabled smart platform (e.g. a smart fridge).

A client application was also developed for testing purposes; the "Smart Home Browser". This application is deployable on various end devices (personal computers, smart phones or tablets) and allows users to discover and control the various DPWS-enabled smart appliances (to get the current contents of the smart fridge, to subscribe to the power consumption readings provided by the smart metering device etc.). A screenshot of the Smart Home Browser prototype implementation appears in Fig. 4.

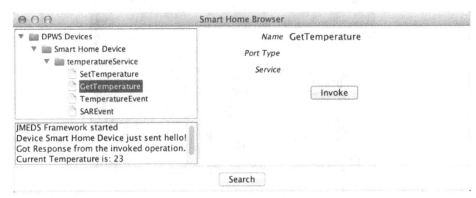

Fig. 4. The "Smart Home Browser"; an application developed to facilitate the discovery of DPWS devices and provide access to their hosted services.

A command line-only variation of this client, programmed to automatically invoke operations and record response times, was developed 'for benchmarking purposes. This benchmark client was used to evaluate the performance of three setups: a simple DPWS device with no PEP implemented (i.e. with direct access to its services), a DPWS device protected by the presented access control entities communicating in plaintext, and a third setup with the entities' communications being protected via WS-Security. This allowed us to separately assess the impact of the access control functionality and the impact of the security mechanisms that may be needed to protect the policy messaging in some deployments.

In addition to the client-side measurements, the CPU and memory utilization was also monitored on both the personal computer that hosted the PDP and PIP/PAP as well as on the PEP-equipped smart device. Furthermore, two different usage scenarios were investigated: In the first scenario, the client issued 100 concurrent requests to invoke the services, allowing the investigation of the performance under heavy load conditions. In the second scenario, the client issued 20 requests, one every 3 minutes, emulating more realistic usage conditions in the context of a smart home environment.

The results of the above assessments in terms of the average response time (i.e. the time the user has to wait before she receives the data she intended to access) are depicted in Fig. 5. In both usage scenarios, the overhead of the access control mechanism are considered acceptable. The impact of the WSS protection is significant in cases of infrequent requests (as in the second scenario, where the connections close between the request timeouts and, thus, have to be reinitiated).

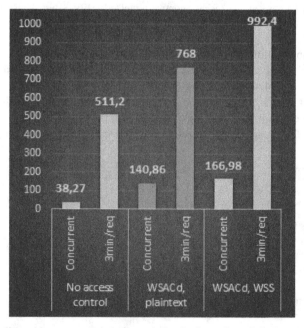

Fig. 5. Average client-side response time (in ms) for the investigated deployments and usage scenario

In terms of the resources consumed on the target, PEP-protected device, and focusing on the most demanding scenario (i.e. concurrent requests), profiling indicated a mild footprint during tests, even in the case of the relatively resource-constrained smart platform used in this setup. Average memory consumption is presented in Fig. 6, where the overhead of the access control mechanisms appears trivial compared to the simpler device.

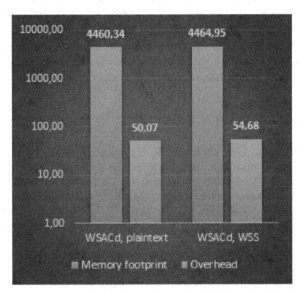

Fig. 6. Memory footprint (in kB, logarithmic scale) on the PEP-protected device, including the overhead compared to the simple DPWS device with no access control protection

The average CPU load was inversely proportional to the client response times (appearing in Fig. 5); when the device has to wait for a reply from the framework (i.e. the PDP) before serving the client, its CPU load is expectedly lower. The recorded values were 11.6%, 9.3% and 8.4% for no access control, WSACd and WSACd with WSS respectively. The same ranking was also documented when monitoring average transmission (TX) and reception (RX) rates on the target device – not depicted here to conserve space. The most taxing scenario network-wise was that of the device with no access control, but in all cases the data rates were relatively low, with the lowest recorded value being 16.13kB (average TX of WSACd, WSS device) and the highest being 26.5kB/sec (average RX of DPWS device without access control).

5   Conclusions and Future Work

This paper presented WSACd, a framework that leverages the benefits of SOAs, and DPWS specifically, to enable the integration of well-studied fine-grained and adaptable access control provided by XACML into smart homes. The intrinsic requirements of the smart home environment, its users and the often resource-constrained nature of its devices fundamentally affected the choice and implementation of the standardized mechanism that form the basis of this work. Thus, WSACd's entities are platform-agnostic, lightweight and interact seamlessly, minimizing the home users' involvement in deploying, setting up and maintaining the system.

Nevertheless, home owners will be responsible for defining some parameters of the active policy set, depending on their requirements and preferences. Thus, an important aspect to be investigated is the provision of user-friendly interfaces for specifying access control policies, e.g. using a GUI with easy to use drop-down menus and tick boxes or having the user answer simple questions, automatically translating the user input to policies. Lastly, while this paper focused on authorization aspects of ubiquitous smart devices, another important building block is the user authentication, which the authors currently investigate and aim to present in future work.

References

1. Fysarakis, K., Hatzivasilis, G., Rantos, K., Papanikolaou, A.: Embedded systems security challenges. In: Measurable security for Embedded Computing and Communication Systems (MeSeCCS 2014), within the International Conference on Pervasive and Embedded Computing and Communication Systems (PECCS 2014), Lisbon, Portugal (2011)
2. Petroulakis, N.E., Askoxylakis, I.G., Tryfonas, T.: Life-logging in smart environments: challenges and security threats. In: IEEE International Conference on Communications, pp. 5680–5684 (2012)
3. Petroulakis, N.E., Askoxylakis, I.G., Traganitis, A., Spanoudakis, G.: A privacy-level model of user-centric cyber-physical systems. In: Marinos, L., Askoxylakis, I. (eds.) HAS 2013. LNCS, vol. 8030, pp. 338–347. Springer, Heidelberg (2013)
4. Parducci, B., Lockhart, H.: eXtensible Access Control Markup Language (XACML) Version 3.0. OASIS Standard, 1–154 (2013)
5. Devices profile for web services, version 1.1, OASIS Standard (2009). http://docs.oasis-open.org/ws-dd/dpws/1.1/os/wsdd-dpws-1.1-spec-os.pdf
6. European Union Agency for Network and Information Security (ENISA): Threat Landscape and Good Practice Guide for Smart Home and Converged Media (2014)
7. Brush, A., Lee, B., Mahajan, R.: Home automation in the wild: challenges and opportunities. In: Proceedings of the SIGCHI Conference on Human Factors in Computing Systems, pp. 2115–2124 (2011)
8. DeCouteau, D., Davis, M., Staggs, D.: OASIS Cross-Enterprise Security and Privacy Authorization (XSPA) Profile of XACML v2.0 for Healthcare. OASIS Standard Specification, pp. 1–21 (2009)
9. Leong, C., Ramli, A., Perumal, T.: A rule-based framework for heterogeneous subsystems management in smart home environment. IEEE Trans. Consum. Electron. **55**, 1208–1213 (2009)
10. Perumal, T., Ramli, A., Leong, C.: Interoperability framework for smart home systems. IEEE Trans. Consum. Electron. **57**, 1607–1611 (2011)
11. Sleman, A.: Moeller R: SOA distributed operating system for managing embedded devices in home and building automation. IEEE Transactions on Consumer Electronics **57**(2), 945–952 (2011)
12. Crockford, D.: The JavaScript Object Notation (JSON) Data Interchange Format. The Internet Engineering Task Force RFC 7159, pp. 1–15 (2006)

13. Bourcier, J., Escoffier, C., Lalanda, P.: Implementing home-control applications on service platform. In: IEEE Consumer Communications and Networking Conference, Las Vegas, USA, pp. 925–929 (2007)
14. Igorevich, R.R., Park, P., Choi, J., Min, D.: iVision based context-aware smart home system. In: The 1st IEEE Global Conference on Consumer Electronics 2012, pp. 542–546. IEEE (2012)
15. Venkatesh, V., Vaithayana, V., Raj, P., Gopalan, K., Amirtharaj, R.: A Smart Train Using the DPWS-based Sensor Integration. Res. J. Inf. Technol. **5**, 352–362 (2013)
16. Garcia Valls, M., Lopez, I.R., Villar, L.F.: ILAND: An enhanced middleware for real-time reconfiguration of service oriented distributed real-time systems. IEEE Trans. Ind. Informatics **9**, 228–236 (2013)
17. Zhou, L., Rodrigues, J.: Service-oriented middleware for smart grid: Principle, infrastructure, and application. IEEE Commun. Mag. **51**, 84–89 (2013)
18. Rantos, K., Fysarakis, K., Manifavas, C., Askoxylakis, I.G.: Policy-Controlled Authenticated Access to LLN-Connected Healthcare Resources. IEEE Systems Journal **PP**(99), 1–11 (2015). doi:10.1109/JSYST.2015.2450313. http://ieeexplore.ieee.org/stamp/stamp.jsp?tp=&arnumber=7160675&isnumber=4357939
19. Dohndorf, O., Krüger, J., Krumm, H., Fiehe, C., Litvina, A., Luck, I., Stewing, F.J.: Towards the web of things: Using DPWS to bridge isolated OSGi platforms. In: 2010 8th IEEE International Conference on Pervasive Computing and Communications Workshops, PERCOM Workshops 2010, pp. 720–725 (2010)
20. Kim, J.E., Boulos, G., Yackovich, J., Barth, T., Beckel, C., Mosse, D.: Seamless integration of heterogeneous devices and access control in smart homes. In: 2012 Eighth Int. Conf. Intell. Environ., pp. 206–213 (2012)
21. Busnel, P., El-Khoury, P., Giroux, S., Li, K.: An XACML-based Security Pattern to achieve Socio-Technical Confidentiality in Smart Homes. J. Smart Home **3**, 17–26 (2009)
22. Faravelon, A., Chollet, S., Verdier, C., Front, A.: Enforcing privacy as access control in a pervasive context. In: IEEE Consumer Communications and Networking Conference, Las Vegas, USA, pp. 380–384 (2012)
23. Jung, M., Kienesberger, G., Granzer, W., Unger, M., Kastner, W.: Privacy enabled web service access control using SAML and XACML for home automation gateways. In: International Conference for Internet Technology and Secured Transactions, Abu Dhabi, UAE, pp. 584–591 (2011)
24. Müller, A., Kinkelin, H., Ghai, S.K., Carle, G.: A secure service infrastructure for interconnecting future home networks based on DPWS and XACML. In: Proceedings of the 2010 ACM SIGCOMM Workshop on Home Networks - HomeNets 2010, p. 31. ACM Press, New York (2010)
25. Lawrence, K., Kaler, C., Nadalin, A., Monzilo, R., Hallam-Baker, P.: Web Services Security: SOAP Message Security 1.1. https://www.oasis-open.org/committees/download.php/16790/wss-v1.1-spec-os-SOAPMessageSecurity.pdf

Secure Devices and Execution Environment

Automatic Top-Down Role Engineering Framework Using Natural Language Processing Techniques

Masoud Narouei[✉] and Hassan Takabi

Department of Computer Science and Engineering,
University of North Texas, Denton, TX, USA
masoudnarouei@my.unt.edu, takabi@unt.edu

Abstract. A challenging problem in managing large networks is the complexity of security administration. Role Based Access Control (RBAC) is the most well-known access control model in diverse enterprises of all sizes because of its ease of administration as well as economic benefits it provides. Deploying such system requires identifying a complete set of roles which are correct and efficient. This process, called role engineering, has been identified as one of the most expensive tasks in migrating to RBAC. Numerous bottom-up, top-down, and hybrid role mining approaches have been proposed due to increased interest in role engineering in recent years. In this paper, we propose a new top-down role engineering approach and take the first step towards extracting access control policies from unrestricted natural language requirements documents. Most organizations have high-level requirement specifications that include a set of access control policies which describes allowable operations for the system. It is very time consuming, labor-intensive, and error-prone to manually sift through these natural language documents to identify and extract access control policies. We propose to use natural language processing techniques, more specifically Semantic Role Labeling (SRL) to automatically extract access control policies from these documents, define roles, and build an RBAC system. By successfully applying semantic role labeling to identify predicate-argument structure, and using a set of predefined rules on the extracted arguments, we were able correctly identify access control policies with a precision of 79%, recall of 88%, and F_1 score of 82%.

Keywords: Role Based Access Control · Role engineering · Semantic role labeling · Natural language processing · Privacy policy

1 Introduction

In computer security, access control is the selective restriction of access to resource. System administrators at the top of any organization ascertain which individuals will be given access to what type of information. Access Control Policies (ACPs) detail controlling access to information and systems. These controls can be exemplified as the management of a number of key issues, including user access, network access controls, passwords, operating system software controls, and higher-risk system

© IFIP International Federation for Information Processing 2015
R.N. Akram and S. Jajodia (Eds.): WISTP 2015, LNCS 9311, pp. 137–152, 2015.
DOI: 10.1007/978-3-319-24018-3_9

access; giving access to files and documents and controlling remote user access; and restricting access.

However, defining proper ACPs is challenging, especially for large organizations. Advanced access control models such as Role Based Access Control (RBAC) [41] promise long-term cost savings through reduced management effort, but manual development of initial policies can be very time consuming, labor-intensive, and error prone [4, 24]. RBAC is the most widely used model for advanced access control in diverse enterprises of all sizes. In RBAC, access permissions are associated with roles instead of users where roles represent functions within a given organization. Users can activate a subset of the roles which they are members of and easily acquire all the required permissions for those roles. Deploying an RBAC system requires identifying a complete, correct and efficient set of roles, and then assigning users and permissions to those roles [44]. This process is known as role engineering and is the most expensive component of an RBAC implementation [19].

There are mainly two approaches to role engineering: the top-down approach and the bottom up approach. The top-down approach takes advantage of a detailed analysis of business processes where organizational business processes are analyzed, particular job functions are defined and decomposed into smaller units. Once the required permissions for performing specific tasks are identified, they can be grouped into appropriate functional roles. The process is repeated until all the job functions are covered. Because of the large number of business processes, users and permissions in an organization, and also as such a process is human-intensive, it is a rather difficult task and hence believed to be slow, expensive, and not scalable. In order to overcome this drawback, researchers have proposed a bottom-up approach to use data mining techniques to discover roles from existing data. Since many organizations already have user-permission assignments defined in some form, it makes sense to identify roles from this existing information. This approach first considers the existing users' permissions before RBAC is implemented, and aggregates them into roles. Such a bottom-up approach is called role mining.

Role mining has raised significant interests in the research community and in recent years, numerous role mining techniques have been developed [17, 18, 23, 34]. While role mining can quickly combine existing permissions into roles, it often leads to roles that are difficult to understand and manage because they don't have business meaning and fail to reflect the business structure of the organization [34]. In order to mitigate this problem, researchers have proposed hybrid role mining techniques that incorporate both top-down and bottom-up approaches [34, 23]. The hybrid role mining approach derives roles not only from the user-permission assignments but also using certain top-down information. This methodology of role development creates roles that are not simply collections of permissions, but are semantically meaningful and bear relevance to the organizational structure. Hybrid role mining generates semantically meaningful roles that are understandable and relevant to practical scenarios and hence makes adoption of RBAC more acceptable to organizations.

In this paper, we propose a substantially different top-down approach to role mining and take the first steps towards using natural language processing techniques to extract policies from unrestricted natural language requirements documents.

Most organizations have high-level requirement specifications that determine how information access is managed and who, under what circumstances, may access what information [24]. These documents define security policies and include a set of access control policies which describes allowable operations for the system. All US federal agencies are required to provide information security by the "Federal Information Security Act of 2002" [14], and policy documentation is part of that requirement [33]. Although private industry is not required to provide such documentation, the significant cost associated with cyber-attacks has led many companies to document their security policies as well. Besides, having security policies documented makes it much easier for organizations to transition from access control lists (ACLs) into a more robust RBAC infrastructure. We refer to these documents (high-level requirement specifications) as Natural Language Access Control Policies (NLACPs) which are defined as "*statements governing management and access of enterprise objects. NLACPs are human expressions that can be translated to machine-enforceable access control policies*" [24]. However, NLACPs are not directly implementable in an access control mechanism as they are normally expressed in human understandable terms. They are unstructured and may be ambiguous and thus hard to convert to formally actionable elements, so the enterprise policy may be difficult to encode in a machine-enforceable form. It is very time consuming, labor-intensive, and error-prone to manually sift through these existing natural language artifacts to identify and extract the buried ACPs. Properly enforcing these security policies requires the ACPs to be translated to machine-readable policies which has been done manually and is a very labor intensive and error prone process [4, 25]. Our goal is to automate this process to reduce manual efforts and human errors. We propose to develop techniques and tools that will support effective development of trustworthy access control policies through automatically extracting formal access control policies from unrestricted natural language documents and transforming them to enforceable policies. Our goal is to allow organizations to use existing, unconstrained natural language texts such as requirements documents for inferring ACPs. Our approach consists of five main steps: (1) apply linguistic analysis to parse natural language documents and annotate words and phrases in sentence (lexical parser), (2) identify whether a sentences contain potential ACP content or not (ACP sentence identification) , (3) infer semantic arguments of each predicate in each sentence using annotated words and phrases (semantic parser), (4) transform these semantic arguments into ACPs (postprocessor), and (5) aggregate the extracted ACPs into roles (role extractor). Our approach automatically generates machine enforceable ACPs and could be used as standalone top-down approach or as hybrid approach in combination with bottom-up role mining approaches.

In this paper, we limit our discussions to the linguistic analysis of natural language documents and extracting semantic arguments of each predicate from each sentence. We also present initial results of applying the technique to a sample of our policy dataset. To the best of our knowledge, there is not much work in the literature that addresses this issue and this is the first report on effectiveness of applying semantic role labeling to large and diverse set of ACPs.

Our contributions in this paper are three-fold:

- We propose an automated top-down role engineering approach;
- We apply semantic role labeling to identify access control policies in unrestricted natural language documents;
- We perform experiments to show efficiency of the proposed approach. Our evaluation results show that the proposed approach can effectively identify access control policies with a precision of 79%, recall of 88%, and F_1 score of 82%.

The rest of this paper is organized as follows: We start with an overview of previous literature in section 2. In section 3, we present our proposed approach and its components. The experiments and results are presented in section 4, and finally, conclusion and future works wraps up the paper.

2   Background and Related Work

This section describes the state of the art in NLP techniques and their application for access control policies and related areas as well as hybrid role mining approaches in the literature.

2.1   Natural Language Processing (NLP)

Most modern NLP semantic parsers include several tasks such as tokenization, sentence segmentation, part-of-speech (POS) tagging, lemmatization, named-entity recognition, syntactic parsing, semantic role labeling, event recognition, and coreference resolution. *Tokenization* detects individual words, punctuation, and other items from the text. *Sentence segmentation* identifies the boundaries of sentences. *Part-Of-Speech (POS) tagging* determines the POS tags such as noun, verb, adjective, etc. for each token. The current state-of-the-art POS taggers achieve 97.3% accuracy for individual tokens [30]. *Lemmatization* generates the common root word for a group of morphologically related words. For instance, sang, sung, and sings are all forms of a common lemma "sing". The state of the art achieves around 99% accuracy for the English language [20]. *Named-entity recognition (NER)* aims to classify phrases into entity types such as people, organizations, locations, times, vehicles, and events [26]. The state-of-the-art for the NER general task has a F_1 score of around 89% [29]. *Syntactic parsing* generates a parse-tree structure for a sentence [26]. The tree structure provides a basis for other tasks within NLP such as question answering, information extraction (IE), and machine translation. State-of-the-art parsers have a F_1 score of around 90% [53]. *Coreference resolution* determines whether or not two expressions in a document refer to the same entity or event. A common subset of this problem occurs within extracting ACPs from NLACP texts in that pronouns must be resolved to their antecedents (the actual role or resource). *Kennedy et al.* introduced an algorithm to resolve pronoun anaphora resolution (match the correct noun to a pronoun) that does not require parsing and achieves 75% accuracy on their test set [28].

2.2   Information Extraction (IE)

Information extraction creates structured data from text [26]. Common targets of IE applications include named-entities, other entities of specific types, relations, events, and their attributes. A relation expresses the relationship among two or more items. Common relation types include "is-a" and "part-of". For example, "a doctor is a healthcare professional (HCP)" is represented by *is_a(doctor, HCP)* and "medical records contain family history" is represented by *contains(medical record, family history)*. State-of-the-art systems for relation extraction (RE) typically have around 85% precision and 70% recall [38]. Another IE technique is shallow parsing (semantic role labeling) which involves identifying the different predicates (verbs) in a sentence along with their semantic arguments [21].

2.3   NLP Techniques for Privacy Policies

Breaux et al. have manually analyzed privacy policies to map natural language policy statements into frame-based and first-order logic representations [5, 6, 8]. They have also analyzed regulatory text and developed natural language heuristics, some expressible as simple regular expressions, that can be used to identify frame-based representations of actions [7] and whether actions on information are permitted, required or prohibited with various conditions, exceptions and purposes [9]. *Ammar et al.* conducted an experiment to use NLP methods and crowdsourced annotations from the "Terms of Service; Didn't Read" project [47] to train a classifier to answer a single question: whether a privacy policy is considered clear by humans about a particular set of procedures pertaining to sensitive user data [1]. The ongoing Usable Privacy Policy Project aims to build on recent advances in NLP, privacy preference modeling, crowdsourcing, and formal methods to semi-automatically extract key privacy policy features from natural language website privacy policies [48]. The focus of this project is website privacy policies while our project is focused on access control policies.

2.4   Controlled Natural Language (CNL) and Access Control

Schwitter defined a Controlled Natural Language (CNL) as "an engineered subset of a natural language whose grammar and vocabulary have been restricted in a systematic way in order to reduce both ambiguity and complexity of full natural language." [42]. While a CNL provides semantic interpretations, it limits policy authors to the defined grammar and requires language-specific tools to stay within the language constraints. The SPARCLE Policy Workbench [10, 27, 11] employs shallow parsing technology [35] to extract privacy policies based on a pre-defined controlled grammar for forming policies in a structured form. The policies are then translated to a machine-readable form, such as EPAL [2] and XACML [36]. *Inglesant et al.* proposed a similar tool, PERMIS, which used a role-based authorization model [25]. However, they reported issues with users not comprehending the predefined "building blocks" imposed by using a CNL. *Shi et al.* presented their approach to authoring policies using a CNL and showed the improved usability of CNL interface [43]. However, their approach is limited in the complexity of the rules that could be created since their supporting tool did not support conditions such as previous actions that must be taken before a user could access data.

2.5   NLP and Access Control

NL sources have been analyzed to infer and generate ACPs. *Fernandez et al.* presented a basic overview of extracting RBAC from use cases [15]. *Fontaine* proposed an approach based upon goal-based requirements engineering to extract authorization and obligation rules from NL texts into a policy language [16]. *He et al.* proposed an approach to generate ACPs from NL based upon available project documents, database design, and existing rules [22]. Using a series of heuristics, developers manually analyze the documents to find ACPs whereas our approach seeks to automatically extract ACPs. *Xiao et al.* proposed Text2Policy for automated extraction of ACPs [49]. It first uses shallow parsing techniques with finite state transducers to match a sentence into one of four possible access control patterns. If such a match can be made, Text2Policy uses the annotated portions of the sentences to extract the subject, action, and object from the sentence. *Slankas et al.* proposed Access Control Rule Extraction (ACRE) [45] which applies inductive reasoning to find and extract ACRs while Text2Policy applies deductive reasoning based upon existing rules to find and extract ACRs. While this work these two early works are promising, they suffer from several weaknesses. ACRE uses a supervised learning approach to identify sentences containing ACRs which requires a labeled dataset similar in structure and content to the document being analyzed. This data is hard to come by. Text2Policy does not require a labeled data set but it misses ACRs that do not follow one of its four patterns. It is reported that only 34.4% of the identified ACR sentences followed one of Text2Policy's patterns [44]. Additionally, Text2Policy's NL parser requires splitting longer sentences as the parser cannot handle complicated sentence structures. These approaches assume all necessary information for an ACP is contained within the same sentence, and they do not handle resolution issues. Neither one of these approaches take into account the presence of contextual information or environment conditions which is a very challenging task.

2.6   Top-Down Role Engineering

Roeckle et al. described a process oriented approach for role-finding to implement Role-Based Security Administration. The core of their work is presenting the data model, which integrates business processes, role based security administration and access control. Moreover, a structured top-down approach is outlined which is the basis for derivation of suitable business roles from enterprise process models [40]. *Baumgrass et al.* identified several tasks in role engineering that are monotonous, time-consuming, and can get tedious if conducted manually. These tasks include the derivation of candidate RBAC artifacts from business processes and scenario models. They presented an approach to automatically derive role engineering artifacts from process and scenario models. They especially discuss the derivation of role engineering artifacts from UML activity models, UML interaction models, and BPMN collaboration models. In particular, they use the XMI (XML Metadata Interchange) representation of these models as a tool and vendor independent format to identify and automatically derive different role engineering artifacts [3]. *Molloy et al.* propose a hybrid role engineering approach where a set of roles has already been derived by the top-down approach and the remaining roles are defined following a bottom-up technique [34]. In this approach, roles that correspond to sensitive job responsibilities are specified manually by the top-down procedure. The proposed hybrid approach combines traditional role mining techniques with an approach that optimizes an existing set of roles. *Hernandez et al.* propose a hybrid role mining method which creates roles from both top-down and bottom-up information collected from a number of sources [23]. Two criteria, one based on the top-down information and the other based on the bottom-up information are used to assign roles to the appropriate users. The bottom-up information is the user permission assignments whereas the top-down information is the various attributes of users.

Frank et al. propose a probabilistic method for hybrid role mining [18]. Their proposed method consists of two steps - (i) identification of business information relevant to the existing user-permission assignments and (ii) including this business information in the process of role mining. Incorporation of business information is achieved by satisfying two objectives: (i) finding a decomposition consisting of UA and PA that best describes the UPA even if new users are added and (ii) agreement of the resulting role assignments with the relevant business information.

3   The Proposed Framework

In order to construct a formal model for an NLACP, we must extract the necessary elements of ACPs from the natural language document. The ACPs describes who has access to what resource in what way. By processing these formal models, our technique will generate corresponding machine readable and enforceable policies. An overall view of the proposed system is shown in Figure 1. In the following sections, we describe each of these steps in details.

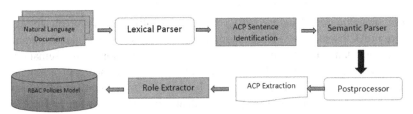

Fig. 1. Overview of the Proposed Framework

3.1   Lexical Parser

We first read the entire NLACPs and perform sentence segmentation and tokenization. Sentence segmentation identifies the boundaries of sentences whereas Tokenization detects individual words, punctuation, and other items from the text.   In order for
the input text to be ready for evaluation, the first step is to identify all sentences and
separating these sentences by a period and a carriage return so that each sentence will
be on a separate line. For this purpose, we use CoreNLP tool kit [31].

Coreference Resolution. Coreference resolution (sometimes written co-reference)
determines whether or not two expressions in a document refer to the same entity or
event. The goal is identify all expressions that refer to the same entity in a text. For
example, consider the following sentence where HCP stands for healthcare professional:

> The **HCP** opens the message to which **he** or **she** wishes to reply.

Here, "HCP," "he," and "she" all refer to the same entity. The goal of coreference
resolution here is to replace all of pronouns with their corresponding referents. Because each sentence will be evaluated separately, having a clear idea of each pronoun
is a key point in identifying the correct ACP elements. We adopt the approach proposed in [12], which is a fast and robust algorithm for this purpose.

3.2   ACP Sentence Identification

Often time NLACPs contain contents that describe functional requirements and are
not necessary related to ACPs. Although these documents also contain ACPs, at-
tempting to extract ACPs from the whole document is an error prone and tedious
process. To correctly extract ACPs from NLACPs, it is very important to find out
those sentences that have potentially ACP content and then perform further analysis
only on those sentences to extract ACP elements.

Slankas et al. proposed a k-Nearest Neighbors (k-NN) classifier to identify sentences containing ACPs. k-NN is an instance based classifier that attempts to locate
the k nearest neighbors of an instance in an instance space and labeling that instance
with the same class as that of most neighbors. As our focus is on correctly identifying
ACP elements, we employ the same approach as the one used in [45].

3.3   Semantic Parser

We use semantic role labeling (SRL) to automatically identify predicate-argument
structure in ACP sentences. SRL, sometimes also called shallow semantic parsing, is a
task in natural language processing consisting of the detection of the semantic arguments associated with the verb (or more technically, a predicate) of a sentence and
their classification into their specific roles. It labels verb-argument structure using the
notation defined by Propbank [37] project, identifying who did what to whom by assigning roles to constituents of the sentence representing entities related to a specific
verb. Recognizing these semantic arguments is a key task in finding the answer to the

questions like: "Who," "When," "What," "Where," "Why", etc., which are especially in use by analyzers trying to extract access control policies from sentences. The following sentence, exemplifies the annotation of semantic roles:

[$_{Arg0}$ John] [$_{ArgM-MOD}$ can] [$_V$ **assign**] [$_{Arg1}$ clerk] [$_{Arg2}$ to users from department A]

Here, the roles for the predicate **assign** (assign.01, that is, the *roleset* of the predicate) are defined in the PropBank Frames scheme as:

V: verb

ArgM-MOD: modal

Arg0: (assigner)

Arg1: (thing assigned)

Arg2: (assigned to)

SRL is very important in making sense of the meaning of a sentence. Such semantic representation is at a higher-level of abstraction than a syntax tree. For instance, the sentence "A professor can review the same project at most one time" has a different syntactic form, but the same semantic roles to "The same project can be reviewed by a professor at most one time".

In general, given any sentence, the task of SRL consists of analyzing the propositions expressed by all target verbs in a sentence and for each target verb, all the constituents in that sentence which fill a semantic role of the verb, will be extracted. Here, we use the following notation to describe ACPs:

$$\{A; B; C\}$$

Where *A* stands for *Argument0*, *B* stands for *predicate* and *C* stands for *argument1*. *Argument0* usually denotes agent or experiencer for that predicate and *Argument1* denotes theme (where predicate affects). In this paper, we use Senna (Semantic/syntactic Extraction using a Neural Network Architecture) semantic role labeler [13], which performs sentence-level analysis. Senna is a multilayer neural network architecture that can handle a number of NLP tasks such as part-of-speech tagging, chunking, named entity recognition, and semantic role labeling with both speed and accuracy. Senna relies on large unlabeled dataset(s) and allows the training algorithm to discover internal representations that prove useful for the requested task. Senna is fast because it uses a simple architecture, it is self-contained because it does not rely on the output of another system, and it is accurate because it offers state-of-the-art or near state-of-the-art performance.

3.4   Postprocessor

After generating predicate-arguments using SRL tool, additional processing is required on the output. This is due to the fact that the NLACPs are typically stated by managers using their own language and grammar because they do not have the technical knowledge of the system, and this makes ACP extraction from their stated sentences more complicated. In order to increase accuracy of the extracted ACPs, we apply named entity recognition and argument expansion to the SRL output as described below.

Named Entity Recognition. Named entity recognition (NER) is the task of identifying named entities and sequences of words in a text belonging to predefined categories such as the names of persons, locations, organizations, expressions of times, quantities, monetary values, percentages, etc. The task here is to produce an annotated text that highlights the names of entities such as the following example:

[ORGANIZATION Customer   Service   Reps],   [PERSON Pharmacists],   and [ORGANIZATION Billing Reps] can collect and use customer name and [TIME date of birth] to help confirm identity.

In this example, *Customer Service Reps* is an organization consisting of three tokens, *Pharmacists*, is a person consisting of one token, *Billing Reps* is an organization consisting of two three tokens, and finally *date of birth* is a time consisting of three tokens.

Argument Expansion. ACPs usually do not conform to a predefined template unless there is controlled grammar being used. Most of the time ACPs are stated by managers using their own language because they do not have the technical knowledge of the system and this makes their stated sentences complicated. One of these complications is that sometimes more than one ACP is stated in a given sentence. Consider the following sentence for example:

Customer Service Reps, Pharmacists, and Billing Reps can collect and use customer name and date of birth to help confirm identity.

There are 15 different ACPs associated with this sentence:

- {customer service rep; collect; customer name}
- {customer service rep; collect; customer date of birth}
- {customer service rep; use; customer name}
- {customer service rep; use; customer date of birth}
- {pharmacist; use; customer name}
- {pharmacist; use; customer date of birth }
- {pharmacist; collect; customer name}
- {pharmacist; collect; customer date of birth }
- {billing rep; collect; customer name}
- {billing rep; collect; customer date of birth }
- {billing rep; use; customer name}
- {billing rep; use; customer date of birth }
- {customer service rep; confirm; identity}
- {pharmacist; confirm; identity}
- {billing rep; confirm; identity}

Now consider the following list of the extracted roles for predicate Collect:

[Arg0 Customer Service Reps, Pharmacists, and Billing Reps] [ArgM-MOD can] [v **collect**] and use [Arg1 customer name and date of birth] [ArgM-PNC to help confirm identity].

As a comparison between the generated semantic arguments and the actual ACPs shows, SRL's output can be interpreted as an abstract form for ACPs, so we have to expand this abstract form to generate all of the related ACPs. This expansion could be in the form of extracting all named entities or other standalone nouns in Arg0 as the possible agents and also extracting independent entities from Arg1 as themes. For example, in this case, Named Entity Recognizer identifies *Customer Service Reps* and *Pharmacists* as organizations. After extracting all of these entities, we list all of the combinations of these entities based on each predicate. For example this verb-argument listing can be expanded as the following rules:

- {customer service rep; collect; customer name}
- {customer service rep; collect; customer date of birth}
- {pharmacist; collect; customer name}
- {pharmacist; collect; customer date of birth }
- {billing rep; collect; customer name}
- {billing rep; collect; customer date of birth }

3.5   Role Extractor

When the SRL tool extracts the ACP components, role extractor utilizes the extracted information to define roles. Then, these roles can be used to build an access control models such as RBAC. The ACPs are in the form of {subject, object, operation} and many of the extracted subjects correspond with the job functions within organization (e.g. doctor, pharmacist, nurse, healthcare professional, etc.) which could represent roles.

A naïve approach would be to just look at the ACPs and find the ones with the same subject and group them together in one role and use all the ACPs with that subject to build the role permission assignment relationships. The object and operation elements of the ACPs are used to define permissions in RBAC and then assign those permissions to roles based on that specific subject using ACP associations. Another approach is to use classifier such as *k*-Nearest Neighbors (*k*-NN) classifier or Naive Bayes classifier to extract roles from the ACPs. However, we leave this to future work as it is not focus of this paper.

4   Experimental Results

In this section, we perform experiments to answer the research question of how effectively the subject, object, and operation elements of ACPs are extracted. In the followings, we explain the datasets and the evaluation criteria used in our experiments. Then, we present the experimental results.

4.1   Datasets

We use documents from multiple domains such as electronic healthcare, educational, and conference management for the experiments. For the electronic health care domain, we use iTrust [32], which is an open source healthcare application that includes various features such as maintaining medical history of patients, identifying primary caregivers, storing communications with doctors, and sharing satisfaction results. For the educational domain, we employ use cases from the IBM Course Registration System used in previous research [39]. For the conference management domain, we use documents from CyberChair [46], which has been used by hundreds of different conferences and workshops. We also use a combined document of 115 ACP sentences collected from 18 sources (published papers, public web sites, etc.) that has been used in previous research [49, 45]. In this paper, we only consider those sentences that are labeled as access control sentence and ignore the rest as ACP identification is not the focus of this paper. For our evaluation, we use the iTrust data set that was used by *Xiao et al.* [27]. This version includes the preprocessed iTrust data set consisting of simplified sentences. For iTrust, there are 418 sentences identified as containing ACP content. The second dataset, IBM Course Registration System consists of eight use cases and there are 169 ACP sentences. The CyberChair dataset consists of 139 ACP sentences and the for Collected ACP documents, there are 115 ACP sentences.

4.2   Evaluation Criteria

We want to know how effectively the semantic arguments of each predicate are extracted from ACP sentences. The results are evaluated with respect to *recall, precision*, and the F_1 measure of the predicate arguments. To calculate these values, we categorize the extractions into four categories: false positives (FP) are cases where we mistakenly identify a word as an ACP element when it is not, false negatives (FN) occur when we fail to correctly extract an actual ACP element, true positives (TP) are correct extractions, and true negatives (TN) are cases where we correctly identified that a word in the sentence was not an ACP element. From these values, we define precision as the proportion of correctly extracted ACP elements against all extractions against the test data. We also define recall as the proportion of ACP elements found for the current data under test. The F_1 score is the harmonic mean—a weighted average of precision and recall—giving an equal weight to both recall and precision. F_1 is computed by equation 1.

$$F_1 = 2 \times \frac{Recall \times Precision}{Recall + Precision} \tag{1}$$

In order to evaluate the effectiveness of our proposed approach, we use the datasets that were manually labeled by *Slankas et al.* [45]. They were able to find a total of 1070 ACPs in iTrust dataset, 375 ACPs in IBM Course Registration System dataset, 386 ACPs in CyberChair dataset and 258 ACPs in Collected ACP documents. More details on how the labeling was done can be found in [45]. The evaluation results as well as comparison with the most recent system (ACRE) are presented in Table 1. As the results show, our approach based on semantic role labeling performs very well and outperforms the ACRE approach in most cases. The algorithm used in ACRE requires repetition in sentence structure as well as subjects and resources throughout the document to perform well. This algorithm performed best on iTrust because it contained repetitions throughout the document but performed poor on the Collected ACP document. That's because there are not enough repetition in that document for finding initial set of known subjects and resources and expanding the patterns. However, semantic role labeling does not require repetition as every sentence will be considered separately, independent of the other sentences. As long as there are role sets defined for that predicate, semantic role labeling can find most of the arguments. This is why the results for semantic role labeling are stable throughout all documents and it provides good results regardless of the structure of the document.

Table 1. Comparison of ACP extraction between ACRE and the proposed system (ICM: IBM Course Registration, CC: CyberChair and CAD: Collected ACP Documents).

Dataset	ACRE			SRL		
	Precision	Recall	F_1	Precision	Recall	F_1
iTrust	80%	75%	77%	75%	88%	80%
IBM	81%	62%	70%	54%	87%	58%
CC	75%	30%	43%	46%	84%	59%
CAD	68%	18%	29%	79%	86%	82%

In terms of precision, however, our approach does not perform very well. One issue with using semantic role labeling is that it extracts all arguments for all of the verbs in a sentence. Sometimes only a portion of these verbs such as (set, add, etc) describe access control policies. Consider the following example:

Only the manager [$_v$ is] [$_v$ allowed] to [$_v$ add] a new resident to the system and to [$_v$ start] or [$_v$ update] the care plan of a resident.

Here, only three of the verbs, namely *add*, *start* and *update* address ACPs. In the experiments, we eliminate "To Be" and "Modal" verbs because usually they are part of other verbs such as *can assign* and do not express ACPs on their own. There are also other verbs such as *click, include*, etc., that do not express ACPs and hence increase the false positive rate. In the future, we plan to create a dictionary of the verbs that are associated with ACPs and will only consider those verbs which will improve the results significantly.

Another issue with our approach is that sometimes the SRL tool is unable to correctly identify all predicates and their arguments. This is due to complex structure of some sentences. We plan to define specific rules to handle this issue and improve the precision.

Although our approach does not perform very well in terms of precision, if we consider the F_1 scores, we can see that our approach outperforms the ACRE and for some dataset(s) the difference is very significant (82% compared to 29% for the Collected ACP documents). Only for the IBM Course Management dataset, SRL is outperformed by ACRE and it is because precision is very low which leads to lower F_1 score. In addition to offering better recall and F_1 score, another advantage of our approach over the ACRE is that it does not require any labeled data set whereas ACRE uses a supervised learning approach and requires a labeled dataset similar in structure and content to the document being analyzed to setup the classifiers. One technical challenge concerning the use of SRL is that sometimes our tool is unable to find the predicate-arguments in some sentences. The reason is that SRL tools are often trained on publicly available corpora such as the Wall Street Journal. This means that the predicate-argument frames are usually general and not well suited for processing information such as access control requirements documents. In the future, we plan to address this issue by adapting the SRL tool to ACP domain so that it can identify all predicate-arguments.

5   Conclusion and Future Work

In this paper, we proposed a new top-down approach towards role engineering in order to extract access control policies from unstructured natural language documents. We applied semantic role labeling techniques to extract policies from natural language requirements documents. The semantic role labeling allowed us to identify predicate-argument structure and by applying a set of predefined rules on the extracted arguments, we were able to successfully identify ACP elements with a recall of 88%, precision of 79%, and F_1 score of 82%. The performance of our system depends on the predefined role sets for each predicate. Currently, the proposed approach considers all predicates in the sentence which results in large number of false positives. In the future, we plan to create a dictionary of the verbs that are usually associated with access control policies and only consider those verbs to improve the results. We also plan to implement the complete system including implementing ACP sentence identification step and role extractor components.

References

1. Ammar, W., Wilson, S., Sadeh, N., Smith, N.: Automatic Categorization of Privacy Policies: A Pilot Study. School of Computer Science, Language Technology Institute, Technical Report CMU-LTI-12-019, December 2012
2. Ashley, P., Hada, S., Karjoth, G., Powers, C., Schunter, M.: Enterprise Privacy Architecture Language (EPAL 1.2) (2003). http://www.w3.org/Submission/EPAL/
3. Baumgrass, A., Strembeck, M., Ma, S.R.: Deriving role engineering artifacts from business processes and scenario models. In: Proceeding of ACM SACMAT 2011, June 15–17, Innsbruck, Austria, pp. 11–20 (2011)
4. Beckerle, M., Martucci, L.A.: Formal definitions for usable access control rule sets from goals to metrics. In: Proceedings of the Ninth Symposium on Usable Privacy and Security (SOUPS), pp. 2:1–2:11. ACM (2013)
5. Breaux, T.D., Antón, A.I.: Deriving semantic models from privacy policies. In: 6th IEEE International Workshop on Policies for Distributed Systems & Networks, pp. 67–76 (2005)
6. Breaux, T.D., Antón, A.I.: Analyzing goal semantics for rights, permissions and obligations. In: Proc. IEEE 13th International Requirements Engineering Conference (RE 2005), Paris, France, pp. 177–186, August 2005
7. Breaux, T.D., Antón, A.I.: Analyzing regulatory rules for privacy and security requirements. IEEE Transactions on Software Engineering, Special Issue on Software Engineering for Secure Systems (IEEE TSE) **34**(1), 5–20 (2008)
8. Breaux, T.D., Antón, A.I., Doyle, J.: Semantic parameterization: a process for modeling domain descriptions. ACM Transactions on Software Engineering Methodology (ACM TOSEM) **18**(2), Article 5 (2008)

9. Breaux, T.D.: Legal Requirements Acquisition for the Specification of Legally Compliant Information Systems. Ph.D. Thesis, North Carolina State University, April 2009
10. Brodie, C.A., Karat, C.-M., Karat, J., Feng, J.: Usable security and privacy: a case study of developing privacy management tools. In: Proc. SOUPS 2005 (2005)
11. Brodie, C.A., Karat, C.-M., Karat, J.: An empirical study of natural language parsing of privacy policy rules using the SPARCLE policy workbench. In: Proc. SOUPS 2006, pp. 8–19 (2006)
12. Charniak, E., Elsner, M.: EM works for pronoun anaphora resolution. In: Proceedings of the European Chapter of the ACL (2009)
13. Collobert, R., Weston, J., Bottou, L., Karlen, M., Kavukcuoglu, K., Kuksa, P.: Natural Language Processing (Almost) from Scratch. Journal of Machine Learning Research (JMLR) (2011)
14. Federal information security management act of 2002. Title III of the E-Government Act of 2002 (Public Law 107-347) (2002)
15. Fernandez, E.B., Hawkins, J.C.: Determining role rights from use cases. In: Proc. ACM Workshop on Role-Based Access Control 1997, pp. 121–125 (1997)
16. Fontaine, P.J.: Goal-Oriented Elaboration of Security Requirements. Université catholique de Louvain (2001)
17. Frank, M., Basin, D., Buhmann, J.M.: A class of probabilistic models for role engineering. In: Proc. 15th ACM Conference on Computer and Communications Security (CCS) 2008, pp. 299–310 (2008)
18. Frank, M., Buhmann, J.M., Basin, D.A.: Role mining with probabilistic models. ACM Transactions on Information and System Security 15(4), 1–28 (2013)
19. Gallagher, M.P., O'Connor, A.C., Kropp, B.: The economic impact of role-based access control. Planning report 02-1, National Institute of Standards and Technology (2002)
20. Gesmundo, A., Samardžić, T.: Lemmatisation as a tagging task. In: Proc. ACL 2012, pp. 368–372 (2012)
21. Gildea, D., Jurafsky, D.: Automatic Labeling of Semantic Roles. Computational Linguistics 28(3), 245–288 (2002)
22. He, Q., Antón, A.I.: Requirements-based Access Control Analysis and Policy Specification (ReCAPS). Information and Software Technology 51(6), 993–1009 (2009)
23. Hernandez, M.H., Laredo, J.A., Mandala, S., Ruan, Y., Sreedhar, V.C., Vukovic, M.: System and Method for Hybrid Role Mining, May 2, 2013.
    http://www.google.com/patents/US20130111583. US Patent App. 13/283,371
24. Hu, V.C., Ferraiolo, D., Kuhn, R., Friedman, A.R., Lang, A.J., Cogdell, M.M., Schnitzer, A., Sandlin, K., Miller, R., Scarfone, K.: Guide to attribute based access control (abac) definition and considerations (final draft). NIST Special Publication 800-162, National Institute of Standards and Technology, September 2013.
    http://csrc.nist.gov/publications/drafts/800-162/sp800_162_draft.pdf
25. Inglesant, P., Sasse, M.A., Chadwick, D., Shi, L.L.: Expressions of expertness: the virtuous circle of natural language for access control policy specification. In: Proc. SOUPS 2008, pp. 77–88 (2008)
26. Jurafsky, D., Martin, J.: Speech and Language Processing: An Introduction to Natural Language Processing, Computational Linguistics, and Speech Recognition. Pearson (2009)
27. Karat, J., Karat, C.-M., Brodie, C., Feng, J.: Designing natural language and structured entry methods for privacy policy authoring. In: Costabile, M.F., Paternó, F. (eds.) INTERACT 2005. LNCS, vol. 3585, pp. 671–684. Springer, Heidelberg (2005)
28. Kennedy, C., Boguraev, B.: Anaphora for everyone: pronominal anaphora resoluation without a parser. In: Proc. Coling 1996, pp. 113–118 (1996)

29. Language-Independent Named Entity Recognition (2003).
    http://www.cnts.ua.ac.be/conll2003/ner
30. Manning, C.D.: Part-of-speech tagging from 97% to 100%: is it time for some linguistics?
    In: Gelbukh, A.F. (ed.) CICLing 2011, Part I. LNCS, vol. 6608, pp. 171–189. Springer,
    Heidelberg (2011)
31. Manning, C.D., Surdeanu, M., Bauer, J., Finkel, J., Bethard, S.J., McClosky, D.: The stan-
    ford CoreNLP natural language processing toolkit. In: Proceedings of 52nd Annual Meet-
    ing of the Association for Computational Linguistics: System Demonstrations,
    pp. 55–60 (2014)
32. Meneely, A., Smith, B., Williams, L.: iTrust electronic health care system: a case study. In:
    Software System Traceability (2011)
33. Minimum security requirements for federal information and information systems. Tech-
    nical report, National Institute of Standards, March 2006. FIPS Pub 200
34. Molloy, I., Chen, H., Li, T., Wang, Q., Li, N., Bertino, E., Calo, S., Lobo, J.: Mining Roles
    with Multiple Objectives. ACM Transactions on Information and System Security 13(4),
    Article 36 (2010)
35. Neff, M.S., Byrd, R.J., Boguraev, B.K.: The Talent System: TEXTRACT Architecture and
    Data Model. Nat. Lang. Eng. 10(3–4), 2004 (2004)
36. OASIS. Privacy Policy Profile of XACML v3.0. (2010). http://docs.oasis-
    open.org/xacml/3.0/xacml-3.0-privacy-v1-spec-cs-01-en.pdf
37. Palmer, M., Gildea, D., Kingsbury, P.: The proposition bank: An annotated corpus of se-
    mantic roles. Comput. Linguist. 31(1), 71–106 (2005). ISSN: 0891-2017
38. Poibeau, T., Piskorski, J., Yangarber, R.: Information extraction: past, present, and future.
    In: Multi-source, Multilingual Information Extraction and Summarization, pp. 23–50.
    Springer, Heidelberg (2013)
39. Roeckle, H., Schimpf, G., Weidinger, R.: Process-oriented approach for role-finding to
    implement role-based security administration in a large industrial organization. In: Pro-
    ceedings of the Fifth ACM Workshop on Role-Based Access Control, RBAC 2000,
    pp. 103–110. ACM, New York (2000)
40. Sagar, V.V.B.R., Abirami, S.: Conceptual modeling of natural language functional re-
    quirements. Journal of Systems and Software 88, 25–41 (2014)
41. Sandhu, R., Coyne, E., Feinstein, H., Youman, C.: Role-based access control models.
    IEEE. Computer 29(2), 38–47 (1996)
42. Schwitter, R.: Controlled natural languages for knowledge representation. In: Proc. CICL-
    ing 2010, pp. 1113–1121 (2010)
43. Sinha, A., Sutton Jr., S.M., Paradkar, A.: Text2test: automated inspection of natural lan-
    guage use cases. In: Proc. ICST, pp. 155–164 (2010)
44. Slankas, J., Xiao, X., Williams, L., Xie, T.: Relation extraction for inferring access control
    rules from natural language artifacts. In: Proceedings of the of 2014 Annual Computer Se-
    curity Applications Conference (ACSAC 2014), New Orleans, LA (2014)
45. Socher, R., Bauer, J., Manning, C.D., Ng, A.Y.: Parsing with compositional vector gram-
    mars. In: Proc. ACL 2013 (2013)
46. Tan, L., Yuan, D., Krishna, G., Zhou, Y.: 21st SOSP 2007, pp. 145–158 (2007)
47. Terms of Service, Didn't Read project. http://tosdr.org/
48. Xiao, X., Paradkar, A., Thummalapenta, S., Xie, T.: Automated extraction of security poli-
    cies from natural-language software documents. In: Proc. 20th FSE, November 2012

Practical and Privacy-Preserving TEE Migration

Ghada Arfaoui[1,3]([⊠]), Saïd Gharout[2],
Jean-François Lalande[3,4], and Jacques Traoré[1]

[1] Orange Labs, 14000 Caen, France
ghada.arfaoui@orange.com
[2] Orange Labs, 92130 Issy-les-moulineaux, France
[3] INSA Centre Val de Loire, LIFO, 18022 Bourges, France
[4] Inria, CentraleSupélec, IRISA, 35576 Cesson-sévigné, France

Abstract. Trusted Execution Environments (TEE) are becoming widely deployed in new smartphone generation. Running within the TEE, the Trusted Applications (TA) belong to diverse service providers. Each TA manipulates a profile, constituted of secret credentials and user's private data. Normally, a user should be able to transfer his TEE profiles from a TEE to another compliant TEE. However, TEE profile migration implies security and privacy issues in particular for TEE profiles that require explicit agreement of the service provider. In this paper, we first present our perception of the deployment and implementation of a TEE: we organize the TEE into security domains with different roles and privileges. Based on this new model, we build a migration protocol of TEE profiles ensuring its confidentiality and integrity. To this end, we use a reencryption key and an authorization token per couple of devices, per service provider and per transfer. The proposed protocol has been successfully validated by AVISPA, an automated security protocol validation tool.

Keywords: TEE · Credential transfer · Privacy

1 Introduction

In the last years, a secure mobile operating system running alongside the standard Rich Execution Environment (REE for short), has emerged: the Trusted Execution Environment (TEE for short). A TEE could have its own CPU and memory, and hosts isolated Trusted Applications (TA for short) that provide secure services to the applications running within the REE. These TAs belong to diverse service providers. Each TA manipulates a profile, constituted of secret credentials and user's private data.

The TEE has been standardized by GlobalPlatform, however, to the best of our knowledge, there is no specification or research work that models the TEE internal architecture or ecosystem. For instance, comparing to smart cards, the GlobalPlatform Card Specifications [12] have worked on such a model and it is now widely deployed and accepted by all the stakeholders. This is why we propose

© IFIP International Federation for Information Processing 2015
R.N. Akram and S. Jajodia (Eds.): WISTP 2015, LNCS 9311, pp. 153–168, 2015.
DOI: 10.1007/978-3-319-24018-3_10

to study in which extent we can apply it for the TEE context: we identified the limitations of the GlobalPlatform Card model, in the TEE context, when the user wants to migrate its profile from one TEE to another one.

A user, who has many devices or gets a new one, shall be able to securely migrate his TEE profiles from a TEE to another compliant TEE. This problem of migration is currently poorly addressed by TEE implementations, standardization and only few papers have worked on designing TEE migration protocols [16,19]. Two main solutions can be considered: the straightforward solution, which consists in encrypting the profile (by TEE source), transferring it and decrypting it (by target TEE), or a Trusted Server based solution. These solutions present privacy weaknesses, as discussed in the next sections.

In this paper, we propose a new approach to transfer the TEE profiles from a TEE to another compliant TEE while preserving its privacy. For this purpose, we propose to organize the TEE into security domains (SD) with different roles and privileges.

This paper is organized as follows. In Section 2, we present the TEE technology and describe the problem of profile migration. Then, in Section 3, we describe the previous works and discuss how different are our objectives. We define our assumptions and requirements in Section 4. Then, in Section 5, we give a detailed description of our transfer protocol. Finally, in Section 7, we present the validation of our protocol and we conclude in Section 8.

2   Backgrounds and Problem Statement

A Trusted Execution Environment (TEE) is completely separated from the Rich Execution Environment (REE). It offers a way to isolate Trusted Applications (TAs) and provide secure functionalities such as cryptographic operations or secure PIN input. As defined by GlobalPlatform [14], three main TEE software components are involved: the trusted OS, the TAs and the hardware secure resources, e.g., trusted peripherals. The TAs can access the trusted resources and exchange with Secure Elements using a private API. From the REE, mobile applications can interact with TAs using public APIs. Additional details about TEEs can be found in [3,5].

Before using a service of the TEE, which is provided by a service provider, several steps should occur, as shown in Figure 1. (1) User enrollment: the user registers to the service provided by the SP, using a secure channel. This step allows to associate the user identity to a dedicated TA inside the device. (2) The TA is personalized inside the TEE by the SP. The necessary application in the REE is also installed. After this step, the service is active. (3) The user could acquire a new device and wish to *securely* transfer its TEE profiles from the first device to the new one. (4) The user may want to destroy its profile, also defined as *disabling* credentials [17].

In this article we focus on step 3, the migration of a TEE profile. Like step 1, step 3 can be threatened by an external attacker. If we suppose that an attacker may have compromised the rich OS or control the network connection

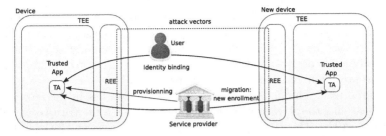

Fig. 1. The life cycle of a TEE service

of the smartphone, then the enrollment or migration steps become challenging tasks. Indeed, as shown in Figure 1, as the interactions with a TEE crosses the REE, the attacker may succeed to migrate the user's profile from a victim to the attacker's smartphone. This attack may succeed because the service provider has no insurance about the TEE security and the user-to-TEE binding. In the next section, we describe the solutions already proposed in the literature in order to show their limitations and motivate a new way of migrating TEE profiles.

3 Related Work

The first papers that studied the security of TEE credentials tried to guarantee its local (within the TEE) confidentiality and integrity. For instance in [2], authors proposed to protect TEE data using a unique PUF (Physical Unclonable Functions) AES encryption key for each device. In [18], authors proposed a TEE key attestation protocol proving that a TEE key has been generated inside the TEE and never left this TEE.

Later, scientists have been interested in the enrollment problem (mainly user-device binding) while assuming that there is no operator responsible for the management of the TEE. For instance, Marforio et al. [19] explained that the user's identity can be bound to the device using a password or a SMS or by collecting the device's IMEI. Unfortunately, an attacker that controls the Rich OS can intercept the protocol exchanges. Thus, Marforio et al. proposed some hardware and software modifications in order to secure the enrollment process. Others, like in [16], assumed that the smartphone is *safe* at the first use. This would enable to store a secret password in the TEE.

The problem of credential migration first appears for Trusted Platform Module (TPM), which is in some way the TEE ancestor. The commands of key migration have been specified in TPM specifications [21] and have undergone many improvements. Later, Sadeghi et al. [20] proposed a property based TPM virtualization in order to have a solution that supports software update and migration. The shortcoming of this solution consists in omitting the service provider during the virtual TPM migration. However, some credential migration requires service provider fresh and explicit agreement.

In the specific context of TEE, Kari et al. have proposed a credential migration protocol in open credential platforms [16]. They proposed to make the credential migration user-friendly based on delegated-automatic re-provisioning. The credentials are backup in clear in a trusted server. Then, the migration process is a re-provisioning from the backup, protected by a secret password only known by the user. The main weakness of this solution lies in the fact that its security, including to user's privacy, is entirely based on a the trustworthy of the trusted server (TS). This latter, as third party, has full access to TEE credentials and user's private data while it is not its owner or provisioner. This proposal implies privacy issues that we propose to solve with our protocol.

GlobalPlatform specifications related to smartcards have been interested in credential management in secure elements (smart cards). However, it seems that the credential privacy in some cases has been overlooked. In GlobalPlatform card specifications [12], the smart card is organized into fully isolated areas called Security Domains (SD). There are a root security domain called ISD for Issuer Security Domain and many Supplementary Security Domains (SSDs) for the different Service Providers. Let us call SPSD the security domain for a given SP. For instance, the ISD could be owned by the Mobile Network Operator (MNO) and the SPSD could be owned by a bank. Once, the SPSD created, there are two modes to manage the content of this SPSD: either directly from SP to SPSD, or through ISD. In the first case, the credential migration process would be naturally implemented in the application of the SP within the smart card: encryption with the target public key, transfer and decryption, provided that the MNO initiates the SP space in the target smart card. In the second case, the MNO plays the role of firewall and proxy for the SPSD without having access to the content between SP and its SSD (SPSD). SPSDs do not have any code enabling to perform a credential transfer.

If we adopt the first model for the TEE, the TEE profile migration would be processed like in the smart card: the TEE profile migration process would be naturally implemented in the TA of the SP: encryption with the target public TEE key, transfer and decryption, provided that the TEE admin - MNO initiates the SP space in the target TEE. As a consequence, each service provider would have to implement a migration process for its service.

If we adopt the second model for the TEE, TEE admin will serve as the single entry point to transfer point-to-point credentials: implementing the migration process would imply privacy issues similarly to the Kari et al. [16] solution. TEE admin would have full access to the SP credentials and user's data in order to encrypt and transfer it. In this paper, we propose a new migration protocol, while adopting the second model, where the TEE Admin plays the role of proxy without having access to SP credentials. We consider the following properties:

- As trusted application profile contains credentials and also personal data (statistics, usage data of the service), during the migration, the profile shall be accessible only by legitimate entities: the SP and the user;
- A special third party, the TEE admin should be responsible of the role of installation, deletion and migration of trusted profiles;

– The trusted application of the SP should not contain any code dedicated to the migration protocol. All the migration software components should be handled by the TEE admin.

4 Attacker Model and Requirements

We assume that the enrollment, provisioning and personalization processes are already achieved: the trusted application is provisioned to the TEE and has access to its credentials and the user's personal data. By the profile, we mean the credentials (allowing the access to the service) and private data (related to personalization and the use of application/service).

We consider three different actors: the user (the devices' owner), the Service Provider (e.g. the bank) and a TEE admin (e.g., Mobile Network Operator or smartphone manufacturer). We consider the following attacker model:

A1: Communication control. We consider that we have a Dolev-Yao [11] attacker model: an attacker has full control over communication channels.

A2: TEE control. We consider that TEEs are enough resistant to physical attacks according the Protection Profile proposed by GlobalPlatform [13] which is EAL2+ certified.

A3: REE control. Given the possible vulnerabilities of the rich OS, we assume that an attacker can compromise the REE of a user's device.

A4: Entities control and trustworthy. We assume that (i) an attacker cannot spoof the SP, cannot compromise its dedicated spaces within the TEE and the SP is honest, (ii) an attacker cannot spoof the TEE Admin and cannot compromise its dedicated spaces within the TEE, however the TEE Admin can be honest-but-curious and, (iii) the user is honest.

While keeping in view the above discussions, we define the security requirements that a migration protocol shall meet as follow:

R1: Integrity. During the migration process, the integrity of the TEE profile should be ensured. For a given profile, only the user and the relevant service provider should be able to eventually modify the profile content.

R2: Confidentiality. During the migration process, the confidentiality of the TEE profile should be ensured. For a given profile, only the user and the relevant service provider should be able to eventually read the profile content.

5 TEE Migration Protocol

Considering the previous requirements, attacker model, and the GlobalPlatform Card Specifications [12], we introduce a new approach for deploying services in a TEE where: TAs of a service provider are hosted in a Security Domain (SD) and a new actor, called TEE admin, has a special SD and implements the migration functionalities. With such a new software architecture, we build a protocol that allows to securely transfer a TEE profile from one device to another one.

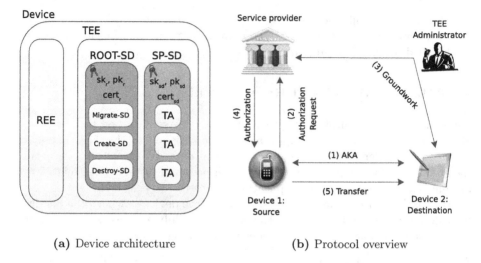

(a) Device architecture   **(b)** Protocol overview

Fig. 2. Architecture and protocol overview

5.1   Architecture Overview

We organize the TEE into Security Domains (SD) [12]. Every SD can contain one or many Trusted Applications (TA) from the same Service Provider. A SD is a fully isolated zone. This functionality could be ensured by memory protection mechanisms, firewall functionalities, data isolation techniques implemented at OS level of the TEE, such as the ones used for Linux systems (SELinux, AppArmor,...). For example, in the commercialized TEE solution of Trustsonic, such an architecture can be implemented using containers. A SD manipulates cryptographic keys which are completely separated from any other SD. These keys enable code execution integrity, credentials and user's private data integrity and confidentiality when using a service. Consequently, a SD must not cipher his credentials or user's private data using any external keys whatever is the case, e.g., transfer. We define two types of SD, represented in Figure 2a: (1) SD without management rights (many per TEE): SP-SD (in green). They contain the trusted applications of a service provider. (2) SD with management rights (only one per TEE): ROOT-SD (in orange). It is responsible of creating and deleting SDs, downloading and installing packages in SDs, and also migrating SDs from a TEE to another compliant TEE.

5.2   Protocol Overview

In order to migrate a TEE profile from a source device to a target one, the user gets the two devices nearby each other in order to establish a wireless communication, such as NFC or bluetooth. Then, the user starts the migration application, noted Migrate-SD in Figure 2a, within the ROOT-SD of the TEE source. In order to do this, the user must be authenticated in both source and target

TEEs. Owing to the authentication procedure, the TEEs check that only the user enrolled by the TEE admin can start the migration process. This authentication can be done through the "Trusted User Interface" [15], or by using the password or the pin code setup at the enrollment phase, or by using a biometry peripheral if available. The next steps of the protocol that involve the two TEEs are presented in Figure 2b and described in the following.

Step 1. An authenticated key agreement takes place between the ROOT-SD of TEE source and the ROOT-SD of target TEE. This prevents the TEE source from disclosing critical information to a malicious environment and prevents the target TEE from accepting malicious data.

Step 2. The TEE source requires a migration authorization from all service providers that have a SD within the TEE source. If a service provider does not agree with the migration of his relevant SD, the migration cannot take place. The migration authorization is temporary and unique per pair of devices, per transfer and per service provider. Indeed, the authorization is related to the date and time of the request that has been initiated. Thus, it is valid only for a given period of time.

Step 3. At that time starts the groundwork for the authorization. First, the service provider checks with the TEE admin whether the target TEE is stated compromised. Then, the service provider checks that the target TEE is not already a client containing a service provider SD. Finally, the service provider asks the TEE admin to set up a specific SD within target TEE, and updates the SD credentials in order to be the unique master of this SD.

Step 4. Finally, the service provider replies to the TEE source with the authorization and necessary migration credentials. The authorization consists of a service provider signature proving his agreement regarding the migration of his SD. The credentials consist of a re-encryption key [8,9]. Using this re-encryption key, the Migrate-SD application will be able to perform the transfer without having access to SD profile. In order to send source profile to the target SD, the source SD provides its profile, encrypted with its public key, to the TA, Migrate-SD, that should re-encrypt it with the re-encryption key. In such a case, even if the TEE Admin is honest-but-curious, it cannot eavesdrop the SD profile.

Step 5. The target TEE must check the validity of the received authorization. At this time, the migration can start.

5.3   TEE Profile Migration Protocol

In the following, we introduce the notations and cryptographic keys used in our protocol. Later, we detail the phases of our protocol: Authenticated key agreement, Service Provider authorization and TEE Profile migration.

Cryptographic Keys and Notations. We denote $(sk_{src}, pk_{src}, cert_{src})$ (resp. $(sk_{tgt}, pk_{tgt}, cert_{tgt})$) the TEE private root key and the certified TEE public root key of the source (resp. target) ROOT-SD. These keys are used to authenticate the TEE and set up a key session with an authenticated TEE. A TEE admin is characterized by a private and public key pair (sk_{Admin}, pk_{Admin}).

Enc(pk, M)   : The encryption of the message M using the public key pk.
MAC(sk, M) : The Message Authenticated Code (MAC) of the message M using the key sk.
$Signature_A$: The signature on the message sent with the signature using the private key of A.
Verify(pk, σ) : The verification of the signature σ using the public key pk corresponding to private
key sk used during the signature generation.

Fig. 3. Cryptographic notations

It controls the ROOT-SD and certifies TEE root keys. A Security Domain SP-SD is characterized by a root keys set (sk_{sd}, pk_{sd}, $cert_{sd}$). This is an encryption keys set that enables to securely store SD profile. We denote $SP - SD_{src}$ (resp. $SP - SD_{tgt}$) the service provider SD within TEE source (resp. target TEE). Consequently, the tuple ($sk_{SP-SD_{src}}$, $pk_{SP-SD_{src}}$, $cert_{SP-SD_{src}}$) (resp. the tuple ($sk_{SP-SD_{tgt}}$, $pk_{SP-SD_{tgt}}$, $cert_{SP-SD_{tgt}}$)) is the root keys set of $SP - SD_{src}$ (resp. $SP - SD_{tgt}$). A service provider is characterized by (sk_{sp}, pk_{sp}) and a unique identifier ID_{SP}. It provides the security domains root keys and is responsible of the re-encryption key and transfer authorization generation. The notations for the different cryptographic primitives are defined in Figure 3.

Authenticated Key Agreement. The authenticated key agreement (AKA, step 1 in Figure 2b) occurs in order to establish a secure session between two TEEs after a mutual authentication. The AKA can be a password based key agreement [1] or a public key authenticated Key agreement [10] and must be a two ways authentication. In the first case, we can use the password or PIN or biometric data introduced by the user during the authentication phase and in the second case, we can use the TEEs root keys. At the end of this phase, the source and target TEEs will share a couple of ephemeral keys (eK_t, eK_m) to secure the migration. eK_t is the private session key, whereas eK_m is used for MAC computations.

Service Provider Authorization. The TEE source requires a migration authorization from all service providers having trusted applications within the TEE source (step 2 in Figure 2b). This protocol is described in Figure 4. For the sake of simplicity, we consider only one service provider.

(1) The migration application within $ROOT - SD_{src}$ sends the request $INIT\_RQ$ with its signature noted $Signature_{ROOT-SD_{src}}$ to the service provider through the TEE admin. The request includes the identity of the service provider (ID_{SP}), the public key of $SP - SD_{src}$ ($pk_{SP-SD_{src}}$) and the certified TEE public root keys of source and target TEE ($cert_{src}$, $cert_{tgt}$). (2) When receiving the request, TEE admin checks the certificates ($cert_{src}$, $cert_{tgt}$), the signature and freshness of the request and a timestamp ($Signature_{ROOT-SD_{src}}$)[1]. It should also check whether source or target TEE are compromised[2] for example using the remote attestation protocols of Baiardi et al. [6]. (3) If checks are successful, the TEE admin transmits the request ($INIT$) to the relevant service provider based on the ID_{SP} received within the request.

---

[1] TEE implementations like TrustZone offer access to trusted clocks for this usage.

[2] This is already the case for SIM card where MNOs checks if a SIM has been revoked.

(4) With the received request, the service provider checks if the TEE source (resp. target TEE) has (resp. has not) an associated SP-SD by checking if $cert_{src}$ (resp. $cert_{tgt}$) is registered in its database. Then, (5) the service provider inquires TEE admin to create a SP-SD within the recipient TEE via the $SD - Create\_RQ(cert_{tgt})$ command. (6) The TEE admin signs the command (the signature $Signature_{TEE_{Admin}}$ is performed on the command and a times-tamp) and forwards it to the trusted application $Create - SD_{tgt}$ in order to create $SP - SD_{tgt}$. (7, 8, 9, 10). The creation is acknowledged by Ack and $Param$ that are returned to the service provider (through the TEE Admin) in order to let him be able to personalize $SP - SD_{tgt}$, as done classically when personalizing TEE security domains. (11) Once the $SP - SD_{tgt}$ installed, the service provider proceeds to the update of $SP - SD_{tgt}$ credentials in order to have the exclusive control over $SP - SD_{tgt}$ [12].

Finally, the service provider generates the migration authorization. It consists of a re-encryption key K_{proxy} and a signature $PERM$. The signature $PERM$ is computed on the SP identifier ID_{SP}, source and target TEE public keys as well as a timestamp: $PERM = \{ID_{SP}, cert_{src}, cert_{tgt}, TimeStamp\}_{sk_{SP}}$. The re-encryption key K_{proxy} is used to re-encrypt the $SD - SP_{src}$ content such that the result will be understandable only by $SP - SD_{tgt}$: $K_{proxy} = rekeygen(pk_{SP-SD_{tgt}}, sk_{SP-SD_{src}})$. In the literature [8,9], K_{proxy} is called a proxy key. (12, 13) The authorization is sent to the TEE Admin who signs it and transmits it (with its signature) to $ROOT - SD_{src}$.

TEE Profile Migration. Using the re-encryption key, the confidentiality and integrity of the migration phase is guaranteed. Any outsider cannot eaves-drop the $SP - SD_{src}$ profile and a honest-but-curious TEE Admin has no visi-bility about the $SP - SD_{src}$ profile. The migration occurs as follows.

As described in Figure 5, $Migrate - SD_{src}$ re-encrypts the protected profile of $SP - SD_{src}$ (P) using the proxy key K_{proxy} to obtain the cipher A. Only $SP - SD_{tgt}$ is able to decrypt A. Afterwards, $Migrate - SD_{src}$ computes B and C. B is the encryption of A and the identifier of the service provider owning $SP - SD_{src}$ (ID_{SP}) using the transfer key eK_t. Regarding C, it is the MAC of A and ID_{SP} using eK_m. At the end of these computations, $Migrate - SD_{src}$ sends A, B, C and $PERM$ to $Migrate - SD_{tgt}$. that proceeds to the verifications of $PERM$ and C. The verification of $PERM$ corresponds to the verification of a signature, its freshness and that its parameters contain the right $cert_{src}$ and $cert_{tgt}$. Next, $Migrate - SD_{tgt}$ decrypts B in order to retrieve A and ID_{SP}. Based on the retrieved ID_{SP}, $Migrate - SD_{tgt}$ transmits A to $SP - SD_{tgt}$.

When the migration finishes, we have two possibilities. On the one hand, the security policy of the service admits to conserve the TEE profile in the source. In such a case, $Migrate - SD_{tgt}$ simply acknowledges that the TEE profile migration is completed successfully (*Signed Ack*). On the other hand, the security policy of the service admits to conserve only one profile. The TEE profile in the source should be destroyed. In order to ensure a fair exchange, exchanges between $Migrate - SD_{src}$ and $Migrate - SD_{tgt}$ must be performed via the service provider. $Migrate - SD_{tgt}$ acknowledges that the TEE profile

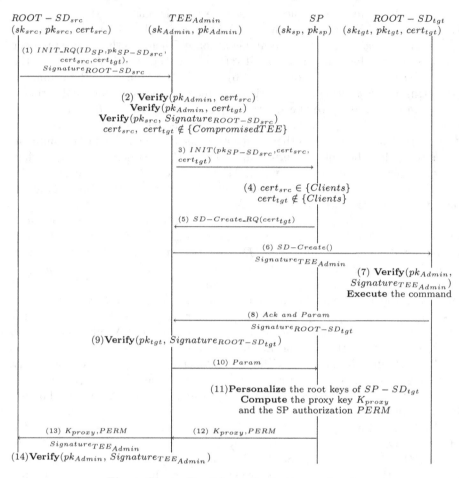

Fig. 4. Service Provider authorization protocol

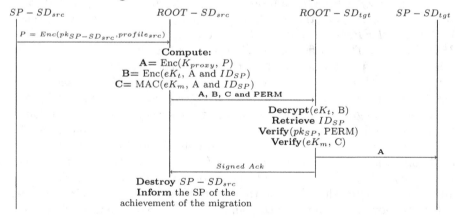

Fig. 5. Profile migration protocol

migration is completed successfully (*Signed Ack*). At this time, $Migrate-SD_{src}$ asks the trusted application $Destroy - SD_{src}$ to destroy the SD corresponding to ID_{SP}. When the operation finishes, $Migrate - SD_{src}$ informs the service provider that the transfer is accomplished. Hence, the service provider will not consider any more TEE source as a client and revoke its corresponding keys.

5.4   Performance Remarks

As current TEE implementation does not give access to low level cryptographic primitives we cannot implement the whole protocol. To give an idea of performances, the reader should note that TEEs exploit the CPU of the smartphone with an amount of RAM of some MBs. Thus performance are comparable with what can be obtained in the Rich OS. For example, a RSA computation is achieved in 20 ms on a Galaxy SIII smartphone. Our reencryption scheme needs lower than a RSA computation: we measured, on a Galaxy SIII a reencryption time of about 4 ms.

6   Security Analysis

User Identification. During a TEE profile migration, it is important to ensure that the target TEE (target device) belongs to the owner of the source TEE (source device). In our model, this is guaranteed by the concept of demonstrative identification [7]. Indeed, we proposed to run the migration protocol over a wireless proximity technology (NFC).

Requirements Analysis. During the migration, an outsider or a curious TEE Admin must not be able to read or modify the transferred TEE profile (R1, R2). This is ensured by using the cryptographic re-encryption method. Indeed, the migration authorization, delivered by the service provider, consists of two components: K_{proxy} and $PERM$. $PERM$ is a signature computed by the service provider on $(ID_{SP}, cert_{src}, cert_{tgt}, timeStamp)$. An attacker would not be able to replay this authorization because of the timestamp. Moreover, the transfer process would fail if $cert_{src}$ (resp. $cert_{tgt}$) does not correspond to the certified root public key used by source TEE (resp. target) during the AKA phase. Regarding the re-encryption key K_{proxy}, it is computed based on the private key of the source SD and the public key of the target SD. This means that a cipher text of source SD, if encrypted using K_{proxy}, will be converted to a cipher text of target SD. Thus, only source SD, target SD and the service provider have access (read / modify) to the TEE profile. If the re-encryption key K_{proxy} is improperly computed, the attacker cannot get the TEE profile content.

TEE Admin Trustworthy. Besides the cryptographic solution, our approach relies on the trustworthy of the TEE Admin. We assume that a TEE Admin can only be honest-but-curious and not malicious (compromised). Indeed, a malicious TEE Admin can get access to service provider credentials and user's private data. However, we estimate that the assumption of a honest-but-curious TEE Admin is reasonable. This is because a malicious TEE Admin (when detected) risks not only huge financial damages but also his reputation. Knowing that this role should be played by the device manufacturer or the mobile network operator. In our opinion, this risk is far from being taken.

7 Protocol Validation

We validated our protocol using the AVISPA [4] tool web interface. AVISPA is an automated tool for the validation of security protocols. It takes as input a protocol modelled in High-Level Protocol Specification Language (HLPSL). This latter is translated into Intermediate Format (IF) and forwarded to the back-end analyser tools.

In Appendix A, we show (the core subset of) our migration protocol model written in HLPSL. In this validation model, we mainly focused on Service Provider authorization protocol (Figure 4) and Profile transfer protocol (Figure 5). Therefore, we assumed that the user authentication and AKA steps have been successfully achieved. Moreover, for the sake of simplicity, we did not consider the $SP - SD_{tgt}$ root key personalization.

We modeled our transfer protocol into six roles in addition to two standard roles (i.e. "session" and "environment"). First, the role "sdSrc" (resp. "sdTgt") refers to the $SP-SD_{src}$ (resp. $SP-SD_{tgt}$). Then, the role "src" (resp. "tgt") represents the Migration TA within TEE source (resp. target TEE). At last, "teeAdmin" and "sp" respectively correspond to the entities TEE admin and Service Provider. Every role is modelled into a state transition system. A state represents the reception and/or the transmission of a message from our protocol. For instance, "State = 0" in the role "teeAdmin" corresponds to the reception of $INIT\_RQ$ by the TEE administrator in Figure 4. Regarding the role called "session", it represents a single session of our protocol where all the other roles are instantiated.

All the roles communicate over Dolev-Yao [11] channels (channel(dy)), i.e., an adversary can fully control the communication channels (A1). The attacker knowledge is defined by the set of constants or variables of the intruder_knowledge set in the main role (environment) (A2, A3). Then, the intruder actions are modeled by the combination of several sessions where the intruder may take part of the sessions running. On the subject of our protocol, besides the initialization of intruder_knowledge, we modeled our attacker by the variable i (i for intruder) such that he can play the role of a honest-but-curious TEE Admin (Line 125) or a honest-but-curious Migration TA in the source (Line 123) or target TEEs (Line 124) (A4-ii). Finally, we note that the attacker i did not compromise the SP nor its SDs (A4-i) because the roles "sdsrc", "sdtgt" and "spagent" are not played by the attacker in the initialized sessions (Lines 122, 123, 124, 125).

The migration authorization, delivered by the service provider, consists of two components: K_{proxy} and $PERM$. $PERM$ is a signature computed by the SP on $(ID_{SP}, cert_{src}, cert_{tgt}, timeStamp)$. Regarding K_{proxy}, it is not a standard cryptographic tool. Thus, AVISPA does not have its predefined predicate. Our model must manually put up all its features. We designed the proxy re-encryption concept owing to the predicate $\wedge$equal({EncSD}_KProxy, {SDCred}_PKSDtgt) at the end of the role "sdSrc". This predicate models the equality between "the encryption of EncSD (the encryption of SDCred using the public key of the source SD) using the proxy key" and "the encryption of SDCred using the public key of the target SD". If this equality does not hold, it means that K_{proxy} is a fake key from an attacker which should be assimilated to a denied authorization of the SP.

The HLPSL language provides four predicates to model security requirements. The predicate secret(E, id, S) declares the information E as secret shared by the agents of set S. This security goal will be identified by id in the goal section. In addition, witness, request and wreuqest are used to model authentication goals. Regarding the security requirements R1 (integrity) and R2 (confidentiality with respect to outsiders and a curious TEE Admin), we defined them in one goal owing to the predicate secret(SDCred, transfer, {SDsrc, SP, SDtgt}) at the end of the role "sdSrc". This predicate expresses that the content of an SD should remain secret between the SD of TEE source, the service provider and the SD of the target TEE.

We successfully validated our protocol with two AVISPA back-ends (AtSe and SATMC). The AtSe back-end extracts attacks that defeat the security properties by translating the model in constraints on the adversary's knowledge. Using a unification algorithm it integrates at each step of the protocol the new constraints. As our protocol is loop free, the search of possible attacks is complete. Regarding the SATMC back-end, it translates the protocol in propositional formulas that can feed an off-the-shelf SAT solver.

8   Conclusion

In this paper, we have introduced a TEE architecture based on security domains. The root security domain is controlled by the TEE admin and the other security domains isolate the service providers trusted applications. With such an architecture, we have proposed a practical and privacy-preserving TEE profile migration protocol. This protocol requires the dynamic interaction of the service provider and the TEE admin. Owing to the security and functional characteristics of the used re-encryption method, the integrity and the confidentiality of the TEE profile, with respect to external attackers and TEE Admin, are guaranteed. Finally, we successfully validated our protocol using the AVISPA tool.

References

1. Coron, J.-S., Gouget, A., Icart, T., Paillier, P.: Supplemental access control (PACE v2): security analysis of PACE integrated mapping. In: Naccache, D. (ed.) Cryphtography and Security: From Theory to Applications. LNCS, vol. 6805, pp. 207–232. Springer, Heidelberg (2012)
2. Areno, M., Plusquellic, J.: Securing trusted execution environments with PUF generated secret keys. In: 11th International Conference on Trust, Security and Privacy in Computing and Communications, Liverpool, England, UK, pp. 1188–1193. IEEE Computer Society, June 2012

3. Arfaoui, G., Gharout, S., Traoré, J.: Trusted execution environments: a look under the hood. In: 2nd IEEE International Conference on Mobile Cloud Computing, Services, and Engineering (MobileCloud), Oxford, UK, pp. 259–266. IEEE Computer Society, April 2014

4. Armando, A., Basin, D., Boichut, Y., Chevalier, Y., Compagna, L., Cuellar, J., Drielsma, P.H., Heám, P.C., Kouchnarenko, O., Mantovani, J., Mödersheim, S., von Oheimb, D., Rusinowitch, M., Santiago, J., Turuani, M., Viganò, L., Vigneron, L.: The AVISPA tool for the automated validation of internet security protocols and applications. In: Etessami, K., Rajamani, S.K. (eds.) CAV 2005. LNCS, vol. 3576, pp. 281–285. Springer, Heidelberg (2005)

5. Asokan, N., Ekberg, J.E., Kostiainen, K.: The untapped potential of trusted execution environments on mobile devices. IEEE Security And Privacy 12(4), 293–294 (2013)

6. Baiardi, F., Cilea, D., Sgandurra, D., Ceccarelli, F.: Measuring semantic integrity for remote attestation. In: Chen, L., Mitchell, C.J., Martin, A. (eds.) Trust 2009. LNCS, vol. 5471, pp. 81–100. Springer, Heidelberg (2009)

7. Balfanz, D., Smetters, D.K., Stewart, P., Wong, H.C.: Talking to strangers: Authentication in ad-hoc wireless networks. In: Network and Distributed System Security Symposium, San Diego, California, USA. The Internet Society (2002)

8. Blaze, M., Bleumer, G., Strauss, M.J.: Divertible protocols and atomic proxy cryptography. In: Nyberg, K. (ed.) EUROCRYPT 1998. LNCS, vol. 1403, pp. 127–144. Springer, Heidelberg (1998)

9. Canard, S., Devigne, J., Laguillaumie, F.: Improving the security of an efficient unidirectional proxy re-encryption scheme. Journal of Internet Services and Information Security (JISIS) 1(2/3), 140–160 (2011)

10. Coron, J.-S., Gouget, A., Paillier, P., Villegas, K.: SPAKE: a single-party public-key authenticated key exchange protocol for contact-less applications. In: Sion, R., Curtmola, R., Dietrich, S., Kiayias, A., Miret, J.M., Sako, K., Sebé, F. (eds.) RLCPS, WECSR, and WLC 2010. LNCS, vol. 6054, pp. 107–122. Springer, Heidelberg (2010)

11. Dolev, D., Yao, A.C.: On the security of public key protocols. In: 22Nd Annual Symposium on Foundations of Computer Science, SFCS 1981, Nashville, USA, pp. 350–357. IEEE Computer Society (1981)

12. GlobalPlatform Card technology. Card specification - v2.2.1, January 2011

13. GlobalPlatform Device Committee. TEE protection profile version 1.2, public release, gpd_spe_021, November 2014

14. GlobalPlatform Device technology. TEE system architecture, v1.0, December 2011

15. GlobalPlatform Device technology. Trusted user interface API, v1.0, June 2013

16. Kostiainen, K., Asokan, N., Afanasyeva, A.: Towards user-friendly credential transfer on open credential platforms. In: Lopez, J., Tsudik, G. (eds.) ACNS 2011. LNCS, vol. 6715, pp. 395–412. Springer, Heidelberg (2011)

17. Kostiainen, K., Asokan, N., Ekberg, J.-E.: Credential disabling from trusted execution environments. In: Aura, T., Järvinen, K., Nyberg, K. (eds.) NordSec 2010. LNCS, vol. 7127, pp. 171–186. Springer, Heidelberg (2012)

18. Kostiainen, K., Dmitrienko, A., Ekberg, J.-E., Sadeghi, A.-R., Asokan, N.: Key attestation from trusted execution environments. In: Acquisti, A., Smith, S.W., Sadeghi, A.-R. (eds.) TRUST 2010. LNCS, vol. 6101, pp. 30–46. Springer, Heidelberg (2010)

19. Marforio, C., Karapanos, N., Soriente, C., Kostiainen, K., Capkun, S.: Secure enrollment and practical migration for mobile trusted execution environments. In: Third ACM Workshop on Security and Privacy in Smartphones & Mobile Devices, Berlin, Germany, pp. 93–98. ACM Press, November 2013
20. Sadeghi, A.-R., Stüble, C., Winandy, M.: Property-based TPM virtualization. In: Wu, T.-C., Lei, C.-L., Rijmen, V., Lee, D.-T. (eds.) ISC 2008. LNCS, vol. 5222, pp. 1–16. Springer, Heidelberg (2008)
21. Trusted Computing Group. TPM main specification (2015). http://www. trustedcomputinggroup.org/resources/tpm_main_specification

A   Our Transfer Protocol in HLPSL

```
 1  role sdSrc (SrcTEE, SDsrc, SDtgt, SP: agent,
 2                PKSrcTEE, PKSDsrc, PKSDtgt, PKSP: public_key,
 3                SDCred: text,
 4                SND, RCV: channel (dy))
 5      played_by SDsrc def=
 6      local
 7          State: nat,
 8          EncSD: text,
 9          KProxy: public_key
10      init State:=0
11      transition
12      0.State=0 /\ RCV(start) =|> EncSD':={SDCred}_PKSDsrc /\ State':=1
13      1.State=1 =|> SND(EncSD)
14      /\ secret(SDCred,transfer,{SDsrc, SP, SDtgt})
15      /\ equal({EncSD}_KProxy, {SDCred}_PKSDtgt)
16  end role
17
18  role src (SrcTEE, SDsrc, TgtTEE, TEEAdmin, SP: agent,
19                PKSrcTEE, PKSDsrc, PKTgtTEE, PKTEEAdmin, PKSP : public_key,
20                SK : symmetric_key,
21                SND, RCV: channel (dy))
22      played_by SrcTEE def=
23      local
24          State : nat,
25          TimeStamp,EncSD: text,
26          Ack: message,
27          KProxy: public_key
28      init State := 0
29      transition
30      0.State = 0 /\ RCV(EncSD) =|> State':= 1 /\ TimeStamp':= new()/\SND(SrcTEE.
                TEEAdmin.PKSP.PKSDsrc. PKSrcTEE. PKTgtTEE.{PKSP. PKSDsrc. PKSrcTEE.
                PKTgtTEE.TimeStamp'}_inv(PKSrcTEE))
31      1.State= 1 /\ RCV(SrcTEE.TEEAdmin.KProxy.{PKSP.PKSrcTEE. PKTgtTEE}_inv(PKSP)
                .{KProxy.{ PKSP.PKSrcTEE. PKTgtTEE. TimeStamp}_inv(PKSP)}_inv(
                PKTEEAdmin)) =|> State':= 2
32      2.State=2/\SND(SrcTEE.TgtTEE.{{EncSD}_KProxy.PKSP}_SK) =|> RCV({SrcTEE.
                TgtTEE.Ack.TimeStamp}_SK)
33  end role
34
35  role teeAdmin (SrcTEE, TgtTEE, TEEAdmin, SP: agent,
36                PKSrcTEE, PKTgtTEE, PKTEEAdmin, PKSP: public_key,
37                SND, RCV: channel (dy))
38      played_by TEEAdmin def=
39      local
40          State : nat,
41          SDCreate, Param, Ack: message,
42          TimeStamp: text,
43          PKSDsrc, KProxy: public_key
44      init State := 0
45      transition
46      0.State=0 /\ RCV(TEEAdmin.SrcTEE.PKSP.PKSDsrc.PKSrcTEE.PKTgtTEE.{PKSP.
                PKSDsrc.PKSrcTEE. PKTgtTEE.TimeStamp}_inv(PKSrcTEE))=|> State':= 1 /\ SND
                (TEEAdmin.SP.PKSDsrc.PKSrcTEE. PKTgtTEE)
47      1.State=1 /\ RCV(TEEAdmin.SP .SDCreate .PKTgtTEE) =|> State':=2 /\ TimeStamp':=
                new()/\SND(TEEAdmin. TgtTEE. SDCreate. {SDCreate.TimeStamp'}_inv(
                PKTEEAdmin))
48      2.State=2 /\RCV(TEEAdmin. TgtTEE.Ack.Param.{ Ack.Param.TimeStamp}_inv(PKTgtTEE
                )) =|> State':=3 /\ SND(TEEAdmin.SP.Param)
49      3.State=3 /\RCV(TEEAdmin.SP.KProxy.{PKSP.PKSrcTEE. PKTgtTEE. TimeStamp}_inv(
                PKSP))=|> SND(TEEAdmin.SP.KProxy.{ PKSP.PKSrcTEE. PKTgtTEE.
                TimeStamp}_inv(PKSP).{ KProxy.{PKSP.PKSrcTEE. PKTgtTEE.TimeStamp}_inv(
                PKSP)}_inv(PKTEEAdmin))
50  end role
51
52  role sp(TEEAdmin, SP: agent,
53          PKTEEAdmin, PKSP: public_key,
54          SND, RCV: channel (dy))
55      played_by SP def=
```

```
56    local
57        State : nat,
58        SDCreate, Param: message,
59        TimeStamp: text,
60        PKSrcTEE, PKTgtTEE, PKSDsrc, PKSDtgt, KProxy: public_key
61    init State := 0
62    transition
63    0.State=0 /\ RCV(SP.TEEAdmin.PKSDsrc.PKSrcTEE.PKTgtTEE) =|> State':=1 /\ SND(
          SP.TEEAdmin.SDCreate.PKTgtTEE)
64    1.State=1/\RCV(Param) =|> TimeStamp':=new()/\PKSDtgt':=new()/\ KProxy':=new()/\
          SND(KProxy'.{PKSP.PKSrcTEE.PKTgtTEE.TimeStamp'}_inv(PKSP))
65    end role
66
67    role tgt(SrcTEE, TgtTEE, TEEAdmin, SDTgt: agent,
68            PKTgtTEE, PKTEEAdmin, PKSP, PKSDtgt: public_key,
69            SK : symmetric_key,
70            SND, RCV: channel (dy))
71    played_by TgtTEE def=
72    local
73        State : nat,
74        TimeStamp, EncSD: text,
75        SDCreate, Ack, Param: message,
76        KProxy: public_key
77    init State := 0
78    transition
79    0.State=0/\RCV(TgtTEE.TEEAdmin.SDCreate.{SDCreate.TimeStamp}_inv(PKTEEAdmin))
          =|> State':=1/\TimeStamp':=new()/\SND(TgtTEE.TEEAdmin.Ack.Param.{Ack.
          Param.TimeStamp'}_inv(PKTgtTEE))
80    1.State=1/\RCV(TgtTEE.SrcTEE.{{EncSD}_KProxy.PKSP}_SK)=|>State':=2/\TimeStamp
          ':=new()/\SND(TgtTEE.SrcTEE.{Ack.TimeStamp'}_SK)
81    2.State=2 =|>SND(TgtTEE.SDTgt.{EncSD}_KProxy)
82    end role
83
84    role sdTgt(TgtTEE, SDTgt: agent,
85            PKTgtTEE, PKSDsrc, PKSDtgt: public_key,
86            SND, RCV: channel (dy))
87    played_by SDTgt def=
88    local
89        State: nat,
90        EncSD: text,
91        KProxy: public_key
92    init State:=0
93    transition
94    0.State= 0 =|> RCV({EncSD}_KProxy)
95    end role
96
97    role session(SDsrc, SDtgt, SrcTEE, TgtTEE, TEEAdmin, SP: agent,
98            PKSDsrc,PKSDtgt,PKSrcTEE,PKTgtTEE,PKTEEAdmin,PKSP: public_key,
99            SK : symmetric_key,
100           SDCred: text)
101   def=
102   local S0, R0, S1, R1, S2, R2, S3, R3, S4, R4, S5, R5 : channel (dy)
103   composition
104   sdSrc (SrcTEE, SDsrc, SDtgt, SP, PKSrcTEE, PKSDsrc, PKSDtgt, PKSP, SDCred, S0, R0)
105   /\ src (SrcTEE, SDsrc, TgtTEE, TEEAdmin, SP, PKSrcTEE, PKSDsrc, PKTgtTEE,
          PKTEEAdmin, PKSP, SK, S1, R1)
106   /\ teeAdmin (SrcTEE, TgtTEE, TEEAdmin, SP, PKSrcTEE, PKTgtTEE, PKTEEAdmin,
          PKSP,S2, R2)
107   /\ sp (TEEAdmin, SP, PKTEEAdmin, PKSP, S3, R3)
108   /\ tgt (SrcTEE, TgtTEE, TEEAdmin, SDtgt, PKTgtTEE, PKTEEAdmin, PKSP, PKSDtgt,
          SK, S4, R4)
109   /\ sdTgt(TgtTEE, SDtgt, PKTgtTEE, PKSDsrc, PKSDtgt, S5, R5)
110   end role
111
112   role environment()
113   def=
114   const
115       sdsrc, sdtgt, srctee, tgttee, teeadmin, spagent, i: agent,
116       pksdsrc,pksdtgt,pksrctee,pktgttee,pkteeadmin,pksp,ki: public_key,
117       sk: symmetric_key,
118       transfer : protocol_id,
119       sdcred: text
120   intruder_knowledge={pksrctee, pktgttee, pkteeadmin, pksp, ki, inv(ki)}
121   composition
122   session(sdsrc, sdtgt, srctee, tgttee, teeadmin, spagent, pksdsrc, pksdtgt, pksrctee, pktgttee,
          pkteeadmin, pksp, sk, sdcred)
123   /\ session(sdsrc, sdtgt, i, tgttee, teeadmin, spagent, pksdsrc, pksdtgt, pksrctee, pktgttee,
          pkteeadmin, pksp, sk, sdcred)
124   /\ session(sdsrc, sdtgt, srctee, i, teeadmin, spagent, pksdsrc, pksdtgt, pksrctee, pktgttee,
          pkteeadmin, pksp, sk, sdcred)
125   /\ session(sdsrc, sdtgt, srctee, tgttee, i, spagent, pksdsrc, pksdtgt, pksrctee, pktgttee,
          pkteeadmin, pksp, sk, sdcred)
126   end role
127
128   goal
129       secrecy_of transfer
130   end goal
131
132   environment()
```

Randomizing the Montgomery Powering Ladder

Duc-Phong Le[1], Chik How Tan[1], and Michael Tunstall[2]([⊠])

[1] Temasek Laboratories, National University of Singapore,
5A Engineering Drive 1, #09-02, Singapore 117411, Singapore
{tslld,tsltch}@nus.edu.sg
[2] Rambus Cryptography Research Division,
425 Market Street, 11th Floor, San Francisco, CA 94105, USA
michael.tunstall@cryptography.com

Abstract. In this paper, we present novel randomized techniques to enhance Montgomery powering ladder. The proposed techniques increase the resistance against side-channel attacks and especially recently published correlation collision attacks in the horizontal setting. The first of these operates by randomly changing state such that the difference between registers varies, unpredictably, between two states. The second algorithm takes a random walk, albeit tightly bounded, along the possible addition chains required to compute an exponentiation. We also generalize the Montgomery powering ladder and present randomized (both left-to-right and right-to-left) m-ary exponentiation algorithms.

Keywords: Montgomery powering ladder · Side-channel analysis · Countermeasures

1 Introduction

Side-channel analysis is one of the most serious threats to the security of a given implementation of a cryptographic algorithm. In the traditional model, a given cryptographic algorithm is typically proven secure against various attacks under assumptions regarding the computational complexity of an attack. However, in a more practical scenario, Kocher noted that the time required to compute a cryptographic algorithm could reveal information on the keys used [1]. This was then extended to analyze differences in the power consumption of a microprocessor [2] and the variations in the surrounding electromagnetic field [3,4]. The simplest such attack is based on the inspection of an acquired power consumption (resp. electromagnetic emanation) trace to derive information. This is referred to as Simple Power Analysis (SPA) (resp. Simple ElectroMagnetic Analysis (SEMA)). The exploitation of statistical differences in the instantaneous power consumption proposed by Kocher et al. [2] is termed Differential Power Analysis (DPA) (resp. Differential ElectroMagnetic Analysis (DEMA)), and alternatives have been proposed using, for example, a model and Pearson's correlation coefficient [5] or mutual information [6].

© IFIP International Federation for Information Processing 2015
R.N. Akram and S. Jajodia (Eds.): WISTP 2015, LNCS 9311, pp. 169–184, 2015.
DOI: 10.1007/978-3-319-24018-3_11

In choosing an exponentiation algorithm for a secure implementation, one needs to consider the possible attacks that could be applied. One can often discount attacks where input values need to be known, such as the doubling attack [7], template attacks [8] or DPA [2]. Such attacks can typically be prevented by blinding input values [9] or by using a suitable padding scheme. That is, these attacks are not typically prevented by choosing a specific exponentiation algorithm. However, one also needs to consider attacks based on inspecting a limited number of traces, such as SPA [2], or power attacks in the horizontal setting [10,11]. The later was first introduced by Walter [10]. His attack, the so-called Big Mac attack, applied to m-ary exponentiation, although only simulated attacks are described. Clavier et al. [12] then exploited the collision correlation between selected points from two subtraces to derive information. Recent work by Bauer et al. [13] has also detailed how one could apply such collision attacks to implementations of scalar multiplications over elliptic curves. Witteman et al. [14] demonstrated that this attack works on an ASIC implementation. Kim et al. [15] also determined how one could apply such an attack to the Montgomery ladder [16,17]. The attack model was extended by Hanley et al. [18] to include an attacker that computes the correlation between carefully chosen points in a trace to detect where the output of one operation is used as the input to another operation.

In this paper, we present randomized variants of the Montgomery powering ladder that are resistant to SPA and power collision correlation attacks in the horizontal setting. The first algorithm is based on an amalgamation of two simple variants of the Montgomery powering ladder, where the content of the registers becomes *unpredicable*. The second algorithm is based on blinding addition chains, i.e. it takes tightly bounded random walks to compute an exponentiation. We also generalize the Montgomery powering ladder and present randomized m-ary exponentiation algorithms.

2 Preliminaries

2.1 Attack Model

In this paper we shall predominantly be considering an adversary that is able to take power consumption traces (or something equivalent) while a microprocessor is computing a group exponentiation algorithm. The adversary is then able to make deductions on what the microprocessor is computing. We shall consider three different attacks that require a limited number of traces when discussing the effects of our modifications to the Montgomery powering ladder.

1. The first attack is Simple Power Analysis (SPA) where one observes differences in the power consumption caused by different operations taking place. This was first demonstrated by Kocher *et al.* [2] who showed that one could, given a naïve implementation, observe the difference between operations during the computation of an exponentiation in $(\mathbb{Z}/N\,\mathbb{Z})^*$.

2. Another attack is the use of Pearson's correlation coefficient to detect collisions in variables to deduce key values [11]. For example, during the computation of an exponentiation in $(\mathbb{Z}/N\,\mathbb{Z})^*$ using Coron's *square-and-multiply-
   always* exponentiation algorithm, one could seek to determine the locations
   of multiplications with the same input. That is, operations that both take
   the same input should show a significant cross-correlation.
3. An extension to the collision correlation attack given above is where an
   adversary is able to detect collisions between the output of one operation and
   the input of another operation. This provides an attack where a complete
   defense is not possible. However, limiting the information available to an
   adversary can make the attack impractical since it has been shown that
   the error rate for this attack is significantly higher than a straightforward
   comparison of operations [18].

We do not consider attacks that require chosen inputs, such as the doubling
attack [7] or statistical differences in the power consumption over time [2,5].
This is because these attacks are typically prevented by padding or blinding
the input by using a redundant representation where the details depend on the
group being used [9,19].

Typically, a blinded exponent is used, which is equivalent to the actual exponent, meaning that each trace must be attacked independently. The discussion
of the security of the proposed algorithms will be largely informal, except where
we wish to make specific claims about the amount of information available to
an adversary.

2.2   The Montgomery Powering Ladder

The Montgomery powering ladder was originally proposed as a means of speeding
up scalar multiplication over elliptic curves [16], and was later shown to be
applicable to all multiplicatively written abelian groups [17].

We recall the description of the Montgomery powering ladder given by Joye
and Yen [17]. We consider the problem of computing $y = x^k$ in $\mathbb{G}$ for inputs
x and k. Let $\sum_{i=0}^{n-1} k_i\, 2^i$ be the binary expansion of κ with bit length n. For
ease of expression we shall also denote this as $(k_{n-1}, \ldots, k_0)_2$. The Montgomery
powering ladder relies on the following observation. Defining $L_j = \sum_{i=j}^{n-1} k_i\, 2^{i-j}$
and $H_j = L_j + 1$, we have

$$L_j = 2\,L_{j+1} + k_j = L_{j+1} + H_{j+1} + k_j - 1 = 2\,H_{j+1} + k_j - 2 \qquad (1)$$

and so we obtain

$$(L_j, H_j) = \begin{cases} (2\,L_{j+1}, L_{j+1} + H_{j+1}) & \text{if } k_j = 0, \\ (L_{j+1} + H_{j+1}, 2\,H_{j+1}) & \text{if } k_j = 1. \end{cases} \qquad (2)$$

If we consider one register containing x^{L_j} and another containing x^{H_j} then (2) implies that

$$(x^{L_j}, x^{H_j}) = \begin{cases} \left(\left(x^{L_{j+1}}\right)^2, x^{L_{j+1}} \cdot x^{H_{j+1}} \right) & \text{if } k_j = 0, \\ \left(x^{L_{j+1}} \cdot x^{H_{j+1}}, \left(x^{H_{j+1}}\right)^2 \right) & \text{if } k_j = 1. \end{cases}$$

Given that $L_0 = \kappa$ one can build an exponentiation algorithm that requires two group operations per bit of the exponent. Joye and Yen give several different versions of such an algorithm [17]. Algorithm 1 describes the most resistant to side-channel analysis version in their paper (as noted by Kim et al. [15] who describe implementations of cross correlation attacks on other versions).

Algorithm 1. Montgomery Powering Ladder

Input: $x \in \mathbb{G}$, an n-bit integer $\kappa = (k_{n-1}, k_{n-2}, \ldots, k_0)_2$
Output: x^{κ}

1 $R_0 \leftarrow 1_{\mathbb{G}}$; $R_1 \leftarrow x$;

2 **for** $i = n - 1$ **down to** 0 **do**
3 $\quad$ $R_{\neg k_i} \leftarrow R_{k_i} \cdot R_{\neg k_i}$;
4 $\quad$ $R_{k_i} \leftarrow (R_{k_i})^2$;
5 **end**

6 **return** R_0

The Montgomery powering ladder, as described in Algorithm 1, has several properties that make it useful when defining a side-channel resistant implementation of an exponentiation. However, the Montgomery Powering ladder also has been shown to be vulnerable to recent collision correlation attacks in the horizontal setting [12,18]. In the reminder of this paper we propose alternative versions of the Montgomery powering ladder to enhance its security against horizontal collision correlation attacks.

Definition 1. *We define a variant of the Montgomery powering ladder as an exponentiation algorithm that has the following properties.*

1. *The algorithm uses two registers in the main loop containing group elements, both of which are updated in each iteration.*
2. *Each iteration of the main loop treats one bit of the exponent and contains no more than two group operations.*
3. *The operands in the first group operation will only involve one or both of the registers used in the main loop.*
4. *The operands in the second group operation can involve one or both of the registers used in the main loop and/or some precomputed value.*

The 3rd and 4th properties allow for variants of the Montgomery ladder to be defined. That is, the Montgomery ladder is in the set of possible algorithms that satisfy these criteria.

For brevity in defining algorithms, we shall concentrate on the main loop of the algorithm. The computation before and after the main loop may contain **if**-statements. We shall not give fully secure versions where solutions are widely known, e.g. dummy operations or redundant representations [9, 19, 20].

3   Randomizing the Montgomery Powering Ladder

We note that when computing x^n using the Montgomery powering ladder, as defined in Algorithm 1, then at the end of each iteration we will have the condition where $R_1/R_0 = x$, or equivalently $R_0 \cdot x = R_1$. Thus, using the notation given above, and we allow some precomputed values to be used in the algorithm, then (2) can be rewritten as

$$(L_j, H_j) = \begin{cases} (2\,L_{j+1}, L_j + 1) & \text{if } k_j = 0, \\ (L_{j+1} + H_{j+1}, L_j + 1) & \text{if } k_j = 1. \end{cases} \tag{3}$$

Implying that

$$(x^{L_j}, x^{H_j}) = \begin{cases} \left(\left(x^{L_{j+1}} \right)^2, x^{L_j} \cdot x \right) & \text{if } k_j = 0, \\ \left(x^{L_{j+1}} \cdot x^{H_{j+1}}, x^{L_j} \cdot x \right) & \text{if } k_j = 1. \end{cases}$$

From which we can define Algorithm 2.

Algorithm 2. A Straightforward Variant I	**Algorithm 3.** A Straightforward Variant II
Input: $x \in \mathbb{G}$, an n-bit integer $\kappa = (k_{n-1}, k_{n-2}, \dots, k_0)_2$ **Output:** x^κ	**Input:** $x \in \mathbb{G}$, an n-bit integer $\kappa = (k_{n-1}, k_{n-2}, \dots, k_0)_2$, and $k_{n-1} = 1$ **Output:** x^κ
1 $R_0 \leftarrow 1_{\mathbb{G}}$; $R_1 \leftarrow x$;	1 $R_0 \leftarrow 1_{\mathbb{G}}$; $R_1 \leftarrow 1_{\mathbb{G}}$;
2 **for** $i = n - 1$ **down to** 0 **do**	2 **for** $i = n - 1$ **down to** 0 **do**
3 $\qquad R_0 \leftarrow R_0 \cdot R_{k_i}$;	3 $\qquad R_1 \leftarrow R_0 \cdot R_{\neg k_i}$;
4 $\qquad R_1 \leftarrow R_0 \cdot x$;	4 $\qquad R_0 \leftarrow R_1 \cdot x$;
5 **end**	5 **end**
6 **return** R_0	6 **return** R_0

Following the reasoning used to define (1), we can instead define $L_j = \sum_{i=j}^{n-1} k_i\, 2^{i-j}$ and $H_j = L_j - 1$, giving

$$L_j = 2\,L_{j+1} + k_j = L_{j+1} + H_{j+1} + k_j + 1 = 2\,H_{j+1} + k_j + 2 \tag{4}$$

and so, as with (3), we obtain

$$(L_j, H_j) = \begin{cases} (H_j + 1, L_{j+1} + H_{j+1}) & \text{if } k_j = 0, \\ (H_j + 1, 2\, L_{j+1}) & \text{if } k_j = 1. \end{cases} \tag{5}$$

If we consider one register containing x^{L_j} and another containing x^{H_j} then (5) implies that

$$(x^{L_j}, x^{H_j}) = \begin{cases} \left(x^{H_j} \cdot x, x^{L_{j+1}} \cdot x^{H_{j+1}}\right) & \text{if } k_j = 0, \\ \left(x^{H_j} \cdot x, \left(x^{L_{j+1}}\right)^2\right) & \text{if } k_j = 1. \end{cases}$$

From which we can define Algorithm 3. We note that at the end of each iteration we will have the condition where $R_0/R_1 = x$, or equivalently $R_1 \cdot x = R_0$.

Suppose that an adversary can distinguish multiplications from squaring operations, then the two above variants of Montgomery powering ladder are not immune to SPA. In line 3 of both algorithms, a squaring operation will occur for certain bit values. That is, a squaring operation will be computed if the bit value $k_i = 0$ in Algorithm 2 and in Algorithm 3 a squaring operation occurs when $k_i = 1$. The following randomized algorithm will deal with this problem.

We observe that Algorithms 2–3 can be blended together. That is, in loop ℓ, for some $\ell \in \{1, \dots, n-1\}$, of Algorithm 2 if $k_\ell = 1$ one could compute $R_1 \leftarrow (R_0)^2$ followed by $R_0 \leftarrow R_1 \cdot x$. Before this step $R_1/R_0 = x$, and afterwards one bit of the exponent is treated and $R_0/R_1 = x$. Hence, one could continue to compute an exponentiation using Algorithm 3.

Likewise, in loop ℓ, for some $\ell \in \{1, \dots, n-1\}$, of Algorithm 3, if $k_\ell = 0$, one could compute $R_0 \leftarrow (R_0)^2$ followed by $R_1 \leftarrow R_0 \cdot x$. Afterwards one bit of the exponent is treated and $R_1/R_0 = x$. Hence, one could continue to compute an exponentiation using Algorithm 2. We define Algorithm 4 as an example of how Algorithms 2 and 3 could be randomly blended together. We use a random generator producing a random bit b to determine when to change from one algorithm to the other, and to determine which algorithm is used to start the exponentiation algorithm. If $b = 0$, the exponentiation is computed by using Algorithm 2, that is $R_1/R_0 = x$. Otherwise, the exponentiation is computed by using Algorithm 3, that is, $R_0/R_1 = x$.

Suppose that an adversary is able to distinguish a multiplication from a squaring operation. Then, she would be able to determine individual bits of the exponent if she could determine if $R_0/R_1 = x$ or $R_1/R_0 = x$. However, the following lemma shows that this information is not available.

Lemma 1. *An adversary analyzing an instance of Algorithm 4 is able to reduce the hypotheses for the exponent from κ to $\kappa^{\frac{11}{12}}$ by distinguishing a multiplication from a squaring operation.*

Proof. If an adversary observes a squaring operation followed by a multiplication in the loop using index i, then the adversary knows one of the following operations has occurred:

Algorithm 4. Randomized Montgomery Powering Ladder

Input: $x \in \mathbb{G}$, an n-bit integer $\kappa = (k_{n-1}, k_{n-2}, \ldots, k_0)_2$, and $k_{n-1} = 1$
Output: x^κ

1 $b \xleftarrow{R} \{0, 1\}$; $R_0 \leftarrow 1_\mathbb{G}$;
2 **if** $b = 0$ **then**
3 $\quad\big|\quad R_1 \leftarrow x$;
4 **else**
5 $\quad\big|\quad R_1 \leftarrow 1_\mathbb{G}$;
6 **end**

7 **for** $i = n - 1$ **down to** 0 **do**
8 $\quad\big|\quad$ **if** $b \oplus k_i = 1$ **then**
9 $\quad\big|\quad\quad\big|\quad b \xleftarrow{R} \{0, 1\}$;
10 $\quad\big|\quad$ **end**
11 $\quad\big|\quad R_b \leftarrow R_0 \cdot R_{b \oplus k_i}$;
12 $\quad\big|\quad R_{\neg b} \leftarrow R_b \cdot x$;
13 **end**

14 **return** R_0

---

1. Where $R_1/R_0 = x$ and $k_i = 0$.
2. Where $R_0/R_1 = x$ and $k_i = 1$.
3. Where $R_1/R_0 = x$ changes to $R_0/R_1 = x$ and $k_i = 1$.
4. Where $R_0/R_1 = x$ changes to $R_1/R_0 = x$ and $k_i = 0$.

At an arbitrary point, each of these occur with probability $\frac{1}{4}$. Likewise, if an adversary observes two multiplications in the loop using index i, hence the adversary knows one of the following operations has occurred:

1. Where $R_1/R_0 = x$ and $k_i = 1$.
2. Where $R_0/R_1 = x$ and $k_i = 0$.

Each of these occur with probability $\frac{1}{2}$. Hence, there is no information available to an adversary since for any observed sequence of operations $\Pr(k_i = 0) = \Pr(k_i = 1) = \frac{1}{2}$.

However, if an adversary observes y consecutive pairs of multiplications then the adversary will know that y consecutive bits have the same value. If an attacker observes a pair of multiplications then the distribution of the number of subsequent pairs W of multiplications is geometric. That is, $W \sim \text{Geometric}(\frac{3}{4})$, since the following bit has to be the same and the randomly generated bit has to be a specific value. The, by definition, the expected length of a run of multiplication is $\frac{4}{3}$ operations, where each observation would therefore provide an expected $\frac{4}{3} - 1 = \frac{1}{3}$ of a bit of the exponent. A pair of multiplications will occur with probability $\frac{1}{4}$, giving an expected $n/4$ bits for an n-bit exponent. For an n-bit exponent an expected $\frac{1}{3} \times \frac{n}{4} = \frac{n}{12}$ bits can expected to be derived. Hence, κ hypotheses can be expected to be reduced to $\kappa^{\frac{11}{12}}$ hypotheses. $\qquad\square$

As with the Montgomery powering ladder shown in Algorithm 1, an attack using collisions based on the reuse of variables is not possible, but a collision attack based in the use of the output of operations is possible. One can attempt to observe whether the second operand in line 11 of Algorithm 4 is created from line 11 or line 12 in the previous iteration of the exponentiation loop. However, an analysis based on this will return the wrong key hypothesis when the algorithm changes from using (3) to (5).

Lemma 2. *An adversary analyzing an instance of Algorithm 4 using a collision attack an adversary would be able to reduce the hypotheses for the exponent from κ to $\kappa^{\frac{3}{4}}$.*

Proof. If we, arbitrarily, consider the ℓ-th loop of the exponentiation loop, we have $\Pr(b \oplus k_i = 1) = \frac{1}{2}$ and the probability that b changes, and hence the algorithm being used, is also $\frac{1}{2}$. An adversary making a deductions using a collision attack will have to guess the value of b in two consecutive loops of the algorithm. Given a correct guess for b it will remain the same with probability $\frac{3}{4}$. On the assumption that an attack will validate b in the first loop the value of b in the second loop will remain the same with probability $\frac{3}{4}$. If it changes an incorrect result will be given. Hence, the probability that a collision would detect an incorrect key bit is $\frac{1}{4}$, and an adversary would be able to determine a given bit with a probability $\frac{3}{4}$ leading to a reduction in the number of hypotheses from κ to $\kappa^{\frac{3}{4}}$. $\qquad\square$

4   Random Walk Method

In this section, we generalize the difference between the two registers used in the Montgomery powering ladder to be some arbitrary power of the input. This leads to an algorithm that computes a group exponentiation taking a random, albeit tightly bounded, walk through the possible addition chains.

If one is working in a group where computing the inverses of an element can be readily computed, then other options for a variant of the Montgomery powering ladder are possible. We note that (2) can be rewritten as

$$(L_j, H_j) = \begin{cases} (H_j - 1, L_{j+1} + H_{j+1}) & \text{if } k_j = 0, \\ (L_{j+1} + H_{j+1}, L_j + 1) & \text{if } k_j = 1. \end{cases} \tag{6}$$

Implying that

$$(x^{L_j}, x^{H_j}) = \begin{cases} (x^{H_j} \cdot x^{-1}, x^{L_{j+1}} \cdot x^{H_{j+1}}) & \text{if } k_j = 0, \\ (x^{L_{j+1}} \cdot x^{H_{j+1}}, x^{L_j} \cdot x) & \text{if } k_j = 1. \end{cases}$$

(6) can be rewritten as follows:

$$(L_j, H_j) = \begin{cases} (L_{j+1} + H_{j+1}, L_j - 1) & \text{if } k_j = 0, \\ (L_{j+1} + H_{j+1}, L_j + 1) & \text{if } k_j = 1. \end{cases} \tag{7}$$

Implying that

$$(x^{L_j}, x^{H_j}) = \begin{cases} \left(x^{L_{j+1}} \cdot x^{H_{j+1}}, x^{L_j} \cdot x^{-1}\right) & \text{if } k_j = 0, \\ \left(x^{L_{j+1}} \cdot x^{H_{j+1}}, x^{L_j} \cdot x\right) & \text{if } k_j = 1. \end{cases}$$

From which we can define Algorithm 5. In previous examples of Montgomery powering ladders presented in this paper R_0 has acted as an accumulator and returned the result. In Algorithm 5 the accumulator, i.e. the register containing the correct power of x at the end of each loop, shifts depending on the value of the bit of the exponent being treated. Hence, $R_{\neg k_0}$ is returned at the end of the algorithm.

Algorithm 5. Variant with Inverses

Input: $x \in \mathbb{G}$, an n-bit integer $\kappa = (k_{n-1}, k_{n-2}, \ldots, k_0)_2$
Output: x^{κ}

1 $R_0 \leftarrow 1_{\mathbb{G}}$; $R_1 \leftarrow x$;
2 $U_0 \leftarrow x^{-1}$; $U_1 \leftarrow x$;

3 **for** $i = n - 1$ **down to** 0 **do**
4 | $\quad R_0 \leftarrow R_0 \cdot R_1$;
5 | $\quad R_1 \leftarrow R_0 \cdot U_{k_i}$;
6 **end**

7 **return** $R_{\neg k_0}$

In analyzing an instance of Algorithm 5, an adversary would not be able to determine any information on bits of the exponent based on distinguishing a multiplication from a squaring operation, since no squaring operations take place. However, a collision attack is possible by observing where the multiplication with U_i, for $i \in \{0, 1\}$, collides with the multiplications used to generate these values in line 2. If an adversary is able to determine whether $U_{k_i} = x^{-1}$ or $U_{k_i} = x$ was used, for some $i \in \{0, \ldots, n - 1\}$, then individual bits of the exponent can be determined.

We can modify (7) by choosing $L'_{j+1} = L_{j+1} + \alpha$ and $H'_{j+1} = H_{j+1} + \beta$, giving

$$(L'_j, H'_j) = \begin{cases} (L'_{j+1} + H'_{j+1}, L'_j - 1) & \text{if } k_j = 0, \\ (L'_{j+1} + H'_{j+1}, L'_j + 1) & \text{if } k_j = 1. \end{cases} \tag{8}$$

where $L'_j = L_j + \gamma$, $H'_j = H_j + \mu$, and $\gamma = \alpha + \beta$. If we choose γ as a random element from $\{-h, \ldots h\}$ for some small integer h, then α and β can be chosen such that $\gamma = \alpha + \beta$. If we assume that α is fixed then $\beta = \gamma - \alpha$, i.e., $H'_{j+1} = H_{j+1} + \gamma - \alpha$. Given that H'_{j+1} is computed from L'_{j+1} this can be done by

$$H'_{j+1} = \begin{cases} L_{j+1} + (\gamma - \alpha - 1) = L'_{j+1} + (\gamma - 2\alpha - 1) & \text{if } k_j = 0, \\ L_{j+1} + (\gamma - \alpha + 1) = L'_{j+1} + (\gamma - 2\alpha + 1) & \text{if } k_j = 1. \end{cases}$$

This also removes the need to have the accumulating register change as described for Algorithm 5. If we define a value $L'_j = L_j + \gamma_j$ then (8) can be rewritten as

$(L_j + \gamma_j, H_j + (\gamma_{j-1} - \gamma_j) =$

$$\begin{cases} (L_{j+1} + \gamma_{j+1} + H_{j+1} + (\gamma_j - \gamma_{j+1}), L'_j + (\gamma_{j-1} - 2\gamma_j - 1)) & \text{if } k_j = 0, \\ (L_{j+1} + \gamma_{j+1} + H_{j+1} + (\gamma_j - \gamma_{j+1}), L'_j + (\gamma_{j-1} - 2\gamma_j + 1)) & \text{if } k_j = 1. \end{cases} \quad (9)$$

If we consider one register containing $x^{L'_j}$ and another containing $x^{H'_j}$ then (9) implies that $(x^{L'_j}, x^{H'_j}) = \left(x^{L'_{j+1}} \cdot x^{H'_{j+1}}, x^{L'_j} \cdot x^{\Delta} \right)$ where

$$\Delta = \begin{cases} \gamma_{j-1} - 2\gamma_j - 1 & \text{if } k_j = 0, \\ \gamma_{j-1} - 2\gamma_j + 1 & \text{if } k_j = 1. \end{cases}$$

Given that $L_0 = \kappa$ one can build an exponentiation algorithm as shown in Algorithm 6 where we set $\gamma_0 = 0$ to produce the correct result. Assume that γ can be arbitrarily chosen from the set $\{-h, \ldots, h\}$ in each iteration of computation, then $\Delta \in \{-3h - 1, \ldots, 3h + 1\}$. Hence, our algorithm makes use of an array of $6h + 3$ elements that stores the required values of x^{Δ}.

Algorithm 6. Blinded Montgomery Powering Ladder

Input: $x \in \mathbb{G}$, an n-bit integer $\kappa = (k_{n-1}, \ldots, k_0)_2$, small integer $h \in \mathbb{Z}$
Output: x^{κ}
Uses: U a $6h + 3$ element array.

1 $U_{3h+1} \leftarrow 1_{\mathbb{G}}$;
2 **for** $i = 1$ **to** $3h + 1$ **do**
3 $\quad$ $U_{3h+1+i} \leftarrow U_{3h+i} \cdot x$;
4 $\quad$ $U_{3h+1-i} \leftarrow U_{3h+2-i} \cdot x^{-1}$;
5 **end**

6 $R_0 \leftarrow 1_{\mathbb{G}}$; $R_1 \leftarrow 1_{\mathbb{G}}$; $\alpha = 0$;

7 **for** $i = n - 1$ **down to** 1 **do**
8 $\quad$ $R_0 \leftarrow R_0 \cdot R_1$;
9 $\quad$ $\gamma \xleftarrow{R} \{-h, \ldots, h\}$;
10 $\quad$ $\ell \leftarrow \gamma - 2\alpha + k_i - \neg k_i$;
11 $\quad$ $R_1 \leftarrow R_0 \cdot U_{3h+1+\ell}$;
12 $\quad$ $\alpha \leftarrow \gamma$;
13 **end**

14 $R_0 \leftarrow R_0 \cdot R_1$;
15 $R_0 \leftarrow R_0 \cdot U_{3h+1-\alpha-\neg k_0}$;

16 **return** R_0

An adversary who is able to distinguish a multiplication from a squaring operation would not be able to determine any information on bits of the exponent used since no squaring operations take place. However, a cross correlation attack is possible by observing where the multiplication with U_d, for $d \in \{0, \ldots, 6h+2\}$, collides with the multiplications used to generate these values in line 11. From these values, an adversary can derive the addition chain that was used to compute the exponentiation. This will not give an adversary the exponent, since there is no means to map the digits used to bits of the exponent, but would give an adversary an equivalent addition chain.

In determining whether an attack is practical Hanley et al. [18] determine that when analyzing an implementation 192-bit exponentiation, the error rate need to be less than 22 bits. This is determined to be less than 2^{54} operations, based on the boundary set for block ciphers by Biryukov et al. [21]. The expected number of operations can be determined using Stinson's algorithm [22], where an t-bit error in a n-bit hypothesis leads to the exponent in time complexity $\mathcal{O}\left(n\sum_{i=0}^{\lceil t/2\rceil}\binom{n/2}{i}\right)$ [22]. Then one can apply a version of Stinson's algorithm where one has to treat all the values that digits can take. Given a small integer h, as defined in Algorithm 6, a t-digit error in an μ-bit hypothesis leads to the exponent in time complexity $\mathcal{O}\left(\mu\binom{\mu/2}{t/2}(2h+1)^{\frac{\mu}{2}}\right)$. That is, there are μ possible divisions of the digits, each of which will have $\binom{\mu/2}{t/2}$ ways of selecting $t/2$ digits and each digit can take $(2h+1)$ values. In practice, t will not be known so the analysis will have time complexity $\mathcal{O}\left(\mu\sum_{i=0}^{\lceil t/2\rceil}\binom{\mu/2}{i}(2h+1)^{i}\right)$ further reducing the required error rate for a successful attack.

We note that an adversary is required to derive the entire exponent as information on part of the exponent is not useful. Moreover, an adversary will not know the exponent but an equivalent addition-chain. If we consider the group exponentiation algorithm used in ECDSA (Elliptic Curve Digital Signature Algorithm) [23] this provides a significant increase in security. Howgrave-Graham and Smart [24] noted that if a few bits of the ephemeral exponent are known for sufficiently many signatures, then the scheme can be broken, based on the so-called hidden number problem introduced by Boneh and Venkatesan [25].

A more memory-efficient version of Algorithm 6 is described in Algorithm 7. This is a security-memory trade off where the value of γ_j is still chosen at random, but the value range depend on the previous value γ_{j+1}. Although the available choices for γ_j decreases, Algorithm 7 requires only $2h+2$ registers to store pre-computed values instead of $6h+3$ registers in Algorithm 6.

5   Generalizing the Montgomery Powering Ladder

The *square-and-multiply* (left-to-right and right-to-left)) exponentiation algorithms are the most efficient implementations for raising x to the power κ when the exponent is treated bit-by-bit. Furthermore, these exponentiation algorithms extend easily to any radix m for the purpose of speeding the computation. In this section, by using the random walk technique, we generalize the (both left-to-right and right-to-left) exponentiation algorithms and present new blinded m-ary exponentiation algorithms.

Algorithm 7. Blinded Montgomery Powering Ladder II

Input: $x \in \mathbb{G}$, an n-bit integer $\kappa = (k_{n-1}, k_{n-2}, \ldots, k_0)_2$, small integer $h \in \mathbb{Z}$, U
 a look-up table of $2h + 2$ precomputed values $x^{-h}, \ldots, x^{h+1}$.
Output: x^{κ}

1 $U_h \leftarrow 1_{\mathbb{G}}$;
2 **for** $i = 1$ **to** h **do**
3 $\quad$ $U_{h+i} \leftarrow U_{h+i-1} \cdot x$;
4 $\quad$ $U_{h-i} \leftarrow U_{h+1-i} \cdot x^{-1}$;
5 **end**
6 $U_{2h+1} \leftarrow U_{2h} \cdot x$; $R_0 \leftarrow 1_{\mathbb{G}}$; $R_1 \leftarrow 1_{\mathbb{G}}$; $\alpha \leftarrow 0$;
7 **for** $i = n - 1$ **down to** 1 **do**
8 $\quad$ $R_0 \leftarrow R_0 \cdot R_1$;
9 $\quad$ **if** $\alpha \geq 0$ **then**
10 $\quad\quad$ $\gamma \xleftarrow{R} \{2\alpha - h, \ldots, h + 1 - k_i\}$;
11 $\quad$ **end**
12 $\quad$ **else**
13 $\quad\quad$ $\gamma \xleftarrow{R} \{-h - k_i, \ldots, 2\alpha + h - 1\}$;
14 $\quad$ **end**
15 $\quad$ $R_1 \leftarrow R_0 \cdot U_{h+\gamma+k_i}$;
16 $\quad$ $\alpha \leftarrow 2\alpha - \gamma$;
17 **end**
18 $R_0 \leftarrow R_0 \cdot R_1$;
19 $R_0 \leftarrow R_0 \cdot U_{h+\alpha+k_0}$;
20 **return** R_0

5.1   Left-to-Right Algorithms

We first consider the left-to-right exponentiation. Let $\kappa = (w_{\ell-1}, w_{\ell-2}, \ldots, w_0)_2$ be the m-ary representation of κ, where $0 \neq w_i < m$, $w_{\ell-1} \neq 0$, and ℓ is the length of κ in radix m. As in Section 2.2, by defining $L_j = \sum_{i=j}^{\ell-1} w_i m^{i-j}$, we have

$$L_j = m L_{j+1} + w_j \tag{10}$$

From then, the exponentiation algorithm will perform $x^{L_j} = (x^{L_{j+1}})^m \cdot x^{w_j}$. Noting that $x^{L_0} = x^{\kappa}$. Using the random walk technique as in Section 4, we modify $L'_j = L_j + \gamma_j$ where γ_j can be chosen from a pre-defined set $\{-h, \ldots, h\}$ for some small integer h. Then (10) can be rewritten as

$$L_j + \gamma_j = m L_{j+1} + \gamma_j + w_j = m L'_{j+1} - m \gamma_{j+1} + \gamma_j + w_j \tag{11}$$

This leads to a randomized algorithm (Algorithm 8) that computes a group exponentiation taking a random, albeit tightly bounded, walk through the possible addition chains. As with Algorithm 7, Algorithm 8 also requires a look-up table of $2(m + 1) h + m - 1$ values to stores precomputed values. Algorithm 8 can be used in the cases where the computation of inversions is cheap, otherwise Algorithm 9 is more suitable.

Algorithm 8. Randomized Left-to-Right m-ary Exponentiation

Input: $x \in \mathbb{G}$, an integer
$\kappa = (w_{\ell-1}, w_{\ell-2}, \ldots, w_0)_m$,
where $0 \le w_i < m$ and
$w_{\ell-1} \ne 0$, small integer
$h \in \mathbb{Z}$, T a look-up table of
$2(m+1)h + m - 1$
precomputed values
$x^{-(m+1)h-m+1}, \ldots, x^{(m+1)h+m-1}$.

Output: x^κ

1 $R \leftarrow 1_{\mathbb{G}}$, $\alpha \leftarrow 0$
2 **for** $i = \ell - 2$ **to** 1 **do**
3 $\quad R \leftarrow R^m$;
4 $\quad \gamma \xleftarrow{R} \{-h, \ldots, h\}$;
5 $\quad R \leftarrow R \cdot x^{m\,\alpha - \gamma + w_i}$;
6 $\quad \alpha \leftarrow \gamma$;
7 **end**
8 $R \leftarrow R^m$;
9 $R \leftarrow R \cdot x^{m\,\alpha + w_0}$;
10 **return** R

Algorithm 9. Randomized Left-to-Right m-ary Exponentiation without Inversions

Input: $x \in \mathbb{G}$, an integer
$\kappa = (w_{n-1}, w_{n-2}, \ldots, w_0)_m$,
where w_i is m-bit words,
small integer $h \in \mathbb{Z}$, T a
look-up table of
$m(h+1) - 1$ precomputed
values $x, \ldots, x^{m(h+1)-1}$.

Output: x^κ

1 $R \leftarrow 1_{\mathbb{G}}$, $\alpha \leftarrow 0$
2 **for** $i = \ell - 2$ **to** 1 **do**
3 $\quad R \leftarrow R^m$;
4 $\quad \gamma \xleftarrow{R} \{0, \ldots, \min(h, m\,\alpha + w_i)\}$;
5 $\quad R \leftarrow R \cdot x^{m\,\alpha - \gamma + w_i}$;
6 $\quad \alpha \leftarrow \gamma$;
7 **end**
8 $R \leftarrow R^m$;
9 $R \leftarrow R \cdot x^{m\,\alpha + w_0}$;
10 **return** R

We note that Algorithm 9 works in a similar way to the Overlapping Windows method [26] for a fixed base $m = 2^{k - h_{OWM}}$ and $m(h+1) = 2^{k}$[1]. The main difference is that our algorithm generates *on-the-fly* a randomized recoding of the binary representation of the secret exponent κ. This allows our algorithm to avoid side-channel attacks in the recoding phase.

5.2 Right-to-Left Algorithm

Likewise, we can devise a randomized *right-to-left* m-ary algorithm. Let $\kappa = (w_{\ell-1}, w_{\ell-2}, \ldots, w_0)_m$, where $w_{\ell-1} \ne 0$, the principle of the *right-to-left* m-ary exponentiation algorithm, as shown by Yao [27], makes use of the is relied on the following equality:

$$x^\kappa = \prod_{\substack{0 \le i \le \ell-1 \\ d_i = 1}} x^{m^i} \cdot \prod_{\substack{0 \le i \le \ell-1 \\ d_i = 2}} x^{2 \cdot m^i} \cdots \prod_{\substack{0 \le i \le \ell-1 \\ d_i = m-1}} x^{(m-1) \cdot m^i} = \prod_{j=1}^{m-1} \left(\prod_{\substack{0 \le i \le \ell-1 \\ d_i = j}} x^{m^i} \right)^j .$$

---

[1] We use the notation h_{OWM} instead of h as in [26] to distinguish it from the notation h in our algorithms.

The *right-to-left* m-ary exponentiation algorithm uses $(m - 1)$ accumulators, $R[1], \ldots, R[m-1]$. At each iteration, it applies w successive squarings to compute $A = x^{m^j}$ from $x^{m^{(j-1)}}$, then multiplies the result to some accumulators $R[k]$. Let $R[k]^{(j)}$ (resp. $A^{(j)}$) denote the value of the accumulator $R[k]$ (resp. A) before entering step j. We have:

$$R[k]^{(j+1)} = R[k]^{(j)} \cdot A^{(j)} \quad \text{for } k = w_j,$$
$$R[k]^{(j+1)} = R[k]^{(j)} \quad \text{for } k \neq w_j,$$

and $A^{(j+1)} = (A^{(j)})^m$. At the end of the loop each accumulator $R[k]$ contains the product $\prod_{\substack{0 \leq j \leq \ell-1 \\ w_j = k}} x^{m^j}$. The different accumulators are finally aggregated as $\prod_{0 \leq j \leq \ell-1} R[k]^k = x^\kappa$. By defining $L_j = \sum_{i=0}^{j} w_i \cdot m^i$, we have

$$L_{j+1} = m^{j+1} \cdot w_{j+1} + Lj \tag{12}$$

Noting that $L_{\ell-1} = \kappa$. Similar, we use the random walk technique and modify $L'_j = L_j - m^{j+1} \cdot \gamma_j$, then equation (12) can be rewritten as:

$$
\begin{aligned}
L_{j+1} - m^{j+2} \cdot \gamma_{j+1} &= m^{j+1} \cdot w_{j+1} + L_j - m^{j+2} \cdot \gamma_{j+1} \\
&= m \cdot w_{j+1} + L'_j + m^{j+1} \cdot \gamma_j - m^{j+2} \cdot \gamma_{j+1} \\
&= (\gamma_j - m \cdot \gamma_{j+1} + w_{j+1})m^{j+1} + L'_j
\end{aligned}
$$

This leads to a randomized *right-to-left* m-ary exponentiation algorithm (Algorithm 10). In this algorithm, we make use of $2(m + 1)h + m - 1$ accumulators $R[j]$, where $-(m + 1)h - m + 1 \leq j \leq (m + 1)h + m - 1$. Each $R[j]$ is initialized to $1_{\mathbb{G}}$, and then updated if $\alpha - m\gamma + w_i = j$. The different accumulators are finally aggregated as $\prod_{j=1}^{h} \left(R[j] \cdot (R[-j])^{-1} \right)^j = x^\kappa$.

6   Conclusion

In this paper we presented variants of the Montgomery powering ladder which have properties that increase the side-channel resistance of the exponentiation algorithm. The first of these operates by randomly changing states such that the difference between the two registers varies, unpredictably, between two states. The second variant of the Montgomery powering ladder that we presented takes a random walk, albeit tightly bounded, among the possible addition chains required to compute an exponentiation. While this variant is not resistant to all side-channel analysis, it will prevent lattice-based attacks when used, for example, in implementations of ECDSA. In other cases, significantly more computation is required to derive any exploitable information and, therefore, an adversary requires a lower error rate to succeed. By applying the random walk method, we also generalized the Montgomery powering ladder and present randomized (both left-to-right and right-to-left) m-ary exponentiation algorithms.

Algorithm 10. Randomized Right-to-Left m-ary Exponentiation

Input: $x \in \mathbb{G}$, an n-bit integer $\kappa = (w_{\ell-1}, w_{\ell-2}, \ldots, w_0)_m$, small integer $h \in \mathbb{Z}$.
Output: x^κ

1 **for** $j = 0$ **to** $(m+1)h + m - 1$ **do**
2     $R[j] \leftarrow 1_\mathbb{G}$; $R[-j] \leftarrow 1_\mathbb{G}$;
3 **end**
4 $A \leftarrow x$; $\alpha \leftarrow 0$;
5 **for** $i = 0$ **to** $\ell - 1$ **do**
6     $\gamma \xleftarrow{R} \{-h, \ldots, h\}$;
7     $R[\alpha - m\gamma + k_i] \leftarrow R[\alpha - m\gamma + k_i] \cdot A$;
8     $\alpha \leftarrow \gamma$; $A \leftarrow A^2$;
9 **end**

10 $A \leftarrow \prod_{j=1}^{h} \left(R[j] \cdot (R[-j])^{-1} \right)^j$;

11 **return** A

References

1. Kocher, P.C.: Timing attacks on implementations of diffie-hellman, RSA, DSS, and other systems. In: Koblitz, N. (ed.) CRYPTO 1996. LNCS, vol. 1109, pp. 104–113. Springer, Heidelberg (1996)
2. Kocher, P.C., Jaffe, J., Jun, B.: Differential power analysis. In: Wiener, M. (ed.) CRYPTO 1999. LNCS, vol. 1666, p. 388. Springer, Heidelberg (1999)
3. Quisquater, J.-J., Samyde, D.: ElectroMagnetic analysis (EMA): measures and counter-measures for smart cards. In: Attali, S., Jensen, T. (eds.) E-smart 2001. LNCS, vol. 2140, p. 200. Springer, Heidelberg (2001)
4. Gandolfi, K., Mourtel, C., Olivier, F.: Electromagnetic analysis: concrete results. In: Koç, Ç.K., Naccache, D., Paar, C. (eds.) CHES 2001. LNCS, vol. 2162, p. 251. Springer, Heidelberg (2001)
5. Brier, E., Clavier, C., Olivier, F.: Correlation power analysis with a leakage model. In: Joye, M., Quisquater, J.-J. (eds.) CHES 2004. LNCS, vol. 3156, pp. 16–29. Springer, Heidelberg (2004)
6. Gierlichs, B., Batina, L., Tuyls, P., Preneel, B.: Mutual information analysis. In: Oswald, E., Rohatgi, P. (eds.) CHES 2008. LNCS, vol. 5154, pp. 426–442. Springer, Heidelberg (2008)
7. Fouque, P.-A., Valette, F.: The doubling attack – why upwards is better than downwards. In: Walter, C.D., Koç, Ç.K., Paar, C. (eds.) CHES 2003. LNCS, vol. 2779, pp. 269–280. Springer, Heidelberg (2003)
8. Chari, S., Rao, J.R., Rohatgi, P.: Template attacks. In: Kaliski Jr., B.S., Koç, Ç.K., Paar, C. (eds.) CHES 2002. LNCS, vol. 2523, pp. 13–28. Springer, Heidelberg (2003)
9. Coron, J.-S.: Resistance against differential power analysis for elliptic curve cryptosystems. In: Koç, Ç.K., Paar, C. (eds.) CHES 1999. LNCS, vol. 1717, p. 292. Springer, Heidelberg (1999)
10. Walter, C.D.: Sliding windows succumbs to big MAC attack. In: Koç, Ç.K., Naccache, D., Paar, C. (eds.) CHES 2001. LNCS, vol. 2162, p. 286. Springer, Heidelberg (2001)

11. Clavier, C., Feix, B., Gagnerot, G., Giraud, C., Roussellet, M., Verneuil, V.: ROSETTA for single trace analysis. In: Galbraith, S., Nandi, M. (eds.) INDOCRYPT 2012. LNCS, vol. 7668, pp. 140–155. Springer, Heidelberg (2012)
12. Clavier, C., Feix, B., Gagnerot, G., Roussellet, M., Verneuil, V.: Horizontal correlation analysis on exponentiation. In: Soriano, M., Qing, S., López, J. (eds.) ICICS 2010. LNCS, vol. 6476, pp. 46–61. Springer, Heidelberg (2010)
13. Bauer, A., Jaulmes, E., Prouff, E., Wild, J.: Horizontal collision correlation attack on elliptic curves. In: Lange, T., Lauter, K., Lisoněk, P. (eds.) SAC 2013. LNCS, vol. 8282, pp. 553–570. Springer, Heidelberg (2014)
14. Witteman, M.F., van Woudenberg, J.G.J., Menarini, F.: Defeating RSA multiply-always and message blinding countermeasures. In: Kiayias, A. (ed.) CT-RSA 2011. LNCS, vol. 6558, pp. 77–88. Springer, Heidelberg (2011)
15. Kim, H., Kim, T.H., Yoon, J.C., Hong, S.: Practical second-order correlation power analysis on the message blinding method and its novel countermeasure for RSA. ETRI J. **32**, 102–111 (2010)
16. Montgomery, P.: Speeding the Pollard and elliptic curve methods of factorization. Mathematics of Computation **48**, 243–264 (1987)
17. Joye, M., Yen, S.-M.: The montgomery powering ladder. In: Kaliski Jr., B.S., Koç, Ç.K., Paar, C. (eds.) CHES 2002. LNCS, vol. 2523, pp. 291–302. Springer, Heidelberg (2003)
18. Hanley, N., Kim, H.S., Tunstall, M.: Exploiting collisions in addition chain-based exponentiation algorithms using a single trace. In: Nyberg, K. (ed.) CT-RSA 2015. LNCS, vol. 9048, pp. 429–446. Springer, Heidelberg (2015)
19. De Win, E., Mister, S., Preneel, B., Wiener, M.: On the performance of signature schemes based on elliptic curves. In: Buhler, J.P. (ed.) ANTS 1998. LNCS, vol. 1423, pp. 252–266. Springer, Heidelberg (1998)
20. Mangard, S., Oswald, E., Popp, T.: Power Analysis Attacks – Revealing the Secrets of Smart Cards. Springer (2007)
21. Biryukov, A., Dunkelman, O., Keller, N., Khovratovich, D., Shamir, A.: Key recovery attacks of practical complexity on AES-256 variants with up to 10 rounds. In: Gilbert, H. (ed.) EUROCRYPT 2010. LNCS, vol. 6110, pp. 299–319. Springer, Heidelberg (2010)
22. Stinson, D.: Some baby-step giant-step algorithms for the low Hamming weight discrete logarithm problem. Mathematics of Computation **71**, 379–391 (2002)
23. X9.62, A.: Public key cryptography for the financial services industry, the elliptic curve digital signature algorithm (ECDSA) (1999)
24. Howgrave-Graham, N.A., Smart, N.P.: Lattice attacks on digital signature schemes. Design, Codes and Cryptography **23**, 283–290 (2001)
25. Boneh, D., Venkatesan, R.: Hardness of computing the most significant bits of secret keys in diffie-hellman and related schemes. In: Koblitz, N. (ed.) CRYPTO 1996. LNCS, vol. 1109, pp. 129–142. Springer, Heidelberg (1996)
26. Itoh, K., Yajima, J., Takenaka, M., Torii, N.: DPA Countermeasures by Improving the window method. In: Kaliski Jr., B.S., Koç, Ç.K., Paar, C. (eds.) CHES 2002. LNCS, vol. 2523, pp. 303–317. Springer, Heidelberg (2003)
27. Yao, A.C.C.: On the evaluation of powers. SIAM J. Comput. **5**, 100–103 (1976)

Challenges of Security and Reliability

How Current Android Malware Seeks to Evade Automated Code Analysis

Siegfried Rasthofer[1]([⊠]), Irfan Asrar[3] , Stephan Huber[2], and Eric Bodden[1,2]

[1] Center for Advanced Security Research Darmstadt (CASED),
Technische Universität Darmstadt, Darmstadt, Germany
`siegfried.rasthofer@cased.de`
[2] Fraunhofer SIT, Darmstadt, Germany
`{stephan.huber,eric.bodden}@sit.fraunhofer.de`
[3] Appthority, San Francisco, USA
`iasrar@appthority.com`

Abstract. First we report on a new threat campaign, underway in Korea, which infected around 20,000 Android users within two months. The campaign attacked mobile users with malicious applications spread via different channels, such as email attachments or SMS spam. A detailed investigation of the Android malware resulted in the identification of a new Android malware family Android/BadAccents. The family represents current state-of-the-art in mobile malware development for banking trojans.

Second, we describe in detail the techniques this malware family uses and confront them with current state-of-the-art static and dynamic code-analysis techniques for Android applications. We highlight various challenges for automatic malware analysis frameworks that significantly hinder the fully automatic detection of malicious components in current Android malware. Furthermore, the malware exploits a previously unknown *tapjacking* vulnerability in the Android operating system, which we describe. As a result of this work, the vulnerability, affecting all Android versions, will be patched in one of the next releases of the Android Open Source Project.

Keywords: Botnet · Android malware · Code analysis · Banking trojans · Vulnerability

1 Introduction

According to a recent study [9], Android has reached a mobile-market share of 81%. There is an app for almost every need, provided by various app stores such as the Google PlayStore with 1.3M applications by July 2014 [36]. Besides apps that are mostly used for amusement, there are also more critical applications that handle confidential data such as mobile banking applications. According to a study of the Federal Reserve Board [28], more and more people switch from using cash and ATMs to using mobile banking with their smartphones.

© IFIP International Federation for Information Processing 2015
R.N. Akram and S. Jajodia (Eds.): WISTP 2015, LNCS 9311, pp. 187–202, 2015.
DOI: 10.1007/978-3-319-24018-3_12

This makes phones a very attractive target for attackers who want to steal money from victims. Indeed, there is a big underground market for trading stolen bank account credentials [38]. For instance, Symantec reported [38] that a single underground group made $4.3 million in purchases using stolen credit cards over a two-year period.

The Android operating system got enhanced with different security features, such as the 'Application verification' in version 4.2. Its goal is to protect the user against harmful applications. Despite those protection mechanisms, banking trojans are still actively spreading [6]; even worse, McAfee is predicting a rapid growth [18]. Very recently, we identified a new threat campaign underway in South Korea that emphasizes McAfee's prediction. The campaign stole, within two months, the credentials of more than 20,000 bank accounts of users residing in Korea. We identified a new malware family `Android/BadAccents` (named after the main component in the first stage of the trojan) that impersonates known banking applications in order to steal the user's credentials. Furthermore, it also steals incoming SMS messages, aborts phone calls and installs a fake anti-virus application.

In this paper, we describe in detail the techniques this malware family uses, and explain the current state-of-the-art of mobile malware development. The malware family clearly illustrates that mobile malware is becoming increasingly complex. In 2010, FakePlayer [11] was one of the first mobile malware families ever discovered. It implemented a simple premium SMS trojan, with only a few lines of Java code. As we show in this paper, however, current malware shows a highly complex structure comprising multiple malicious components and complex interactions between these components. In the case of Android/BadAccents, the complexity is further enhanced by an included zero-day-exploit (a vulnerability that was previously not known).

Many malware-detection frameworks, such as the one used in Google Play [13], or the ones used by anti-virus companies, however, aim at (semi-)automatically distinguishing between benign and malicious applications. To be able to initiate further actions, such as the take-down of a botnet, it is moreover crucial to be able to identify the actual malicious components. Given that every single day thousands of new apps, and versions of apps, are uploaded to the larger app stores, it is crucial that such an analysis can be conducted efficiently. Any manual analysis therefore must be supported by automated or semi-automated program-analysis tools. In this work we show, however, that current pieces of malware such as Android/BadAccents are raising significant challenges to static as well as dynamic code-analysis techniques. While we do not reiterate the well-known limitations from literature of both approaches [1,3], instead we demonstrate new challenges that are related to Android and which have to be considered on top of the well-known ones. For instance, the hiding of sensitive information in native code is no longer a theoretical problem for static analysis; it is already being exploited in the wild. The usage of multi-stage command and control (C&C) protocols is growing into a challenge for dynamic code-analysis techniques as well. Even malware-analysis frameworks that try to circumvent emulator-detection mechanisms [29] are not well prepared for current Android malware. There is still a big need for a proper environment setup, such as specific files on the SD card or specific apps installed, as otherwise the malicious behavior does not get triggered and hence cannot be observed. These are significant challenges that future code-analysis approaches will need to address.

The rest of the paper is organized as follows. Section 2 describes the details of the malware including an AOSP vulnerability. In Section 3 we identify the challenges for current state-of-the-art code analysis techniques and Section 4 describes the related work in the field of Android security while Section 5 concludes the paper.

2   Android/BadAccent Malware

During a threat-campaign investigation, we spotted an interesting malware sample that targets Korean users (more details in our technical report[31]). The threat campaign employed tactics such as social engineering to distribute Android malware. In particular, it distributed a new form of banking trojans that we designated as Android/BadAccents (named after the main component in the first stage of the trojan). Such mobile malware targeting Korea in many ways represents the best of breed practices when it comes to mobile malware development. In general, Android/BadAccents is a banking trojan that tries to steal bank-account credentials through a phishing attack. The victim is asked to enter her confidential data into a Graphical User Interface (GUI) that looks identical to the one of a benign mobile banking application. But the malware's GUI is designed by the attacker, and is instrumented to steal the credentials instead. Figure 1 shows such a fake GUI component which appears after a fake security message which prompts the user for some action.

Android/BadAccents demonstrates the complexity of current Android banking trojans. Different interactions, environment settings and conditions are necessary before a specific malicious behavior gets triggered. The malware sample uses different techniques to hide the malicious behavior as long as possible. Figure 2 gives an overview of the main components in the Android/BadAccents malware and shows the complexity of environment settings, workflow and external events that are involved. Especially the *Intercept SMS* components show that

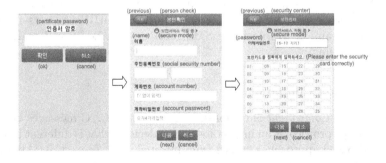

Fig. 1. Phishing of confidential banking credentials

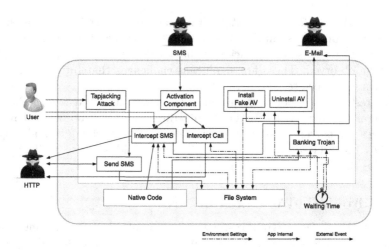

Fig. 2. Interactions and environment settings necessary for triggering malicious behavior in the Android/BadAccents Malware

current attackers do not only rely on a single channel for transmitting sensitive data. Instead they use several ones, in this case e-mail and HTTP connections. In the following we will describe each component individually in detail, and its requirements for triggering a malicious behavior. The resulting requirements for code-analysis tools are described afterwards.

2.1 Send SMS

The *Send SMS* component gets activated at application startup time and is responsible for sending SMS messages to all contacts on the phone that have more than 5 digits as a phone number. It first initializes a connection to the C&C server, using the victim's device's phone number for identification, from which it receives the text for the SMS message. Additionally, it saves all phone numbers of the contacts into a global storage (*SharedPreferences* file). After receiving the text, the component immediately sends a message containing that text to all contacts. This mechanism is probably used for spreading the malware to all contacts. We assume that the text from the C&C server contains spam messages together with a download link to the Android/BadAccents malware. The attacker's aim is to infect the SMS receiver with additional malware by clicking on the link.

2.2 Activation Component

The *Activation Component* is responsible for receiving C&C messages via SMS. Using SMS as a protocol is an important design decision that is different from traditional IP-based approaches known from infected PCs. Zeng et al. [44] already illustrated this design in 2012. The main advantages of an SMS-based approach instead of IP-based are the fact that it does not require steady connections, that SMS is ubiquitous, and that SMS can accommodate offline bots easily.

The *Activation Component* is implemented as a broadcast receiver, which is active from the time the application starts. This broadcast receiver registers 63 different actions it can react to. However, it uses only a single one of them, the SMS-received action. It intercepts all incoming SMS messages and triggers the malicious behavior only if the message contains special commands. More concretely, it is responsible for activating the *Intercept SMS* and *Intercept Call* component (details below). The Android/BadAccents malware contains two specific checks on the incoming SMS number. It checks for '+84' and '+82' numbers, which indicates that the malware expects SMS from a C&C SMS server either located in China or South Korea. The message has to have a special format that contains either 'sd_$\langle MESSAGE \rangle$', 'ak40_0', 'ak40_1' 'call_0' or 'call_1' and can be concatenated with '_' (e.g., 'ak40_1_call_0'). The 'ak40' command is responsible for the *Intercept SMS* component and activates that component with 'ak40_1' and deactivates it with 'ak40_0'. The 'call' command is responsible for the *Intercept Call* component and 'call_1' activates and 'call_0' deactivates it. Activating a component is implemented by storing activation-flags (e.g. $\langle call, 1 \rangle$) into a SharedPreferences file, deactivating components is done by storing deactivation-flags (e.g. $\langle call, 0 \rangle$). The individual components get called in a specific time interval in which they first check for the appropriate activation-flag before running it. This is indicated as dotted arrows in Figure 2 from both components to *File System*. The 'sd_$\langle MESSAGE \rangle$' command is equivalent to the functionality of the *Send SMS* component (see section 2.1). The main difference is the communication channel. Instead of receiving the text of the message body via HTTP (*Send SMS* component), it uses only the SMS channel by taking the message from the incoming C&C SMS ($\langle MESSAGE \rangle$).

Intercept Call. The *Intercept Call* component intercepts all incoming calls and checks whether the caller is stored as a contact on the device or not. If this is not the case, the call gets aborted and the entry in the call log gets deleted. We assume that the attackers want to abort calls from the bank which could have detected suspicious transactions caused by the banking trojan.

Intercept SMS. This component intercepts all incoming SMS messages that do not contain any C&C command and leaks the information to the attacker via HTTP and E-mail. It uses two channels in parallel for a more reliable data theft. The credentials of the E-mail account are hidden in native code, which makes the detection hard for static analysis approaches that operate purely on the Dalvik bytecode. Listing 1.1 shows two native methods that return the constant username and password (original credentials are removed) that get called in the `onCreate` method (listing 1.2) and stored into a SharedPreferences file (`setValue` method). Before sending the email, the credentials are extracted from the SharedPreferences file in order to authenticate against the email server.

```
1 void Java_com_MainActivity_stringUser() {
2   return "USERNAME";
3 }
4
5 void Java_com_MainActivity_stringPassword() {
6   return "PASSWORD";
7 }
```

```
1 public native java.lang.String
       stringPassword();
2 public native java.lang.String stringUser();
3
4 public void onCreate(Bundle b) {
5 ...
6 user = stringUser();
7 setValue("musername", user);
8 pw = stringPassword();
9 setValue("mpass", pw);
10 ...
11 }
```

Listing 1.1. Methods in Native Code   **Listing 1.2.**   Accessing   Native
Methods within Java

2.3   Install/Uninstall

The Install/Uninstall component first removes one particular app, the 'AhnLab
V3 Mobile Plus 2.0'[1] app in case it is installed on the device. This is a malware-
scanner application especially designed for detecting banking trojans. In the
Banking Trojan component, a fake 'AhnLab V3 Mobile Plus 2.0' application
gets installed which impersonates the original app and which contains malicious
components similar to Android/BadAccents.

2.4   Banking Trojan

The *Banking Trojan* component tries to hide the application's icon from the
launcher. This is possible with a singe API call (*setComponentEnabledSetting*
in *PackageManager*) and does not require any permission. After a delay of 30
minutes, the malware looks for DER-formatted certificates stored under a specific
folder on the SD card. If found, the malware checks whether the user has installed
specific Korean banking applications such as Shinhan Bank, Woori Bank or NH
Bank. This indicates that the threat campaign primary targets user from Korea.
Next, if one of these applications is installed, it dynamically creates a new view
impersonating this app. The 'fake' app uses social engineering in showing security
warnings that should convince the user to provide the attacker her data.

After accepting the security messages, the attacker tries to steal the banking
victim's credentials. Figure 1 shows the individual GUI fields the user has to go
through. It is worth mentioning that input into the fields has to satisfy specific
criteria such as the certificate password has to be entered twice or the password
in the *security center* has to have more than 5 digits. If everything got filled out
correctly, all the data, together with the certificate gets sent to the malicious
e-mail account. Similar to the *Intercept SMS* component (see section 2.2), the
e-mail-account credentials are loaded through native methods.

2.5   Gain Administration Privilege

Besides the malicious components above, we also found a zero-day vulnerability of the AOSP abused by the malware. The Android/BadAccents malware

---

[1] https://play.google.com/store/apps/details?id=com.ahnlab.v3mobileplus

tries to obtain Android Device Administration privileges [39] without the user's knowledge.

The Android Device Administration API was introduced for applications to support enterprise features [39]. It provides functions on the system level with varying security impact. An application that is granted such privileges can, for example, lock the device screen, encrypt user data, or initiate a factory reset of the device. The full set of supported system functions is described in the developer documentation [40].

When an application requests administration privilege, the Android OS shows a warning message to the user, who then has to accept or deny the request. The malware abuses the mentioned vulnerability to trick the user into accepting the administration request by a so-called *tapjacking* attack [24] where the user clicks on a seemingly benign object, but instead activates the Device Administration. To the best of our knowledge this attack form is currently the only way to obtain administration privilege without resorting to some root exploit or without an explicit visible user confirmation.

Tapjacking Attack Summary. The following subsection gives a short summary about the concept of tapjacking attacks. The formal name or most common name in research for a tapjacking attack is UI redressing [24] and subsumes tapjacking as a specific case.

The basic idea behind tapjaking on Android is not to directly exploit some system vulnerability, instead its focus is to force the user to an interaction without her knowledge and to hide the system or application information which is shown as a consequence of this hidden interaction. A harmlessly looking overlay window is brought to the foreground, hiding the real application behind the overlay window. The design of such an overlay window can be freely defined, for instance posing as a game or some generic application dialog (see figure 3).

The requirements for such an attack are all provided by the Android user interface (UI) design API. Such attacks can be performed in different ways, but the main premise is to generate a UI element which can be layered over applications and routes touch gestures to the underlying application. An additional requirement for successful tapjacking is the hidden start of the victim application or a part of the application [7] behind the overlay. Exported activities or defined intent-filters in applications can facilitate such hidden starts. System applications or Android settings can be accessed via system intents. To route taps through underlying applications, Android provides settings that make a widget transparent for touches.

Analysis of the Tapjacking Vulnerability. After a detailed analysis of the malicious application, we isolated the code responsible for the tapjacking attack and reassembled it into a stand-alone proof-of-concept implementation. The malware uses the described tapjacking attack to obtain Android Device Administration privilege and thus the ability to lock the device screen. Another aspect is the uninstall protection. Once the admin privilege is granted, antivirus tools can

```
1 | private void setupLayoutParams() {
2 |     layoutParams = new WindowManager.LayoutParams(WindowManager.LayoutParams.TYPE_SYSTEM_OVERLAY,
3 |                         WindowManager.LayoutParams.FLAG_FULLSCREEN,
4 |                         WindowManager.LayoutParams.FLAG_SCALED);
5 |         layoutParams.flags = WindowManager.LayoutParams.FLAG_NOT_TOUCHABLE;
6 |         ...
7 | }
```

Listing 1.3. Settings for ovelay window layout paramters

no longer remove the malware. The attack can be illustrated as shown in figure 3. The victim only sees an application window requesting *"Please update to the*

Fig. 3. Tapjacking Attack on Android Device Administrator App

latest version" with a *confirmation* and a *cancel* button. Pressing *confirmation* she activates the device administration feature.

Therefore the tapjacking attack at first starts the admin request dialog by sending the system intent `android.app.action.ADD_DEVICE_ADMIN`. Due to the asynchronous execution character of Android the application does not stop after calling the administration activity and executes a method showing the overlay window hiding the administration activity (see figure 3). The overlay window is an extended `LinearLayout` class defining specific layout properties (see listing 1.3). The first layout option is the overlay definition itself. The last option (`FLAG_NOT_TOUCHABLE`) is the crucial factor. It makes the window transparent for touches and therefore every touch gestures on it were received on the application behind it. Considering the malware example the victim assumes she confirms the update request, but in reality she activates the administration privilege. This form of attack is working to Android Kitkat version 4.4 and older Android versions.

In the newer Lollipop version (Android 5) this part of the malware is not working correctly anymore. Thus the victim would detect the attack. With a slight modification of the isolated proof of concept code we could show that the attack is still possible and that there is no tapjacking protection for the administration activity. We informed Google about our discovery and provided a patch preventing such an attack.

Bug Fix and Counter-Measures. As a counter measure against *tapjacking* Android provides some specific protection mechanism. It was introduced in API level 9 and is enabled by the method `setFilterTouchesWhenObscured()` which discards touches whenever the view's window is obscured by another visible window. As a result, clicking on the overlay window does not affect the underlying window. Alternatively, view elements can be protected on the level of XML declarations by defining the attribute `android:filterTouchesWhenObscured`.

Our provided patch introduces these functions to the accept- and deny-button for the administration activity. The patch code can be found here [2]. An attacker app thus can no longer trick the user into obtaining administrator privileges without her explicit consent. The described blacklisting approach of the Android OS is currently the only way to protect applications against such tapjacking attacks. To mitigate or completely prevent such attacks every critical android system application and also every provided Android application from the PlayStore should activate the protection. A better way would be some generic protection approach integrated in the Android OS.

Besides the counter measures from the AOSP, there already exists other mitigations from different researchers. For instance, Niemietz et al. [24] introduced an additional security layer into the AOSP consisting of a transparent layer over each foreground application. If a malicious application tries to get above the victim activity to set up a tapjacking attack, the security layer can catch all the touches trying to reach the protected app. We believe that a concept directly integrated into the AOSP, without further additions by the developer, would be simpler to maintain and should be integrated into Android.

3 Mobile Malware Analysis Challenges

The previous section describes in detail a representative malware family that shows the state-of-the-art for current Android banking malware. Mobile malware differs from PC malware in different aspects [25] resulting in the need for more complex analysis. One important aspect is the sensor-based event system of mobile devices, which allows the malware to react to incoming SMS, location changes etc., adding more complexity for automated malware-analysis approaches. Also the modular design of Android applications is an important factor for the need of more sophisticated analysis techniques, given that apps can use services and activities [10], and can combine different programming languages (e.g. JavaScript or native code) in one application.

Nevertheless, the goal in PC and mobile malware analysis always remains the same: *to identify the threat and take the necessary actions to eliminate the threat.* In case of a trojan stealing personal information, it is necessary to know *what*

---

[2] https://android-review.googlesource.com/#/c/127602/

data are stolen and *where* are they sent to. These are very important questions for security analysts in the case of active malware, because the analyst has to initiate further steps to remove the threat, for instance a C&C server takedown. The first question usually poses *dataflow questions* [3] whereas the latter one poses *reachability questions* [4]. Answering these questions in an automatic way would save a lot of time and money during investigation. Generally, two code-analyses approaches can be used: static or dynamic analysis techniques, or—more likely— a combination of both. Both approaches have well-known limitations [1,3], but the Android OS itself introduces new additional challenges.

In the following we look more concretely into the different challenges for static and dynamic analysis approaches that will arise during an analysis of the Android/BadAccents example. Challenges such as emulator detection mechanisms, obfuscation techniques or packers are not covered, since they are already described in previous work [29,37]. We use the Android/BadAccents malware as a representative for the complexity of current Android malware since it is implemented in a high-end engineering manner and contains various malicious components.

3.1   Static Analysis Challenges

In general, static analysis is a very powerful technique since one can reason about all execution paths in the application. This is especially useful to answer the *what* question in an investigation, i.e., what data are leaked.

Unfortunately, Android applications raise new challenges to static dataflow analysis, which are not only a theoretical problem anymore, as Android/BadAccents demonstrates. Recall that the malware sends sensitive data via e-mail where the origin of the data-source is stored in native code (Section 2). By answering the question *What is the username and password of the email account?*, one would either use a forward [3] or backward [14] dataflow analysis (*dataflow problem*) across language borders. The fact that the dataflow analysis has to deal with multiple code representations (Dalvik and native ARM) makes it more complex. Moreover, there is a need for new concepts how to handle *inter-language dataflows*. A new research direction could be the design of a common intermediate representation of Dalvik and native code which is not easy since both languages (Java and C/C++) have significant differences such as the pointer handling in native code. To the best of our knowledge, there is currently no real solution to this practical problem. But even an analysis of just the Java part raises new challenges for code-analysis approaches. The so-called *inter-component* dataflow tracking is well-known from literature [19,27], but the approaches do not yet scale in practice, due to path-explosion problems [19]. Besides the inter-component problem, Android/BadAccents has shown another interesting problem, namely the dataflow through persistent storages (e.g., SharedPreferences) where the data-source flows to a persistent storage and gets read at some later point from it to continue the flow to the sink-method. The current solution for such cases is an over-approximation of the dataflows where all data read from persistent storages are assumed to be 'sensitive' even if this is not the case. In practice, this produces too many false positives, which over-whelms an analyst with false-warnings. This is especially noticeable for Android applications, in comparison to applications in the PC world, since Android has a lot of API support for (temporary) storing data, which is actively used by developers as the Android/BadAccents sample shows (see Listing 1.1). Post-analysis approaches [43] that try to reduce false-positives after the main data-flow analysis are an interesting research area, but do not solve the main issue. Static code-analysis approaches for Android have to get advanced by adding new algorithms such as *quantitative information flows* [22] to reduce the false-positive problem.

As a summary, static analysis is very useful in general, but the analysis of Android applications include more challenges for which no concrete solution exists yet.

3.2 Dynamic Analysis Challenges

For all the above reasons, dynamic analysis or *behavior analysis* [33] has been advocated in the context of malware analysis [20, 35]. Furthermore, the answer to the *what* question is usually given by a dynamic analysis. To be complete however, dynamic analysis requires a set of execution traces that are representative of all the possible program behaviors. While observing all the program behaviors of a complex program is impractical, several coverage criteria have been proposed in the software testing literature to approximate full behavior coverage; their effectiveness however is still debated [15, 16]. Different facts in Android significantly hinder the triggering of malicious behavior by dynamically executing the code. For the example of Android/BadAccents we summarize the major problems in the following three categories: external events, environment settings and user interaction.

External Events. The Android OS is a sensor-based event-driven environment that reacts to various events and executes the registered event handlers. For instance, an incoming phone call is modeled as an Android internal event, called intent [41], which can be intercepted through a corresponding callback defined in the application. This produces the first challenge: a simple dynamic analysis is insufficient if it fails to generate the proper events. Researchers have proposed several approaches [34,45] for fuzzy testing Android components by sending abnormal/random intents to the components in order to identify security bugs. Nevertheless, section 2.2 shows that the malicious behavior gets only triggered if, for instance, the incoming SMS or HTTP request have the proper format. Furthermore, the ordering of events can also matter. For instance, the *Intercept SMS* component described in section 2.2 gets only activated if the attacker first sends an 'activation-command' and second the user sends an SMS to the victim. This makes a fully automated triggering of the original *Intercept SMS* component extremely difficult.

Environment Settings. A successful analysis of Android malware with a *behavior analysis* requires a properly setup environment, since many malware families check for clues of an emulated environment before they trigger their malicious behavior. The environment thus must be set up in such a way that it *emulates* all aspects of a proper smartphone. To some extent, this is impossible. For instance, emulators will always expose timing and cache behavior that is clearly distinguishable from real phones [29]. But not only emulator checks complicate dynamic analysis. The problem of *time bombs*, were the malware waits for a specific time until it triggers its malicious behavior (see section 2.2) poses a serious problem to dynamic analyses. This problem is similar to malware in the PC world, but has a much higher impact as the Wall Street Journal reported this year[3]. The Android malware went undetected in the Google Play store due to a time bomb and infecting close to 10 million devices. Time bombs can be 'evaded' by speeding up the time in the environment. Unfortunately, this might still be insufficient with state-of-the-art malware samples. Android/BadAccents requires specific files in the file system (DER-formatted files), specific contact data stored on the device and specific apps installed on the device (Korean banking apps) before the banking trojan gets activated. Since there is an exponential amount of combinations for different settings, it is very difficult to come up with a proper setting of an environment that emulates all that.

User Interaction. Mobile applications give a user a lot more possibilities for interaction since smartphones are in general an event-driven system. Interactions include the clicking on buttons, swiping objects, the reaction on incoming messages or filling out forms. Many of these interactions may need to be emulated to facilitate a meaningful dynamic analysis. Again, there has been a lot of research in the area of Android GUI testing [1,8] but to the best of our knowledge none of these approaches would successfully work on Android/BadAccents. For instance, the first GUI in figure 1 requires the user to input her password two times. Randomly inserting some values and automatically clicking on the 'ok'-button would not result in a page switch. Also the password in the first and third screen page has to have more than 5 digits, otherwise the GUI will not switch to the next one and the malicious behavior of stealing the credential data (shown in figure 2) would not be triggered. Figuring out the right combination of inputs would require the most sophisticated techniques, such as symbolic execution, which are hard to scale in general. Further research in this field is clearly required.

4   Related Work

In this section, we describe a number of related work in the context of Android malware analysis that addresses attacks and threats.

Abusing the device administration privileges in order to make the uninstallation of applications more difficult is a common technique used in Android

---

[3] http://blogs.wsj.com/personal-technology/2015/02/04/
   android-malware-removed-from-google-play-store-after-millions-of-downloads/

malware. For instance, the Android malware OBAD [42] requests administration privileges. Additionally it uses an Android vulnerability (fixed in Android 4) to hide its entry from the device administration list. This means it was also not possible for a user to manually revoke the admin privileges for uninstalling the malware. Another Android vulnerability [2], which got fixed in version 4.4.3, shows that it is even possible to prevent the installation of an arbitrary app on the device. Also different ransomware applications like Android/Koler [17] try to gather administration privileges to lock the device and encrypt the data storage. Another related malware in the context of banking trojans and C&C is the Zeus [23] trojan. This banking trojan exists despite of Android also for different mobile platforms like Blackberry, Windows Mobile or Symbian. The focus of the first Zeus trojan was to steal mTAN numbers through sms interception. Newer versions of Android trojans are aiming on stealing credit cards through wireless connection. Zhou et al. showed [47] a first global study about different types of Android malware. They showed that normal applications were enriched with malicious content and found different apps containing similar malware code. Depending of this payload they grouped them in different families.

Besides the internal threat detection framework of AV companies, there exist also other open-source approaches that crawl various app-stores for detecting malicious applications. Lindorfer et al. [21] propose a framework for discovering multiple instances of a malicious Android application in a set of alternative application markets. Based on some lightweight indicators, such as the package name or the hash of an application, they found various malicious applications in different markets. DroidSearch [30] is another framework that crawls different app stores and stores for each application meta-data into a database. The database can be queried afterwards for detecting vulnerabilities or malicious applications.

Isolated environments for analyzing and detecting Android malware are a well-established technique in the context of mobile malware analysis. Andrubis [20] or the Mobile Sandbox [35] are two examples. Usually, they use lightweight static analysis techniques to find concrete malware patterns [5] in combination with a lightweight dynamic code analysis approach that monitors the application in a secure environment. The results are used to detect suspicious behavior or evaluate the risk factor [26] of an application. Due to the nature of the lightweight analysis, the proposed techniques reaches its limitations when it comes to sophisticated malware that triggers malicious behavior only under specific circumstances.

Signature based approaches [46] are a well-known techniques used by many anti-virus applications. Zheng et al. [46] proposed a new signature methodology that was able to easily discover repackaged malicious applications or even zero-day malware samples. Apposcopy, a tool proposed by Feng et al. [12] improves signature based approaches by a semantic based approach that specifies signatures that describe semantic characteristics of malware families. Both approaches rely on static information extracted from the bytecode. Hardening or even packers complicates the detection of malicious applications as shown by different researchers [32].

5 Conclusion

In this paper, we have described an investigation of a new malware family that infected more than 20,000 mobile devices in Korea. We described in detail the components of current state-of-the-art mobile malware development. Furthermore, we compared each individual technique of the malware with current state-of-the-art malware-analysis techniques. Our results show that current malware poses many challenges to malware analysis techniques in order to trigger malicious behavior, showing the need for further research in this area. We furthermore demonstrated a new tapjacking attack that is exploited by the Android/BadAccents malware. It causes a security threat, as the user can be tricked into clicking/tapping on objects that trigger unintended behavior. The Android Security Team confirmed the attack and our proposed patch will be integrated in the next major release of Android.

Acknowledgments. This work was supported by the Deutsche Forschungsgemeinschaft within the project RUNSECURE, the BMBF within EC SPRIDE and ZertApps, by the Hessian LOEWE excellence initiative within CASED, and by the DFG Collaborative Research Center CROSSING.

References

1. Anand, S., Naik, M., Harrold, M.J., Yang, H.: Automated concolic testing of smartphone apps. In: Proceedings of the ACM SIGSOFT 20th FSE, FSE 2012. ACM, New York (2012)
2. Arzt, S., Huber, S., Rasthofer, S., Bodden, E.: Denial-of-app attack: inhibiting the installation of android apps on stock phones. In: Proceedings of the Fourth ACM SPSM Workshop. ACM, November 2014. https://github.com/secure-software-engineering/denial-of-app-attack
3. Arzt, S., Rasthofer, S., Fritz, C., Bodden, E., Bartel, A., Klein, J., Le Traon, Y., Octeau, D., McDaniel, P.: Flowdroid: precise context, flow, field, object-sensitive and lifecycle-aware taint analysis for android apps. In: Proceedings of the 35th ACM SIGPLAN PLDI. ACM, June 2014
4. Basin, D., Mödersheim, S., Vigano, L.: An on-the-fly model-checker for security protocol analysis. Springer (2003)
5. Bläsing, T., Schmidt, A.-D., Batyuk, L., Camtepe, S.A., Albayrak, S.: An android application sandbox system for suspicious software detection. In: 5th International MALWARE 2010, Nancy, France
6. Castillo, C.: Phishing attack replaces android banking apps with malware, June 2013. Blog
7. Chen, Q.A., Qian, Z., Mao, Z.M.: Peeking into your app without actually seeing it: UI state inference and novel android attacks. In: Proceedings of the 23rd USENIX Security Symposium (2014)
8. Choi, W., Necula, G., Sen, K.: Guided gui testing of android apps with minimal restart and approximate learning. In: Proceedings of the 2013 ACM SIGPLAN OOPSLA, OOPSLA 2013, New York, NY, USA (2013)
9. International Data Corporation. Worldwide quarterly mobile phone tracker 3q12, November 2012. Blog

10. Android Developer. Application fundamentals, April 2015. http://developer. android.com/guide/components/fundamentals.html
11. Dunham, K.: Android Malware and Analysis. CRC Press (2014)
12. Feng, Y., Anand, S., Dillig, I., Aiken, A.: Apposcopy: semantics-based detection of android malware through static analysis. In: Proceedings of the 22Nd ACM SIGSOFT FSE, FSE 2014. ACM, New York (2014)
13. Google. Android security 2014 year in review, April 2014
14. Hoffmann, J., Ussath, M., Holz, T., Spreitzenbarth, M.: Slicing droids: program slicing for smali code. In: Proceedings of the 28th Annual ACM SAC, SAC 2013, New York, NY, USA (2013)
15. Hutchins, M., Foster, H., Goradia, T., Ostrand, T.: Experiments of the effectiveness of dataflow- and controlflow-based test adequacy criteria. In: Proceedings of the 16th ICSE, ICSE 1994, Los Alamitos, CA, USA (1994)
16. Inozemtseva, L., Holmes, R.: Coverage is not strongly correlated with test suite effectiveness. In: Proceedings of the 36th ICSE, ICSE 2014, New York, NY, USA (2014)
17. Bitdefender LABS. Reveton / icepol ransomware moves to android. blog
18. McAfee Labs. Threats predictions (2015)
19. Li, L., Bartel, A., Bissyande, T., Klein, J., Le Traon, Y., Arzt, S., Rasthofer, S., Bodden, E., Octeau, D., McDaniel, P.: Iccta: detecting inter-component privacy leaks in android apps. In: Proceedings of the 37th ICSE, ICSE 2015. ACM (2015)
20. Lindorfer, M., Neugschwandtner, M., Weichselbaum, L., Fratantonio, Y., van der Veen, V., Platzer, C.: Andrubis - 1,000,000 apps later: a view on current android malware behaviors. In: Proceedings of the 3rd International Workshop BADGERS (2014)
21. Lindorfer, M., Volanis, S., Sisto, A., Neugschwandtner, M., Athanasopoulos, E., Maggi, F., Platzer, C., Zanero, S., Ioannidis, S.: AndRadar: fast discovery of android applications in alternative markets. In: Dietrich, S. (ed.) DIMVA 2014. LNCS, vol. 8550, pp. 51–71. Springer, Heidelberg (2014)
22. Lovat, E., Oudinet, J., Pretschner, A.: On quantitative dynamic data flow tracking. In: Fourth ACM Conference CODASPY (2014)
23. Maslennikov, D.: Zeus-in-the-mobile - facts and theories, October 2011. Blog
24. Niemietz, M., Schwenk, J.: Ui redressing attacks on android devices (2014). Black-Hat Asia
25. Nigam, R.: A timeline of mobile botnets, April 2015
26. NViso. http://apkscan.nviso.be/
27. Octeau, D., McDaniel, P., Jha, S., Bartel, A., Bodden, E., Klein, J., Le Traon, Y.: Effective inter-component communication mapping in android: an essential step towards holistic security analysis. In: Proceedings of the 22nd USENIX Security Symposium, USENIX, Washington, D.C. (2013)
28. Board of Governors of the Federal Reserve System. Consumers and mobile financial services 2014, March 2014
29. Petsas, T., Voyatzis, G., Athanasopoulos, E., Polychronakis, M., Ioannidis, S.: Rage against the virtual machine: hindering dynamic analysis of android malware. In: Proceedings of the Seventh European Workshop on System Security, EuroSec 2014, New York, NY, USA (2014)
30. Rasthofer, S., Arzt, S., Huber, S., Kohlhagen, M., Pfretschner, B., Bodden, E., Richter, P.: Droidsearch: a tool for scaling android app triage to real-world app stores. In: Proceedings of the IEEE SAI 2015, July 2015

31. Rasthofer, S., Asrar, I., Huber, S., Bodden, E.: An investigation of the android/badaccents malware which exploits a new android tapjacking attack. Technical report, TU Darmstadt, Fraunhofer SIT and McAfee Mobile Research, April 2015
32. Rastogi, V., Chen, Y., Jiang, X.: Droidchameleon: evaluating android anti-malware against transformation attacks. In: Proceedings of the 8th ACM SIGSAC ASIA CCS, ASIA CCS 2013, New York, NY, USA (2013)
33. Rieck, K., Trinius, P., Willems, C., Holz, T.: Automatic analysis of malware behavior using machine learning. J. Comput. Secur. **19**(4) (2011)
34. Sasnauskas, R., Regehr, J.: Intent fuzzer: crafting intents of death. In: Proceedings of the 2014 Joint International Workshop on Dynamic Analysis (WODA) and Software and System Performance Testing, Debugging, and Analytics (PERTEA), WODA+PERTEA 2014. ACM, New York (2014)
35. Spreitzenbarth, M., Freiling, F., Echtler, F., Schreck, T., Hoffmann, J.: Mobilesandbox: having a deeper look into android applications. In: Proceedings of the 28th Annual ACM SAC, SAC 2013. ACM, New York (2013)
36. statista, July 2014. http://www.statista.com/statistics/266210/number-of-available-applications-in-the-google-play-store/
37. Strazzere, T.: Android hacker protection level 0. Defcon 22
38. Symantec. Symantec report on the underground economy (2008)
39. Android Developer Team. Device administration. http://developer.android.com/guide/topics/admin/device-admin.html
40. Android Developer Team. Device policymanager. http://developer.android.com/reference/android/app/admin/DevicePolicyManager.html
41. Android Developer Team. Intent. http://developer.android.com/reference/android/content/Intent.html
42. Tinaztepe, E., Kurt, D., Güleç, A.: Android obad. Technical report, COMODO, July 2013
43. Tripp, O., Guarnieri, S., Pistoia, M., Aravkin, A.: Aletheia: improving the usability of static security analysis. In: Proceedings of the 2014 ACM SIGSAC CCS, CCS 2014. ACM, New York (2014)
44. Zeng, Y., Shin, K.G., Hu, X.: Design of sms commanded-and-controlled and p2p-structured mobile botnets. In: Proceedings of the Fifth ACM WISEC Conference, WISEC 2012. ACM, New York (2012)
45. Zhang, Y., Yang, M., Xu, B., Yang, Z., Gu, G., Ning, P., Wang, X.S., Zang, B.: Vetting undesirable behaviors in android apps with permission use analysis. In: Proceedings of the 2013 ACM SIGSAC CCS Conference, CCS 2013, pp. 611–622. ACM, New York (2013)
46. Zheng, M., Sun, M., Lui, J.C.S.: Droid analytics: a signature based analytic system to collect, extract, analyze and associate android malware. In: Proceedings of the 12th IEEE International TRUSTCOM Conference, TRUSTCOM 2013. IEEE Computer Society, Washington, DC (2013)
47. Zhou, Y., Jiang, X.: Dissecting android malware: characterization and evolution. In: Proceedings of the 2012 IEEE S&P, SP 2012. IEEE Computer Society, Washington, DC (2012)

On Linkability and Malleability in Self-blindable Credentials

Jaap-Henk Hoepman[1], Wouter Lueks[1], and Sietse Ringers[2]([✉])

[1] Radboud University, Nijmegen, The Netherlands
{jhh,lueks}@cs.ru.nl
[2] Johann Bernoulli Institute for Mathematics and Computer Science,
University of Groningen, Groningen, The Netherlands
s.ringers@rug.nl

Abstract. Self-blindable credential schemes allow users to anonymously prove ownership of credentials. This is achieved by randomizing the credential before each showing in such a way that it still remains valid. As a result, each time a different version of the same credential is presented. A number of such schemes have been proposed, but unfortunately many of them are broken, in the sense that they are *linkable* (i.e., failing to protect the privacy of the user), or *malleable* (i.e., they allow users to create new credentials using one or more valid credentials given to them). In this paper we prove a general theorem that relates linkability and malleability in self-blindable credential schemes, and that can test whether a scheme is linkable or malleable. After that we apply the theorem to a number of self-blindable credential schemes to show that they suffer from one or both of these issues.

1 Introduction

The indiscriminate collection and processing of personal data, and the consequences to the privacy of citizens, has been getting more and more attention over the last few years. As a result, there is an increasing demand for technologies that put privacy and control back in the hands of the user. In the case of digital identity management, in particular, it is both highly desirable and non-trivial to have privacy-friendly solutions.

Anonymous credentials are a promising technique for secure and privacy-friendly identity management. They are given by an issuer to the user, who can then prove possession of it to other parties. This showing should be such that it is infeasible for the issuer, the verifier or any other party to determine whether two transactions did or did not originate from the same user (this property is called *multi-show unlinkability*, or just unlinkability for short). Additionally, credentials have to be unforgeable, in the sense that the user cannot create his own credential, or modify one or more existing ones in order to obtain a new credential (this kind of forgeability is called *malleability* and plays and important role in this paper). A number of such systems already exist; we mention, for example, Idemix [4,10] and U-Prove [3,12]. Both of these are *attribute based*, meaning that

© IFIP International Federation for Information Processing 2015
R.N. Akram and S. Jajodia (Eds.): WISTP 2015, LNCS 9311, pp. 203–218, 2015.
DOI: 10.1007/978-3-319-24018-3_13

a credential may contain multiple attributes (which are pieces of information or statements, generally about the owner of the credential). These systems tend to be complex, however, which is why considerable effort has gone into simpler credential systems that have no attributes (for example [9]; see also Example 31). Instead, such credentials are either valid or invalid, resulting in simpler constructions that are easier to study and potentially more efficient, allowing for practical implementations of such credentials on smart cards. Naturally, such credential schemes still have to be unlinkable and unforgeable.

A simple method to construct (not necessarily anonymous) credentials would be to sign the user's public key (for example in the form of an X.509 certificate). The signature, together with the public key, then form the credential. To prevent replay attacks (e.g., a malicious verifier reusing a user's public key and signature to authenticate itself elsewhere), when showing the credential the user proofs knowledge of the private key of his credential without disclosing the private key to the verifier (using, for example, a zero-knowledge proof or a challenge-response). A problem with this simple scheme, however, is that the user presents the same certificate on each use, making all uses of the same credential linkable. One technique for preventing such linkability is to modify the credential before each showing, in such a way that it remains valid. This is called *blinding*, and credential schemes that use this technique are called *self-blindable credential schemes*. The first example of such a scheme was given by Verheul in the same paper that defines the notion of self-blindability [13]. The advantage of blinding credentials in such a way is that it is easy for the user (blinding is usually cheap) and for the verifier (verifying a blinded signature is generally not much different from verifying an ordinary signature).

In the past decade, a number of such self-blindable credential schemes have been proposed [4,7,9,11,13]. Unfortunately, many of them are broken, in the sense that transactions are linkable or the credentials are malleable, or even both. In this paper we uncover a common theme in the cause of the problem of each of these schemes: the dependence of the public key and signature on the private key of the credential can often be exploited to achieve linkability or malleability. This suggests there is a trade-off between the two. After having introduced and defined the relevant concepts in Section 3, we show this by proving a general theorem in Section 4 that makes it easy to determine whether a self-blindable credential scheme is linkable. The theorem exhibits an interesting and strong relationship between linkability and malleability of the credential scheme. We then apply this theorem in Section 5 to show that several proposed self-blindable schemes in the literature are linkable, and present explicit counter-examples as well. The theorem also indicates in which directions to look for self-blindable credential schemes that are both unlinkable and unmalleable.

2   Notations and Conventions

In this paper we use the following notations and conventions. A bilinear group pair (G_1, G_2) consists of two cyclic groups (that we will write additively), both of prime order p, such that there exists a a *bilinear map* or *pairing*; that is, a map $e: G_1 \times G_2 \to G_T$ (with G_T a multiplicative group of order p) satisfying the following properties:

- *Bilinearity*: for all $G, G' \in G_1$ and $H, H' \in G_2$ we have $e(G + G', H) = e(G, H)e(G', H)$ and $e(G, H + H') = e(G, H)e(G, H')$.
- *Non-degeneracy*: Denoting the generators of G_1 and G_2 with $P \in G_1, Q \in G_2$ respectively, the element $e(P, Q)$ is a generator of G_T (that is, it is unequal to $1 \in G_T$).
- *Computability*: There exists an efficient algorithm for computing $e(G, H)$ for any $G \in G_1$, $H \in G_2$.

Such pairings exist for some special classes of elliptic curves. Usually, three distinct types of bilinear group pairs are distinguished:

- Type 1: $G_1 = G_2$.
- Type 2: $G_1 \neq G_2$, but there exists an efficiently computable group isomorphism $\phi: G_2 \to G_1$.
- Type 3: $G_1 \neq G_2$, and there is no known efficiently computable group isomorphism $\phi: G_2 \to G_1$.

For more information about bilinear group pairs and pairings we refer to [8]; see also, for example, Chapters I and X from [1].

We consider the coefficient k of a group element $K = kP$ to be an element of $\mathbb{Z}_p = \mathbb{Z}/p\mathbb{Z}$. Blinding factors will be denoted with Greek letters α, β, γ. We denote variables which have been blinded with a bar on top of them, for example $\overline{K}$.

3   Self-blindable Credentials

A credential scheme is a set of protocols in which an *issuer* (or *identity provider*) can issue a credential to a user, who can then show this credential to a *verifier* (or *service provider*), so that the verifier becomes convinced that the user indeed has the credential, and that it was given to him by the issuer. For the purposes of this paper we assume that there is a single issuer, and that he creates all certificates using the same private key (our results easily extend to the general case). Such credential schemes must provide at least the following two protocols:

Issue: This is an interactive protocol between a user and the issuer. The user provides the issuer with the information it needs (if the issuer does not already know this information) in order to create the credential C. The issuer checks whether the user is allowed to have the credential C, and if so, creates it and sends it to the user.

ShowCredential: This is an interactive protocol between a user and a verifier, in which the user convinces the verifier that he owns a credential C and that it is valid (i.e., that it was given to him by the issuer, and if the credential scheme allows for revoking, that it has not been revoked).[1]

A credential scheme may also allow for credentials to be revoked; in that case there is also a Revoke protocol, which revokes (invalidates) a credential. Additionally, during the ShowCredential protocol an algorithm RevocationCheck is executed, which checks if a credential has been revoked.

We expect any credential scheme, be it attribute-based, self-blindable or both, to satisfy the following properties.

– *Multi-show unlinkability*: It should be impossible for any party to tell whether two executions of the ShowCredential protocol involved the same credential or two different ones.[2]
– *Issuer unlinkability*: The issuer cannot decide if a run of the Issue and a run of the ShowCredential protocol did or did not originate from the same credential.
– *Unforgeability*: Only the issuer can create valid credentials.
– *Offline issuer*: The issuer is not involved in the verification of credentials.
– *Non-transferability*: Users cannot transfer their credentials to other users.

3.1 Definitions

In all self-blindable credential schemes that we know of, a credential consists of a private key k, a corresponding public key K, and a signature S over the public key that the issuer gives to the owner of the credential. That is, a credential C is of the form

$$C = (k, K, S) \in \mathcal{P} \times \mathcal{K} \times \mathcal{S}$$

where $\mathcal{P}$, $\mathcal{K}$ and $\mathcal{S}$ are the sets of private keys, public keys and signatures, respectively. We shall write $\mathcal{C}$ for the product $\mathcal{C} = \mathcal{P} \times \mathcal{K} \times \mathcal{S}$. Let us say that an element $(k, K, S) \in \mathcal{P} \times \mathcal{K} \times \mathcal{S}$ is *valid* when k is the private key corresponding to K and S is a valid signature over K with respect to the issuer's signing key.

Self-blindable credentials, introduced by Verheul [13], are credentials that the user modifies each time before he shows it to a verifier, in such a way that

---

[1] Attribute-based credential schemes such as U-Prove and Idemix generally also allow selective disclosures of attributes. Such disclosures, however, necessarily reduces the anonymity set of the credential (and may even identify it uniquely).

[2] In the case of attribute-based credential schemes, the unlinkability that the first and second properties describe only need to hold within the set of credentials that have disclosed the same attributes. That is, for example, given two executions of the ShowCredential protocol in which the same attributes with the same values were disclosed, it should be impossible to tell whether one or two credentials were involved. A similar adaptation holds for the second property.

   In the remainder of this paper, we assume for simplicity that no attributes are disclosed in the ShowCredential protocol.

it remains valid, and such that multiple transactions cannot be linked to each other. We define this notion as follows.[3]

Definition 3.1. *A credential scheme is called* self-blindable *if*

1. *There exists a blinding-factor space $\mathcal{B}$ and an efficiently computable map*

$$B: \mathcal{C} \times \mathcal{B} \to \mathcal{K} \times \mathcal{S},$$

   such that if the credential $C = (k, K, S) \in \mathcal{C}$ is valid and $B(C, \alpha) = (\overline{K}, \overline{S})$ for $\overline{K} \in \mathcal{K}$ and $\overline{S} \in \mathcal{S}$, then $\overline{S}$ is a valid signature over $\overline{K}$ for any $\alpha \in \mathcal{B}$;
2. *In the ShowCredential protocol, the credential C is blinded to $(\overline{K}, \overline{S}) = B(C, \alpha)$ for a random $\alpha \in_R \mathcal{B}$, after which $\overline{K}$ and $\overline{S}$ are used as the public key and signature respectively in the remainder of the ShowCredential protocol.*

Most self-blindable credential schemes that we know of have a ShowCredential protocol of the following form:

1. The user blinds K and S using the blinding map B and sends the blinded values $\overline{K}$, $\overline{S}$ to the verifier, who then non-interactively checks that $\overline{S}$ is a valid signature over $\overline{K}$.
2. Afterwards, the user and verifier engage in a (possibly zero-knowledge) proof in which the user convinces the verifier that he knows the private key k and blinding factor α from which he calculated $\overline{K}$ (i.e., the first element from the tuple $(\overline{K}, \overline{S}) = B((k, K, C), \alpha)$).

We purposefully do not include the private key in the blinded credentials (that is, we do not demand that $B(C, \alpha) = (\overline{k}, \overline{K}, \overline{S})$, where $\overline{k}$ is the private key corresponding to $\overline{K}$), because if such a map B were to exist then anyone can, given one credential, create arbitrary new ones. That is, there would be no distinction between the creation of new credentials by the issuer and blinding an existing credential. In terms of Definition 3.3, the system would then be 1-malleable.

Example 31. As a first example we consider the self-blindable credential by Hoepman et al. [9], which is based on the original scheme by Verheul [13]. Here we use the Chaum–Pedersen [6] signature scheme, as follows. Consider a Type 1 pairing $e: G_1 \times G_2 \to G_T$, with all groups of prime order p, and take generators P and Q for G_1 and G_2 respectively. Then the private signing key of the issuer is a number $a \in \mathbb{Z}_p$, and the corresponding public key is $A = aQ \in G_2$.

The space of private keys of credentials is $\mathcal{P} = \mathbb{Z}_p$, and for a private key $k \in \mathbb{Z}_p$ the corresponding public key is $K = kP \in G_1$. The signature on K is then a Chaum–Pedersen signature $S = aK$, which can be verified by

$$e(K, A) \stackrel{?}{=} e(S, Q).$$

---

[3] In [13], Verheul puts four extra demands on the blinding map B besides item 1 in our definition, that are meant to exclude edge cases that could never lead to desirable properties in a credential schemes. Instead of including these four extra properties, we describe the role of the blinding map B more directly in the second item in Definition 3.1.

Thus, we have $\mathcal{K} = \mathcal{S} = G_1$.

Blinding the public key is done by multiplying it by a random number $\alpha \in \mathbb{Z}_p$, that is, $\overline{K} = \alpha k P$, and similarly for the signature: $\overline{S} = \alpha a k P$. The verification equation then becomes

$$e(\overline{K}, A) \stackrel{?}{=} e(\overline{S}, Q).$$

If $\overline{K}$ and $\overline{S}$ are blinded by the same value $\alpha \in \mathbb{Z}_p$, and if the unblinded signature is a valid Chaum–Pedersen signature over the unblinded public key K, then this equation holds.

The problem of this system is not linkability, but malleability. Given a credential (k, K, S) on its private key k the user can easily create a new credential $(\alpha k, \alpha K, \alpha S)$ on any other private key αk. This means that a user that has access to the internals of his credential can create a new credential over any private key $\overline{k} \in \mathbb{Z}_p$, without involving the issuer. (Hoepman et al. mitigate this attack by storing the private key on a smart card, so that the user cannot access it directly. It is, however, still a problem, for example because revocation in such a system would be impossible, because there is nothing that binds the private key to the user.)

We will examine this form of forgeability more closely in Definition 3.3 and Example 53. In this case, it is a consequence of the linearity of the Chaum–Pedersen signature S in the private key k. Later on, in Example 51, we will see how using a signature scheme that is nonlinear in k results in linkability.

This paper is mostly concerned with how the blinded public key $\overline{K}$ and blinded signature $\overline{S}$ depend on the private key k and blinding factor α. Taking the blinded public key $\overline{K}$, we will denote the dependency of $\overline{K}$ on k by writing

$$\overline{K} = \mathsf{PubKey}(k, \alpha)$$

for a certain function $\mathsf{PubKey} \colon \mathcal{P} \times \mathcal{B} \to \mathcal{K}$. Similarly,

$$\overline{S} = \mathsf{Sig}_{SK}(k, \alpha).$$

for a certain function $\mathsf{Sig}_{SK} \colon \mathcal{P} \times \mathcal{B} \to \mathcal{S}$. Here SK is the issuer's private key. Using these functions PubKey and Sig_{SK}, we can express the blinding map B as follows:

$$B((k, K, S), \alpha) = (\overline{K}, \overline{S}) = (\mathsf{PubKey}(k, \alpha), \mathsf{Sig}_{SK}(k, \alpha)).$$

We stress that these functions PubKey and Sig_{SK} need not correspond to any algorithm that is run by one of the involved parties (typically, for example, the user will calculate the blinded public key using the unblinded public key, not directly from the private key). The purpose of these functions is purely to make the dependence on the private key and blinding factor explicit.

3.2 Security Properties

Having defined the basic structures and the notion of self-blindability, we next turn to the security properties that we expect credential schemes to satisfy.

Definition 3.2 (Unlinkability). *A self-blindable credential scheme is* unlinkable *if no adversary can win the following game with non-negligible advantage.*

Setup. *The challenger sets up the system and creates n credentials with identifiers $1, \ldots, n$. It sends the public parameters to the adversary.*

Queries. *For any $i \in \{1, \ldots, n\}$ the adversary may issue the following queries:*

    Verify(i). *The adversary acts as the verifier in the ShowCredential protocol for the credential i, with the challenger acting as the user. The adversary sees the same interaction as a normal verifier would see.*

    Corrupt(i). *The adversary requests the credential i to be corrupted. The challenger gives him the internal state of credential i.*

Challenge. *The adversary selects two uncorrupted credentials i_0, i_1 from the set $\{1, \ldots, n\}$ and informs the challenger of his choice. The challenger then picks a bit $b \in_R \{0,1\}$ at random, and runs ShowCredential on credential i_b with the adversary playing the role of the user while the adversary acts as the verifier. The adversary outputs a bit b'. He wins if $b = b'$.*

This definition of linkability includes a stronger notion of linkability where the adversary only gets to see two traces, and has to decide whether they belong to the same user. Given such an adversary $\mathcal{A}'$ we can then build an adversary $\mathcal{A}$ satisfying the definition above by having it perform the following actions:

Setup. $\mathcal{A}$ sets up the unlinkability game with his challenger.

Queries. $\mathcal{A}$ chooses two credentials i_0 and i_1 at random from the list of credentials $\{1, \ldots, n\}$ and queries his challenger on i_0. He stores the trace of the protocol run.

Challenge. $\mathcal{A}$ informs his challenger that he has chosen the credentials i_0 and i_1 from the previous phase. He engages in the ShowCredential protocol on i_b and stores the trace. Then, he uses the algorithm $\mathcal{A}'$ to compare the traces from i_0 and i_b. If $\mathcal{A}'$ returns that i_0 and i_b have the same public key then $\mathcal{A}$ outputs $b' = 0$ as his guess; otherwise he outputs $b' = 1$.

Then the algorithm $\mathcal{A}$ satisfies the definitions above.

Definition 3.3 (n-malleability). *Let $\{(k_1, K_1, S_1), \ldots, (k_n, K_n, S_n)\} \in \mathcal{C}^n$ be a tuple of n valid credentials. If there exists an efficiently computable map $F \colon \mathcal{C}^n \to \mathcal{C}$ which outputs a valid credential on a new private key (that is, if*

$$(k, K, S) = F\Big((k_1, K_1, S_1), \ldots, (k_n, K_n, S_n)\Big)$$

then (k, K, S) is valid and $k \neq k_i$ for all $i = 1, \ldots, n$) then we say that the credential scheme is n-malleable.

Although malleability is nothing more than a particular kind of forgeability, it warrants a separate definition because it occurs in a number of existing credential schemes, and because it plays an important role in the theorem below. The problem that the definition above aims to capture is that new credentials can be made without the involvement or knowledge of the issuer, if the user has n credentials. We see that the credential scheme from Example 31 has 1-malleability: in that scheme, given a credential (k, K, S) and any $\alpha \in \mathbb{Z}_p$, the credential $(\alpha k, \alpha K, \alpha S)$ is a new valid credential. This is a problem, because the blinded credential should still be bound to the original private key k.

Note, however, that if the scheme is not attribute-based but credentials are either valid or invalid, then malleability is not necessarily a problem. Modifying an existing credential into a new one does not change any of its key properties: it was valid and it remains valid, so nothing has really changed. On the other hand, we can think of the following cases in which it would be a problem.

- The public key K may contain meaningful information such as attributes (as is the case in, for example, U-Prove). In this case, the user should not be able to manipulate this meaningful data, so it should be impossible by exploiting the malleability to obtain a new valid credential whose public key contains different information. In particular, the user should not be able to create a credential whose public key is $\overline{K}$ when given a credential with public key K.
- In a self-blindable credential scheme that is not attribute-based (for example the one from Example 31), issuers may issue multiple credentials (signed by different keys) instead of a single credential with multiple attributes. For example, a public key signed with private key a_1 may mean that the user is over 18, while one signed with private key a_2 could mean that he is a German citizen. In such a setting it should be impossible to combine credentials issued to different users. In this case, an underage German citizen should not be able to use his foreign friend's over 18 credential to prove that he is both over 18 and a German citizen. Normally, such a proof would show that the signed public keys in both credentials are identical, thus preventing credentials from being combined. However, malleability might make it possible to change a credential over one public key (say the foreign friend's) into another public key (say of the underage German citizen). This would make credential pooling trivial.
- Similarly, the unchecked randomization of the signed public key can make revocation – an essential feature of anonymous credential systems – all but impossible.

In the next section, we show that malleability has a strong link with linkability, and then examine a number of credential schemes that suffer from these issues.

4   Relating Malleability and Linkability

In the credential schemes considered in this paper, the public key $K \in \mathcal{K}$ depends linearly on the private key $k \in \mathcal{P}$. Any signature over K obviously depends on

K, and therefore also on k. Thus, when considering suitable signature schemes, if the set of signatures is a group then we may take one that is either linear or not linear in k. The theorem and its corollary below then say the following: if the signature scheme is *not* linear in k, then there is linkability, while if it is linear in k then the scheme *may* be malleable. Loosely speaking, this is because if the public key and the signature do not depend on the user's private key and the blinding factor in precisely the same way, then this can be exploited. Let us now make this more precise.

We assume henceforth that $\mathcal{P}$, $\mathcal{K}$ and $\mathcal{S}$ are all groups, that we will write additively. From the corollary below and onwards it will moreover be the case that the latter two are vector spaces over $\mathcal{P}$, meaning that elements from $\mathcal{K}$ and $\mathcal{S}$ can be multiplied on the left by elements from $\mathcal{P}$: for example, $kK \in \mathcal{K}$ for $k \in \mathcal{P}$ and $K \in \mathcal{K}$. We recall the following definition.

Definition 4.1. *A map $L \colon V \to W$, with V and W being vector spaces over $\mathcal{P}$, is* linear *if $L(v + v') = L(v) + L(v')$ and $L(kv) = kL(v)$ for all $v, v' \in V$ and $k \in \mathcal{P}$.*

We denote with $\mathsf{Verify}_{PK} \colon \mathcal{K} \times \mathcal{S} \to \{\mathsf{true}, \mathsf{false}\}$ the verification function of the signature scheme under consideration, where PK is the public key of the issuer. That is, Verify_{PK} is such that

$$\mathsf{Verify}_{PK}\left(\mathsf{PubKey}(k, \alpha), \mathsf{Sig}_{SK}(k, \alpha)\right) = \mathsf{true}$$

for all k, α. On the other hand, whenever $k \neq k'$ or $\alpha \neq \alpha'$ (or both), we should have (with overwhelming probability)

$$\mathsf{Verify}_{PK}\left(\mathsf{PubKey}(k, \alpha), \mathsf{Sig}_{SK}(k', \alpha')\right) = \mathsf{false}.$$

Theorem 4.1. *Consider a self-blindable credential scheme. Suppose that for each $k, k' \in \mathcal{P}$ and $\alpha, \alpha' \in \mathcal{B}$ there exist $\ell \in \mathcal{P}$ and $\beta \in \mathcal{B}$ such that*

$$\mathsf{PubKey}(k, \alpha) + \mathsf{PubKey}(k', \alpha') = \mathsf{PubKey}(\ell, \beta). \tag{1}$$

If Sig_{SK} also has this property for the same ℓ, β, that is,

$$\mathsf{Sig}_{SK}(k, \alpha) + \mathsf{Sig}_{SK}(k', \alpha') = \mathsf{Sig}_{SK}(\ell, \beta) \tag{2}$$

but only when $k = k'$, then there is linkability. On the other hand, if Sig_{SK} always has this property, and

- *the $\mathsf{ShowCredential}$ protocol allows the user to present $(\ell, \mathsf{PubKey}(\ell, \beta), \mathsf{Sig}_{SK}(\ell, \beta))$ as a valid credential,*
- *the user can efficiently compute ℓ and β,*

then there is 2-malleability.

Proof. Assume that Sig_{SK} has the stated property only when $k = k'$, and that equation (1) always holds. Then if $k = k'$ we have $\mathsf{Sig}_{SK}(k, \alpha) + \mathsf{Sig}_{SK}(k', \alpha') = \mathsf{Sig}_{SK}(\ell, \beta)$ and similarly for PubKey, so

$$\mathsf{Verify}_{PK}\left(\mathsf{PubKey}(k, \alpha) + \mathsf{PubKey}(k', \alpha'),\ \mathsf{Sig}_{SK}(k, \alpha) + \mathsf{Sig}_{SK}(k', \alpha')\right)$$
$$= \mathsf{Verify}_{PK}\left(\mathsf{PubKey}(\ell, \beta), \mathsf{Sig}_{SK}(\ell, \beta)\right) = \mathsf{true}.$$

On the other hand, if $k \neq k'$, then $\mathsf{Sig}_{SK}(k, \alpha) + \mathsf{Sig}_{SK}(k', \alpha')$ does not evaluate to $\mathsf{Sig}_{SK}(\ell, \beta)$. Therefore

$$\mathsf{Verify}_{PK}\left(\mathsf{PubKey}(k, \alpha) + \mathsf{PubKey}(k', \alpha'), \; \mathsf{Sig}_{SK}(k, \alpha) + \mathsf{Sig}_{SK}(k', \alpha')\right)$$
$$= \mathsf{false}.$$

Thus, the function Verify_{PK} returns true when applied to the sum of the two credentials involved if and only if $k = k'$, so that the scheme is linkable.

The second part of the statement is obvious: if the ShowProtocol protocol does not prevent the user from using $(\ell, \; \mathsf{PubKey}(\ell, \beta), \mathsf{Sig}_{SK}(\ell, \beta))$ as a valid credential then he can present it to verifiers, even though $\mathsf{Sig}_{SK}(\ell, \beta)$ was not given to him by the issuer.

Corollary 4.2. *Suppose the function* PubKey *is linear in both arguments. If* Sig_{SK} *is linear in the second but not the first argument, then there is linkability. If* Sig_{SK} *is linear in both arguments, then there is 1-malleability.*

Proof. Suppose Sig_{SK} is linear in the second but not the first argument, and that $k = k' \in \mathcal{P}$. Then

$$\mathsf{PubKey}(k, \alpha) + \mathsf{PubKey}(k', \alpha')$$
$$= \mathsf{PubKey}(k, \alpha) + \mathsf{PubKey}(k, \alpha')$$
$$= \mathsf{PubKey}(k, \alpha + \alpha'),$$

and since Sig_{SK} is also linear in the second argument, we will also have $\mathsf{Sig}_{SK}(k, \alpha) + \mathsf{Sig}_{SK}(k', \alpha') = \mathsf{Sig}_{SK}(k, \alpha + \alpha')$. Thus $\mathsf{Sig}_{SK}(k, \alpha + \alpha')$ will be a valid signature over $\mathsf{PubKey}(k, \alpha + \alpha')$.

On the other hand, if $k \neq k'$ then

$$\mathsf{PubKey}(k, \alpha) + \mathsf{PubKey}(k', \alpha')$$
$$= k\mathsf{PubKey}(1, \alpha) + k'\mathsf{PubKey}(1, \alpha')$$
$$= k\alpha\mathsf{PubKey}(1, 1) + k'\alpha'\mathsf{PubKey}(1, 1)$$
$$= (k\alpha + k'\alpha')\mathsf{PubKey}(1, 1)$$
$$= \mathsf{PubKey}(k\alpha + k'\alpha', 1),$$

but now $\mathsf{Sig}_{SK}(k, \alpha) + \mathsf{Sig}_{SK}(k', \alpha') \neq \mathsf{Sig}_{SK}(k\alpha + k'\alpha', 1)$, because Sig_{SK} is not linear in its first argument. Hence the verification function Verify_{PK} over the sum of both credentials will distinguish $k = k'$ and $k \neq k'$, so that the credential scheme is linkable.

Concerning the second statement of the corollary, if both PubKey and Sig_{SK} are linear in both arguments, then

$$\mathsf{PubKey}(k, \alpha) = \alpha\mathsf{PubKey}(k, 1) = \mathsf{PubKey}(\alpha k, 1),$$

and similarly $\mathsf{Sig}_{SK}(k, \alpha) = \mathsf{Sig}_{SK}(\alpha k, 1)$, so that $(\alpha k, \mathsf{PubKey}(k, \alpha), \mathsf{Sig}_{SK}(k, \alpha))$ is a valid credential. Therefore, there is 1-malleability.

Essentially, the corollary implies that when the verification function is used directly in the ShowCredential protocol, then it is very difficult to assure that it is neither linkable nor malleable. Indeed, if the public key is linear in the private key while the signature is not, then there is likely linkability through the verification equation of the signature scheme. On the other hand, if they are both linear in the private key then it is likely that the system suffers from malleability.

In spite of this difficulty we do not believe that it is impossible to create a self-blindable credential scheme that is neither malleable nor linkable; we will discuss this in more detail in Section 6. In the next section, we discuss a number of self-blindable credential schemes, that all suffer from one of these problems.

5   Broken Self-blindable Credential Schemes

Example 51. For this example we reuse the PubKey function from Example 31, but this time we use the (weak) Boneh–Boyen signature scheme [2] instead. In this scheme the public and private keys of the issuer are $a \in \mathbb{Z}_p$ and $A = aQ \in G_2$ respectively, as before. A signature on $k \in \mathbb{Z}_p$ is $S = \frac{1}{a+k}P$. Setting $K = kQ \in G_2$ (note that now $K \in G_2$, contrary to Example 31), the signature S may be verified by checking that $e(S, A + K) \stackrel{?}{=} e(P, Q)$.

We still blind the public key and signature by multiplying it with a random number α, i.e.,

$$\overline{K} = \mathsf{PubKey}(k, \alpha) = \alpha k Q$$

and

$$\overline{S} = \mathsf{Sig}_a(k, \alpha) = \frac{\alpha}{a + k}P.$$

In addition, the user will also have to send $\overline{A} = \alpha A$, $\overline{P} = \alpha P$ and $\overline{Q} = \alpha Q$ to the verifier. The verification is done by checking

$$e(\overline{S}, \overline{A} + \overline{K}) \stackrel{?}{=} e(\overline{P}, \overline{Q}).$$

The ShowCredential protocol of this scheme might look as follows.

	User	Verifier
	choose blinding $\alpha \in_R \mathbb{Z}_p$	
	send $\alpha K, \alpha S, \alpha A, \alpha P, \alpha Q \longrightarrow$	into $\overline{K}, \overline{S}, \overline{A}, \overline{P}, \overline{Q}$
		verify $e(\overline{S}, \overline{A} + \overline{K}) \stackrel{?}{=} e(\overline{P}, \overline{Q})$
	$\mathrm{PK}\{(\kappa) : \overline{K} = \kappa P\} \longleftarrow$	

Fig. 1. Self-blindable credential scheme from Example 31 modified to use the Boneh–Boyen signature scheme.

In this case, if $k = k'$ then $\mathsf{PubKey}(k, \alpha) + \mathsf{PubKey}(k', \alpha') = \mathsf{PubKey}(k, \alpha + \alpha')$, and similarly $\mathsf{Sig}_a(k, \alpha) + \mathsf{Sig}_a(k', \alpha') = \mathsf{Sig}_a(k, \alpha + \alpha')$, so that Verify_A will return true. On the other hand, if $k \neq k'$, then

$$\mathsf{PubKey}(k, \alpha) + \mathsf{PubKey}(k', \alpha') = \mathsf{PubKey}(\alpha k + \alpha' k', 1)$$

while

$$\mathsf{Sig}_a(k, \alpha) + \mathsf{Sig}_a(k', \alpha') \neq \mathsf{Sig}_a(\alpha k + \alpha' k', 1)$$

so Verify_A will return false. Thus, this system is linkable.

Example 52. Like the scheme from Example 31, the self-blindable credential scheme from Kiyomoto and Tanaka [11] uses Chaum-Pedersen signatures, but this time on a Type 1 curve (i.e., $G_1 = G_2 = G$ and $P = Q$). The issuer's public key is $A = aP$.

The private key here consists of two numbers $(\kappa, \kappa') \in \mathbb{Z}_p^2$, where κ is random while $\kappa' = m\kappa$ is a *non-repudiation private key*; here m is a number encoding some valuable piece of information related to the user. This would discourage users from sharing their credential, because if another party learns κ and κ' then it could recover m. Setting $k := \kappa + \kappa'$, the corresponding public key and signature are $K = kP$ and $S = aK = akP$. The $\mathsf{ShowCredential}$ protocol of this scheme is shown in Figure 2.

User	Verifier
choose blinding $\alpha \in_R \mathbb{Z}_p$	
send $\alpha K, \alpha S \longrightarrow$	into $\overline{K}, \overline{S}$
	verify $e(\overline{K}, A) \stackrel{?}{=} e(\overline{S}, P)$
	choose nonce $\eta \in_R \mathbb{Z}_p$
into $N \longleftarrow$	send ηP
send $\alpha\kappa N, \alpha\kappa' N \longrightarrow$	into $\overline{M}, \overline{M}'$
	verify $e(\overline{M} + \overline{M}', P) \stackrel{?}{=} e(\overline{K}, \eta P)$
	run $\mathsf{RevocationCheck}(\overline{K}, \overline{M})$

Fig. 2. Self-blindable credential scheme by Kiyomoto et al. [11] (simplified).

This scheme suffers from a number of problems. First, the relation $k = \kappa + m\kappa$ is nowhere enforced by the $\mathsf{ShowCredential}$ protocol, in the sense that the user could use $\lambda, k - \lambda$ for some random $\lambda \in \mathbb{Z}_p$ instead of κ, κ'. This means that users can easily share credentials after all, without fear of disclosing the valuable information encoded by m.

Second, without going into the details of the revocation mechanism, we remark that it relies on how k splits into $k = \kappa + \kappa'$, so that the problem above allows users to present revoked credentials without problems. (In addition, the revocation mechanism introduces linkability.)

Third, since both the public key K and signature S are linear in both the blinding factor α and private key k, by Corollary 4.2 the scheme is 1-malleable. For any α and valid credential $((\kappa, \kappa'), K, S)$ the user can present the credential $((\lambda, \alpha k - \lambda), \alpha K, \alpha S)$. (Actually, because the public key $A = aP \in G$ lives in the same group as the signatures $S = akP \in G$, anyone can easily create his own credential by setting $K = (\kappa + \kappa')P =: kP$ for some random $\kappa, \kappa' \in \mathbb{Z}_p$, and $S = kA$ – that is, the system is actually 0-malleable.)

Example 53. Some of the problems of the credential scheme above were pointed out by Emura et al. [7], who came up with an improved protocol that we will examine in this example. In this protocol the malleability is solved through the use of Boneh-Boyen signatures. Theorem 4.1 shows, however, that it is linkable. We explain the problem here.

User	Verifier
	choose nonce $\eta \in_R \mathbb{Z}_p$
into $N \longleftarrow$	send ηQ
choose blinding $\alpha \in_R \mathbb{Z}_p$	
send $\alpha S, \alpha k N, \alpha A, \alpha N, \alpha P \longrightarrow$	into $\overline{S}, \overline{K}, \overline{A}, \overline{Q}, \overline{P}$
	verify $e(\overline{P}, A) = e(P, \overline{A})$
	verify $e(\overline{P}, \eta Q) = e(P, \overline{Q})$
	verify $e(\overline{S}, \eta \overline{A} + \overline{K}) = e(\overline{P}, \overline{Q})$
	run RevocationCheck$(\overline{A}, \overline{K}, \overline{Q})$

Fig. 3. Self-blindable credential scheme by Emura et al. [7] (simplified).

The ShowCredential protocol is shown in Figure 3. As in Example 51, the Boneh-Boyen signature is of the form

$$\left(A, P, Q, S = \frac{1}{a+k} P \right);$$

we include the values A, P and Q explicitly in the signature because these are blinded as well in the ShowCredential protocol. The blinding factor is (η, α), where η is chosen by the verifier and α by the user. The blinded signature is then $(\alpha A, \alpha P, \alpha \eta Q, \alpha S)$, while the blinded public key is $\alpha \eta K$.

Theorem 4.1 is directly applicable to this scheme; we now describe the resulting linkability attack. Suppose the ShowCredential protocol is executed twice, and let (η_i, α_i) be the blinding factors used in two runs of the ShowCredential protocol, for $i = 1, 2$. Let $\overline{A}_i, \overline{P}_i, \overline{Q}_i, \overline{S}_i, \overline{K}_i$ be the values that the user sends to the issuer. We take the sum of two traces as follows:

$$\overline{A} = \eta_1 \overline{A}_1 + \eta_2 \overline{A}_2 = (\alpha_1 \eta_1 + \alpha_2 \eta_2)A,$$
$$\overline{P} = \overline{P}_1 + \overline{P}_2 = (\alpha_1 + \alpha_2)P,$$
$$\overline{Q} = \overline{Q}_1 + \overline{Q}_2 = (\alpha_1 \eta_1 + \alpha_2 \eta_2)Q, \tag{3}$$
$$\overline{S} = \overline{S}_1 + \overline{S}_2 = \alpha_1 S_1 + \alpha_2 S_2,$$
$$\overline{K} = \overline{K}_1 + \overline{K}_2 = \alpha_1 \eta_1 K_1 + \alpha_2 K_2.$$

Now we put these values in the third verification equation as follows:

$$e(\overline{S}, \overline{A} + \overline{K}) \stackrel{?}{=} e(\overline{P}, \overline{Q}). \tag{4}$$

If $K_1 = K_2$, then also $S_1 = S_2$ holds, and the lower two equations of (3) become $\overline{S} = (\alpha_1 + \alpha_2)S$, $\overline{K} = (\alpha_1 \eta_1 + \alpha_2 \eta_2)K$. Then equation (4) will hold. On the other hand, if $K_1 \neq K_2$ then equation (4) will not hold. Thus, transactions are linkable by the third verification equation.[4]

6   Can Unmalleable, Unlinkable Self-blindable Credential Schemes Exist?

Let us briefly consider a number of ways in which the pitfall outlined by Theorem 4.1 might be avoided. Suppose first that both the public key and the signature are linear in the private key, and that the sum of a trace of the ShowCredential protocol again constitutes a valid public key and signature. Then this can only be abused by a malicious user if he is able to calculate the corresponding private key. Therefore, if this is not feasible (perhaps because the private key k can only be calculated by the issuer, or because not all private keys are valid or allowable), then the system would not be malleable in the sense of Definition 3.3.

As another approach, one might take a public key and signature scheme that are both nonlinear in the private key k, or both nonlinear in the blinding factor α. In that case neither of the statements of Theorem 4.1 would be applicable. Going further, the ShowCredential protocol may be such that it is not necessary to send the public key to the verifier at all, so that it can play no role in either linkability

---

[4] Note, however, that only the verifier can calculate the element $\overline{A} = \eta_1 \overline{A}_1 + \eta_2 \overline{A}_2$ (which is needed in order to perform this linking attack), as it contains η_1, η_2 which are never sent to the user. This differs from the linkability described in Example 51, in which anyone that can eavesdrop on the communication between the user and verifier can execute the attack. On the other hand, transactions can also be linked by checking the following equation:

$$e(\alpha_1 P, \alpha_2 S_2) = e(\overline{P}_1, \overline{S}_2) \stackrel{?}{=} e(\overline{P}_2, \overline{S}_1) = e(\alpha_2 P, \alpha_1 S_1)$$

which will hold if and only if $S_1 = S_2$; that is, when the signatures are the same. This attack can be done by any eavesdropper.

or malleability. (This approach is taken in Idemix; see Example 61 below. For this reason, as well as the fact that Idemix does not satisfy Definition 3.1, we do not consider Idemix to be self-blindable.)

Example 61. The Idemix credential scheme [4,10] is an attribute-based credential scheme which is neither linkable nor malleable, and indeed, Proposition 4.1 does not apply to Idemix. This is because the ShowCredential protocol is substantially different from the ones of the other schemes discussed so far. In short, it goes as follows: the user partially blinds the Camenisch–Lysyanskaya [5] signature (A, e, v), resulting into $(\overline{A}, e, \overline{v})$, and sends $\overline{A}$ to the verifier. After that, they engage in an interactive zero knowledge-proof in which the user shows that he knows e, $\overline{v}$, and his private key, without disclosing any of these. This has the following consequences:

- There is no clear separation between the sending and verification of the public key and signature on the one hand, and a proof of knowledge of the secret key on the other hand. Both of these happen in a single interactive algorithm.
- In fact, the user does not directly send the public key to the verifier at all, blinded or otherwise. As a result, the map PubKey does not play any role in the ShowCredential algorithm.
- The map Sig_{SK} is not linear in the blinding factor.

Summarizing, we do not believe that it would be impossible to create self-blindable credential schemes that are unlinkable and unmalleable, but since the margin for error seems to be small, getting it right may be difficult. Such systems would certainly be useful and interesting, however, so we would not discourage further research in this direction.

7 Conclusion

Creating a self-blindable credential scheme which is neither malleable nor linkable is hard, and indeed all self-blindable credential schemes that we have studied are broken. There is a common theme in their failures: the use of the verification equation of the signature scheme in the ShowCredential protocol may cause linkability or malleability. We believe that this observation in the form of Theorem 4.1 and Corollary 4.2, together with the examples showing the consequences of this observation, will be of help in the creation of new, secure and anonymous self-blindable credential schemes.

References

1. Blake, I.F., Seroussi, G., Smart, N.P. (eds.): Advances in Elliptic Curve Cryptography. Cambridge University Press (2005), Cambridge Books Online
2. Boneh, D., Boyen, X.: Short signatures without random oracles and the SDH assumption in bilinear groups. J. Cryptology **21**(2), 149–177 (2008)

3. Brands, S.: Rethinking Public Key Infrastructures and Digital Certificates: Building in Privacy. MIT Press (2000)
4. Camenisch, J.L., Lysyanskaya, A.: An efficient system for non-transferable anonymous credentials with optional anonymity revocation. In: Pfitzmann, B. (ed.) EUROCRYPT 2001. LNCS, vol. 2045, pp. 93–118. Springer, Heidelberg (2001)
5. Camenisch, J.L., Lysyanskaya, A.: A signature scheme with efficient protocols. In: Cimato, S., Galdi, C., Persiano, G. (eds.) SCN 2002. LNCS, vol. 2576, pp. 268–289. Springer, Heidelberg (2003)
6. Chaum, D., Pedersen, T.P.: Wallet databases with observers. In: Brickell, E.F. (ed.) CRYPTO 1992. LNCS, vol. 740, pp. 89–105. Springer, Heidelberg (1993)
7. Emura, K., Miyaji, A., Omote, K.: A certificate revocable anonymous authentication scheme with designated verifier. In: Proceedings of the Forth International Conference on Availability, Reliability and Security, ARES 2009, Fukuoka, Japan, March 16–19, 2009, pp. 769–773. IEEE Computer Society (2009)
8. Galbraith, S.D., Paterson, K.G., Smart, N.P.: Pairings for cryptographers. Discrete Applied Mathematics 156(16), 3113–3121 (2008)
9. Hoepman, J.H., Jacobs, B., Vullers, P.: Privacy and security issues in e-ticketing - optimisation of smart card-based attribute-proving. In: Cortier, V., Ryan, M., Shmatikov, V. (eds.) Proceedings of the Workshop on Foundations of Security and Privacy, FCS-PrivMod 2010, Edinburgh, UK, July 14–15, 2010, July 2010
10. IBM Research Zurich Security Team: Specification of the Identity Mixer cryptographic library, version 2.3.4. Tech. rep., IBM Research, Zurich, February 2012
11. Kiyomoto, S., Tanaka, T.: Anonymous attribute authentication scheme using self-blindable certificates. In: Proceedings of the IEEE International Conference on Intelligence and Security Informatics, ISI 2008, Taipei, Taiwan, June 17–20, 2008, pp. 215–217. IEEE (2008)
12. Paquin, C., Zaverucha, G.: U-prove cryptographic specification v1.1 (revision 3), December 2013. http://research.microsoft.com/apps/pubs/default.aspx?id=166969, released under the Open Specification Promise
13. Verheul, E.R.: Self-blindable credential certificates from the weil pairing. In: Boyd, C. (ed.) ASIACRYPT 2001. LNCS, vol. 2248, pp. 533–551. Springer, Heidelberg (2001)

Device Synchronisation: A Practical Limitation on Reader Assisted Jamming Methods for RFID Confidentiality

Qiao Hu, Lavinia Mihaela Dinca, and Gerhard Hancke[✉]

City University of Hong Kong, Hong Kong, China
qiaohu2-c@my.cityu.edu.hk, gp.hancke@cityu.edu.hk

Abstract. Radio frequency identification (RFID) is a core component of the Internet-of-Things. In certain cases the communication between the tag and the reader needs to be confidential. Some passive RFID tags have very limited computational power and can therefore not implement standard cryptographic mechanisms. This has led to several proposals where data sent by the RFID tag is 'hidden' by noisy signals generated by the RFID reader. The RFID reader can remove the noise but third-party adversaries cannot, thereby ensuring a confidential backward-channel for tag data without the need for cryptography. Although this is a promising research direction there are also some practical limitations on the effectiveness of such schemes. This paper shows that at least one recent scheme is vulnerable to data recovery despite varying the reader's transmission power if there is a slight difference in the phase of the reader's blocking signal and the tag's data. We experimentally verify our attack and conclude that our eavesdropping and data recovery approach is effective and realistic. Finally we test three possible mitigation methods and show that two of the three approaches can provide protection against our attack while having little impact on the bit error rate of the reader in decoding the tag data.

Keywords: RFID · Jamming · Eavesdropping · Physical-layer security

1 Introduction

Radio frequency identification (RFID) is one of the main technologies enabling the Internet-of-Things. There are many types of RFID systems, which cover devices from contactless payment smart cards to item-identification tags. The latter type of inexpensive RFID tags have several limitations, including storage, computational capability and power [1]. Given the popularity of RFID technology in various types of systems, security services have become an important aspect of RFID systems, including within the Internet-of-Things [2],. There are generally two major kinds of security concerns [2]: privacy and authentication. In this paper we focus on mechanisms that provide data encryption for the purpose of ensuring data confidentiality and privacy. As RFID uses wireless communication, eavesdropping is potentially an effective attack to obtain tag information

© IFIP International Federation for Information Processing 2015
R.N. Akram and S. Jajodia (Eds.): WISTP 2015, LNCS 9311, pp. 219–234, 2015.
DOI: 10.1007/978-3-319-24018-3_14

and has been demonstrated against RFID systems [5,6]. In general, to protect against eavesdropping attacks, we usually apply some cryptography to encrypt messages that will be transmitted over the air [7]. However, this approach obviously needs some computational ability, which adds costs to minimalist tags. This resulted in research work on how tags responses could be 'encrypted' without the need for dedicated cryptographic mechanisms on the tag.

Recently, Huo et. al. [3] has proposed a new physical-layer security method (we will refer to it as Power Varying in the rest of our paper). Passive tags derive their power from the radio carrier transmitted by the RFID reader. Tags also do not transmit their own radio signals, due to power constraints, but rather modulate their response data on the reader's carrier. The reader can observe this 'backscatter' approach to determine the tag's response. Huo's scheme requires the reader to vary the amplitude of the carrier during the tag's response. This means that the response is modulated onto a 'noisy' signal. The reader, as it is sending this signal can cancel it out and determine the tag's response. A third party, who observes the mixed signal, cannot recover the response. The basic concept had been proposed before [4,12,13] but this scheme used a simpler, non-random step function as the intentionally introduced noise.

In this paper, we show that under certain realistic conditions we can reliably circumvent the basic Power Varying scheme. If the reader noise signal and the tag's response are not exactly in phase, i.e. perfectly synchronized, we can successfully start to recover tag response data from the mixed signal. Although RFID tags are generally adapt at loosely synchronizing responses with each other and to the timings expected by the reader there are in practice still variations in the response times. In publishing our research we wish to illustrate that, even though this general approach shows some promise, designs should carefully take into account the actual channel environments and device characteristics of RFID systems. Not doing so could have unintended consequences that could compromise the security of the entire scheme.

The rest of our paper is organized as follows: Section II provides a brief overview of related work and introduces the details of the Power Varying method by Hou et. al. We then describe how we can break this method with only one eavesdropper in section III, and demonstrate our attack through realistic simulation. In section IV, we show how the scheme could be improved using ideas from existing literature and show the effectiveness of mitigation methods on our earlier attack.

2   Background and Related Work

2.1   RFID System

In the Power Varying scheme the authors mention using a 915 MHz carrier as the signal from the RFID reader. We therefore assume that the scheme is primarily intended to work with RFID systems adhering to ISO/IEC 18000-6 (although the idea could feasibly also be applied to 13.56 MHz systems like ISO/IEC 14443/15693). As such, we will provide a brief overview of the communication

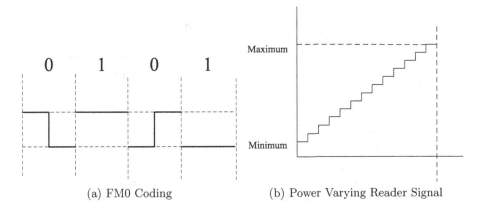

(a) FM0 Coding   (b) Power Varying Reader Signal

Fig. 1. Basic concepts of RFID tag response and Power Varying

channel specified in this standard in terms of the encoding and modulation characteristics of the response transmitted by the tag.

In ISO/IEC 18000-6, the tag transmits data to the reader through backscatter modulation, i.e. modifying and 'reflecting' the incident reader signals. Data that is transmitted by the tag is coded with the FM0 technique, as shown in Fig. 1.a, For logic bit 1, we can just see an instant electrical level change at the start of the symbol period. For logic bit 0, we can see not only an instant electrical level change at the start of the symbol period but also at the middle of the symbol period. The modulation method adopted is 10% Amplitude Shift Keying (ASK). If the logic bit is 1, the amplitude is α, otherwise it will be β. A modulation index of 10% means that $(\alpha - \beta)/(\alpha + \beta)$ is equal to 10%.

2.2   The Power Varying Method

Power Varying aims to prevent eavesdropping by changing the power/amplitude of the transmitted reader's signal. Huo et. al. [3] claims that the changing amplitude can effectively hide the backscattered signal transmitted by tags from eavesdroppers. Given that the reader is responsible for the power variation it can effectively cancel out this variation and reliably recover the noise. The basic format of the power varying signal is shown in Fig. 1.b. First, it will choose a minimum amplitude that satisfies the minimum power needed to activate and power the passive tags. Next, the amplitude of the signal will increase step-by-step until it reaches the maximum chosen amplitude. It will then return to the minimum amplitude and the cycle will start again.

The authors describes the variations of this step signal. In the first variation the period of the signal is equal to the bit period of the tag's response. The second variation uses a varying signal that has a period that is 10% of the bit period. The basic scheme defines that the changing step amplitude is equal to the difference between the amplitude of tag signals containing logic bit 0 or

1. In other words, when a symbol period of tag containing logic bit 0 arrives, the amplitude of the signal observed by eavesdropper will be the same as the amplitude of the signal during the previous step if the symbol period of the tag containing logic bit 1 arrived. We give an example of the first variation of this scheme in Fig. 2. From this figure, we can observe that amplitude differences between two continuous signals received by the attacker are different depending on the logic bit carried by corresponding tag signals. For example, the amplitude difference between two periods with logic bits sequence in 10 is near zero. And the amplitude difference between two periods with logic bits sequence in 01 is almost double of that with sequence in 11. This means that if we know which logic bit is carried during a step period, we can deduce the previous or next logic bit by the amplitude difference between these periods. How to know the logic bit? If we observe near zero amplitude difference, which happens quite often, we know that these two periods represent logic bits 00.

As this constant amplitude increasing method is vulnerable, its authors suggest to use random amplitude. Fig. 3.a illustrates this improved method

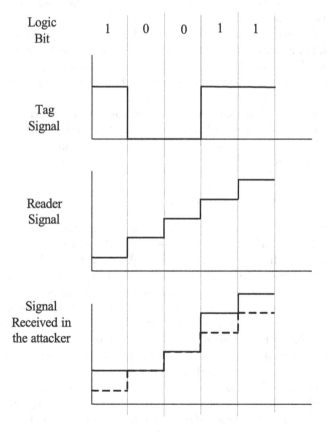

Fig. 2. Signals received by an attacker under the constant amplitude increasing method

in the first variation mentioned above. We can see that the amplitude difference between two continuous step periods has no relationship with the logic bit sequence. Even the logic bit sequence is 10, there is also a large amplitude difference. In other words, it is unclear whether the 2th bit is a large step with a logic 0 or a smaller step with a logic 1.This result demonstrates that the randomly increasing amplitude method has fixed the previous vulnerability.

2.3 Related Work

There are several works on physical-layer security and cryptographic-less encryption based on the general concept put forward by Wyner in the 1970s [16]. The foundation of all these schemes are that the legitimate receiver is less effected by, or can cancel out, noise. This allows for reliable reception of data while an eavesdropper cannot recover the data. At first schemes relied on environmental noise, but to ensure that there is sufficient noise to hide the data, schemes started introducing intentional noise. For example, the introduction of friendly jamming, where the system could either use multiple antennas in one node or multiple trusted nodes, could co-operate to transmit 'friendly' noise that is known to the receiver [9]. Subsequently many researchers tried to apply this idea to RFID technology, e.g [4,10,11], where either the reader or other tags would transmit noise to cover data signals transmitted by the tag of interest. There has also work been done on how to generate appropriate noise for jamming high-frequency RFID devices[13]. This method has also been applied to other technologies, such as short-range audio communication channels in mobile phones. In such cases, one device would transmit data and the receiving device would transmit noise [14,15].

There has not much work been done on attacking jamming schemes in practical environments. Hancke [12] showed that the natural variation in modulation index, which derives from the inherent impedance of the tags between the device transmitting the response data and the device transmitting the blocking noise, could reveal the hidden response. In this paper we investigate the effect of variations on the response time of the tags, i.e. difference in phase of the blocking noise and the response.

3   Overview of Our Attack

3.1   Adversarial Model

In this subsection we introduce the adversarial model used throughout this work. In the rest of this paper we apply the increasing amplitude Power Varying scheme. We calculate the number of steps m by the following formula proposed in [3].

$$m = \frac{x_{high} - x_{low}}{\alpha \overline{x}} \tag{1}$$

x_{high} and x_{low} mean the maximum and minimum amplitude of the reader signal respectively. $\overline{x}$ is given by:

$$\overline{x} = \frac{x_{high} - x_{low}}{2} \tag{2}$$

We set α as 0.1, then m equals 21. Given that there is no standard prescribed in the Power Varying scheme we take two approaches. We attack the scheme assuming that no specific standard is used, i.e. non-return to zero encoding with basic amplitude modulation, and then analyse the scheme if it was implemented as per the ISO/IEC 18000-6 standard. In our adversarial model we have one RFID reader communicating with one passive RFID tag. The adversary is a passive attacker and only obtains the combined signal resulting from the tag response and the varying signal. We do not specify the position of the adversary relative to the tag and reader but assume that the attacker cannot derive any additional advantage from directional monitoring techniques to isolated reader and tag transmissions. Our attacker has knowledge of the standard used, i.e. the communication parameters, and of the Power Varying scheme. This means that the attacker knows that a step function is used to vary the power and he knows the period of the steps, but not necessarily the amplitude of the steps.

3.2   Analysis of Power Varying

1) General Attack

We first analyze the scheme taking into consideration no specific standard. We accept that the method is secure when the mixed signal received by the attacker is as shown in Fig. 3. We can see from Fig. 3 that the data is effectively hidden if the symbol period and the step period is synchronized, with the attacker unable to distinguish the response data as we talked about in Section 2. However, in reality it is unlikely that the reader would be able to perfectly synchronise his step function to the response of the tag. As shown is [11], even similar tags, i.e. same technology and manufacturer, exhibit slighlty different modulation and timing characteristics. We refer to this desynchronisation as the phase offset, or offset for short. The result of an offset on the combined signal is illustrated in Fig. 4, where the step period is not synchronized with the symbol period. In Fig. 3, there is no amplitude change during each symbol period. However, in Fig. 4, due to the desynchronization, the attacker could infer the effect of the step. For example, if two logic 1's are transmitted we expect the second to have a higher amplitude due to the step, but ideally there should be an uncertainty whether it might also be a large step with a logic 0. If we notice that halfway through the first one the signal increases that is evidently the size of the step. If there is then an additional increase if the next bit period starts we also know that the bit is a one. Therefore, depending on these amplitude discontinuities caused by the offset we can distinguish the logic bits of the response.

2) Results of the General Attack

We simulate the general attack in Matlab. In this experiment, we consider no specific standard and the tag signal is as shown in Fig. 4. And we also assume that there is no additional environmental noise. Between the minimum amplitude and the maximum amplitude there are 10 step periods (we use this setting at the

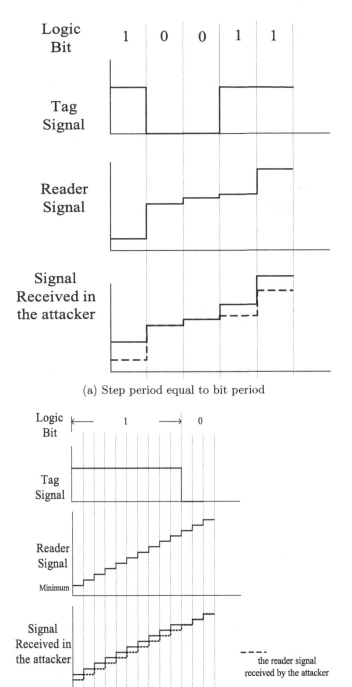

(a) Step period equal to bit period

(b) Step with period equal to 10% of bit period

Fig. 3. Signals received by an attacker with perfect synchronization

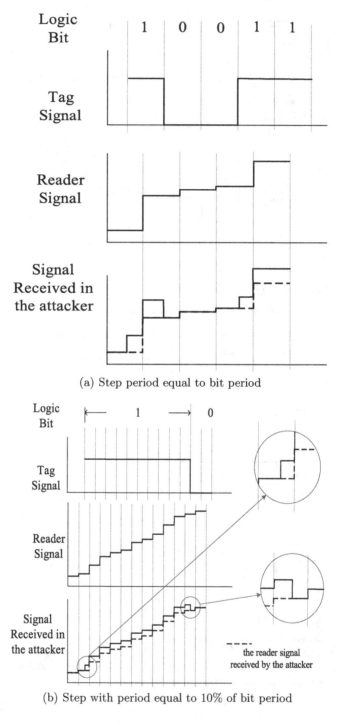

(a) Step period equal to bit period

(b) Step with period equal to 10% of bit period

Fig. 4. Unsynchronized signals received by the Attacker

rest of our experiments). This means that the power signal is a periodic signal with a 10 step cycle (with step period equal to either the bit period or 10% of the bit period). The only factor that may effect the result of our attack is the degree of desynchronization (or phase offset) between the two signals. For step equal to bit period, we set the offset from zero to a step period with interval equals to one fifth of a step period. For the step period 10% of the bit period, we set the offset from zero to two and a half step periods with interval equals to half of a step period. We use bit error rate(BER) to evaluate our experimental results. Our results show that apart from the case where the offset is 0 the resultant BER was always 0 for any amount of offset.

3) Specific Attack under ISO/IEC 18000-6

We then attempted the same attack as in the previous section, but we use the FM0 coding scheme as per ISO 18000-6. This means there is a slight variation in the signal when a logic 0 is encoded in that there is a signal change in the middle of the period, which results in a slightly different combined signal as shown in Fig. 5. Although this case appears at first similar there is now some uncertainty as to whether a discontinuity in the middle of the bit period is caused by the step of the logic 0 transition in some cases. If there is an instant level change at the beginning of each symbol period or at the middle of the period then the symbol represents logic 0. If the step period and the symbol period are not well synchronized, during one step period, we may also observe a similar level change.

We therefore need two steps to recover logic bits. First, we need to find the start of the tag response signal. If there is no tag signal, then there is no amplitude difference in one step period. Because we know the time of all step periods, we can distinguish whether the amplitude difference is caused by the tag signal or by the power signal. So we assume that the first amplitude difference means the start of the tag signal. Then we can calculate the middle area of each symbol period to search for the level change to judge the logic bit of this symbol period, as each symbol period has the same length. These two steps seem the simplest to find amplitude differences caused by electrical level changes.

4) Results of the Specific Attack under ISO/IEC 18000-6

We also simulate the specific attack in Matlab. In this experiment, we have the same configuration as with the previous experiment. We also do the experiment under one or one tenth of a symbol period situation. We set the offset as we do in the general attack experiment. Interestingly the results differ from the general case as shown in Figure 6. Let's first see the result of a situation with a period ratio equals to 1, which means a step period is equals to a symbol period shown in Fig 5.a. We can observe three high BER periods. The first and the last period happen when the offset nears zero or one step period, which means the starting point of a symbol period is overlapping with the beginning of a step period. The second period happens with a 1/2 step period offset, which represents the overlap between the middle point of a symbol period and the beginning of a step period. The result of a period ratio equal to 10 has a similar but a little different

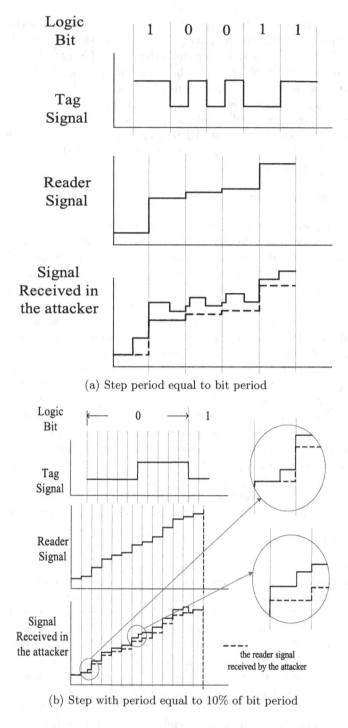

(a) Step period equal to bit period

(b) Step with period equal to 10% of bit period

Fig. 5. Unsynchronized signals received as per ISO/IEC 18000-6

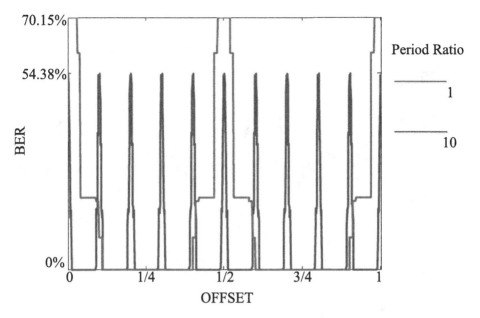

Fig. 6. Results of the attack on ISO 18000-6

reason as the previous result. The difference is that the distance between the starting point and the middle point of a symbol period can be divided by a step period, which is illustrated in Fig 5.b. If the starting point of a symbol period is overlapping with the beginning of a step period, we may get a high BER at the attacker. We can observe that except for the area of overlapping, the BER is 0, which means the attack is a success.

5) Eavesdropping in a Noisy Environment

Up to now the attack implementation did not consider any additional noise. However, this is not a realistic assumption in real operating environments. Therefore we also consider our attack against Power Varying in the presence of background noise. Such noise should in theory hinder the attacker and the valid receiver. We only analyze the impact of noise for the attack scenario against ISO 18000-6. As noise will change the amplitude of signals, we should calculate the average amplitude to deduce the impact of noise.

To evaluate the impact of additional background noise, we add Additive White Gaussian Noise (AWGN) to our simulation. We set the SNR (Signal to Noise Ratio) of the received signal in the attacker as ∞ (no noise), 20dB and 30dB. These are realistic noise figure in radio environments, e.g. WiFi under normal conditions operates at around 40 dB. We again run the experiment with the two kinds of step period length. The final

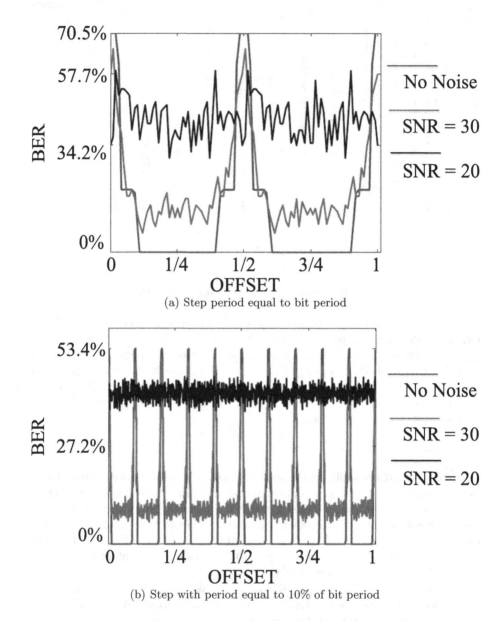

(a) Step period equal to bit period

(b) Step with period equal to 10% of bit period

Fig. 7. Impact of noise on the attack

result, as shown in Fig. 7, is as expected. It shows the BER of the attacker increasing but large parts of the message could still be recovered.

4   Mitigation Methods

In this section we consider ways to mitigate the weaknesses of the basic scheme. As we only analyze the randomly increasing amplitude method, we try to analyze the random amplitude method that allows the amplitude increasing or decreasing. We will refer to this as the random amplitude method. Another approach is to use the reader signal and a phase shifted version of the reader signal as the reader's signal. This is similar to the approach in [4] where noise and noise phase shifted by $\pi/2$ are used to hide the data. We randomly create two reader signals with just one cycle from the minimum amplitude to the maximum amplitude. So these two randomly created signals have different amplitudes even in the same step period. Then we multiply one reader signal by the normal carrier and the other one by the carrier phase-shifted by $\pi/2$. We add them together to form a new reader signal. During one step period, α and β are the amplitude of two reader signals, and the amplitude of the new reader signal in this step period can be calculated by:

$$Amp = \alpha cos(2\pi * 915000000 * t) + \beta cos(2\pi * 915000000 * t - \frac{\pi}{2}) \qquad (3)$$

This formula tells us that the new reader signal is a cyclic signal with a period of 2π during one step period. We refer to this as the artificial noise method. Finally, we propose that we can improve the random amplitude method by also adding a random variation of the step length. In other words, choose the step period length randomly. We call it the random step period and amplitude method. We implement these three methods for the ISO/IEC 18000-6 standard and repeat the attacks tests in the previous sections. In experiments on the first two methods, we set the period ratio as 1. We also evaluated these methods if the SNR of the received signal at the attacker are ∞ (no noise), 30db and 20db.

Results of these tests are shown in Fig 8. Thise figure show that when the energy of noise is very low compared to the mixed signal, the first two methods increase the BER by a small amount but the third method utilizing both the random step size and random step amplitude works much more effectively. We believe this is because our attack depends mostly on the amplitude difference caused by the tag signal and the time of amplitude changes caused by the power signal can be calculated by us. As the first method only change the amplitude of the power signal and the second method only change the original power signal to another power signal with the same cycle time, these have minimal effect on our attack. The last method is also successful at causing the attack to calculate the incorrect start point which would lead to error decoding most of the message.

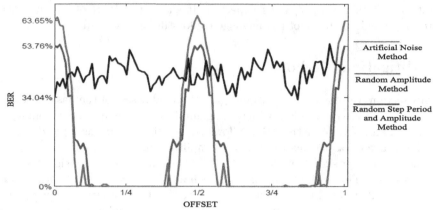

(a) BER at the Attacker of Three Methods with no noise

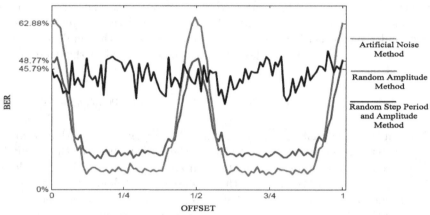

(b) BER at the Attacker of Three Methods with SNR equals to 30db

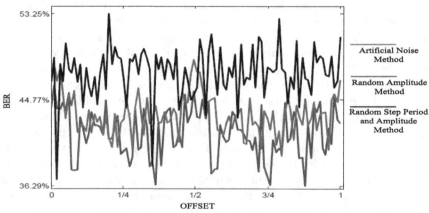

(c) BER at the Attacker of Three Methods with SNR equals to 20db

Fig. 8. Results of Noise Impact on Communication based on Specific Standard

5   Conclusion

In this article, we analyze the vulnerability of Power Varying method proposed by Hou et. al. [3]. This method can be broken when the step period of the signal from a reader and the symbol period of the backscatter signal from a tag are not well synchronized. This desynchronization causes amplitude differences in the step period which can be used to distinguish tag signals. We describe our attack under general situation and for communication adhering to ISO/IEC 18000-6. Then we analyze factors including noise and phase offset that can affect our attack. Results show that our attack works well in less noisy environment and that even a small phase offset can result in effective recovery of the tag's response. Lastly, we test three mitigation methods: a random step amplitude method, artificial noise addition method and a combined random step period and amplitude method. Results show that the latter approach, which is propose by us, is the best mitigation method. The combined random step period and amplitude method can protect communication from recovery while have little impact on the bit decoding error rate of the tag signal at the reader.

References

1. Grover, A., Berghel, H.: A Survey of RFID Deployment and Security Issues. Journal of Information Processing Systems **7**, 561–580 (2011)
2. Hancke, G.P., Markantonakis, K., Mayes, K.E.: Security Challenges for User-Oriented RFID Applications within the Internet of Things. Journal of Internet Technology **11**(3), 307–313 (2010)
3. Huo, F., Yang, C., Gong, G., Poovendran, R.: A framework to securing RFID transmissions by varying transmitted reader's power. In: 9th Workshop on RFID Security, pp. 57–68. IOS Press, Amsterdam (2013)
4. Archard, F., Savry, O.: Cross-layer approach to preserve privacy in RFID ISO/IEC 15693 systems. In: 2012 IEEE International Conference on RFID-Technologies and Applications (RFID-TA), pp. 85–90. IEEE (2012)
5. Hancke, G.: Practical Eavesdropping and Skimming Attacks on High-Frequency RFID Tokens. Journal of Computer Security **19**, 259–288 (2011)
6. Hancke, G.: Eavesdropping attacks on high-frequency RFID tokens. In: 4th Workshop on RFID? Security, pp. 100–113 (2008)
7. Juels, A.: RFID security and privacy: A research survey. IEEE Journal on Selected Areas in Communications **24**, 381–394 (2006)
8. Bolic, M., Simplot-Ryl, D., Stojmenovic, I.: RFID systems: Research Trends and Challenges. John Wiley & Sons, Hoboken (2010)
9. Negi, R., Goel, S.: Secret communication using artificial noise. In: IEEE Vehicular Techonology Conference, vol. 62, pp. 1906–1910 (2005)
10. Castelluccia, C., Avione, G.: Noisy tags: pretty good key exchange protocol for RFID tags. In: Smart Card Research and Advanced Applications Conference, pp. 289–299 (2006)
11. Haselsteiner, E., Breitfuss, K.: Security in near field communication (NFC). In: Workshop on RFID Security, pp. 12–14 (2006)
12. Hancke, G.: Noisy carrier modulation for HF RFID. In: First International EURASIP Workshop on RFID Technology, pp. 63–66 (2007)

13. Savry, O., Pebay-Peyroula, F., Dehmas, F., Robert, G., Reverdy, J.: RFID noisy reader how to prevent from eavesdropping on the communication? In: Paillier, P., Verbauwhede, I. (eds.) CHES 2007. LNCS, vol. 4727, pp. 334–345. Springer, Heidelberg (2007)
14. Nandakumar, R., Chintalapudi, K., Padmanabhan, V., Venkatesan, R.: Dhwani: secure peer-to-peer acoustic NFC. In: ACM SIGCOMM Computer Communication Review, vol. 43, pp. 63–74 (2013)
15. Zhang, B., Zhan, Q., Chen, S., Li, M., Ren, K., Wang, C., Ma, D.: PriWhisper: Enabling Keyless Secure Acoustic Communication for Smartphones. IEEE Internet of Things Journal 1, 33–45 (2014)
16. Wyner, A.D.: The Wire-Tap Channel. Bell Systems Technical Journal 54, 1355–1387 (1975)

Short Papers

Normalizing Security Events with a Hierarchical Knowledge Base

David Jaeger(✉), Amir Azodi, Feng Cheng, and Christoph Meinel

Hasso Plattner Institute, University of Potsdam, Potsdam, Germany
{david.jaeger,amir.azodi,feng.cheng,christoph.meinel}@hpi.de

Abstract. An important technique for attack detection in complex company networks is the analysis of log data from various network components. As networks are growing, the number of produced log events increases dramatically, sometimes even to multiple billion events per day. The analysis of such big data highly relies on a full normalization of the log data in realtime. Until now, the important issue of full normalization of a large number of log events is only insufficiently handled by many software solutions and not well covered in existing research work. In this paper, we propose and evaluate multiple approaches for handling the normalization of a large number of typical logs better and more efficient. The main idea is to organize the normalization in multiple levels by using a hierarchical knowledge base (KB) of normalization rules. In the end, we achieve a performance gain of about 1000x with our presented approaches, in comparison to a naive approach typically used in existing normalization solutions. Considering this improvement, big log data can now be handled much faster and can be used to find and mitigate attacks in realtime.

Keywords: Network security · Event logs · Normalization · Knowledge base

1 Introduction

During the last years, the number and complexity of cyber-attacks has dramatically increased [1,2]. An important instrument for the monitoring and mitigation of attacks is the logging of suspicious activities in networks and on hosts. This logging is usually performed by operating systems, applications or security software [3] and creates huge amounts of log events for even relatively small networks. Handling these amounts of events manually or automatically by software with typical normalization approaches is almost impossible. Besides that, the incoming information cannot be handled in realtime, which is extremely important to detect ongoing attacks.

A difficult challenge that has to be mastered in software are the variety of formats for event logs that do not follow a common standard. Additionally, the formats usually represent a major part of the activity in an unstructured textual format, which is easy to read for humans, but not for machines [3].

© IFIP International Federation for Information Processing 2015
R.N. Akram and S. Jajodia (Eds.): WISTP 2015, LNCS 9311, pp. 237–248, 2015.
DOI: 10.1007/978-3-319-24018-3_15

At the moment, most solutions that gather and interpret event logs, so called Security Information and Event Management (SIEM) systems, only focus on structured event information and do not sufficiently interpret the unstructured information. Only a few SIEMs and log interpreters, such as HP's ArcSight[1] or Flowerfire's SawMill[2], actually interpret the contents of unstructured data but lack in performance when it comes to huge amounts of events or when data of different formats is mixed.

Although the use of structured log-formats is encouraged, they can also bring up new challenges for normalization, i.e. the structure often introduces a hierarchy of sub-formats. At the moment, there is only limited research on how such hierarchically structured formats can be efficiently normalized.

This paper provides a solution for effective normalization of events in general and for hierarchical log-formats in particular and is structured as follows. Section 2 gives an overview of related work to event normalization. Section 3 shows how a single event can be normalized. The following Section 4 then introduces the concept of a knowledge base for event normalization and shows two possible designs for it. Then, in Section 5, the hierarchical design is further detailed and features are described, that can improve normalization performance. In order to show the applicability of the mentioned concept, Section 6 shows performance values for two concrete scenarios. In the end, Section 7 gives a conclusion and an outlook to further research.

2 Related Work

2.1 Log-Formats

Several efforts have been made to normalize log-formats and simplify the interpretation by machines. Examples for such efforts are the general purpose formats *Syslog* [4], *Common Event Expression* (CEE) [5] or the *Common Event Format* (CEF) [6]. Another set of formats have been introduced for specific domain applications, such as *Cyber Observable eXpression* (CybOX) [7] for network and host-based detection systems.

However, all of the formats allow event normalization on very different levels of detail. Whereas the popular Syslog-format only provides rudimentary semi-structured normalization, the rarely used CybOX provides normalization for almost every imaginable information. Due to this situation, log information is mostly available in semi-structured formats and requires further processing to obtain relevant information.

In this paper, we focus on the Object Log Format (OLF) [8], which combines extensibility and object orientation of CEE and the variety of attributes of CEF.

---

[1] ArcSight Enterprise Security Management - http://www8.hp.com/us/en/software-solutions/arcsight-esm-enterprise-security-management/

[2] SawMill - http://sawmill.co.uk

2.2   Event Normalization and Analysis

The normalization and analysis of log events has already been implemented in a variety of methods and has been integrated into many existing software solutions.

Normalization Methods. There are mainly four normalization methods that can be observed on the market and the research community.

Rule Matching (e.g., Regular Expressions). The normalization of each event log type is described in a rule that specifies how important information can be extracted from a concrete event. A popular approach in this category are regular expressions, especially Named-Group Regular Expressions (NGRE) [9]. This method associates information in the event to concrete event fields, which can be very useful for normalization. However, choosing the right regular expression for a random event type is processing intensive.

Tokenization. A concrete event log is split up into tokens. These tokens could be the words of the human readable part of the log event or even phrases or certain notations in the log. The most common approach for tokenization is by word, which allows to group event logs containing the same words. However, this method heavily relies on static words in logs. A concrete implementation for tokenization is Apache Lucene[3].

Natural Language Processing (NLP). A human readable log line is decomposed by its language structure into subject, object, verbs and more. Once the information is extracted, it can be used to understand the meaning behind the phrase, as a human reader would see it. However, the method relies on the human readability of the log. Examples for NLP implementations are Stanford's CoreNLP library or SAP HANA's text analysis capabilities [10]. A concrete usage of this technique for log analysis has been proposed by Kobayashi et al. [11].

Custom Normalization. The most effective but also most complex method is to use custom code for the normalization of each log format. As an example, one format is read with a CSV parser, while another one is parsed with a special Syslog parser and yet another one is handled with a combination of multiple regular expressions being applied in order. This type of normalization can be partially observed in the log analysis tools Logstash[4] and Sawmill.

Normalization Software. There are a variety of software solutions that perform normalization based on event logs. Log analysis tools like the OSSEC IDS[5] monitors important event log files and extracts potential threats from these using regular expressions. On the other hand, there are complex SIEM systems

---

[3]   Apache Lucene - http://lucene.apache.org/
[4]   Elasticsearch Logstash - https://www.elastic.co/products/logstash
[5]   OSSEC - http://www.ossec.net

like HP's ArcSight and RSA Security Analytics[6]. Both solutions have limited capabilities when it comes to normalization and hence also for complex attack detection. Firstly, event streams have to be associated with the right log-format to be used for normalization. Secondly, log events are mostly normalized by their structured parts and only a few log events are normalized completely.

3   Basic Normalization of Log Events

Different log sources produce events in different formats and encodings. Whereas almost all log sources produce logs in a textual way, the formats are different. The information in event log-formats can usually be categorized into dynamic, static and semantic parts.

Listing 1.1. Log Event in the Syslog-Format with categorized information parts (static, dynamic, semantic)

```
Jan 31 15:08:43␣combo␣sshd[29819]:␣Failed password␣for␣root␣from␣70.84.72.68␣port␣35933␣ssh2
```

Listing 1.1 applies the concept of different information categories on a Syslog event.

The *static* information defines the structure of the log, including white spacing and glue words, such as *for* or *from*, for the dynamic parts. Because of the structure-defining property of the static information, it perfectly fits the purpose of identifying the type of log that is at hand.

The *dynamic* information bears the explicit information for a concrete instance of an event type. This information can change for each log event, but still has a common format, such as a time or a number. For example the port number and IP address in the listing are dynamic, but always have a certain format.

Besides the explicit information, *semantic* information provides a classification of the event through tagging. In the example, the marked text *Failed password* indicates that the event refers to a *failure* for a *login* activity on an *account*. So, the semantic tags for the given event could be *failure*, *login* and *account*.

Azodi et al. [12,13] describe the process of extraction into the OLF-format in detail.

4   Knowledge Base Approaches

An event can theoretically be normalized with the help of a knowledge base that consists of entries of regular expressions and corresponding static fields and tags. However, as soon as multiple log-formats have to be supported for normalization, choosing the right entry becomes an issue. Assuming a KB of n normalization rules would mean that on average $\frac{n}{2}$ entries have to be checked, i.e. applying the entry's NGRE on the event, before the right matching entry is found.

---

[6] RSA Security Analytics - http://www.emc.com/security/security-analytics/

To overcome this processing overhead, NGREs have to be applied more efficiently to a given event. The following subsections show different approaches for applying regular expressions more efficiently by changing the organization of the KB.

For a better demonstration of the concepts, the two example log events in Figure 1 are chosen. Both are Syslog events typically created by Snort and have a similar structure, but they are of different event types.

Listing 1.2. Event #1 for a Snort event of type 648, i.e. an attempt to execute shellcode

Listing 1.3. Event #2 for a Snort event of type 1807, i.e. an attempt to inject commands over HTTP

```
Mar  1 16:02:40 bastion snort: [1:648:7]
    SHELLCODE x86 NOOP [Classification:
    Executable code was detected] [
    Priority: 1]: {TCP} 4.152.207.238:3521
    -> 11.11.79.83:80
```

```
Mar  1 16:03:01 bastion snort: [1:1807:10]
    WEB-MISC Chunked-Encoding transfer
    attempt [Classification: Web
    Application Attack] [Priority: 1]: {
    TCP} 4.152.207.238:3718 ->
    11.11.79.84:80
```

Fig. 1. Two log events produced by Snort with a similar structure

4.1 Flat Knowledge Base

The simplest approach to organize a KB is to have one normalization rule per possible event type. We call it flat KB, because there is no multi-level organization of the rules. Rather, each rule describes an event type in its entirety, including an NGRE matching the entire event text and all static fields. Figure 2 demonstrates the processing of the two log events from Figure 1.

There are two raw events to be normalized. In a flat KB, there is a separate normalization rule for each event. Rule #1 handles a Snort event of type 648, which is embedded into a Syslog event. Rule #2 handles a Snort-event of type 1807. Looking closer at the two rules, it can be seen that the rule parts for Syslog and Snort are identical. The only difference in the rules is the inner part being specific to the concrete Snort rule. It is obvious that flat normalization rules have many redundancies that can be eliminated with a more sophisticated KB approach.

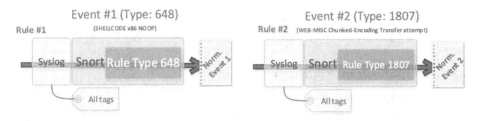

Fig. 2. Normalization with a flat KB

4.2   Hierarchical Knowledge Base

The structure of typical logs is that more specific log parts are wrapped in parent formats, such as Syslog. In the case of Snort log events, there is an intermediary Snort wrapping format, as already indicated in the processing of the flat KB in Figure 2. An approach to overcome the redundancies in normalization rules of a flat KB is to organize normalization rules in multiple levels, i.e. hierarchically.

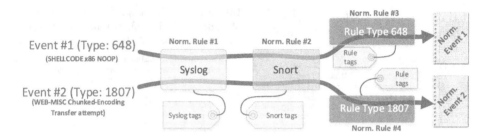

Fig. 3. Normalization with a hierarchical KB

Our hierarchical KB has one rule per identified parent format and one rule per event type. All these rules are loosely coupled by specifying possible parents for each rule. A concrete example for the events from Figure 1 is illustrated in Figure 3.

In the example, there could be four normalization rules. There are the two parent formats, for Syslog and Snort, being specified in rule #1 and #2. #2 has a link to #1 as possible parent. Rule #3 and #4 specify the concrete parts of the two given event types and both link to rule #2 as parent.

In order to match one of the given log events, we look for rules that are applicable in the current matching context. We call these rules *candidate rules*. This means, at the beginning we first check all rules that can stand alone, which in this case is only Syslog, because it has no parents. When the Syslog part is matched, its message part is used to match the next-level rule, which has the Syslog-rule as its parent. In our concrete example, this would be the Snort-rule. Once Snort is matched, the rule's message part is extracted and then checked against the rules that have the Snort-rule as parent. This could be rule #3 and #4. According to the concrete content, the right rule would be matched.

4.3   Comparison of Approaches

Structuring. Taking the effort of defining rules, the hierarchical approach is much more organized, if many event types of similar structure have to be described. For example, taking the thousands of existing Snort rules, the hierarchical approach only defines Syslog and the basic Snort event once and then specifies Snort's event type specific parts in separate simple normalization rules. In the flat approach, all parts, especially Syslog and Snort, have to be repeated for every Snort-rule.

Another benefit with the hierarchical approach is that static fields and tags can be defined at parent-level rules. As an example, to tag an event as a network-related event (expressed with `tag.domain = net`), a corresponding tag only has to be attached to the Snort-rule, because Snort only deals with network data.

Performance. When it comes to performance, the structuring can help to improve the performance of normalization significantly, too. Let us assume there are logs and normalization rules for two different applications, namely `Snort` and `sshd` being wrapped in Syslog.

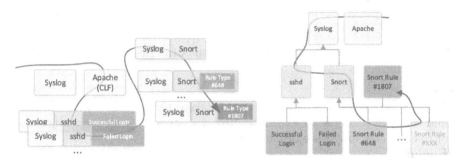

Fig. 4. Matching with a flat KB

Fig. 5. Effective matching with a hierarchical KB

For the flat approach, as seen in Figure 4, in the worst case a Snort event has to be checked against all sshd-related normalization rules until the Snort normalization rule is found as a match.

For the hierarchical approach, as seen in Figure 5, in the worst case only a single Syslog- and sshd-rule is checked until the Snort normalization rules are found as a match. So taking the fact that log events of many applications have to be supported by the KB, the hierarchical approach can have major performance benefits.

5   Improving Knowledge Base Matching Performance

While the main idea, to organize the KB hierarchically, can already bring major performance benefits, further improvements can speed up the normalization even further. Following subsections give an overview of the different approaches we have evaluated. Additionally, we point out which technologies and libraries have been used for our implementation in the Java programming language. The evaluation results of the approaches are presented in Section 6.

5.1   Rule Indexing

When working with hierarchical rules, it is important to choose the right candidate rules as fast as possible. These candidate rules are selected by a number of criteria that effectively filter the number of rules to be applied on a given log fragment. We came up with following criteria:

- **Standalone:** This rule matches an event that can stand on its own. These rules do not require a parent.
- **Level:** Logs are constructed in multiple levels. There are global wrapper formats, such as Syslog, application wrappers, such as Snort, and event parts that are specific to the event type. Based on the current level, rules of upper levels do not have to be checked again.
- **Parent:** Some event parts can only appear as a child of another format. As an example, a specific Snort rule can only appear in the general Snort wrapper. This property can rule out most of the available rules.

Based on these criteria, we tried three different strategies to search applicable rules more efficiently.

Iteration
In the easiest case, the program would iterate through all available rules and check the criteria for each rule. However, iteration over large amounts of rules creates major performance impacts.

CQEngine
A straight-forward approach is to index all available rules by the presented criteria. For our evaluation, we used a library called CQEngine[7], a NoSQL indexing and query engine.

Lucene
Another approach is to create a similarity measure between a given event and the events a rule is able to match. A detailed description of this approach for a flat knowledge base can be found in a paper [13] by Azodi et. al.

5.2   Rule Selectors

Log-formats with many different event types as a child give an indication of the child's type. For example, Syslog has an application name that indicates what kind of application logs are in the message part. Such indicators can be used to directly select the right normalization rules without searching through all possible candidate rules for the parent. An example of this rule selection can be seen in Figure 6.

5.3   Result Caching

The searching for candidate rules can be seen as one of the most processing intensive tasks in the normalization process. We propose to cache the search results for a given set of criteria. Caching can then make candidate rules directly accessible and improve normalization of logs without format indicators.

---

[7] CQEngine - https://code.google.com/p/cqengine/

Fig. 6. Rule selector approach on log event from Listing 1.2

5.4 Priority Lists

A feature that can be added in conjunction with result caching is the ordering of all candidate rules by their frequency they have been used for the normalization of previous events. Creating a priority list with every log event is unfeasible, because the sorting would result in major performance drops. Rather, ordering by frequency should be performed in a time interval that takes the required processing overhead and the actuality of the frequencies into account.

6 Evaluation

We have implemented all of the above mentioned knowledge bases, indexing strategies and other proposed improvements into our Real-time Event Analysis and Monitoring System (REAMS) [14] and ran performance tests for various combinations of these on two data sets. Each combination was run 10 times per data set, so that a mean runtime could be calculated. As our implementation is highly parallelized and can run multiple normalization threads simultaneously, we decided to run the performance tests on eight parallel normalization threads on our server[8].

6.1 Experiment 1: Normalizing Hierarchical Logs

In the first experiment, we have normalized all Snort event logs, i.e., *69039 log events*, from Honeynet Challenge #34 [15]. We have generated normalization rules for all Snort rules from the rule snapshot[9] for registered users and the emerging threats open rules[10]. These rules, altogether 55547, cover all Snort events that were present in the challenge's logs. The performance results of normalization are visualized in the box and whisker diagram in Figure 7.

We see that the flat KB performs at least a magnitude worse than the hierarchical KB. This is because the handling and checking of more and longer rules as used with the flat KB is more time consuming than with a hierarchical one. Both factors have a major impact on hierarchically structured formats as used by Snort.

We can also deduce that direct indexing with CQ is faster for the hierarchical KB than normal iteration. The better indexing with CQ is not relevant for

---

[8] Virtual Machine (Debian 7.8, 32GB RAM(dedicated), 8 cores(dedicated)) on VMware ESXi host with 256GB RAM and 8x Intel Xeon X7560 CPUs @ 2.27GHz
[9] Snort Ruleset (Registered User) - https://www.snort.org/downloads
[10] ETOpen Ruleset - https://portal.emergingthreats.net/etpro/open

the flat KB, because there is almost no data to index. The Lucene indexing generally performs better than iteration and CQ, but because of its mechanisms the rules cannot be further cached or prioritized. Unfortunately, Lucene cannot outperform the benefits of caching and prioritization.

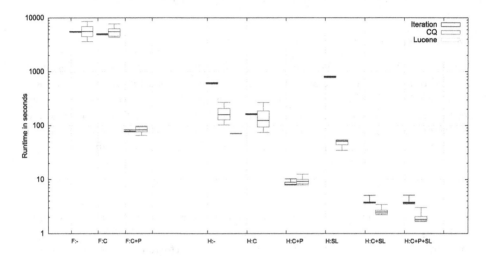

Fig. 7. Evaluation results for normalizing 69039 Snort log events, **left (F)** - flat knowledge base, **right (H)** - hierarchical knowledge base (**C** - Cache, **P** - Prioritization, **SL** - Rule Selector)

Within the hierarchical performance results, prioritization and rule selectors achieve the biggest performance benefits. Both concepts can reduce the number of rules to be checked per log event dramatically. In comparison to the plain KB performance, both concepts also bring the most stable runtime values. The other concepts all heavily rely on the ordering of the rules, because they match rules in the order they are stored in memory. Prioritization and rule selectors mostly choose the right rule directly. It should be mentioned that we intentionally did not fix the rule order, because in reality the correct order is not known and is highly dependent on the concrete distribution and order of log events.

The caching of results can bring benefits, if a large number of varying data lookups would have to be performed. As an example, it is not so relevant for caching of big data sets (e.g. H:- ↔ H:C), but for caching of smaller data sets that apply to only a few log events (e.g.: H:SL ↔ H:C+SL).

6.2   Experiment 2: Normalizing Mixed Logs

In the second experiment, we applied our algorithm to mixed logs consisting of Snort and Apache events, i.e., *76659 log events*, from Honeynet Challenge #34 [15]. In comparison to experiment 1, the performance test results are almost unchanged, because there are only roughly 11% more events now, which are even easier to normalize.

6.3   Summary

Altogether, a combination of a hierarchical KB with CQ indexing, caching, prioritization and rule selectors seems to have the best normalization performance. In our experiments, we could reach a normalization speed of 37,000 events/s for a highly hierarchical log-format on eight threads.

7   Conclusion and Future Work

In this paper, we have shown how the speed of event log normalization can be drastically improved by using normalization algorithms that consider the typical hierarchical structure of log events. We have performed normalization with Lucene on a flat KB before, which did not perform well enough for big data. However, by using hierarchical normalization rules in combination with CQ indexing, caching and prioritization of rules we could speed up normalization by approximately 3 orders of magnitude. Altogether, we were able to normalize around 37,000 events/s, which should already be enough for large network environments. This fast speed can even be achieved, if logs with different parent formats are intermixed, like in real world log environments.

A starting point for further research could be the improvement of the normalization speed in a way that even event logs of companies with multiple billion events per day can be handled. One direction could be the parallelization of the processing on multiple machines.

Additionally, normalized logs can be used for further analysis. For example, inventory information can be extracted from logs to create an overview of machines, software and users in a network. Furthermore, the log information can be used to detect or prevent intrusions in a network environment.

Acknowledgments. We would like to thank HPI FutureSoC lab for providing us with the latest and powerful computing resources, which make the testing and experiments specified in the paper possible.

References

1. United States Computer Emergency Readiness Team (US-CERT). USCERT Year in Review CY 2012. Tech. rep. US Department of Homeland Security (2012)
2. US Office of Management and Budget. Fiscal Year 2012 Report to Congress on the Implementation of The Federal Information Security Management Act of 2002 (March 2013)
3. Kent, K., Souppaya, M.: Guide to Computer Security Log Management. In: NIST special publication (September 2006). http://212.200.39.245:81/CrnaRupa/2009-2010/FIM/ZIS/Literatura/GuidetoComputerSecurityLogManagementSP800-92.pdf
4. Gerhards, R.: The Syslog Protocol. RFC 5424 (Proposed Standard). Internet Engineering Task Force (March 2009). http://www.ietf.org/rfc/rfc5424.txt
5. Chuvakin, A., Marty, R., et al.: Common Event Expression. White Paper, MITRE (June (2008)

6. Hewlett-Packard. Implementing ArcSight CEF. 20. Hewlett-Packard (June 2013)
7. Barnum, S., Martin, R., et al.: The CybOX Language Specification. Draft 1. The MITRE Corporation (April 2012)
8. Sapegin, A., Jaeger, D., et al.: Hierarchical Object Log Format for Normalisation of Security Events. In: Proceedings of the 9th International Conference on Information Assurance and Security (IAS 2013), Yassmine Hammamet, Tunisia, pp. 25–30 (December 2013)
9. Friedl, J.E.F.: Mastering Regular Expressions. In: Oram, A. (ed.) 3rd edn. O'Reilly Media (August 2006)
10. Sparvieri, L.: SAP HANA Text Analysis. SAP (January 2014). http://scn.sap.com/community/developer-center/hana/blog/2013/01/03/sap-hana-text-analysis
11. Kobayashi, S., Fukuda, K., Esaki, H.: Towards an NLPbased log template generation algorithm for system log analysis. In: Proceedings of The Ninth International Conference on Future Internet Technologies, p. 11 (2014)
12. Azodi, A., Jaeger, D., et al.: Pushing the limits in event normalisation to improve attack detection in IDS/SIEM systems. In: Proceedings of the First Internation Conference on Advanced Cloud and Big Data (CBD 2013), Nanjing, China (December 2013)
13. Azodi, A., Jaeger, D., et al.: A new approach to building a multi- tier direct access knowledge base for IDS/SIEM systems. In: Proceedings of the 11th IEEE International Conference on Dependable, Autonomic and Secure Computing (DASC 2013), Chengdu, China (December 2013)
14. Real-time Event Analysis and Monitoring System (REAMS). http://hpi.de/en/meinel/security-tech/network-security/securityanalytics/reams.html (visited on November 5, 2015)
15. The Honeynet Project. Honeynet Challenges: Scan of the Month 34. Web Site (2005). http://old.honeynet.org/scans/scan34/ (visited on May 4, 2013)

Attack Tree Generation by Policy Invalidation

Marieta Georgieva Ivanova[1], Christian W. Probst[1]([⊠]), René Rydhof Hansen[2], and Florian Kammüller[3]

[1] Technical University of Denmark, Lyngby, Denmark
{mgiv,cwpr}@dtu.dk
[2] Aalborg University, Aalborg, Denmark
rrh@cs.aau.dk
[3] Middlesex University, London, UK
f.kammueller@mdx.ac.uk

Abstract. Attacks on systems and organisations increasingly exploit human actors, for example through social engineering, complicating their formal treatment and automatic identification. Formalisation of human behaviour is difficult at best, and attacks on socio-technical systems are still mostly identified through brainstorming of experts. In this work we formalize attack tree generation *including* human factors; based on recent advances in system models we develop a technique to identify possible attacks analytically, including technical and human factors. Our systematic attack generation is based on invalidating policies in the system model by identifying possible sequences of actions that lead to an attack. The generated attacks are precise enough to illustrate the threat, and they are general enough to hide the details of individual steps.

1 Introduction

Many attacks against organisations and how to prevent them are well understood. Traditional and well-established risk assessment methods often identify these potential threats, but due to a technical focus, often abstract away the internal structure of an organisation and ignore human factors. However, an increasing number of attacks do involve attack steps such as social engineering.

Attack trees [1] are a loosely defined, yet (or therefore) widely used approach for documenting possible attacks in risk assessment; they can describe attack goals and different ways of achieving these goals by means of the individual steps in an attack. The goal of the defender is then to inhibit one or more of the attack steps, thereby prohibiting the overall attack, or at least making it more difficult or expensive. While attack trees for purely technical attacks may be constructed by automated means [2], this is currently not possible for attacks exploiting the human factors. Actually, only few, if any, approaches to systematic risk assessment take such "human factor"-based attacks into consideration.

Our work closes this gap by developing models and analytic processes that support risk assessment in complex organisations *including* human factors and physical infrastructure. Our approach simplifies the identification of possible

© IFIP International Federation for Information Processing 2015
R.N. Akram and S. Jajodia (Eds.): WISTP 2015, LNCS 9311, pp. 249–259, 2015.
DOI: 10.1007/978-3-319-24018-3_16

attacks and provides qualified assessment and ranking of attacks based on the expected impact. Based on earlier work [3,4] we describe a systematic approach for the generation of attack trees for attacks that may include elements of human behaviour. These attack trees can be used as input to a traditional risk assessment process and thereby extend and support the brainstorming results. System models such as ExASyM [5] and Portunes [6] have been used to model and analyse organisations for possible attacks [7]. The models contain both physical infrastructure and information on actors, access rights, and policies; consequently, analysis of such models can include social engineering in the identified attacks. The generated attack trees are complete with respect to the model, that is, our method identifies all attacks that are possible in the model. This is achieved by basing the attack tree generation on invalidation of policies; policies in our model describe both access control to locations and data, as well as system-wide policies such as admissible actions and actor behaviour.

The rest of this paper is structured as follows. After introducing our socio-technical system model and a running example in the next section, we discuss policies in Section 3. These policies are at the core of the attack generation, which is described in Section 4. After evaluating our approach and discussing related work in Section 5 and Section 6, we conclude the paper with an outlook on future developments.

2 Modelling Socio-technical Systems

Our model represents the infrastructure of organisations as nodes in a directed graph [5], representing rooms, access control points, and similar locations. A location may belong to several *domains*, *e.g.*, it can be part of the building and the network. Actors are represented by nodes and are associated with behaviour. Assets model any data relevant in the modelled organisation, and can be annotated with a value and a metric, *e.g.*, the likelihood of being lost. Nodes also represent assets that can be attached to locations or actors; assets attached to actors move around with that actor. Actors perform actions on locations, including physical locations or actors. Actions are restricted by policies that represent both access control and the behaviour as expected by an organisation from its employees. Policies consist of required credentials and enabled actions, representing what an actor needs to provide in order to enable the actions in a policy, and what actions are enabled if an actor provides the required credentials, respectively.

In contrast to Klaim [8], we attach processes to special nodes that move around with the process. This makes the modelling of actors and items carried by actors more intuitive and natural. The metrics mentioned above can represent any quantitative knowledge about components, for example, likelihood, time, price, impact, or probability distributions. The latter could describe behaviour of actors or timing distributions.

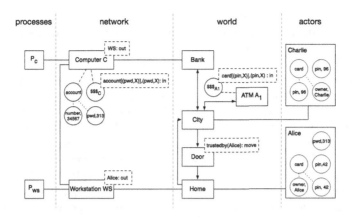

Fig. 1. Graphical representation of the running example. The small rectangles represent locations, the big rectangles represent actors and contain the assets known or owned by the actor, the round nodes represent assets, and the small squares represent process nodes. Solid lines represent the physical connections between locations, while dashed lines indicate containment of information and assets. The dashed rectangles in the upper right part of some nodes represent the policies assigned to these nodes.

2.1 Running Example

We use a running example based on actor Alice, who receives some kind of service, *e.g.*, care-taking, provided by actor Charlie. Charlie's employer has a company policy that forbids him to accept money from Alice. Figure 1 shows the example scenario, consisting of Alice's home, a bank with a bank computer, and an ATM. Alice has a card with a pin code to obtain money, and a password to initiate online transfers from her workstation. The policies in the model require, *e.g.*, a card and a matching pin to obtain money from the ATM.

Actor nodes can also represent processes running on the corresponding locations. The processes at the workstation and the bank computer represent the required functionality for transferring money; they initiate transfers from Alice's home (P_{WS}), and check credentials for transfers (P_C).

3 Policy Language

Our model supports *local policies* for annotating elements with access control polices, and *global policies* for annotating the model with organisational policies. *Local policies* consist of a set of required credentials and a set of *actions* that are enabled by the required credentials: $LocalPolicies \subseteq ReqCred \times Actions$ with $Actions \subseteq \{\textbf{in}, \textbf{out}, \textbf{move}, \textbf{eval}\}$. The actions come from the set of actions supported by the modelling formalism acKlaim [5]. To ease presentation, we treat credentials as terms from the term algebra over a suitable signature, yielding a flexible and expressive, yet simple, formalisation. The signature is chosen based on a concrete system model, and contains enough structure to represent the model's important features. In our running example, we would expect the signature to at least contain such elements as cards, pin codes, locations, accounts, and actor ids. As signatures depend on the model, we only assume the existence of relevant signatures Σ for assets and predicates, and define required credentials as $ReqCred = \mathcal{P}\left(T\left(\Sigma\right)\right)$ where $T(\Sigma)$ is the term algebra generated by Σ.

Checking whether an actor provides the required credentials of a policy is based on the set of concrete credentials $ProvCred = \mathcal{P}\left(T\left(\Sigma\right)\right)$ that an actor has. Using first order unification as defined by Robinson [9] we determine if a set $c \subseteq ProvCred$ of credentials is valid with respect to a given set $r \subseteq ReqCred$ of required credentials: if c and r can be successfully unified, then the credentials c are sufficient to satisfy the required credentials r of a given policy.

Our policy language supports variables for generic policies; these are left out for space reasons. The system model also supports predicates in credentials. Predicates are used to establish facts about actors; in the example a predicate *isEmployee* could express that the actor is an employee of the service provider, and *isCustomer* could express that the actor is a customer of the company. Predicates are specified in the model, and become part of the knowledge base used in unification, and consequently the term algebra.

Global policies express organisational policies in the system model, describing a state or actions that are disallowed in the system and are to be enforced system-wide. We assume two basic kinds of organisational policies: action-based global policies forbid actors to perform certain actions, and location-based global policies forbid data to reach certain locations. Action-based global policies are specified like local policies with required credentials and a set of actions, and contain a component identifying the attacker: $GlobalActionPolicies = (Actors \cup Vars) \times Credentials \times Actions$. Of course, the set of actions here specifies the prohibited actions. Location-based global policies are considerably simpler, since they only specify an asset and a location $GlobalLocationPolicies = Asset \times Location$.

In the rest of this paper we only consider action-based global policies, which generalise location-based global policies: for data to reach a location it either must be co-located with an actor, who must have input the data, or it must have been output at that location, which in turn again requires that an actor has input the data. Location-based policies can therefore be translated to an action-based global policy that forbids inputing the data in question.

In the example from Figure 1, the global action-based policy could specified to be $not(\{X, isEmployee(X), card[(owner, Y)], isCustomer(Y)\}, \{\mathbf{in}\})$, stating that an actor X is not allowed to use a card as credential when performing an **in** action, if the predicate *isEmployee* is true for X and the card is owned by an actor Y, for whom the predicate *isCustomer* holds. In the example, the only possible binding for X is Charlie, and the only possible binding for Y is Alice, and the **in** action would represent obtaining money at an ATM.

4   Policy Invalidation and Attack Tree Generation

We are now ready to present the main contribution of our work, the generation of attack trees by invalidating policies. We choose attack trees as a succinct way of representing attacks; they are defined by

Definition 1. $AT := (N_i \,\dot\cup\, N_l, n, E, L)$ *is an attack tree with inner nodes* $N_i :=$ $N_\wedge \,\dot\cup\, N_\vee$ *and leaf nodes* N_l, *a root node* $n \in N_i$, *directed edges* $E \subseteq N_i \times N_i \,\dot\cup\, N_l$, *and a labelling function* $L := N \to \Sigma^*$. *Nodes in* AT *are conjunctions* $(N_\wedge)$ *or disjunctions* $(N_\vee)$ *of sub-attacks, or basic actions* (N_l). *Let* $\mathcal{N}^{label}$ *be the attack tree that only contains one node* n *that is mapped by* L *to label. For* $AT_1 = (N_1, n_1, E_1, L_1)$ *and* $AT_2 = (N_2, n_2, E_2, L_2)$, *kind* $\in \{\vee, \wedge\}$, *label being a string, and* $n \in N_{kind}$, *we define the addition of attack trees as* $AT_1 \oplus_{kind}^{label} AT_2 :=$ $(N_1 \cup N_2 \cup \{n\}, E_1 \cup E_2 \cup \{(n, n_1), (n, n_2)\}, n, L_1 \cup L_2 \cup \{(n, label)\})$.

We assume an implicit, left to right order for children of conjunctive nodes. For example, an attacker first needs to move to a location before being able to perform an action.

On a high level, our approach for invalidating a policy consists of four basic steps:

1. Choose the policy to invalidate, and identify the possible actors who could do so; these are the potential attackers.
2. Identify a set of locations where the prohibited actions can be performed. Since there might be several possible actions, this results in a set of pairs of location and action.
3. Recursively generate attacks for performing these actions. This will also identify required assets to perform any of these actions, and obtain them.
4. Finally, move to the location identified in the second step and perform the action.

It should be noted that all rules specified below either block if no valid result can be computed, or return an empty attack tree, for example, if no credentials are required. The rules take as input an infrastructure component $\mathcal{I}$, which represents the socio-technical security model described in Section 2, and an actor component $\mathcal{A}$, which stores identities, locations, and assets collected and reached by an actor during an attack. Also note that we extend rules from working on singular elements to sets by unifying the results of rule applications.

Identify Attackers. To start attack generation from a global policy (see Figure 2), we compute the unification of the global policy and the set of all actors, identify the set of attackers by means of function $getAttacker$, which replaces a variable with the identified bindings, or returns an explicitly specified attacker:

$$getAttacker_{\mathcal{I}}(a, \sigma) := \begin{cases} \{a\} \text{ if } a \in \mathsf{N}_a \\ \sigma(a) \text{ if } a \in Vars \end{cases}$$

$$\frac{\sigma = unify_{\mathcal{I}}(Actors, credentials)}{\mathcal{I}, attackers, goals \vdash_{goal} trees} \qquad \frac{goals = applicableAt_{\mathcal{I}}(credentials, enabled, \sigma)}{\mathcal{T} := \oplus_{\vee}^{\text{"perform any actions"}} trees}$$

$$\mathcal{I}, not(actor, credentials, enabled) \vdash_{P} \mathcal{T}$$

Fig. 2. Attack generation starts from the global action-based policy $not(actor, credentials, enabled)$. Attack trees are generated for all possible policy violations. As every attack tree represents a violation of the policy, the resulting attack trees are combined by an *or* node.

$$\frac{\mathcal{I}, \mathcal{A}, goto(location) \wedge perform(action) \vdash_{GP} \mathcal{T}}{\mathcal{I}, \mathcal{A}, (location, action) \vdash_{goal} \mathcal{T}}$$

$$\frac{\mathcal{I}, \mathcal{A}, goto(l) \vdash_{goto} \mathcal{T}_{goto}, \mathcal{A}' \qquad \mathcal{I}, \mathcal{A}', perform(a) \vdash_{perform} \mathcal{T}_{action}, \mathcal{A}''}{\mathcal{I}, \mathcal{A}, goto(l) \wedge perform(a) \vdash_{GP} \mathcal{T}_{goto} \oplus_{\wedge}^{\text{"goto } l \text{ and perform } a\text{"}} \mathcal{T}_{action}, \mathcal{A}''}$$

Fig. 3. For each identified goal (consisting of a location and an action) an attacker moves to the location and performs the action. The rules result in an attack tree and a new state of the attacker, which includes the obtained keys and reached locations.

Identify Target Locations. We then compute all locations at which one of the actions in *enabled* could be applied using the credentials specified in the policy. The function *applicableAt* identifies all these locations in the system model and returns goals as pairs of actions and locations.

Attack Generation. The rules in Figure 3 connect the identified goals with the generation of attack trees. For each goal we generate two attack trees: moving to the location and performing the action. While moving to the location new credentials may be required; as a result, the actor acquires new knowledge, which is stored in the actor component $\mathcal{A}$. The rules in Figure 4 and Figure 5 generate attack trees for moving around, performing actions, and obtaining credentials, resulting in attack trees for every single action of the attacker. The resulting trees are combined in the overall attack tree. The function *missingCredentials* uses the unification described above to match policies with the assets available in the model. This implies that all assets that can fullfil a policy are identified; the attack generation then generates one attack for each of these assets, and combines them with a disjunctive node.

For space reasons we do not discuss the interaction between actors and processes, and for the global policy chosen in this example, this is not necessary either. Another global action-based policy could forbid in general to obtain money that has been "owned" by a customer before. In this case, the processes defined in Section 2.1 for the work station and the bank computer would become important, as they allow to transfer money from Alice's to Charlie's account. When invalidating this global policy one has to consider asset flow.

$$paths = getAllPaths_{\mathcal{I}}(\mathcal{A}, l) \qquad \mathcal{I}, \mathcal{A}, paths \vdash_{path} trees, \mathcal{A}'$$
$$\frac{\mathcal{T} := \oplus_{\vee}^{\text{“find path to } l\text{”}} trees}{\mathcal{I}, \mathcal{A}, goto(l) \vdash_{goto} \mathcal{T}, \mathcal{A}'}$$

$$missing = missingCredentials_{\mathcal{I}}(\mathcal{A}, path) \qquad \mathcal{I}, \mathcal{A}, missing \vdash_{credential} trees, \mathcal{A}'$$
$$\frac{\mathcal{T} := \oplus_{\wedge}^{\text{“get credentials”}} trees}{\mathcal{I}, \mathcal{A}, path \vdash_{path} \mathcal{T} \oplus_{\wedge}^{\text{“get credentials and pass path”}} \mathcal{N}^{\text{pass path}}, \mathcal{A}'}$$

Fig. 4. Going to a location and performing an action results in two attack trees. The function *getAllPaths* returns all paths from the current locations of the actor to the goal location l, and the resulting attack trees are alternatives for reaching this location.

$$\frac{i \notin identities \implies \mathcal{T} = \mathcal{N}^{\text{obtain identity } i}}{\mathcal{I}, (identities, locations, assets), identity\ i \vdash_{credential} \mathcal{T}, (identities \cup \{i\}, locations, assets)}$$

$$\mathcal{A} = (identities, locations, assets) \wedge a \notin assets \implies$$
$$\frac{goals = availableAt_{\mathcal{I}}(a) \qquad \mathcal{I}, \mathcal{A}, goals \vdash_{goal} trees, \mathcal{A}' \qquad \mathcal{T} := \oplus_{\vee}^{\text{“get a”}} trees}{\mathcal{I}, \mathcal{A}, asset\ a \vdash_{credential} \mathcal{T}, \mathcal{A}'}$$

$$\frac{\mathcal{I}, \mathcal{A}, predicate\ p(arguments) \vdash_{predicate} trees, \mathcal{A}' \qquad \mathcal{T} := \oplus_{\vee}^{\text{“fullfil predicate } p\text{”}} trees}{\mathcal{I}, \mathcal{A}, predicate\ p(arguments) \vdash_{credential} \mathcal{T}, \mathcal{A}'}$$

Fig. 5. Depending on the missing credential, different attacks are generated. If the actor lacks an identity, an attack node representing an abstract social engineering attack is generated, for example, social engineering or impersonating. If the missing credential is an asset, the function *availableAt* returns a set of pairs of locations from which this asset is available, and the according **in** actions. If the missing credential is a predicate, a combination of credentials fulfilling the predicate must be obtained.

Post-Processing Attack Trees. The generated attack trees do not contain annotations or metrics about the success likelihood of actions such as social engineering, or the potential impact of actions. Also the likelihood of a given attacker to succeed or fail is not considered. Computing qualitative and quantitative measures on attack trees is beyond the scope of this work. The generated attack trees also often contain duplicated sub-trees, due to similar scenarios being encountered in several locations, for example, the social engineering of the same actor, or the requirement for the same credentials. This is not an inherent limitation, but may clutter attack trees. Similar to [2], a post-processing of attack trees can simplify the result.

5 Evaluation

We now describe briefly the attack generation based on the results of a prototype implementation. The attack tree shown in Figure 6 is generated from

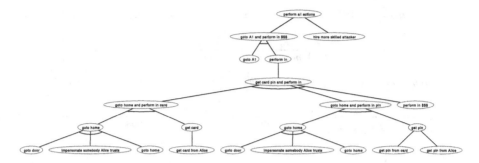

Fig. 6. Attack tree generated by the prototype implementation for the example shown in Figure 1.

the example scenario. As mentioned in the previous section, we assume the global policy that an employee is not allowed to use a customer's card to obtain money: $not(\{X, isEmployee(X), card[(owner, Y)], isCustomer(Y)\}, \{in\})$. Using the rule from Figure 2, we compute the substitution $\sigma = [X \mapsto Charlie, Y \mapsto Alice]$ for variables X, Y: Charlie has the role employee, and Alice has the role customer. In the next step, the attacker is identified to be X, and based on the system specification from Figure 1, the only location with a policy restricting the **in** action is the money location at the ATM A1. The location and action pair $\{(A1, \mathbf{in})$ is therefore the only goal, and next $\vdash_P$ from Figure 4 generates the attack tree for moving to $A1$ and performing the **in** action.

Going to the location does not require additional credentials, but performing the **in** action does. The *missingCredentials* function returns the card and the pin, which combined with the requirement from the goal policy, that the owner of the card must be Alice, implies that the attacker needs Alice's card and pin. The second rule $\vdash_{credential}$ in Figure 5 identifies where they are: Alice has the card and the pin, and the pin code is also stored in the card. Our approach generates an attack tree for going to the location "home", and in doing so the attacker must fullfil the policy "trustedBy(Alice)", meaning that he must impersonate somebody trusted by Alice. Then the attacker can either "input" the card and the pin, or only the card and try to extract the pin code from the card.

The stealing and the extraction of the pin code are not represented in the model since they are context and technology dependent. In a given scenario, they can be instantiated with the matching "real" actions. After the assets have been obtained, the attacker moves to the ATM location and performs the action.

6   Related Work

System models such as ExASyM [5,7] and Portunes [10] also model infrastructure and data, and analyse the modelled organisation for possible threats. However, Portunes supports mobility of nodes, instead of processes, and represents the social domain by low-level policies that describe the trust relation between people to model social engineering. Pieters *et al.* consider policy alignment to address different levels of abstraction of socio-technical systems [11], where policies are interpreted as first-order logical theories containing all sequences of actions and expressing the policy as a "distinguished" prefix-closed predicate in these theories. In contrast to their use of refinement for policies we use the security refinement paradox, *i.e.*, security is *not* generally preserved by refinement.

Attack trees [12] specify an attacker's main goal as the root of a tree; this goal is then disjunctively or conjunctively refined into sub-goals until the reached sub-goals represent basic actions that correspond to atomic components. Disjunctive refinements represent alternative ways of achieving a goal, whereas conjunctive refinements depict different steps an attacker needs to take in order to achieve a goal. Techniques for the automated generation of attack graphs mostly consider computer networks only [13,14]. While these techniques usually require the specification of atomic attacks, in our approach the attack consists in invalidating a policy, and the model just provides the infrastructure and methods for doing so.

7   Conclusion

Threats on systems are often described by attack trees, which represent a possible attack that might realise the described threat. These attack trees are usually collected by experts based on a combination of experience and brainstorming. Earlier work has tried to formalise this approach for threats on technical systems. The increasingly important human factor is often not considered in these formalisations, since it is not part of the model.

In this work we have formalizes attack tree generation *including* human factors using recent advances in system models. Our approach supports all kinds of human factors that can be instantiated once an attack has been identified. To the best of our knowledge this is the first formalisation of an approach to generating attack trees including steps on the technical and social level.

The generated attacks include all relevant steps from detecting the required assets, obtaining them as well as any credentials needed to do so, and finally performing actions that are prohibited in the system. The generated attacks are precise enough to illustrate the threat, and they are general enough to hide the details of individual steps. The generated attacks are also complete with respect to the model; whenever an attack is possible in the model, it will be found. Our approach is also sound; all results of our generator do represent attacks.

The combination of system model and automated generation enables us to trade in precision of the model for details in the attack trees. For example, the modelling of the ATM is very imprecise in the example from Figure 1. A more detailed formalisation would represent that an actor puts the card and the pin code into the ATM and receives money after a check with the bank. In this model, the attack tree generator is able to find out that one can obtain the pin code from the ATM, since it is input into the system. Note that the first action in the second line only verifies whether the pin code entered into the ATM is the one stored on the card. To handle more general global policies that might, for example, prohibit to own money obtained by some other actor, we can use techniques such as tainting to trace which actor or credentials have been used to obtain or handle an asset. In the example described in Section 2.1, using Alice's credit card would result in the withdrawn money being tagged with her id.

We are currently working on further evaluations and domain-specific languages to extend the model's expressivity, and are extending the attack generation to simplify the generated attack tree during generation.

Acknowledgment. Part of the research leading to these results has received funding from the European Union Seventh Framework Programme (FP7/2007-2013) under grant agreement no. 318003 (TRESPASS). This publication reflects only the authors' views and the Union is not liable for any use that may be made of the information contained herein.

References

1. Schneier, B.: Attack Trees: Modeling Security Threats. Dr. Dobb's Journal of Software Tools **24**(12), 21–29 (1999)
2. Vigo, R., Nielson, F., Nielson, H.R.: Automated generation of attack trees. In: Proceedings of the 27th Computer Security Foundations Symposium (CSF), pp. 337–350. IEEE (2014)
3. Kammüller, F., Probst, C.W.: Invalidating policies using structural information. In: 2nd International IEEE Workshop on Research on Insider Threats (WRIT 2013). IEEE (2013)
4. Kammüller, F., Probst, C.W.: Combining generated data models with formal invalidation for insider threat analysis. In: 3rd International IEEE Workshop on Research on Insider Threats (WRIT 2014). IEEE (2014)
5. Probst, C.W., Hansen, R.R.: An extensible analysable system model. Information Security Technical Report **13**(4), 235–246 (2008)
6. Dimkov, T., Pieters, W., Hartel, P.: Portunes: representing attack scenarios spanning through the physical, digital and social domain. In: Armando, A., Lowe, G. (eds.) ARSPA-WITS 2010. LNCS, vol. 6186, pp. 112–129. Springer, Heidelberg (2010)
7. Probst, C.W., Hansen, R.R., Nielson, F.: Where can an insider attack? In: Dimitrakos, T., Martinelli, F., Ryan, P.Y.A., Schneider, S. (eds.) FAST 2006. LNCS, vol. 4691, pp. 127–142. Springer, Heidelberg (2007)
8. de Nicola, R., Ferrari, G.L., Pugliese, R.: KLAIM: A kernel language for agents interaction and mobility. IEEE Trans. Softw. Eng. **24**(5), 315–330 (1998)
9. Robinson, J.A.: A machine-oriented logic based on the resolution principle. J. ACM **12**(1), 23–41 (1965)
10. Dimkov, T.: Alignment of Organizational Security Policies - Theory and Practice. University of Twente (2012)
11. Pieters, W., Dimkov, T., Pavlovic, D.: Security policy alignment: A formal approach. IEEE Systems Journal **7**(2), 275–287 (2013)

12. Salter, C., Saydjari, O.S., Schneier, B., Wallner, J.: Toward a secure system engineering methodology. In: Proceedings of the 1998 Workshop on New Security Paradigms (NSPW), pp. 2–10 (September 1998)
13. Phillips, C., Swiler, L.P.: A graph-based system for network-vulnerability analysis. In: Proceedings of the 1998 workshop on New security paradigms NSPW 1998, pp. 71–79 (1998)
14. Sheyner, O., Haines, J., Jha, S., Lippmann, R., Wing, J.M.: Automated generation and analysis of attack graphs. In: Proceedings of the 2002 IEEE Symposium on Security and Privacy (S&P 2002), vol. 129, pp. 273–284 (2002)

Lightweight Password Hashing Scheme
for Embedded Systems

George Hatzivasilis[1]([⊠]), Ioannis Papaefstathiou[1], Charalampos Manifavas[2],
and Ioannis Askoxylakis[3]

[1] Department of Electronic and Computer Engineering,
Technical University of Crete, Chania, Crete, Greece
`gchatzivasilis@isc.tuc.gr, ygp@mhl.tuc.gr`
[2] Department of Informatics Engineering,
Technological Educational Institute of Crete, Heraklion, Crete, Greece
`harryman@ie.teicrete.gr`
[3] Foundation for Research and Technology – Hellas (FORTH),
Heraklion, Crete, Greece
`asko@ics.forth.gr`

Abstract. Passwords constitute the main mean for authentication in computer systems. In order to maintain the user-related information at the service provider end, password hashing schemes (PHS) are utilized. The limited and old-fashioned solutions led the international cryptographic community to conduct the Password Hashing Competition (PHC). The competition will propose a small portfolio of schemes suitable for widespread usage until 2015. Embedded systems form a special application domain, utilizing devices with inherent computational limitations. Lightweight cryptography focuses in designing schemes for such devices and targets moderate levels of security. In this paper, a lightweight poly PHS suitable for lightweight cryptography is presented. At first, we design two lightweight versions of the PHC schemes Catena and PolyPassHash. Then, we integrate them and implement the proposed scheme – called LightPolyPHS. A fair comparison with similar proposals on mainstream computer is presented.

Keywords: Password hashing · PHC · Catena · PolyPassHash · Lightweight cryptography · LWC · Embedded systems

1 Introduction

Attacks on widely known organizations have exposed mounts of user accounts and credentials. The poor password protection practises are exploited by the attackers in order to recover the user passwords from the stolen data. These attacks lead to negative and significant loss in the vendor's market value.

Advanced password hashing schemes (PHS) are proposed to fortify the secure maintenance of such information. PBKDF2 [1], bcrypt [2] and scrypt [3] are currently the most common solutions. However, the evolving parallel computing and

© IFIP International Federation for Information Processing 2015
R.N. Akram and S. Jajodia (Eds.): WISTP 2015, LNCS 9311, pp. 260–270, 2015.
DOI: 10.1007/978-3-319-24018-3_17

hardware dedicated devices enable attacks [4] that overcome the PHS protection. GPUs, FPGAs and ASICs implement efficient password crackers that try out several attempts in parallel, gaining a significant boost in disclosing the user information. PBKDF2 and bcrypt are vulnerable to such attacks. Memory-hard PHSs can counter password scrambling. The memory elements in parallel platforms are considered expensive. All parallel components share the same memory and the access to it is bounded. Thus, attackers are significantly slowed-down when PHSs with high memory requirements are applied. The goal is to derive password scrambling on parallel cores not much faster than it is on single cores. scrypt is the current solution of memory-hard PHS. Unfortunately, it is vulnerable to other attacks, like cache-timing [5] and garbage-collector [6]. The limited and old-fashioned solutions led the international cryptographic community to conduct the Password Hashing Competition (PHC) [7] in 2013. It targets in modern and secure designs for password hashing, with 22 initial candidates being submitted. In 2014, 9 finalists were selected based on security, efficiency, simplicity, and the extra features that they provide. A comprehensive survey and benchmark analysis of the 22 PHC submissions and the 3 current solutions for password hashing is presented in [7]. In 2015, a small portfolio of schemes will be announced based on further performance and security analysis. The winners are expected to become "de facto" standards and be further examined by organizations like NIST for formal standardization.

PHSs are applied in several domains (e.g. general applications on mainstream computers, web applications and embedded systems) with diverse features and properties. The candidate scheme must comply with them. Typically, a PHS utilizes core cryptographic primitives, such as block ciphers and hash functions, that constitute the main computational components of the scheme. The mainstream cryptographic solutions provide high levels of security, ignoring the requirements of resource constrained devices. The research field of lightweight cryptography (LWC) [8,9] focuses in designing schemes for devices with constrained capabilities in processing, power supply, connectivity, hardware and software. They are mainly applied in embedded systems [10] that are deployed in pervasive and ubiquitous computing [11–13]. Security is just a part of the whole functionality and the lightweight designs consume low computational resources and memory. In case of most constraint devices (e.g. sensors) only a few KBs of memory are devoted to provide moderate level of security [14]. Regarding passwords, embedded systems maintain a small amount of authentication-related data. Device-to-device and short-term communication forms the most common interaction (e.g. in wireless sensor networks), making session key deviation from passwords a desirable goal to enhance security. The garbage-collector attacks [6] can be countered by build-in memory safety techniques [15].

In this paper, we present LightPolyPHS – a lightweight poly PHS for embedded devices and LWC. To our knowledge this is the first scheme that targets constrained devices. Section 2, introduces the background theory and related work regarding passwords and LWC. Section 3, analyses the LightPolyPHS design and its subcomponents. In section 4, the proposed scheme is applied and evaluated on real embedded devices. A comparative analysis is held with similar schemes on mainstream computers. Finally, section 5 concludes.

2   Background Theory and Related Work

2.1   Password Hashing

User passwords are human-memorable secrets, consisting of 8-12 printable characters and form the main mean for authentication in computer systems. The service provider maintains a pair of the user's name and password-related information for each active account. To authenticate himself and login the service, the user must inputs this information first. Passwords can also be used for the generation of cryptographic keys. Key Deviation Functions (KDF) [16] parse a password and derive one or more related keys. The keys are used on cryptographic operations, like session encryption. Ordinary passwords are 8 characters long (8 bytes). The deriving secrets may produce low entropy and be vulnerable to relative attacks. In exhaustive search, an attacker tries out all character combinations until he finds the right password. Then, he owns the relevant account, like the legitimate user does.

The typical method to counter these attacks with PHSs, is key stretching. A hash function parses the password and produces a fixed-length output, acting as the new password. The hash password is longer (usually 32-64 bytes long), making the attacks less feasible. The hash function is iterating several times to further fortify the hash result. The attacker is slowed down by a factor of 2^{i+o}, where i is the iteration count and o is the number of the output bits. However, the user is also slowed down. Thus, the key stretching parameters are also bounded by the user's tolerance to compute a robust hash password. In modern services, a high volume of users must be verified simultaneously. The load on the server may become unmanageable and lead to denial of service. Server relief (SR) protocols are established and balance the total effort between clients and the server. A client may perform part of the PHS computations while the server performs the rest steps and the account verification. The server might need to increase security (e.g. increase the hash size or PHS iterations). Hash password upgrade techniques independent from the user (HUIU) enhances the convenience of the user and enables the seamless operation of the service. The server upgrades the security of the stored hash passwords without prior-knowledge of the initial passwords or the user's involvement. It is quite common for a user to utilize the same password in different services or many users of a service to have the same password. The hash passwords would be the same too. The disclosure of a single account erases security issues for the rest ones. To prevent this correlation a small parameter of random bytes, called salt (usually 8 bytes long), is utilized. The salt also hardens dictionary (try hundreds of likely possibilities to determine the secret) [5] and rainbow table attacks (ability to use tables of precomputed hashes) [6]. Typically, the salt is generated when the user account is created and is concatenated with the password during hashing. Thus, the same password produces different hash passwords. At the server-end, the salt is stored in plaintext along with the hashed password. They are used in the authentication process to validate the password of a login request.

2.2   Poly Password Hashing

Strong PHS can protect the password data that are maintained at the service-end. However, attackers have proven themselves adept at cracking large amounts of passwords once the stored data is compromised. To further fortify security, poly (many) password hashing (PPH) schemes have been recently proposed. They leverage cryptographic hashing and threshold cryptography by combining strong PHS with shares.

Cryptographic hashing and PHSs are described in the previous subsection. A cryptographic (k, n)-threshold scheme protects secret information, by deriving n different shares from this information. The threshold determines how any k shares out of total n can recover the secret information. If fewer than k shares are known, no secret information is disclosed. The Shamir Secret Sharing (SSS) [17] is a fundamental threshold scheme in this domain. It computes $k - 1$ random coefficients for a $k - 1$ degree polynomial $f(x)$ in a finite field. The kth term comprises the secret (usually the constant term of the polynomial). The share is identified by a share value x, taking values between 1 and the order of the field. The share x is the polynomial value of $f(x)$. The secret can be reconstructed by interpolating the values of k shares to find the constant term of the polynomial (i.e., the secret). Interpolation is computationally optimized and only the constant term is revealed.

In the PPH domain, there is one share for each account. The share is XORed with the relevant PHS result and is maintained by the server (instead of the pure PHS result). The shares are derived from a master key. This key is only known to the service provider and is not stored on disk in order to prevent attacks that would disclose the key along with the stolen password data. When the server starts, k clients must login and be correctly verified in order to reconstruct the shares. Implementations of SSS provide integrity check mechanisms to detect if incorrect shares are parsed. After this startup phase, the server operates in the ordinary manner. The attacker has to crack a threshold of password hashes before being able to recover passwords. At a small additional cost by the server, security increases by many orders of magnitude. Poly password hashing is easily implemented and deployed on a server without any changes to clients and can be integrated to current forms of authentication (e.g. two factor authentication and hardware tokens). It is also efficient in terms of storage, memory and computational demands.

2.3   Password Hashing Competition

Secure cryptographic hash functions or HMACs constitute the most common solution for PHSs and KDFs. PBKDF2, bcrypt and scrypt are currently the widely-used PHSs and KDFs for mainstream applications. The Password-Based Key Derivation Function 2 (PBKDF2) [1] is the only standardized scheme (RSA

Laboratories' Public-Key Cryptography Standards (PKCS) series (PKCS #5 v2.0) and the RFC 2898). The input password and salt are processed by an HMAC. PBKDF2 is not memory-hard and can be implemented as a small circuit wit low RAM requirements. This is evinced in a main drawback as cheap brute-force attacks are enabled on GPUs and ASICs. bcrypt [2] is based on the block cipher Blowfish [18] and is the default PHS of the BSD operating system. It uses 4KB RAM and is slightly stronger than PBKDF2 in defending attacks on parallel computing platforms and dedicated hardware devices. However, these memory requirements render efficient attacks on FPGAs. scrypt [3] was announced as an Internet Draft by the IETF in 2012, with the intention to become an informational RFC. It utilizes the PBKDF2 and the stream cipher Salsa [19] and uses arbitrarily large amounts of memory. scrypt is the most resistant widely-used scheme. The cost of a hardware brute force attack is considered around 4000 and 20000 times larger than in bcrypt and PBKDF2 respectively. However, the huge memory requirements can derive denial-of-service (DoS) attacks on servers, when large amounts of simultaneous login requests are handled. Also, scrypt is vulnerable to new types of attacks, like cache-timing [5] and garbage-collector attacks [6].

Password Hashing Competition (PHC) [7] advances our knowledge in designing secure and efficient PHSs and KDFs. At the first round 22 new PHSs were evaluated in terms of security, performance and flexibility. A survey and benchmark analysis of the 3 aforementioned widely-used PHSs and the 22 candidates is presented in [7]. The parameters t_cost and m_cost are introduced to adjust the timing and memory requirements respectively. The defender adjusts the PHS iteration count and memory requirements to design secure schemes. The finalist Catena is one of the most notable submissions and is intended to be included in the winners list. It implements the full functionality of PHS, KDF, SR, and HUIU, is well-documented and analysed, and is one of the most efficient candidate in terms of execution time and memory usage. Catena exhibits low code size and memory requirements, making it suitable for embedded systems. A PPH scheme, called PolyPassHash, is also presented in the competition. It is actually a protocol that recovers a symmetric key used to encrypt passwords and does not constitute a pure PHS. Thus, it is not included in the finalists. Still, Poly-PassHash demonstrates state-of-the-art features regarding PPH and is efficient in terms of storage, memory and computational requirements. We utilize the PHC candidates Catena and PolyPassHash to design our lightweight proposal. Both schemes are analysed in the following section.

2.4 Lightweight Cryptographic Mechanisms

Traditional cryptography targets high level of security. The main primitive types that are investigated in this paper include block ciphers and hash functions. The block cipher AES [20] is considered a landmark in this field. Standardized or widely-used hash functions for mainstream applications are SHA2 [21] and BLAKE [22]. However, these mainstream ciphers and functions are too large to fit in many types of embedded systems.

Lightweight cryptography (LWC) [14] focuses in designing cryptographic primitives for resource constraint devices. The main design goals in software are the reduction of processing and memory requirements. Embedded software implementations are optimized for throughput as well as memory and power savings. Lightweight primitives provide moderate levels of security from 80 to 128 bits. 80 bit security is adequate for constrained devices, like RFID tags and micro-controllers, while 128 bits is typical for mainstream applications. In recent years, a high variety of lightweight proposals are presented [14]. The standardized primitives for LWC are referred in the ISO/IEC standard 29192 [23]. The part 2 of the standard includes block ciphers and the upcoming part 5 includes hash functions. Regarding embedded software, CLEFIA [24], designed by SONY, is the standardized block cipher and PHOTON [25] is a lightweight hash function considered for inclusion in the standard. The proposed LightPolyPHS scheme utilizes CLEFIA for cryptographic operations and PHOTON for hashing.

3   Lightweight PHS and PPH

LightPolyPHS is a lightweight PHS and PPH, designed for embedded systems and constrained devices. The overall system complies with the principles of LWC. First, we replace the inner cryptographic primitives that are utilized by the PHS Catena and the PPH PolyPassHash and implement two relevant lightweight schemes. Then, we integrate them by using the lightweight Catena as the PHS for the lightweight PolyPassHash and implement the proposed LightPolyPHS.

3.1   Mainstream and Lightweight Catena PHS

Catena is suitable for multiple environments, like multi-core CPUs, databases, and low-memory devices. It is a composed cryptographic operation based on a cryptographic hash function and is simple and easy to analyse. The design constitutes a graph-based structure, called "Bit-Reversal Graph", that is instantiated by the cryptographic hash function. Any strong hash function can be embodied. The reference implementation selects SHA512 and BLAKE2b. SHA512 is standardized and widely-implemented in many platforms. BLAKE2b supports the Simple Instruction Multiple Data (SIMD) approach and protects massively parallel attacks on GPUs. The scheme is well-documented with thorough security analysis. The time-memory tradeoff analysis is based on the pebble-game approach [6]. Catena provides lower bounds on the time-memory tradeoff, preimage security, indistinguishability from random and resistance against side-channel (e.g. cache-timing attacks [5]). The computational cost for massively parallel crackers on GPUs, ASICs and FPGAs is high.

The lightweight Catena utilizes PHOTON-256 as the cryptographic hash function, which outputs a 256-bit digest. This results in a smaller datapath and implementation size than the original scheme as well as lower computational and memory requirements. The output size complies with the relevant primitive in PolyPassHash and provides moderate level of security. The security level of the

Catena is determined by the underlying hash function. Consider that Catena-sha512, Catena-blake2b and Catena-photon256 offer 2^{512}, 2^{481} and 2^{244} bits security respectively.

3.2 Mainstream and Lightweight PolyPassHash PPH

PolyPassHash is a PPH scheme that provides protection above PHS. It is composed of two building blocks: the aforementioned SSS threshold scheme and the standardized SHA256 [21] hash function. The computational complexity of SSS is based on the k degree polynomial over a finite field. For PolyPassHash, the default k value is 3 and it is assigned as the t_cost parameter. SHA256 simple parses the password and the salt. The hashes are also encrypted with the AES. At the server-side, PolyPassHash processes the password file when the system restarts. Then, a threshold of users must login before the passwords can be verified. After startup, the login requests are processed with similar computational overhead as in PHS-only systems. The memory overhead is about 1KB independent of the number of passwords and the storage cost is one byte per user account (the share value). An alternative partial verification process is also supported that allows users to login immediately after the restart without the need to verify a threshold of users. No modification of the client applications or the login process is required. PolyPassHash is solely based on software and the system administrator can adjust the threshold value without affecting the users. The attacker must guess 3 passwords simultaneously. On GPUs, PolyPassHash imposes about 23 orders of magnitude more effort than on PHS-only systems. On CPUs, even a threshold of 2 secrets provides sufficient security.

The lightweight PolyPassHash replaces SHA256 with the lightweight PHO-TON256. AES is substituted by CLEFIA with the same key size. The two schemes exhibit the same datapath size and the resource saving is low. The security level of the lightweight version is similar to the original one. In both schemes, the disk space requires 1 additional byte for each account to store the share value, in contrast to PHS-only solutions. The server must also store the polynomial coefficients for the SSS in memory. The total size is small: the XORed share and hash (256 bits long) multiplied by the threshold value (usually 2-5). In real systems, this value would result in a few hundred bytes.

3.3 Mainstream and Lightweight PolyPHS

In PolyPassHash, passwords are simply parsed by SHA256. To further increase security, we replace the hash function with the Catena PHS. The PHS enhances resistance against attacks but is more resource demanding than SHA256. Also, Catena exhibits larger output size (512-bits) and the integrated implementation size is higher.

The original Catena offers high level of security but it can not be applied on constrained devices. The lightweight Catena offers moderate level of security and is appropriate for the targeted systems. To fill the gap, the lightweight PolyPassHash is applied to increase security. The simple hash function is replaced by the PHS. Lightweight Catena uses the same datapath size as the SHA256 of PolyPassHash and provides higher password protection. With 3 shares as the threshold, an attacker must guess 3 lightweight-Catena passwords simultaneously to recover the password file. The security level is increased by 23 magnitudes on GPUs, resulting in $2^{244} * 10^{23} \approx 2^{320}$ bits security.

4   Evaluation

The examined PHSs, PPHs, and the core cryptographic primitives are evaluated under an Intel Core i7 at 2.10GHz CPU with 8GB RAM, running 64-bit operating systems. Reference C or C++ implementations are utilized in order to provide a fair comparison with the unoptimized versions of PHC. All implementations are installed on Windows 8.1 Pro and are executed on cygwin. The different primitives are assessed under common assumptions. We measure the code size, memory consumption, execution time and throughput of each scheme.

Table 1 summarizes the software evaluation of the examined PHSs and PPHs based on the default sizes for output, password and salt, and the indicative t_cost and m_cost parameters as reported by each scheme. The standardized PBKDF2 is not memory-hard and consumes neglected memory. bcrypt has low memory requirements and achieves similar performance as scrypt. scrypt is the first widely-used memory-hard PHS and exhibits the higher memory consumption and larger implementation size. Catena is a novel PHS that applies memory hardness to enhance security. Three versions are evaluated based on the underlying hash function. Catena-blake2d is the fastest and consumes similar memory as Catena-sha512. Catena-photon256 reduces memory demandings around 50% in exchange of lower performance. All three versions produce similar code size. PolyPassHash is a novel PPH that utilizes the hash function SHA256 and the block cipher AES. It is quite efficient and has low and constant memory requirements. The Light-PolyPassHash version uses the hash function PHOTON and the block cipher CLEFIA. It decreases the code size and accomplishes slightly lower memory consumption and worsen speed.

The security of the initial scheme is fortified by replacing the hash function with a PHS. The PHS constitutes the most resource demanding component. The t_cost parameter determines the k shares of the SSS component and linearly affects the execution time. As t_cost increases, the number of password hashing operations, which are performed by the PHS, also increases. PolyPHS uses the Catena-blake2b ($t\_cost = 3$, $m\_cost = 18$) as the PHS of PolyPassHash. LightPolyPHS uses the Catena-photon256 ($t\_cost = 3$, $m\_cost = 18$) as the PHS of Light-PolyPassHash.

Figure 1, illustrates the evaluation results of the 10 PHS and PPH schemes. For $k = 2$, LightPolyPHS has slightly worsen performance than bcrypt and scrypt. The memory-hard Catena-photon256 component enhanced with the SSS provide adequate security for around 39 times lower memory consumption and 2.3 smaller implementation size than scrypt.

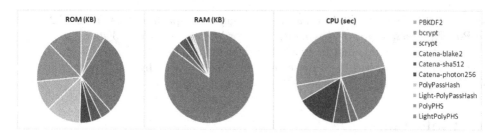

Fig. 1. Comparison of the examined PHSs

Table 1. Software implementations of PHSs and PPHs

PHS	Password (bytes)	Salt (bytes)	Output (bytes)	t_cost	m_cost	ROM (KB)	RAM (KB)	CPU(secs)
PBKDF2	24	8	64	1000	0	30	0	0.002024
	24	8	64	2048	0	30	0	0.004150
bcrypt	12	16	54	12	0	27	492	2.668653
scrypt	8	32	64	5	0	182	450656	2.837654
Catena–	8	16	64	3	18	25	16384	0.353742
blake2b	8	16	64	3	20	25	65596	2.619238
Catena–	8	16	64	3	18	25	16496	0.783590
sha512	8	16	64	3	20	25	65720	5.389355
Catena–	8	16	32	3	18	26	8188	1.749200
photon256	8	16	32	3	20	26	32760	13.065627
PolyPassHash	16	16	32	2	0	78	3412	0.000055
	16	16	32	4	0	78	3412	0.000055
Light–	16	16	32	2	0	66	3410	0.000068
PolyPassHash	16	16	32	4	0	66	3410	0.000080
PolyPHS	16	16	64	2	0	89	19794	0.707538
	16	16	64	4	0	89	19794	1.415020
LightPolyPHS	16	16	32	2	0	77	11579	3.498454
	16	16	32	4	0	77	11579	6.996854

5   Conclusions

The maintenance of user passwords constitutes a significant factor related to the provided security of a service. Security breaches on famous applications have reveal massive amounts of user data, harming the reliability of their providers. The poor password hashing techniques and the limited available solutions lead the international cryptographic community to organize the Password Hashing Competition (PHC). The competition intends to delivery a small portfolio of modern and secure schemes for password hashing and key deviation. This paper presents the LightPolyPHS - a lightweight poly password hashing scheme for embedded systems and lightweight cryptography. We held a comparative analysis with similar schemes on a mainstream computer. LightPolyPHS is the first lightweight password hashing and poly password hashing scheme suitable for constrained devices. Compared to current solutions it requires around 39 times less memory and 2.3 times smaller code size.

References

1. Kaliski, B.: RSA Laboratories: RFC 2898 - PKCS #5: Password-Based Cryptography Specification Version 2.0. Technical report, IETF, 2000 (2000)
2. Provos, N., Mazires, D.: A Future-Adaptable Password Scheme. In: USENIX Annual Technical Conference, pp. 81–92 (1999)
3. Percival, C.: Stronger Key Derivation via Sequential Memory-Hard Functions. presented at BSDCan2009 (May 2009)
4. Orman, H: Twelve Random Characters: Passwords in the Era of Massive Parallelism. IEEE Internet Computing 17(5), 91–94 (2013)
5. Forler, C., Lucks, S., Wenzel, J.: Catena: A memory-consuming password scrambler, Cryptology ePrint Archive, Report 2013/525 (2013)
6. Forler, C., Lucks, S., Wenzel, J.: The Catena Password Scrambler, PHC submission (May 15, 2014)
7. Hatzivasilis, G., Papaefstathiou, I., Manifavas, C.: Password Hashing Competition - Survey and Benchmark, Cryptology ePrint Archive, Report 2015/265 (2015)
8. Hatzivasilis, G., Theodoridis, A., Gasparis, E., Manifavas, C.: ULCL: an Ultra-Lightweight Cryptographic Library for embedded systems. In: MeSeCCS, PECCS, 2014, Lisbon, Portugal (2014)
9. Hatzivasilis, G., Floros, G., Papaefstathiou, I., Manifavas, C.: Lightweight authenticated encryption for green networking. In: IEEE AFRICON 2015 Green Innovation for African Renaissance, Addis Ababa, Ethiopia. IEEE (2015)
10. Fysarakis, K., Hatzivasilis, G., Rantos, K., Papanikolaou, A., Manifavas, C.: Embedded systems security challenges. In: MeSeCCS, PECCS, Lisbon, Portugal (2014)
11. Petroulakis, N.E., Askoxylakis, I.G., Traganitis, A., Spanoudakis, G.: A privacy-level model of user-centric cyber-physical systems. In: Marinos, L., Askoxylakis, I. (eds.) HAS 2013. LNCS, vol. 8030, pp. 338–347. Springer, Heidelberg (2013)
12. Siris, V., Askoxylakis, I., Conti, M., Bruno, R.: Enhanced, ubiquitous and dependable broadband access using MESH networks. In: ERCIM News, vol. 73 (2008)
13. Markantonakis, K., Mayes, K., Sauveron, D., Askoxylakis, I.G.: Overview of security threats for smart cards in the public transport industry. IEEE International Conference on e-Business Engineering, pp. 506–513. IEEE (2008)
14. Manifavas, C., Hatzivasilis, G., Fysarakis, K., Rantos, K.: Lightweight cryptography for embedded systems – a comparative analysis. In: Garcia-Alfaro, J., Lioudakis, G., Cuppens-Boulahia, N., Foley, S., Fitzgerald, W.M. (eds.) DPM 2013 and SETOP 2013. LNCS, vol. 8247, pp. 333–349. Springer, Heidelberg (2014)
15. Dhurjati, D., Kowshik, S., Adve, V., Lattner, C.: Memory safety without garbage collection for embedded applications. ACM TECS 4(1), 73–111 (2005)
16. NIST: Recommendation for Password-Based Key Derivation. NIST Special Publication 800–132 (December 2010)
17. Shamir, A.: How to share a secret. Communications of the ACM 22(11), 612–613 (1979)
18. Schneier, B.: Description of a new variable-length key, 64-bit block cipher (Blowfish). In: Anderson, R. (ed.) FSE. LNCS vol. 809, pp. 191–204. Springer, Heidelberg (1994)
19. Bernstein, D.J.: The Salsa20 family of stream ciphers, eSTREAM project (2007)
20. Moradi, A., Poschmann, A., Ling, S., Paar, C., Wang, H.: Pushing the limits: a very compact and a threshold implementation of aes. In: Paterson, K.G. (ed.) EUROCRYPT 2011. LNCS, vol. 6632, pp. 69–88. Springer, Heidelberg (2011)

21. NIST: Secure Hash Standard, FIPS 180–2 (April 1995)
22. Aumasson, J.-P., Neves, S., Wilcox-O'Hearn, Z., Winnerlein, C.: BLAKE2: Simpler, smaller, fast as MD5. In: Jacobson, M., Locasto, M., Mohassel, P., Safavi-Naini, R. (eds.) ACNS 2013. LNCS, vol. 7954, pp. 119–135. Springer, Heidelberg (2013)
23. ISO/IEC 29192:2012, International standard for lightweight cryptographic methods, ISO/IEC (2012)
24. Akishita, T., Hiwatari, H.: Very Compact Hardware Implementations of the Blockcipher CLEFIA. Sony Corporation, Technical Paper (2011)
25. Guo, J., Peyrin, T., Poschmann, A.: The PHOTON family of lightweight hash functions. In: Rogaway, P. (ed.) CRYPTO 2011. LNCS, vol. 6841, pp. 222–239. Springer, Heidelberg (2011)
26. Guo, J., Karpman, P., Nikolic, I., Wang, L., Wu, S.: Analysis of Blake2, Cryptology ePrint Archive, Report 2013/467 (2013)

Secure and Authenticated Access to LLN Resources Through Policy Constraints

Konstantinos Rantos[1], Konstantinos Fysarakis[2]([✉]), Othonas Soultatos[3], and Ioannis Askoxylakis[4]

[1] Department of Computer and Informatics Engineering,
Eastern Macedonia and Thrace Institute of Technology, Kavala, Greece
`krantos@teiemt.gr`
[2] Department of Electronic & Computer Engineering,
Technical University of Crete, Chania, Crete, Greece
`kfysarakis@isc.tuc.gr`
[3] Department of Computer Science, University of Crete, Heraklion, Crete, Greece
`sultatos@csd.uoc.gr`
[4] Institute of Computer Science, Foundation for Research and Technology - Hellas
(FORTH), Heraklion, Greece
`asko@ics.forth.gr`

Abstract. Ubiquitous devices comprising several resource-constrained sensors and actuators while having the long desired Internet connectivity, are becoming part of many solutions that seek to enhance user's environment smartness and quality of living. Their intrinsic resource limitations however constitute critical requirements, such as security, a great challenge. When these nodes are associated with applications that might have an impact in user's privacy or even become life threatening, the security issues are of primary concern. Access to these resources should be appropriately controlled to ensure that such wearable nodes are adequately protected. On the other hand, it is very important to not restrict access to only a very closed group of entities. This work presents a service oriented architecture that utilizes policy-based, unified, cross-platform and flexible access control to allow authenticated entities consume the services provided by wearable nodes while protecting their valuable resources.

Keywords: Body sensor networks · Policy-based access control · XACML · SAML · DPWS · Web services · Security

1 Introduction

In recent years, we have experienced a lot of innovation in the Internet of Things (IoT) space. Collections of nodes typically bearing sensors and actuators are becoming part of a networking infrastructure and gain connectivity to the Internet. The corresponding technologies are becoming mature enough to start looking into more advanced and comprehensive solutions that can enable these nodes to integrate smoothly with existing infrastructures while, however, expanding existing attack surfaces.

© IFIP International Federation for Information Processing 2015
R.N. Akram and S. Jajodia (Eds.): WISTP 2015, LNCS 9311, pp. 271–280, 2015.
DOI: 10.1007/978-3-319-24018-3_18

There are many application areas where these nodes flourish with even more being introduced to take advantage of the services that they can offer. They can be deployed as standalone nodes serving a single purpose, or as part of an infrastructure that consists of nodes with similar characteristics comprising a so called low power and lossy network (LLN). The current trend for all these nodes characterised by their limited resources in terms of computing power, memory, storage space and energy, is to adopt existing networking technologies and be reachable over the Internet, abandoning proprietary closed solutions.

Sensor nodes and Service Oriented Architectures (SOAs) have become convergent technologies with several standards emerging from these efforts. SOAs evolved from the need to have interoperable, cross-platform, cross-domain and network-agnostic access to devices and their services. At the same time, studies [1] and published reports[1] reveal that current deployments have not adequately considered the threats that these nodes face when connected to the Internet, hence the lack of the security measures. Such negligence is bound to inhibit any efforts made towards using these pervasive devices to handle our personal sensitive data. The expanded attack surface that results from the integration of LLNs with the Internet, needs new or adapted mechanisms to mitigate these new threats.

This paper defines an architecture that controls access to services provided by resource-limited nodes. Among the main concerns of the proposed architecture are the nodes' protection from unauthorised and unjustifiable use of their resources and the need to be able to control access through a well-established set of policy rules that can change and adapt to new environmental parameters. The work builds upon the eXtensible Access Control Markup Language (XACML) reference model for policy based access control infrastructures and proposes certain modifications to provide flexibility in terms of the authentication mechanism being used and satisfy requirements stemming from the limited resources of nodes.

2   Background and Related Work

Standardisation and research efforts in the area of Service Oriented Architectures have been taking place for more than a decade. Several schemes have been proposed and standardised regarding service discovery, registration, access and protection, and the corresponding communication protocols that enable the interoperable exchange of messages among remote participating entities.

In terms of the way that access to web services is controlled, the eXtensible Access Control Markup Language (XACML) [2], provides an access control language and a model for processing requests to resources while the Security Assertion Markup Language (SAML) focuses on the way the requester is authenticated and assertions are being transferred among participating entities. WS-Trust is another web services oriented that defines how security tokens are being issued,

---

[1] http://fortifyprotect.com/HP_IoT_Research_Study.pdf

renewed and validated (WS-Trust). This paper focuses more on the area of securing access to resources through policy-based access control, hence it is related and utilises these security related standards mentioned above, while proposing certain modifications mentioned below to fit best to the restricted environment of LLNs.

Many access control schemes have been proposed for wireless sensor networks, yet most of them focus on authentication and authorization schemes and on enhancing basic access control models to address privacy matters. Such schemes can be found in [3–6]. Little work has been carried out on policy-based access control (PBAC). The EU-project Internet-of-Things Architecture (IoT-A) worked on the adoption of XACML in the Internet of Things [7] and proposed a generic model whose functional modules are mapped to a set of well-defined components that comprise the IoT-A. The authors use a logistics scenario for demonstration purposes.

In [8] the authors also utilize XACML but focus on the privacy of e-Health data within the mobile environment. In contrast to the work presented here, a complete framework is not included and, moreover, the authors choose computationally intensive security mechanisms such as XML encryption digital signatures. In [9], the authors propose a lightweight policy system for body sensors but they do so by presenting a custom API and policy definitions, thus sacrificing interoperability with existing standards and infrastructures.

3   Requirements

IP based networking in LLNs changes the way that participating nodes can be accessed and their respective services can be consumed. For instance, there is no need for a dedicated application server that will intervene between a node and a remote party that wants to access the node's resources [10]. However, one of the problems that these nodes face in such a deployment, is that they have limited resources which do not suffice for the deployment of strong protection mechanisms. Without those mechanisms however, nodes are exposed to direct access from the Internet without having the capacity to handle unlimited requests. Therefore, several issues arise regarding the protection of nodes resources, that have to be addressed. The main aim is to protect the limited resources of a node that implements a service oriented architecture, to provide access to data and mechanisms that the node has under control. In this paper we are looking at these issues aiming for a smooth integration of web-services technology, adopted by serving nodes, with the Web.

Within this context, the proposed architecture is designed to satisfy the following requirements:

- Provide services using of Service Oriented Architecture technologies;
- Provide fine-grained access control to nodes' resources;
- Authenticate remote entities wishing to access protected nodes resources;
- Control access to nodes' resources through well-defined policies;

- Protect sensitive nodes from unauthorised access and unnecessary consumption of valuable resources including network and energy;
- Comply with existing standards to satisfy interoperability among the participating entities, such as between the identity provider chosen by the requester and the service orchestrator, regarding the exchange of authentication messages, assertions or user metadata and attributes.

In the following section we describe the proposed architecture that satisfies the above.

4   Proposed Architecture

The architecture proposed in this paper is an enhanced policy based access control scheme that seeks to provide flexibility regarding the chosen authentication mechanism while satisfying the aforementioned requirements, typically imposed by nodes' resource limitations. For this purpose, certain modifications to the OASIS standardised policy-based access control scheme are proposed to accommodate these needs.

The scheme utilizes and seeks compliance with the following technologies:

- XACML: an XML-based OASIS standard that defines a policy and an access control decision request/response language. An XACML-based architecture typically consists of the following main components:
  - *Policy Enforcement Point (PEP):* Performs access control, by making decision requests and enforcing authorization decisions [2,11].
  - *Policy Decision Point (PDP):* Evaluates requests against applicable policies and renders an authorization decision [2].
  - *Policy Administration Point (PAP):* Creates and manages policies or policy sets [2].
  - *Policy Information Point (PIP):* Acts as a source of attribute values [2].
- SAML 2.0 specification to protect, transport, and request XACML schema instances and other information needed by an XACML implementation [12].

In the XACML data-flow model the PEP, via the context handler, is considered as the device that orchestrates the exchange of messages among the requester, the PDP, the Attribute Authority and the Attribute Repository. According to the XACML specifications the PEP is considered as "part of a remote-access gateway, part of a Web server or part of an email user-agent, etc". Therefore all initial requests, valid or not, are sent to the PEP which will act as a routing device between the requester and the back-end key entities that examine the requests and make decision based on policy rules and other parameters, such as the requester's and/or resource's attributes.

While this model is appropriate for typical application gateways, it cannot be considered as such for resource-constrained nodes that only have the capacity to accept requests from a limited number of clients. Beyond this threshold, valuable node resource consumption is not acceptable as it leads to battery drainage and service unavailability. In this context, resource-constrained devices have to participate in the decision making process only if absolutely necessary and only to authorized entities to save valuable resources. As such, they cannot assume the role of a PEP as this is defined in the XACML standard [2].

Moreover, the flow model currently defined by XACML, considers that the PIP has all the required attributes for the requester, and that the PDP gets all the information from the PIP, which might be queried twice for the required attributes, once from the PEP and once from the PDP. Use of specific PIP implies that services will only be provided to entities subscribed to the specific scheme, thus narrowing down flexibility. This is in contrast to a more flexible approach where services are offered to a broader group of users, subject to policy restrictions.

The proposed architecture is depicted in Figure 1. In this proposal we assume that nodes bearing sensor and actuators, expose their functionality as web services. This can either be done through the device that the node is attached to, e.g. a mobile device, or directly by the node, assuming that it is powerful enough to accommodate such functionality. All these nodes are part of a dispersed environment where there is not necessarily a single gateway or web server to assume the role of PEP as this is defined in the XACML standard. Besides that, the service owner might want to register these services with multiple servers. As a result, the PEP functionality cannot be assigned to a gateway but it should be on the device that exposes this functionality, i.e. the mobile device or the micro/power node. For a given PEP, one of these web servers is assumed to play the role of the orchestrator as described below.

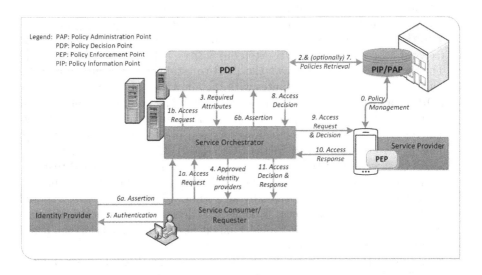

Fig. 1. Authenticated Access Control for LLNs

The core component of the proposed scheme is the Service Orchestrator (SO) which acts as a proxy for certain operations, such as relaying queries and messages exchanged among participating entities, yet not for handling the information the PEP exchanges with the requester.

Initially, the node, which assumes the role of a PEP, registers its services, defines the connection point to be the SO and sets the policy rules for its resources. This is accomplished once during the set-up phase. Following that, the data flow of the proposed architecture includes the following steps:

- A requester, who wants to access the service, formulates an appropriate request based on the advertised service rules, and sends it to the SO (step 1a). Note that this is in contrast to the XACML specifications which opted for sending the request directly to the PEP, introducing significant overhead that a limited-resources device cannot handle.
- The SO forwards the request to the PDP (step 1b) which, based on the requested target, fetches all applicable policies from the PAP (step 2) and informs the SO about the needed user attributes (step 3). As a result, the SO presents a list of approved Identity Providers (IdP) for the requester to authenticate (step 4).
- The requester chooses the appropriate IdP and the SO issues a (signed) authentication request (`<AuthnRequest>`) together with an attribute query (`<AttributeQuery>`) [12] to the chosen IdP. Upon successful authentication (step 5) the requester consents for the disclosure of certain attributes that the SO requires. Note that the IdP might be an entity that operates within the same environment as the SO. The authentication method used by the IdP is outside the scope of this paper.
- The IdP formulates a proper assertion for the necessary attributes and sends it to the SO via the Requester (step 6a). As a result, the SO forwards the received assertion to the PDP (Step 6b) [13].
- The forwarded assertion allows the PDP to establish a security context by combining the supplied attributes with the applicable policy rules which the PDP obtained from the PAP (step 2). Note that additional policy rules, might be obtained at this point (step 7), based on the requestes' attributes. The typical XACML decision making process can take place during this step.
- The access decision is sent to the SO (step 8). If the decision is to grant access, a signed or MAC-protected ticket is forwarded to the PEP together with details about the request (step 9). This is the first time that the node is contacted, and is only performed by an authorized party, hence not exposed to the outside world. If access is denied the decision is simply forwarded to the Requester. The Service Provider might also be informed on that based on appropriate pre-configurations.
- Now the PEP can respond to the service request through the SO (step 10). The SO can in turn send to the requester the Access Decision and the response to the Access Request. The Access Decision can be used as a token for re-accessing the same service without undergoing the authentication process.

5 Implementation Approach

There are many open-source implementations of the XACML handling and decision-making process that can be utilized for the proposed architecture. The authors chose Suns XACML [14] for this implementation, as it remains popular among developers and is actually the basis of various current open source and commercial offerings.

All of the frameworks entities are implemented using DPWS. This facilitates the discovery and description of the devices involved, and also offers control and eventing mechanisms which assist in the communication of the necessary information among the entities. Web Services for Devices (WS4D) [15] is an open source initiative which provides a number of toolkits for various platforms. The authors APIs of choice is the WS4D-JMEDS (Java-based) [16] stack as it is the most advanced and active work of the WS4D initiative, supporting almost all of the existing DPWS features and providing portability to a wide range of platforms.

The exact implementation of the frameworks entities and their communication interfaces are detailed below.

Service Orchestrator to Policy Decision Point. The SO is implemented as a DPWS peer (i.e. both a client and a server). Other than the necessary mechanisms needed to interface with the approved identity providers (which will vary depending on the specific scenario/deployment examined), it also features an "Attribute_Requirements operation. Similarly, the PDP has an "Access_Request_Operation. The latter is invoked by the SO as soon as an access request arrives from a service consumer, relaying the request for evaluation. As soon as the XACML decision-making process is completed, the PDP replies to the invocation with its access decision. As detailed in the information flow above, prior to providing a decision, it may need to invoke the "Attribute_Requirements operation on the SO, in order to inform it of the needed user attributes, getting the proper assertion as an answer.

Service Orchestrator to Policy Enforcement Point. The Policy Enforcement Point must reside on every device with resources that must be protected from unauthorized access. Other than the functional elements of the devices which the framework intends to protect (e.g. access to its sensors), one extra operation must be present on each DPWS device, namely the PEP_Operation. The SO, acting as a client, invokes this operation providing the service consumers access request along with the decision (pre-issued by the PDP) as input. If the decision accompanying the invocation is positive, the PEP replies to the SO with the resource (e.g. temperature reading) that the service consumer originally tried to access. This information is then relayed to the service consumer/requester. The above DPWS-based communication mechanisms are depicted in the figure below.

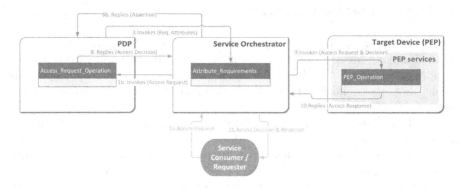

Fig. 2. DPWS-based implementation of the authentication scheme

6 Security Analysis

One of the main concerns in accessing services and issuing commands, is the protection of the data being exchanged among the participating entities. In the proposed scheme the service provider has a pre-established relationship with the SO, PDP and PAP. Note that all these three entities are only functional components and therefore the exact needs in secure channel establishment depend on the actual deployment choice and cannot be specified. In a simplified approach, the SO, PDP and PAP can be part of the same entity and therefore a secure channel establishment using pre-shared keys is a viable and efficient option.

Regarding the underlying message security mechanisms, common methods that provide end-to-end security like TLS [17], (Transport Layer Security) [17] protocol and its counterpart proposed for securing UDP messages, namely DTLS [18], are considered suitable for this architecture. The cost of using TLS however, between the Requester and the SO is that the secure channel breaks at the SO and the SO has to re-encrypt the communication using the security parameters set for the link between the SO and the service provider. At the network layer solutions like the IPsec protocol and its variants that utilize header compression [19–21] can provide similar levels of protection. An alternative approach would be to utilize a subset of the mechanisms detailed in the WS-Security [22] specification, but the X509-based public key schemes included in said specification can impose a significant performance overhead [23].

7 Conclusions

As computing becomes ubiquitous, researchers and engineers aim to exploit the potential of pervasive systems, including nodes with sensors and actuators interconnected via LLNs, in order to introduce new types of services and address inveterate and emerging problems. Nevertheless, a key factor in the wide adoption and success of these new technologies will be the effectiveness with which the various security and privacy concerns are tackled. A necessary instrument in successfully addressing said issues is the presence of robust access control mechanisms.

To this end, this paper presents a work in progress on an architecture for providing access control services to heterogeneous resource-constrained devices. The authors chose the use of standardized access control mechanisms based on XACML. Moreover, the core PEP functionality is separated from the rest of the network and the decision-making process, keeping the core resource provision with the device that has the resources, while relieving it from the additional essential, yet very heavy computations that the XACML standard defines. Moreover, this approach shelters the device from direct user interaction, helping alleviate concerns that are typical to resource-constrained devices, like Denial of Service attacks.

Acknowledgments. This work was partially supported by the Greek General Secretariat for Research and Technology (GSRT), under the ARTEMIS JU research program nSHIELD (new embedded Systems arcHItecturE for multi-Layer Dependable solutions) project. Call: ARTEMIS-2010-1, Grant Agreement No.:269317.

References

1. Cui, A., Stolfo, S.J.: A quantitative analysis of the insecurity of embedded network devices: results of a wide-area scan. In: Proceedings of the 26th Annual Computer Security Applications Conference, ACSAC 2010, pp. 97–106. ACM, New York (2010). http://doi.acm.org/10.1145/1920261.1920276
2. Parducci, B., Lockhart, H., Rissanen, E.: eXtensible Access Control Markup Language (XACML) Version 3.0, pp. 1–150 (2003). http://docs.oasis-open.org/xacml/3.0/
3. He, D., Bu, J., Zhu, S., Chan, S., Chen, C.: Distributed Access Control with Privacy Support in Wireless Sensor Networks. IEEE Transactions on Wireless Communications 10(10), 3472–3481 (2011)
4. Yu, S., Ren, K., Lou, W.: FDAC: Toward Fine-Grained Distributed Data Access Control in Wireless Sensor Networks. IEEE Transactions on Parallel and Distributed Systems 22(4), 352–362 (2011)
5. Askoxylakis, I.G., Markantonakis, K., Tryfonas, T., May, J., Traganitis, A.: A face centered cubic key agreement mechanism for mobile ad hoc networks. In: Granelli, F., Skianis, C., Chatzimisios, P., Xiao, Y., Redana, S. (eds.) MOBILIGHT 2009. LNICST, vol. 13, pp. 103–113. Springer, Heidelberg (2009)
6. Manifavas, C., Fysarakis, K., Rantos, K., Kagiambakis, K., Papaefstathiou, I.: Policy-based access control for body sensor networks. In: Naccache, D., Sauveron, D. (eds.) WISTP 2014. LNCS, vol. 8501, pp. 150–159. Springer, Heidelberg (2014)
7. Serbanati, A., Segura, A.S., Oliverau, A., Saied, Y.B., Gruschka, N., Gessner, D., Gomez-Marmol, F.: Internet of Things Architecture, Concept and Solutions for Privacy and Security in the Resolution Infrastructure. EU project IoT-A, Project report D4.2 (2012). http://www.iot-a.eu/

8. El-Aziz, A., Kannan, A.: Access control for healthcare data using extended XACML-SRBAC model. In: 2012 International Conference on Computer Communication and Informatics, Dept. of Information Science & Technology, Anna University, pp. 1–4. IEEE, January 2012

9. Zhu, Y., Keoh, S., Sloman, M., Lupu, E.: A lightweight policy system for body sensor networks. IEEE Transactions on Network and Service Management **6**(3), 137–148 (2009)

10. Colitti, W., Steenhaut, K., De Caro, N.: Integrating wireless sensor networks with the web. In: Proc. of Extending the Internet to Low Power and Lossy Networks, Chicago, IL, USA (2011)

11. Westerinen, A., Schnizlein, J., Strassner, J., Scherling, M., Quinn, B., Herzog, S., Huynh, A., Carlson, M., Perry, J., Waldbusser, S.: Terminology for Policy-Based Management, pp. 1–22 (2001). http://www.ietf.org/rfc/rfc3198.txt

12. Anderson, A., Lockhart, H.: SAML 2.0 Profile of XACML, Version 2.0 (2005). http://docs.oasis-open.org/xacml/2.0/access_control-xacml-2.0-saml-profile-spec-os.pdf

13. Hughes, J., Cantor, S., Hodges, J., Hirsch, F., Mishra, P., Philpott, R., Maler, E.: Profiles for the OASIS Security Assertion Markup Language (SAML) V2.0 (2005). http://docs.oasis-open.org/security/saml/v2.0/saml-profiles-2.0-os.pdf

14. Sun Microsystems Laboratories, XACML. http://sunxacml.sourceforge.net

15. Web Services for Devices (WS4D). http://ws4d.e-technik.uni-rostock.de

16. WS4D-JMEDS DPWS Stack. http://sourceforge.net/projects/ws4d-javame/

17. Dierks, T., Rescorla, E.: RFC 5246 - The Transport Layer Security (TLS) Protocol Version 1.2, pp. 1–104 (2008). http://tools.ietf.org/rfc/rfc5246.txt

18. Rescorla, E., Modadugu, N.: Datagram Transport Layer Security, pp. 1–31 (2012). http://tools.ietf.org/rfc/rfc6347.txt

19. Rantos, K., Papanikolaou, A., Manifavas, C.: Ipsec over ieee 802.15.4 for low power and lossy networks. In: Proceedings of the 11th ACM International Symposium on Mobility Management and Wireless Access, MobiWac 2013, pp. 59–64. ACM, New York (2013)

20. Rantos, K., Papanikolaou, A., Manifavas, C., Papaefstathiou, I.: Ipv6 security for low power and lossy networks. In: 2013 IFIP Wireless Days (WD), pp. 1–8, November 2013

21. Raza, S., Duquennoy, S., Chung, T., Yazar, D., Voigt, T., Roedig, U.: Securing communication in 6LoWPAN with compressed IPsec. In: Proceedings of the 7th IEEE International Conference on Distributed Computing in Sensor Systems (IEEE DCOSS 2011), Barcelona, Spain, June 2011

22. Lawrence, K., Kaler, C., Nadalin, A., Monzilo, R., Hallam-Baker, P.: Web Services Security: SOAP Message Security 1.1, pp. 1–76 (2006). http://docs.oasis-open.org/wss/v1.1/

23. Lascelles, F., Flint, A.: WS-Security Performance (2006). http://websphere.syscon.com/node/204424

Author Index

Printed in the United States
By Bookmasters